THE MAVERICK AND THE MACHINE

*The Maverick and the Machine:*
*Governor Dan Walker*
*Tells His Story*

**Dan Walker**

Edited by Peggy Lang

Southern Illinois University Press
*Carbondale*

10  09  08  07    4  3  2  1

Library of Congress Cataloging-in-Publication Data
Walker, Daniel, 1922–
The maverick and the machine : Governor Dan Walker tells his story / Dan Walker; edited
by Peggy Lang.
p. cm.
Includes index.
ISBN-13: 978-0-8093-2756-0 (cloth : alk. paper)
ISBN-10: 0-8093-2756-2 (cloth : alk. paper)
1. Walker, Daniel, 1922– 2. Governors—Illinois—Biography. 3. Illinois—Politics and
government—1951–. I. Lang, Peggy. II. Title.
F546.4.W35A3 2007
977.3'043092—dc22
[B]                                                                    2006032130

Printed on recycled paper. ♻

The paper used in this publication meets the minimum requirements of American National
Standard for Information Sciences—Permanence of Paper for Printed Library Materials,
ANSI Z39.48-1992. ♾

*For David Green,*
*without whom I never would*
*have become governor*

# Contents

*Contents*

# *Illustrations*

Office meeting with David Green, William Goldberg, Victor De Grazia, and Norton Kay

With Mayor Richard J. Daley

Greeting President Gerald Ford

Greeting Emperor Hirohito of Japan

Greeting presidential candidate Jimmy Carter

With former governors Stratton and Shapiro

With second wife, Roberta Nelson Walker, Richard Burton, and Elizabeth Taylor

Walker family

With third wife, Lillian M. Stewart

With grandsons Jimmy Kollar, Kenny Okamoto, and Chris Vaught

With sons Dan and Charles

# Preface

The first draft of this book was a very lengthy autobiography in which I detailed in chronological order all that I thought had any relevance to the story of my life. Then I hired experienced editor Peggy Lang, who dismantled much of my text. Working closely with me, she reorganized and reassembled the story, rewriting parts of it. We also added some portions, notably the prison scenes. As to these, she required me to write out my memories of these difficult events, often challenging what I had written and almost literally "pulling" details out of my memory where I had buried them. The resulting book would not have been possible without her participation, and to call her an "editor" hardly does justice to the critical role she played.

As to sources, the major (and even some of the minor) events depicted in this book are matters of public record and have been covered, often extensively, in the mass media. The story of the statewide campaign walk is documented in an existing walk journal. The journal is a compilation of the descriptions I recorded daily in a pocket recorder and sent to the Chicago campaign office for transcription. As to the prison experiences, I used a code to record key events in a prayer book I kept under my mattress, and I still have that book. I used a code because the guards regularly searched inmates' rooms, including personal lockers, which had to remain open at all times. Other experiences are recorded in the numerous letters I wrote to my children. The manuscript has been read for errors by several people who were close to me during my public life.

The Sangamon State University Oral History Project includes extensive interviews of both me and Victor De Grazia, who served as deputy to the governor and as my campaign manager. These were conducted not long after I left office, and I have referred to them repeatedly. I have also used the excellent biography *The Glory and the Tragedy,* by Taylor Pensoneau and Bob Ellis, both talented and experienced reporters. For historical matter regarding the Chicago machine and Mayor Richard J. Daley, I have used the published sources cited in the text.

The talented editorial staff at SIU Press has made this a better book. They include Karl Kageff, editor in chief; Wayne Larsen, project editor; Barb Martin, editorial, design, and production director; and John Wilson, copy editor. All true professionals, they have my deep gratitude.

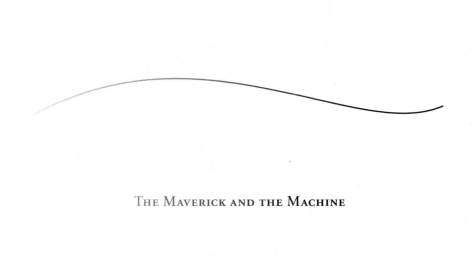

The Maverick and the Machine

# Introduction

Illinois, my chosen state, is truly heartland America. From the hilly land of Galena and Ulysses S. Grant in northern Illinois, to the flat, rich farmland of Springfield and Abraham Lincoln in central Illinois, to the hills, valleys, and river towns of southern Illinois and Mark Twain, the state is rich in American lore. To an unfair extent, the city of Chicago dominates the state. Largely because of Chicago, the state, which historically was usually strong Republican territory, went Democratic for Bill Clinton in 1996 and 2000 and stayed solid blue in 2004, alone among the heartland states.

I chose Illinois as the place where I would practice law and grow my large family. Entranced with the governmental ideals so eloquently elucidated by governor and presidential candidate Adlai Stevenson in 1952, I persuaded myself that here I could pursue my legal career and at the same time satisfy my yearning for political and governmental involvement. This account of my variegated life, during which I "broke my lance" in my long joust with law and government, could perhaps best begin with the "state of the state" in 2006. I can then describe how and why Illinois has not lived up to the governmental ideals voiced by two of its famous sons, Abraham Lincoln and Adlai Stevenson; how and why the state that proudly proclaims itself on license plates as the "Land of Lincoln" has become the land of the Boss Daleys, father and son, and my personal role in that drama; and how and why Illinois has been labeled the center of a "culture of corruption" by columnist John Kass and "a petri dish for corruption" by a speaker unidentified by the press at the 2006 national meeting of state prosecutors.

Perhaps it all began years ago with the infamous secretary of state "Shoe Box" Paul Powell. Receiving a salary of no more than thirty thousand dollars a year (most often less), he left an estate of $4.7 million, $794,000 of which was found in cash, mostly small bills, in closets and shoe boxes when he died.

Illinois's congressmen and governors and Chicago's mayor have all been in the national news during 2006. Senator Richard Durbin, the majority whip, now in his third term in the Senate, is mentioned as a possible vice presidential candidate. Senator Barack Obama is a viable presidential candidate. Congressman Dennis Hastert was Speaker of the House.

But recently the *Chicago Tribune* has concluded that Illinois is becoming "the nation's most notorious hotbed of crime in government." The scandals made headlines throughout 2006 when they were exposed by Chicago newspapers and U.S. Attorney Patrick Fitzgerald. They certainly rank among the worst that have ever hit state and local government. *Chicago Sun-Times* reporter Scott Fornek has done the arithmetic. No fewer than 119 persons had been convicted as felons, either by guilty plea or jury verdict, by September 2006, with more on the way. *Tribune* columnist John Kass ran a contest for a new state slogan. The winner: "Will the defendant please rise?" Perhaps that is about as cynical as the city slogan coined by the great Chicago columnist Mike Royko: *Ubi est mea?* or "Where's mine?"

Perhaps the worst scandal so far involves George Ryan, who served as lieutenant governor, secretary of state, and governor. Ryan was convicted on sixteen counts, including mail fraud, tax fraud, accepting bribes, lying to FBI agents, and leading a criminal racketeering conspiracy, all resulting in a six-and-a-half-year jail sentence. The evidence showed that funds for his many campaigns were solicited by state employees, including bribes for driver's licenses. One notorious case involved an unqualified truck driver who, after paying a bribe to a Ryan underling to obtain a diver's license, caused an expressway crash that killed six children. The U.S. attorney traced the money flow to Ryan's campaign.

Viewing the systemic corruption in state government under Ryan, one *Chicago Sun-Times* reporter called it a "muck of dirty deals." And perhaps it hasn't changed much since Republican Ryan left office. The current governor, Democrat Rod Blagojevich, is under federal investigation, "being pounded by a scandal a day," according to the *Chicago Sun-Times.* Thus far involved in the U.S. attorney's investigation are allegations of state pension-fund kickback schemes, repeated patronage hiring in violation of federal law, and pay-to-play contract cronyism practices that, according to the *Sun-Times*, involved what one investigator called "complete and utter contempt for the law." Nonetheless, Blagojevich was reelected in November 2006.

As to Chicago, after numerous city employees were indicted or found guilty by juries in the widespread $40 million "hired truck" scandal that erupted in 2006, Mayor Richard M. Daley, son of the famous boss Richard J. Daley, was quoted repeatedly in the Chicago newspapers as saying, "I know nothing about it." He has also denied the existence in Chicago of the Mob, or Outfit, in the face of federal indictments of eighteen mobsters for murder. The federal investigation was code-named "Operation Family Secrets," and the final indictment said that it "lifts the veil of secrecy and exposes the violent underworld of organized crime." The Chicago Crime Commission calls the Chicago Outfit "one of the most prolific organized crime enterprises in the United States." A main money source for the mobsters today is the thousands of video poker machines placed in bars, taverns, and restaurants throughout the Chicago area. Just one of those machines can yield six-digit annual profits, and the Mob collector makes weekly rounds to collect its share.

There have also been revelations that a longtime friend of the current Mayor Daley, a member of the notorious Mob-related Roti family, has become a millionaire by trucking the city's trash. It's a family affair. His grandfather was the infamous Bruno Roti Sr., associate of Al Capone, and his late uncle, Alderman Fred B. Roti, openly bragged that he represented the Mob on the city council and went to prison for bribery in zoning cases while old Boss Daley was mayor. The Roti family's trucks have rolled for the city under both Daleys; two family members are charged in the current investigation.

Boss Daley's son stood by in 2006 while his city water department was labeled a "racketeering enterprise" that raked in more than half a million dollars in bribes. Its leader was now-convicted felon Donald Tomczak from Bridgeport in the Eleventh Ward—the same ward that has produced so many mayors, including both Daleys. It was ward boss Tomczak who supplied a horde of precinct captains to help elect Congressman Rahm Emmanuel in another part of the city.

Some say that the famed Chicago machine is dead and gone, but Tomczak and others like him holding high-powered jobs in city government under the new Daley administration have used illegal means to build a patronage army that rivals the accomplishments of the efficient precinct captains of the old Daley machine. The powerful Eleventh Ward boss and ward committeeman is John Daley, the mayor's brother, who also wields power as a Cook County commissioner. Little has changed. Federal prosecutors have charged that businessmen are constantly "strong armed" by city employees to make political contributions and that minority set-aside programs are abused by city hall favorites who use minority members as fronts while they, Daley's friend and associates, profit from city business.

Young Daley's friend and patronage chief, Robert Sorich, has been sentenced to four years for an illegal fraudulent hiring scheme. Judge David Coar called it "corruption with a capital *C*." Another Daley crony and fund raiser, James Duff, was sentenced to nearly ten years in prison and $22 million in fines for defrauding the city by taking contracts meant for minorities and women.

Nonetheless, nobody doubts that Richie Daley will triumph in his current campaign for a sixth term as mayor. He has worked some wonders in Chicago, making the city considerably more beautiful and tackling some tough problems in city schools and public housing. However, the plain fact remains that under Richie Daley, as under his father, those in power look the other way and brag of the municipal greatness of Chicago, how well "the city works," just like the magician who diverts the eyes of his audience while he does his sleight of hand. The fact is, the Chicago Democratic political machine still lives and works, even though it may be dressed in different clothes.

That's the city government in Chicago, and that's the state government in Illinois today, the product of a rotten political system that has existed for years in the once-proud Land of Lincoln. Campaigning and governing, I called it a nefarious "club system" involving top politicians of both parties. *Chicago Tribune* columnist John Kass calls it "the combine." What follows is the story of how I acquired the courage to confront that system. The story develops from my upbringing and my naval and legal careers, and once the pieces fall into place, it tells how I jump-started my political career by walking the length and breadth of the state as a maverick fighting the machine. But I give you fair warning: there is no storybook ending. As F. Scott Fitzgerald once wrote long ago, "show me a famous figure and I'll show you a tragedy."

**I**

## *A Tough Father, a Loving Wife, and a Growing Family*

Iam traumatized and not in touch with reality. My sons, professionals with busy lives, drive me from Chicago to a minimum-security prison in Duluth, Minnesota, in January of 1987 for what is surely the saddest journey of my life. I wish I had thought to include my daughters as a part of this farewell trip. My second wife isn't here because she isn't close with my family, and I only know how much I need my sons. Dan, my oldest, is driving, and Charles and Will sit in the back—all three trying to keep my spirits up. They reminisce or try to get a rise out of me. They pretend to chide me for my ignorance of the sports world.

"Remember when you didn't know that the Senators and the Nats were the same team?"

I don't take the bait. I control myself, steel myself, summon what I have always believed was my formidable self-discipline.

Charles asks, "Dad, if you could change one thing in your life, what would it be?"

I merely grumble, "Hell if I know." Then, "Isn't it pretty damn obvious?"

They have tried every approach, but there is nothing my sons can say that will lift my despair, and they stop trying. The lapse into silence turns deadly grim on the eight-hour drive. I have no idea what to expect. The prison is where I·will serve a seven-year sentence.

A former World War II air force base, the prison sits on a wind-swept bluff above Duluth. We circle the place before my report-in time. All around my new home, an imposing fence rises to its crown of triple-strand barbed wire. There is only one gate. My sons embrace me, eyes bleak with sadness. They murmur encouragement, promise to visit, and leave me there.

I watch Dan's Chevrolet recede. Will, alone now in the back seat, is the last one to look at me. He waves, and they are soon gone. The temperature is below zero, and a strong blast of frigid air whips across the tarmac, but the cold barely registers. The few belongings I was instructed to bring are crowded into the small satchel at my side. I am sixty-five years old.

The gate guards send me to a nearby building where two young men, both black, wait in a reception area. Nobody talks. I assume they are gang members, and for the first time, it hits me viscerally that I will be living with all kinds of criminals.

Long wait. Deliberate, I'm sure. Time to reflect on those famous words that will come to mind many times in the long days ahead. *Stone walls do not a prison make, nor iron bars a cage.*

Finally, a guard arrives. Silently, he motions to us to follow him down a hall, where we enter a small room with no furniture. "Okay, guys. Strip for a search before you get your prison garb."

Now naked, we pile our clothes in front of us on the floor.

The guard says, "This is your first experience with our narcotics control procedures. I'm gonna search all body cavities. We don't want any dope brought in here." He pulls on rubber gloves and does as he said. He commands, "Spread your cheeks." Roughly, he finishes his job.

I'm shocked, still fighting to control myself, but I will not let them see my despair.

"Stay stripped," he says. "Put your clothes in your bags and wait."

We stand and wait. After what seems an interminable time, he opens the door and motions for us to follow him. Still naked, we walk into a room where a few men and women are standing behind the counter. They size us up with their eyes, ask each of us for our basic measurements, and then stack some clothes and shoes on the counter. Undershirt and shorts, khaki trousers and shirts, ankle-high boots, jacket, poncho.

"Okay, you guys. You're cons now. Do what we tell you to do and keep your mouths shut. Don't expect nothing and you won't be disappointed."

I know what they are up to. We are deliberately being dehumanized, stripped—not just of our clothes, but also of our pride—and forced to realize that normal life as we knew it is gone. We will live at the behest and whim of guards who do not give a damn about us as humans.

My first job is in the prison furniture factory, but I soon get a better job as a clerk to the chaplain and begin to feel that this might not be so terrible. I am about to report in to the chaplain when a new warden stops me outside the mess hall. It's another freezing day. The warden has short, cropped hair and walks with a West Point strut, a martinet with a potbelly. He hands me a three-foot-long stick with a nail sticking out of the end.

"You're fired from your cushy chapel job. Every day from 10:00 to 12:00 and from 2:00 to 4:00 you'll come over to the area around the administration building. Using that stick, you'll pick up all the cigarette butts and put them in a tin can you'll carry. I don't give a damn if the temperature outside is below zero. It's your shtick and your stick, Walker." He hands it to me. It has *governor's stick* burned into the wood.

"I'm going to tell all visitors, 'Look at that guy; he's a former governor.'"

Governor to convict. All my expectations in life, all my beliefs, my idealism—how could they have led me to prison? As I walk away, I think again, as I have a thousand times, that I still haven't figured it out. I battle the desire to say, "I don't deserve this." But I will not fall into what my dad used to call the PLOM trap. *Poor Little Old Me.*

The fact is, I am here. And I must understand, must look in the mirror and ask myself why, demanding an answer. The answer to my son's question isn't obvious at all. I look back at my life and begin to consider what I might have done differently and what on earth made me decide to take that hard road that ultimately led to prison.

---

### TRYING ON JACKETS

At age seventeen, I started out following in my brother's footsteps, wearing the jacket of an apprentice seaman, though I wanted very much to become a lawyer. My brother had begun a wonderful career in the navy and made my dad, an ex-navy man, proud. My brother and I grew up understanding the critical importance of doing exactly that.

The Old Man, as I affectionately call him, had imprinted his name twice onto my brother. In addition to naming him Lewis Walker Jr., Dad also gave his firstborn son the nickname from his own navy days: Waco. The Old Man had picked up this name when someone heard he was from Texas and mentioned the town of Waco, mispronouncing it "Wacko," and the name must have stuck because it seemed to evoke my father's eccentricities. My brother will always be "Waco" (pronounced "Wacko") to me.

One of the strongest lessons of my youth concerned my brother. The Old Man posed a question to me one day. "You're the judge, and your brother comes before you charged with a serious crime." His expression revealed no particular gravity or intensity. "How would you treat him?"

I responded quickly, "I would treat him fairly and in accordance with the law." I expected to be commended.

My dad stared at me in silence. Then, "You mean that if he was guilty you would send him to jail?"

I paused, beginning to wonder if I were headed for trouble. I thought the correct answer was obvious. I reviewed the lessons the Old Man drilled into us, often starting early in the day. "Breakfast sermons," he called them: "Self-esteem becomes ego when you let it show." "Do as I teach and become a better man than me." "Admit your mistakes and make amends." Other lessons were monologues. They stressed the virtues of independence and nonconformity and the dangers of conventional wisdom, or they hammered the need for self-discipline or the delight of new ideas. The most constant sermon subject, though, was the need to combine hard work with thinking, always thinking. "Never open your mouth without thinking first." "Never be one of the herd." "Be an achiever and think, think, think." When finished, he would say, "That's your sermon for the day."

I couldn't think of any of the lessons that would help me out with this question about my brother and the law. So, I finally responded, "Yes."

The Old Man looked at me hard for a long time. Then, apparently having reached a decision, he said, "Dan, I'll see you out behind the henhouse." When we got there, he said tersely, "Okay, take down your britches."

I complied.

"Your answer to my question about your brother was dead wrong. *Dead* wrong. Your brother is your blood. Blood comes before everything else. I said, *everything* else. I want to make sure you never forget that. No matter anything else, no matter who you are, no matter what he did, you will always put your brother first and protect him and help him. Now, I'm going to make sure you never forget this."

He took off his belt and whipped me soundly. He had never done that before and never did it again. Instead, he enforced his discipline with his firm, modulated voice, the power of his mind, and the look in his eyes.

The loyalty issue never came up with Waco. Though younger, I was perceived as being more like the Walker clan than like my mother's side of the family and therefore in need of intense molding and prodding. I went home from grammar school during noon recess once with a bloody nose.

Dad asked, "Is your opponent still standing?" I admitted he was, and Dad said, "You go right back and finish it, son. When the going gets tough, fight harder."

For many years, a bearskin rug sprawled on our living room floor, its claws reaching out and huge yellow-toothed jaws gaping open, one bullet hole in the head—a daily reminder of what my father could do. In Alaska, he had taken my uncle and several other Texans bear hunting. Tracks in the snow on a mountain trail led directly to a silvertip grizzly bear. The huge bear growled and charged. Dad jumped aside, letting the next hunter have the shot. The bullet hit its massive chest, but the grizzly merely roared. The Texan pumped five more shots and failed to stop the oncoming bear, now blowing bloody froth out of its mouth. Dad aimed his .3006 caliber heavy-load rifle just as the eight-foot grizzly fell dead at his companion's feet.

Its hide was the Texan's trophy, but the men encountered another bear several days later. They trekked through the snowy forest, crossing streams on teetering logs, and reached a cabin. Dad pushed the door all the way open. He faced a grizzly, ransacking the place, quickly raised his rifle, and killed the bear with one shot to its head.

Yes, I wanted to please this man.

He deeply desired success for both my brother and me. And he taught repeatedly that the two keys to success for a man with a good mind were hard work and imagination. "Hard work comes first. If you always—every hour and every day—work harder than others, then inevitably you're going to be noticed, and you'll get ahead." And then comes the mind. "Use your imagination to outthink others."

Walkers belong in the "top 10 percent," he said. "Never forget that." Over and over again: "Spell your last name out loud: W-A-L-K-E-R. Go on, let me hear you spell it again, louder. You are a Walker and destined to succeed. Walk like a man. Keep your head up, your shoulders back, your chin in, your chest out, your belly in." Those lessons were drummed into our heads a thousand times.

And so in high school, I regularly achieved the honor society. I joined ROTC, worked on the school newspaper and the student council, and eventually ran for class president—losing badly. Debating was great fun, and my partner and I managed to win matches all the way to the all-state finals. I also won the high school oratorical contest. These skills came naturally to me, and the Old Man was proud. He assured me I would make a fine lawyer someday.

In 1939, I wanted to start applying to colleges, but the Nazis were on the move in Europe, and the Japanese expanded throughout the Pacific. The Old Man knew we would get into it. Waco had joined the naval reserve, and Dad practically chained him to the dining room table for months of studying seven days a week to apply to Annapolis. Mom brought meals to the table and asked that he be given time off. Dad would have none of that. We held a family celebration on the day Waco ran into the house with the letter saying he had been selected to enter the Naval Academy—Dad's lifelong ambition for Waco.

The Old Man said to me, "No son of mine will be drafted into the army. So it's the navy for you."

I enlisted and served three years as a sailor and then took the competitive examination with thousands of other sailors and managed to win admission to the U.S. Naval Academy at Annapolis. Graduating in 1945, I added the gold stripe of an ensign to my dress jacket, raising my position in the world. I served two years on "tin can" destroyers in the Pacific, working up to the rank of lieutenant. I had come to love the navy, yet I wanted to leave it. I felt my true calling was the law. I had this nagging feeling, however, that I had neither done enough for my country, nor had I fully repaid the debt I owed Annapolis.

While at the academy, I met, dated, and fell in love with Roberta Marie Dowse, a good Catholic girl from Kenosha, Wisconsin. Anxious to finally begin a life of conjugal bliss, we married upon my return from the Pacific and honeymooned in the mountains of West Virginia at The Homestead—a resort that offered carriages, high tea, and other trappings of colonial heritage.

"It's time for me to make my move, honey," I told her as we rode in a horse-drawn carriage in April, passing a few patches of snow alongside the first spring flowers. "I've decided to leave the navy and apply to law school. This means we'll have very little to live on."

"I know," she said, "but I don't need fancy things, darling. We'll get by." The frosty air brought out a lovely blush in her cheeks.

"Well . . ." I squeezed her hand, hesitating to approach something I knew absolutely nothing about. "What if . . . ? What about . . . ?"

"Are you wondering what would happen if . . ." She whispered so the coachman wouldn't hear. "I got pregnant?"

"Yes," I whispered back.

She continued in a whisper. "Don't worry. That's up to me. I've learned how to use the rhythm method."

"Oh," I said, unable to fathom what that could possibly mean.

She cupped my ear with her hand and whispered the mysteries of menstrual cycles.

"Oh," I said, mulling things over. "And is this rhythm stuff as reliable as other methods of birth control?"

Her eyes widened. "Dan, we can't even think about those other methods. Birth control is a sin, and I won't do it."

"Oh." We rode along in silence except for the clopping of hooves and birds chirping. "So, your . . . uh . . . rhythm, is it predictable?"

"Dan, if I get pregnant, we'll just figure out a way to get by."

### FINDING ANOTHER LOVE

In 1947, I enrolled at Northwestern University School of Law in Chicago, one of the nation's top ten law schools, having no idea how lucky I was. I didn't know the difference between a debit and a credit; understood little about the development of the English, French, or Russian governments; and knew even less about Plato, Aristotle, and Marx. Fortunately, the law school gave special consideration to veterans. A few years later , I would not have gotten into one of the top law schools with a Naval Academy education without first taking supplemental courses.

To save rent, we spent the summer at Roberta's home in Kenosha. I had to earn as much money as possible. Even with the G.I. Bill paying my tuition, it would be difficult to get by. However, the highest pay available in Kenosha was at the Nash automobile plant, where the boring, assembly-line work of applying nuts to bolts on car wheels for eight hours a day drove me out of my mind. I learned a little about labor union politics, though, when the union shop steward refused to accept my reason for quitting.

"You can't be serious," he said. "No one quits a good job just because it's boring." Eager for a dispute with management, he said, "They must be harassing you."

I finally managed to avoid being the subject of a labor relations dispute, quit Nash, and sought other employment in the home office of Snap-On Tools. When law school time arrived, we had a total of about $2,500 saved—a sum we thought would suffice if we budgeted closely and if I worked part-time. By attending summer school, I could finish law school in thirty months instead of the usual thirty-six.

Roberta's rhythm system failed, and she became pregnant, just before we left for Chicago and law school. The difficulty of finding an apartment in those postwar times shocked us. Anything decent would require buying the used furniture—at a seriously inflated price—from the previous inhabitants. We settled on a second-story, two-bedroom walk-up with reasonable rent on the far west side of Chicago, but we had to pay $1,250 for inadequate furniture. This *debit*—a concept I soon understood all too well—nearly demolished our savings. At least we were near a streetcar line that would take me to Northwestern.

Unlike my experience at the Naval Academy, where boredom contributed to keeping my GPA unremarkable, I found law school intellectually stimulating and was surprised that top grades came easily. I took a part-time job with the Veterans Administration and then typed papers at home for ten cents per page, using a small portable typewriter purchased secondhand.

Kathleen Marie Walker arrived in March of 1948 during my first year in law school, and Daniel Walker Jr. followed in the second year. Roberta had her hands full. I loved our babies but had to work late and study even later and couldn't help much. We never ate in a restaurant or went out for a movie. Roberta never visited a beauty parlor. Many veterans shared the same experience of combining new marriage, children, hard work, and college under the G.I. Bill. But, like them, we were happy, and I soon fell totally in love—with the law.

I was not just learning how to use the law but also why and how the law came to be the way that it was and how it fit into government. The concept of the law as noble had never occurred to me before—that the rule of law could provide the very foundation for a free nation. Law was no longer a dry subject of study, but a way to build an exciting career and provide tools to make life better for people. The chance to do just that thrilled me. If my vision of myself as a lawyer had previously been a vague sense of what felt right, it became a clear mission that would fill my life.

A young man's dreams are nourished in unlooked-for ways. We finally managed to buy a cheap used car and visited Roberta's parents and then her Aunt Gertrude and Uncle David van Patten in rural northern Illinois. Uncle Dave, a longtime member of the Lake County Board of Supervisors, fascinated me with his insight on the workings of local government. He said, "State government tends to forget those of us at the county level." I never forgot those words. Roberta's uncle had unknowingly given me a vital direction.

I jumped into politics. In 1948, Colonel Jake Arvey, chairman of the Cook County Democratic Central Committee—the undisputed boss of the party—amazed all the Chicago machine regulars by putting together the ticket of a scrappy independent South Side alderman named Paul Douglas, also a professor, for the U.S. Senate, and Adlai Stevenson for governor. Adlai, an Ivy League lawyer often called a liberal egghead, and Douglas became my heroes. I had always been a Democrat, as my father had been. But these men showed me that idealism belonged in the Democratic Party. People who saw Adlai as only an egghead overlooked the fact that this was the man who helped found the United Nations. Neither Douglas nor Stevenson was given much chance, but I campaigned my heart out for those two.

A young law school graduate and I formed Veterans for Douglas and Stevenson, and cofounded the postwar Young Democrats of Illinois. I became its North Side vice president and enthusiastically licked many an envelope. Hard campaigning paid off. Douglas and Stevenson won the same year that Harry Truman scored his surprising national upset victory, and I was proud to have been a part of it.

When I was pounding the pavements for the campaign, Chicago's diverse ethnicity came as a cultural shock to me. In rural San Diego where I grew up, I had never heard of Armenians, our landlords' nationality. (I wasn't at home much, and they kindly treated Roberta almost as if she were family.) Nor was I familiar with Poles, Germans, Greeks, Sicilians, Lithuanians, Russians—or for that matter, Jews in skullcaps, and especially Hassidic Jews in black hats and curled locks. For the first time in my life, I encountered serious anti-Semitism and racism. I knew none of the Yiddish terms that my classmates in law school used easily. To my amazement, people used parish names like St. Marks or St. Andrews for geographic references. Whole families crowded into noisy Irish taverns while the menfolk guzzled beer. I took Roberta and the kids to Maxwell Street, a perpetual ethnic flea market where ripe cheeses hung on ropes alongside garlicky sausages and piles of unwrapped breads. Hungarian goulash steamed in open pots. Fruits and vegetables were piled onto pushcarts. Cookware, clothing, shoes, tools, an occasional bit of Irish lace—all were for sale.

I received blank looks when I tried to interest these people in voting for Stevenson and Douglas on the basis of issues. They had little idea how government could serve them. The street reality of politics required acceptance of the diversity of real people, not just of an unleavened, abstract mass. Such diversity moved me away from idealism and theory. Even though the law could provide a way to change these people's lives for the better, you couldn't have good law without the concrete reality of good, practical politics. Idealistic politicians like Paul Douglas and Adlai Stevenson could make laws work for real people. And so could I.

### THE BEST JACKET

In 1949, I was chosen to be editor-in-chief of both *Northwestern University Law Review* and the *Journal of Criminal Law and Criminology*, jobs that traditionally went to the person at the top of the class—an accomplishment I had, in fact, managed to pull off, despite juggling the political work, home life, legal studies, and a part-time job. Those editorial jobs finally forced me to cut back on part-time work. Two babies, rent due, and food to be put on the table—I could often see worry in Roberta's eyes.

"Dan, why this editor position on top of everything else? You already don't spend enough time with your children. Let somebody else do it!" She was almost in tears.

"Sweetheart, don't you see? This editor job is a sure ticket into the nation's best law firms. I can't pass it up. Once I take on a job, it has to be full tilt. Nothing halfway."

I doubt that she ever understood my compulsion to not only excel in my intended career path but also to demonstrate leadership qualities. I wanted to do what my father had taught me: Be the best, the top at whatever I undertook. I honestly can't explain why I so readily accepted the concept that achieving goals in life had a higher priority than spending time with family. I would have died for my family, but I couldn't live the quiet life for them. Yet, I was just about to step down from my exciting editorial jobs for their sakes.

A modest cash grant from a foundation based on my law school standing saved the day. Freed from the part-time job, I couldn't just be an editor for Northwestern's publications; I had to create a first, an annual conference of law review editors from throughout the nation. And even that wasn't enough. I also became an unpaid intern for the Chicago Crime Commission, then the nation's most prestigious citizens' crime commission, specializing as a watchdog over the Mafia in Chicago. My task was to work on proposed state anticrime legislation. Somehow, I found time to draft the bills for an attorney, Tom Mulroy, the chairman of the commission's legislative committee.

This was my first real cause and one that gripped me. There had to be a compelling cause for seeking high office. The law and politics were not enough. Along with fighting organized crime, improving mental health care became an important cause for me, and I worked with Lieutenant Governor Sam Shapiro to draft a new mental health code for Illinois. If government wouldn't help the helpless, who would? Someone once said that the best measure of good government is how it treats the unfortunate among us—including particularly those in jails and mental institutions.

One of my favorite professors, Willard Wirtz—who taught labor law and would later become secretary of labor under President Kennedy—chaired a meeting of students, faculty, and alumni in a wood-paneled grand room that displayed portraits of former deans and distinguished graduates. I was to be recognized, and for my introduction I thought he would simply recite the usual summary of accomplishments.

He began his remarks by saying, "I want to introduce a guy who someday will become governor of Illinois."

I was stunned. Afterwards, I asked him why he had said such a thing.

"Because that's what you have talent to be," he said.

His compliment excited me, offering a surprising and attractive vision of myself bringing the law to life through real governing power. During my time in the navy, I had felt like I was wearing someone else's ill-fitting, uncomfortable jacket. Imagining myself as governor one day was like trying on a dearly expensive coat that fit perfectly.

Such a goal seemed utterly beyond my reach now, with two kids and Roberta carrying our third. She could never understand just how much this picture captivated her husband's heart and mind. My dad taught me that dreams were useless without facing facts. Guts, dedication, and imagination were essential—I thought I could supply those—but realities had to be taken into account. As a neophyte to the strange political system of Illinois, I couldn't see how this could be done. Common sense told me this was only a pipe dream. I should simply work hard and become the best lawyer possible. However, I still aimed to be a politically involved attorney, and the governor-dream would not die.

January of 1950 brought law school graduation. Roberta, heavily pregnant, left our two babies at home with our landlords, the Armenian couple, for the occasion. I was named to the prestigious Order of the Coif, a legal honorary society, and received the John Henry Wigmore award for outstanding contributions to the law school. Then, Willard Pedrick, one of my professors, approached the rostrum. He announced that I had been selected to be a law clerk at the U.S. Supreme Court. I was a young man on fire.

Afterward, Roberta hugged me. "I'm very proud of you, honey. I see now how your hard work has paid off."

I told her how happy her reaction made me. She was still curious.

"Out of all the country's top law graduates, how did they pick you for this top job?"

I explained to her that Willard Pedrick had served as a law clerk for Fred Vinson when Vinson was a judge on the Federal District of Columbia Circuit Court of Appeals. President Harry Truman promoted Vinson to the Supreme Court, and then, as now, justices of the Supreme Court looked to professors at the nation's top law schools to recommend students to become their law clerks. Everyone knew this job was an excellent entrée into the legal profession. Vinson was named chief justice, and he turned to Pedrick for his clerks. These were two-year jobs working for the chief, even better than the one-year term clerking for other justices. The "chief," as he is informally called at the Court, is not chief justice of the U.S. Supreme Court; rather, he is chief justice of the United States. I would become the chief's junior law clerk starting in July of that year, 1950.

I called my father and told him about my honors and the exciting clerkship.

"That's great," he said. "You're on your way. Now, go to work."

Work was the foundation of success for him, never resting on laurels. Resting was not the problem, though. There was absolutely no danger of that. If anything, I was overactive and headstrong. Nothing could stop me.

And yet, much later, something *would* stop me. As my father would have put it, this law I loved so much would turn around and bite me in the ass.

## 2

## *The War, Law School, and the*
## *U.S. Supreme Court*

The temperature in the prison yard is about twenty degrees, and a light snow covers the ground outside the prison office building. I'm shivering, and my hands keep sticking to the "governor's stick." It's hard to stab a cigarette butt when your hands are nearly frozen. Even in the best weather, it's tough. My can holds about two dozen, and it's only half full.

Returning to his office, the new warden sees me and stops to watch. This bastard likes to see me suffer from the cold. He obviously enjoys my misery. Most of the inmates agree he is a prime son of a bitch, but I think he especially relishes humiliating men of former high position.

"Come with me, Walker," he says.

We walk into his office. At least it's warmer inside. He sits and leaves me standing.

"I have an additional job for you."

He pretends to be busy, deliberately keeping me in suspense. A picture of himself as a West Point cadet hangs behind him on the stark walls. Maybe this man expected more of himself and must take his frustration out on others. "Let's see how a governor scrubs bathroom floors and toilets," he says.

The toilets I am to clean are in the prison's clothing store. Not just those used by inmates but also those used by male and female staff workers. I must also scrub and polish all the tiled floors.

I am determined to view this assignment as a challenge and show that I can do these tasks better than anyone else possibly could. I had done all this before, cleaning heads and scrubbing decks when I served as an apprentice seaman in the navy a long time ago. It didn't get to me then, and I won't let it get to me now.

I get up early enough to get some ice cubes from a machine before going to breakfast. A prison guard asks, "What are you doin' with all that ice?"

"They call this place a country club, right?"

He scoffs. The ice is just a part of my plan to make these bathrooms the absolute best. For the toilets, I scrounge ice cubes twice daily to place in the urinals, just as they do in gentlemen's clubs, to dissipate the odor. I'm not sure why it works; I only know that it does. I also scrub floors and then polish the tiles to a high gloss several times daily to keep the shine clear enough to see your face reflected. I even buy cheap perfume at the prison store and spray it frequently on the freshly cleaned toilets used by women staffers.

Not only does this satisfy my "do each job better than anyone else" compulsion, I am also getting back at that warden. I can just see his reaction. Believing that someone will tell him what I do—since every detail of prison happenings is reported to the warden—I positively enjoy the thought of his frustration at his inability to humiliate or break me. *Damn you,* I think, *you're not demeaning me; you're just giving me an opportunity to prove that I'm a better man.*

I defy him even more openly and actively by teaching the inmates how to seek legal redress for violations of their constitutional rights by filing petitions for habeas corpus. I hate the sloppy legal practices that have deprived a number of these prisoners of their sentencing rights. Such a class is permitted by the prison regulations of the Department of Justice, so the warden cannot stop me.

———————

## WONDERLAND

After graduating in January 1950, I was determined to make the best use of my time—as The Old Man had always prodded me to—before reporting to the Supreme Court in July. Adlai Stevenson, then serving as governor, had created the CSSG, the Commission to Study State Government, with an eye to simplifying a maze of agencies, boards, commissions, and departments that reported to the governor. Professor Walter Schaefer, who had first introduced me to Stevenson and who had joined his administration as counsel to the governor, became the CSSG chairman. Schaefer, in turn, asked me to work on the CSSG staff for those six interim months.

Roberta and I and the kids moved two hundred miles south to Springfield into a small, furnished house. I began another love affair—one with state government—and it was quite passionate. In studying all those agencies and commissions that made up state government, my innate idealism kicked in. I wanted not to just simplify complicated government; I also wanted to see it work better for people. Streamlining that structure was only part of the challenge. Moving the pieces of government around was not enough. I went to Jack Isakoff, the staff director, with my idea.

"Jack, why can't we include with our report, not just ways to make state government more efficient, but ways to make it *work* better for more people? For example, ways to guide people with problems through this bureaucratic maze, making government not just more efficient, but more productive."

Jack smiled and chuckled. "That's all very noble, Dan. Now get back to work. Just do the simple task I've assigned to you. Get over to the Department of Insurance. That has too many offices. Just figure out a way to simplify it."

While working on that assignment, I learned that the department was a haven for legislators' mistresses. With offices near the House and Senate chambers, it was a handy place for legislators to place mistresses in clerical or secretarial positions with a department head anxious to go along in order to protect appropriations.

Mike Royko, the noted Chicago columnist, once wrote that these women were called "monkey girls" because they "held their jobs with their tails." They enjoyed what were called "floor privileges" that allowed them to visit their men when the legislature was in session. I learned from old-timers in the insurance department how they watched with amusement a senator's wife looking on from the balcony at an attractive woman down on the floor bringing her husband a cup of coffee, having no idea of their real relationship.

I gave Jack a paper proposing to eliminate some useless functions and to add a new one to simplify complicated insurance policies with straightforward language telling people what they were getting for their money. At the end of the paper, I wrote, "And get rid of the legislators' mistresses, replacing them with employees who would put more of their energies into working for the state, rather than taking care of their boyfriends." The commission was interested in the structure of government, but not in day-to-day operations. The monkey girls kept swinging.

I also went up to the balcony once to see Governor Stevenson's wife, who occasionally came over from the Executive Mansion to watch the proceedings. I met her once at the mansion when invited to attend a party. Her much-gossiped-about bathroom was lined with heavy mirrors, including the floor. Some had kinky theories as to why she had installed them, but no one really knew. I got a firsthand look at the contrast between the outward appearances of state government and what really went on, as if stepping into the looking glass, entering political wonderland. I was fascinated.

A staff member showed me the governor's office on the first floor of the mansion where Adlai spent most of his office hours, not caring for the large, formal office in the State House that was so accessible to legislators, lobbyists, and opportunists. I confess that after looking to see that nobody was watching, I tried sitting in the governor's chair. I liked this office.

While in Springfield, our third child, Julie Ann, arrived. For the first time in our married life, I was able to join Roberta and the children for family time every evening. And we could occasionally afford some nights out. The time in Springfield was brief, however, and when I headed for Washington, Roberta went to stay with her mother in Kenosha until we were ready to settle down in Washington. I was eager to start my new job with the chief justice, and this filled my mind. Yet I still thought about Springfield. My gut told me that I would be back.

### HEARING JUSTICE THINK

In July 1950, I went to work at the U.S. Supreme Court. First, though, I found an apartment in Arlington, Virginia, about ten miles from where I was born. It was big enough for our growing family, and one we could afford on my monthly salary of $300. The work exhilarated me, allowing me to deal with major cases, raise critical points of law, and handle cases that made front-page news across the nation. We wrote memos on the petitions for review in those cases, petitions for writs of *certiorari*, as they are called. And we researched law points where the chief wanted our help. Sometimes, though rarely, the chief asked us to prepare drafts of opinions for him—thrilling assignments, especially for someone right out of law school.

Getting to know the other justices was also a rewarding experience. These famous men were not mere judges. They were to be the embodiment of their title: justice. And I had the opportunity to "hear them think." I remember heady occasions when Justice Felix Frankfurter would wander into our office to discuss pending cases and actually listen to our views. Justice William Douglas, who was talked about as a candidate for the presidency, had a public reputation as a man of the people. The clerks, however, found him aloof. They had crudely printed on a cardboard badge "Justice Douglas spoke to me," and it was awarded on the rare occasion when the justice returned a law clerk's greeting in the Court's corridors. On one occasion near Christmas, when the clerk for Douglas asked for a few days off to get married in California, his callous response was, "Get married on your own time." With such an attitude, he wasn't particularly popular with the clerks for the other justices.

Our dealings with Vinson, the chief, on the other hand, were very relaxed. I recall the red telephone on his desk. When that phone rang, we had been told to immediately and quietly leave his office. It was a direct line to his good friend Harry Truman. Vinson told us they talked about their poker games. Needless to say, that kind of conviviality between a chief justice and the president would not be acceptable today.

The chief regularly discussed with us the Court's work, much more than other justices did with their clerks. Each week, after the conference where preliminarily votes were taken on pending cases, he would fill us in on the details—who voted which way on each important case. We were able in this way to understand the politics of the Court, the jousting and the often shifting coalitions.

And then came one of the most powerful challenges to the First Amendment in our history. The Supreme Court would decide the constitutionality of making membership in the Communist Party a crime. Chief Justice Vinson had trouble putting together the solid support he wanted for this important case. The very idea of legitimizing the party offended several justices, but the chief wanted no less than a unanimous decision. He argued with them by phone and traipsed from office to office, challenging those who were troubled about the free speech issue inherent in legitimizing the Communist Party, and finally building consensus out of disputation. He wanted to let the public know that the Court spoke with one voice on critical national issues.

Other clerks were always anxious to hear what we could relate about these disputes, though we carefully followed the chief's admonitions as to what was confidential. To this day, I dislike reading reports of Supreme Court law clerks giving what should be confidential information about the Court's work to reporters or authors of books. A good example is Bob Woodward's *The Brethren*, in which he described—based on such information—"what the justices were thinking and discussing" about pending cases. I blame the clerks for making the disclosures and Woodward for printing them, particularly where he presumed to know what the justices were thinking.

Overall, the majesty of the law and the Supreme Court's vital place in our system gripped me powerfully—not just theoretically, but in real cases involving head-on collisions with tough legal issues. Nobody could succeed in government without truly grasping the role of the judiciary as one of our three branches of government. This was an irreplaceable career education for me.

The chief called me into his office one morning to say that I was being called back into active duty with the navy, cutting the normal two-year clerk-ship term to one. The secretary of the navy had informed him as a matter of courtesy, telling him that because of the Korean conflict they were calling back all reserved members of my Naval Academy class.

The chief said, "I hope you understand, Dan, that I could not urge the Secretary to skip you, much as I like your work here."

"I understand, Sir. This has been an amazing experience, and I'm grateful, but I don't really mind another stint in the navy. I have a blue and gold streak up my back." It was true. Love of country and the navy was an obligation I was raised to understand and accept. I recommended my old friend Newt Minow from law school as my replacement. (Years later, Newt would serve as chairman of the Federal Communications Commission, holding that position when he famously denounced television programming as "a vast wasteland.")

### SOME KIND OF HOT STUFF

I was ordered to report in San Diego, California, to the USS *Kidd* (DD 661) as communications officer. Roberta, a good sport about the constant changes in jobs, and the three kids joined me in the trip cross-country in January 1951. After a disastrous car failure at night in a snowstorm, a car-stopping dust storm in Kansas, and a dangerous ice storm in El Paso, Texas, we finally arrived safely at my parents' home in Encanto, a small rural community outside San Diego. We rented a home in Chula Vista, a nearby town, where Roberta and the kids would stay while my ship went over to Korea. I had been told to expect two years of service. My ship, the *Kidd*, was nicknamed "Pirate of the Pacific" in World War II, and while it emerged from the mothballs at the San Diego destroyer base—a two-month process—I did my best to help Roberta get ready to handle the family while I was gone. She didn't drive, so she would have to rely on Mom to take her shopping, and would have to walk across Chula Vista with three little children to go to church.

Strangely, I have no memory of that trip across the Pacific to Sasebo on the southern tip of Japan. *Kidd* was ordered to "firing line" duty off the coast of Korea in the Sea of Japan, lobbing five-inch shells into North Korean–Chinese Communist troop positions. Their artillery returned fire constantly, and occasionally stray Chi-Com fighters in Russian-made MIGs tracked us, but a rapidly maneuvering destroyer is an elusive target for both shore artillery and fast-flying jets.

After several months of this duty, I received a letter from Chief Judge Robert Quinn of the U.S. Court of Military Appeals in Washington, D.C. He informed me that Congress had recently established this court under the new Uniform Code of Military Justice for the purpose of hearing appeals from courts-martial. Then the chief judge wrote politely that he had learned of my desire to become one of three deputy chief commissioners for the new court.

*What?* I had absolutely no idea what he was talking about.

He added that one deputy was to be appointed from each of the services—the Army, the Navy, and the Marine Corps. The Air Force had supplied the chief commissioner.

All news to me. When I read out loud the last line of his letter, "Stop by my office when you get a chance," my fellow officers laughed with me. Many thousands of miles away on the far side of the world, I puzzled over what it was all about and did not take the letter seriously. In fact, with the long working hours and under considerable stress, I soon forgot it.

About two weeks later, we were operating with a large aircraft carrier task force. Two fast cruisers and twenty-four destroyers formed a huge, circular screen to protect two aircraft carriers. While in this position and watching out for MIGs one night when I was officer of the deck on the bridge, my chief radioman came up with a dispatch. He shined the beam on the message clipboard and spoke softly so no one else could hear.

"Boss, you'd better look at this before I take it to the captain."

Actually, he was violating protocol since the captain should have seen the message first. I was both startled and amazed when I read the message from the navy's top admiral, the chief of naval operations in Washington (called "CNO").

> To Commanding Officer *Kidd* (DD 661)
> Lieutenant Daniel Walker USN ordered detached *Kidd* proceed first available
> transportation report SecNav Washington D.C.

As you might guess, "SecNav" was the secretary of the navy in the president's cabinet. "First available transportation" meant just that. A copy of the message going to the task force commander informed him that *Kidd* was required to leave the task force immediately and deliver me to a port where I could get air transportation to Washington.

On the other side of the bridge, the captain read the message and walked over to me. "Read this," he said. "You must be some kind of hot stuff, Mr. Walker. Referencing this dispatch, inform the task force commander that *Kidd* is proceeding independently in accordance with CNO orders, and then shape a course that'll take us to Sasebo."

Coming directly from the CNO, this couldn't possibly be a routine transfer. In wonderment, I quickly complied with both orders, having no idea whatsoever what was in store for me. I never thought of myself as hot stuff, of course, but I was certainly ambitious to get to the top, somehow, some way.

When the *Kidd* reached Sasebo, I caught a military plane to Tokyo and then another to Washington, D.C. I hated flying, especially when it entailed sitting in hard metal bucket seats for many hours. After reaching stateside, I telephoned Roberta. She and the kids were managing well. I told her I was on my way east to Washington. My answer to all her questions was, "I just don't know what's up. I'm in the dark."

Arriving in Washington after the exhausting trip, I reported to the Navy Department and finally learned the facts. My old buddy Newt Minow—as a thank-you for my recommending him as replacement law clerk for the chief justice—had made a pitch for me. He happened to encounter at a cocktail party the man who was assembling the new Court of Military Appeals and who described to him the position of deputy chief commissioner, saying they had filled the other deputy spots but as yet had no one from the navy. Newt told him, "I've got just the guy for you," and gave him my name. The matter went up to the top, where the decision was made. Such is the way things often get done in Washington.

The secretary of the navy's staff duty officer crisply informed me that the navy wanted me to take the job and that I would be immediately released from active duty if the chief judge of the new court wanted me. This was wonderful news. I could continue fulfilling my military obligation while at the same time furthering my career—a plum of a job.

After an interview, the chief judge did want me. I called Roberta and told her to bring the family east. On the way, she spent some time in Kenosha with her parents and finally learned how to drive. In Washington, we settled down in an apartment and enjoyed life. That was 1951. The court job was not hard. My cohorts and I had fact-finding power, and I mostly did research and wrote opinions for the chief judge in court-martial appeal cases.

Election year 1952 arrived, and then-governor Adlai Stevenson called to say that Newt Minow, who was already working with him, had recommended me to join his growing staff. Once again my friend Newt helped me. Eager to participate, I persuaded the chief judge, a former governor of Rhode Island who also liked Adlai, to grant me a leave of absence from the court. This abrupt departure was almost too much for Roberta. All the changes began taking a toll. As soon as possible after our fourth child was born, I brought Roberta and Carol Sue home from the hospital and left immediately for Springfield, Illinois, feeling terrible about abandoning her, but also feeling that I couldn't pass this up.

My 1952 job as Adlai's administrative assistant was actually more with Illinois government than with the national campaign. Because of my Schaeffer Commission background (CSSG), Adlai needed me to help deal with governmental crises while he was out of the state, immersed in the campaign. I worked on state issues with Carl McGowan, one of my law school professors and now counsel to the governor.

Lieutenant Governor Sherwood Dixon officially took over when Adlai left the state, and I also spent a lot of time with him, adding considerably to my knowledge of state government. While others working for Adlai dreamed of positions in the federal government, I felt happy right where I was in state government. And some of my experiences played to my dreams, such as the time I rode to a disaster area in a state police car with sirens screaming, just like a real governor.

During the campaign, I thoroughly enjoyed getting to know Adlai. Talking with him about Truman's performance as president and his own role in the formation of the United Nations fascinated me. This was my desired milieu; government at the highest level. However, Adlai's frequent indecisiveness on critical issues, such as the threat of Communism, bothered me and other voters as well. Also, he often allowed the Chicago political bosses to have what I thought was undue sway on state legislative issues. He regularly yielded power to the party machine leaders on matters affecting Chicago instead of making the decisions himself. He even went so far in one speech as to call Richard J. Daley, then a leading official in the Chicago machine, a "four-square friend of reform," and the machine itself "an inspiration to the rest of the country." Not fond of machine politics even then, I found this hard to swallow.

Yet I loved Adlai and gathered nervously with the rest of the workers to watch the returns. There were so many bright, young, impassioned people among us. I felt energized in a way I could never get from my home life. I cried when Adlai lost the race for president. So did the pretty campaign aide I was working with during this emotional time. I reached out to her for a comforting hug, and she readily responded. Hugging led to kisses.

The whole time though, a little voice was shouting at me, "Dan, you're a married man!" The next morning, I called Roberta to reassure her of my love, promising myself this would not happen again. It was just the intensity of the campaign, I told myself, since I had an extremely strong commitment to marriage and family and still considered myself a moral person. My father had warned me that my attraction to pretty women could be my undoing. I would have to be very careful to resist such available temptations.

After Adlai's loss, I quickly bounced back to the military appeals court. Even though I was not obligated to stay there, I felt compelled to complete my two-year stint, just as my Annapolis classmates in the reserves completed theirs. I found time during the workday to write my first book. *Military Law* was designed as a textbook for the military justice courses then becoming prevalent in the nation's law schools. In addition, I taught military law to night classes at American University School of Law in Washington.

I was comfortable with letting Roberta take care of the kids because I felt strongly that it was my duty to pursue my career and become successful—for the family's sake as well as my own. I never discussed it with her, confident that she was raised with the same priorities. Some people would say I was a workaholic, even an overachiever, but I just thought I was doing what a man at the head of a family was supposed to do.

**3**

*My Introduction to Machine Politics*

I am walking from the barracks to the law class I'm giving for the inmates. It is another bitterly cold day, below zero, with a north wind lashing the compound.

A guard stops me. "Strip and spread!" he commands as he pulls a rubber glove over his right hand.

I remember these words from my initial experience on entering prison. He orders me to remove all clothing and hold my buttocks apart while he searches the anal orifice. The guards never stop looking for drugs, knowing that some way, somehow, prisoners manage to get them into the prison. I have learned that the searches are not just routine efforts to find drugs, however. They are a part of the subjugation and control system, another way to demean, depersonalize, and control the inmates.

"Okay, Walker. Right now."

The guys I'm walking with hurry away; others nearby stop and watch. Some men enjoy seeing others humiliated.

"Sir," I ask, "can't we go inside to do this? It's damn cold out here."

"Who do ya think you are, Walker? You think you're a big shot, better than the rest of the shit in this prison? Get to it, guy; you know the routine. And you better strip fast. We'd all like to see how you could cope with solitary."

I remove my hooded flannel jacket, shirt, pants, undershorts, socks, and boots. Bare feet on the cold tarmac, I comply. I submit, trying to think of other things. I, who revere the law and served in the highest court in the land, am considered a criminal and will be late to a class teaching criminals about the law because a supposed upholder of the law enjoys his job of inflicting such intimate humiliation. The irony is as shocking as the cold air and the man's rough handling.

In prison, one thing that keeps me going is the belief that I'm trying to help people. I arrive at my class for the inmates, freezing cold and holding myself rigid to keep from shivering in front of the men in the class, some of whom must know what just happened. I am determined to continue teaching. The guys keep gathering in the chapel building after supper for the weekly two-hour class.

Law books were allowed in the prison library, which was also legally required to make available a full set of prison regulations. The criminal justice system changed during this time. Previously, sentences were indeterminate, with a prisoner's release based on applications for parole. With good behavior, prisoners usually served only about one-third of their sentence. Naturally, this led to plea-bargaining by prosecutors carrying very heavy caseloads. They would offer a reduced sentence, knowing that only one-third of it would be served—the alternative being a not-guilty plea and the risk of a much longer sentence if the defendant were convicted.

By the late 1980s, when I was in prison, Congress had dramatically changed the federal criminal sentencing law. Sentences were now determinate or fixed, with only a small reduction for good behavior. Parole had been abolished. Every defendant would serve at least 85 percent of his sentence. Yielding to political pressure from people increasingly concerned about rising crime rates and the widely varying sentences being handed down by judges for the same offense, Congress enacted a law imposing uniform, mandatory, and more severe sentences, taking away judges' power to impose a sentence with a range of years: for example, two to ten for armed robbery. The new law decreed, say, twelve years for armed robbery. Period. No judicial discretion. Only a short reduction, up to 15 percent of the total sentence, depending on time served, was allowed.

I was convicted and sentenced under the old law, but now the new law had gone into effect, and inmates sentenced under it had no right whatsoever to parole. This created considerable problems among the prisoners. A man convicted in 1987, for example, could look forward to a realistic possibility of parole after serving one-third of a nine-year sentence with good behavior. Another man convicted in 1988 of exactly the same crime has had no hope for parole and would have to serve a minimum of seven years of a nine-year sentence, regardless of his behavior.

Because of my conviction date, I am still eligible for parole, and I am strategizing about how soon to attempt it, but I feel I can offer other prisoners possible alternatives. Unfortunately, many neighborhood or small-town lawyers are not aware of the changes in the law and have continued to let their clients expect to get out after one-third of their sentence.

One prisoner the guards pick on, partly because he is pudgy and wears glasses, is Sheffield, or "Sheff" for short. He was a bookkeeper arrested on a federal drug offense involving a small amount of cocaine. The mandatory sentence under the federal guidelines was ridiculous: twelve years. He pleaded guilty, having been told erroneously by his lawyer that he would have to serve only one-third of the sentence. He had figured that one-third of twelve was his best gamble. Imagine his outrage over such lousy legal advice from his lawyer when he learned that his sentence was fixed.

Sheff told me his story at the end of one of my classes, and I advised him to file a motion to have his sentence reduced on the basis of his lawyer's erroneous advice—a clearly incompetent counsel. He took my advice, the judge reduced his sentence to time already served, and he walked out of prison. Neither the guards nor the warden were happy about my role in getting this young man out of their reach.

In my class, I teach the men not only about their right to challenge sentences from prison, I also teach them how to prepare and file petitions for habeas corpus in the federal court in Duluth. I cover other aspects of the law, other ways that men can get court relief for their problems, including any mistreatment they have received while in prison.

The day after Sheff walked, I again heard the guard commanding a search and probe of a sixty-five-year-old man for narcotics. Me. I am utterly humiliated as those watching simply stare.

At least the weather is a little above freezing this evening. In the yard, I am astonished to see a familiar face among the black inmates: former Chicago alderman Dick Kelley who, I later found out, was a kind of kingpin among the black inmates, despite the fact that his light complexion allowed him to move among both blacks and whites.

### THE MACHINE

In 1953, I was ambitious and ready to seriously pursue my career in law, and if opportunities arose, work my way into politics—my true dream. With a growing family, however, I needed to begin earning the kind of income I had long been promising Roberta. Carl McGowan, Adlai Stevenson's legal counsel, had earlier wanted me to join him in practicing law in Chicago. Now he had become a "name partner" in an old-line, well-established Chicago law firm renamed Dailey, Dines, Ross, McGowan, and O'Keefe. He asked me to join the firm. This was the kind of law firm my dad had in mind when he told me not to be a lawyer making a living by handling DUIs and misdemeanors and chasing ambulances. Like his brother after whom I was named, Dad wanted me to be a more significant lawyer, representing important clients.

In those days, beginners were called "clerks" just as they were in the 1800s, not "associates" as they now are. We moved to Chicago in early 1954 and rented a home at 11427 South Longwood Drive in the Morgan Park community, a part of Chicago's Nineteenth Ward. I wanted a place with a short train ride to the Loop. A former law school classmate, Al Scheele, whom I had worked with in Veterans for Stevenson-Douglas in 1948, helped me find a place. Al, Louise, and their two children became close family friends.

That summer, we drove from Chicago to San Diego in our first memorable visit to California. We had four kids by then, and we all piled into a station wagon for the drive west in July. No air conditioning. Horribly uncomfortable, we drove across Texas, New Mexico, and Arizona. When the time arrived to return to Chicago, I was absolutely unwilling to repeat those days on the hot southwestern highways. I sold the car, and we flew back.

I missed the exciting days of the Stevenson campaign. One of my heroes, Paul Douglas, was up for reelection as U.S. senator, so after we returned from our trip, my neighbor Al Steele asked me to work with him in ward politics, and though Roberta wasn't too pleased, I insisted on making time. I officially became an assistant Democratic precinct captain in Chicago's Nineteenth Ward, an experience that would force me to define myself politically in ways I hadn't imagined. I was about to encounter machine politics, where organizational efficiency constantly trumped idealism. I had read, of course, of the infamous Tammany Hall in New York City, the Boss Hague machine in New Jersey, and the Kansas City machine that yielded Harry Truman. So I knew that the Chicago variety had as its principal occupation the turning out of votes on Election Day—for the Democratic candidates, of course. But nothing I had read prepared me for the real thing.

I very much wanted to be a working member of the Democratic Party apparatus to understand just how it was so successful in electing Democratic candidates. I was, and proudly remain, a Yellow Dog Democrat, like my father—I would vote for a yellow dog if the party ran him as a candidate. I strongly endorsed straight ticket voting. The Democratic Party, I always believed, is the party of the people. This is the party that gave us Social Security and gave the labor unions power to check the excesses of large corporations who were interested only in bigger and bigger profits, a party that doesn't want big business running America. Its leaders were my personal heroes: George Ball and Dean Acheson, who helped create the Marshall Plan that so effectively rebuilt Europe after World War II; Adlai Stevenson, my hero from law school days.

And most Democratic Party leaders had what old-timers called "fire in the belly," a burning desire to make government work better for people. If a Yellow Dog ran on the Democratic ticket, he was, at least, accountable to the party's platform and would therefore serve the people better than a Republican. The answer to any possible corruption within the party was not to abandon priorities and switch to the party that favored big business over the people, but to always keep the people's welfare as the top priority and work for change within the party.

That passionate party loyalty was about to undergo the crucible of the Chicago machine. Chicago was divided into fifty wards and over a thousand precincts. Each precinct, like mine in the Nineteenth Ward, had a captain appointed by a ward committeeman, and many captains had assistants. The voters of each ward elected an alderman, similar to a city councilman, except the ward committeemen usually handpicked the candidate. Politically, the committeemen owed their loyalty not to the precinct captains who elected them but to the chairman of the Cook County Democratic Central Committee that comprised all the ward committeemen. Through the years, this chairmanship has been the most powerful political job in Chicago. Irish Catholic males dominated the Nineteenth Ward organization, so it was a little unusual that my precinct captain was a middle-aged woman. Another Catholic stronghold was the Eleventh Ward, particularly a community called Bridgeport (later called the "Mother of Mayors") near the stockyards that bordered on the predominantly black South Side areas. Nearby were the notorious "river wards" strung along the Chicago River running south out of the Loop, where the machine regularly turned out top-heavy votes for Democratic candidates. I would concentrate on my Nineteenth Ward, but I longed to know and understand the whole system.

My first job involved door-to-door canvassing, following the Chicago machine's plus-minus-zero system, an amazingly efficient procedure that went back to Abraham Lincoln's days in local politics. I saw myself using it in future campaigns. Precinct captains and workers talked to every voter in the precinct about six weeks before the election, recording a plus for a sure vote, minus for a negative reaction, and zero for uncommitted or unsure. We would follow up several weeks later to record changes, but we never called on minus voters. We only ensured that the pluses were solid and attempted to convert zeros to pluses.

The first night of canvassing, Al and I stopped at a tavern for a beer, and he warned me, "Dan, most folks in Morgan Park are scared of the blacks taking over their neighborhood. Also, this is a very Catholic ward. Keep this in mind in your conversations with these people. You've gotta know how this city really works. You have to understand ethnic likes and dislikes if you want to be active at any level of politics. At least in this ward, we don't have to hear people being called Polacks or Spics."

I was nonplussed. "I'm just not used to this ethnic stuff," I said.

"You have to get used to it. There's a saying about Chicago: 'The Jews own it, the Irish run it, and the blacks live in it.' And the machine makes it all work."

I knew Al wasn't really a racist; it was just the way many Chicagoans talked. I realized that there was a big difference in recognizing differences in ethnicity and being racist, and that politicians had to be realistic about people's feelings. Still, there was no question that, in their hearts, many Chicago politicians were thoroughly racist, at least insofar as the blacks were concerned.

This both bothered and shocked me. I wanted to treat everyone just like I had treated people in San Diego. Common sense told me that the racism had to change, and my idealism dictated that I become a part of eliminating it. But for the moment, I just concentrated on learning. A black precinct worker I knew asked if I wanted to canvass voters with him in the heavily black First Ward, where John D'Arco was the ward committeeman. Curious, I agreed.

Common knowledge held that D'Arco was the semiofficial link between the Mob and the machine. Policy wheel gambling was still prevalent at that time. These were "wheels," or stations—small but highly profitable lotteries with runners selling the tickets. Reportedly D'Arco used Mob pressure to collect an estimated $3,000 per month personally from all the bars and strip clubs on South State Street, where black men routinely lost their wages to the Mob.

While canvassing the First Ward with my black friend, who was talking with an unemployed man, I spoke with his wife in the kitchen.

I said to her, "Ma'am, we really need you to get out and vote next week. Paul Douglas has a tough fight on his hands, and we need him in the U.S. Senate."

"For what?" she said.

"Well, for one thing, he's a strong voice for integrating our schools and for helping to see that your kids get a better education in the Chicago schools. That's a big issue for the Democrats in Washington."

The black woman laughed. "Who you kiddin'? Whitey don't give a damn about our schools."

At this point, my friend came into the kitchen. "I've got some food stamps for you, Miz Johnson."

"And I'll bet you gave my old man a pint," she said, laughing.

My friend took my arm, guiding me out of the room, and we went on our way.

"Dan, you've got a lot to learn about canvassing. For God's sake, don't talk about schools and education and stuff like that. Everybody knows that the schools on the South Side are in terrible condition with lousy teachers, so that's the last thing we want to talk about. All you'll do is get those folks upset. We don't want them upset; we want them to vote the ticket. So shut up about the damn issues. Just give 'em something, prate the pep talk, ask for the straight ticket vote, and get the hell out."

I was amazed. Not talk about issues? Elected government officials were not only not protecting people from crime, they were allowing it, promoting segregation, and neglecting schools. This was mind-boggling to me, and I had to understand why this was tolerable to people. Ethnicity wasn't the only thing that was radically different from anything I had ever encountered before. I faced requests that I found strange and disconcerting.

### THE BASKET OF VEGETABLES

An elderly woman said to me, "You haven't brought me anything."

I handed her some campaign literature.

"Huh!" She refused the materials. "I remember back in the days of Push-cart Tony Cermak,[1] the precinct captain always brought me candy or a policy wheel ticket. Or, if he thought I needed it, a pound of hamburger. Sometimes even now I get a turkey."

I didn't know what to say. Others asked unexpected things as well. One night while working on 95th Street, I was approached by two people who asked me to fix their traffic tickets. One guy thought I could help him with his DUI. "Write it down," he said. "Take it to the man." He meant, of course, the ward committeeman.

When finished that night, I took my tally of pluses, minuses, and zeros to ward headquarters and told all this to an old Irish precinct captain named Pat.

"Help them with their personal problems," he said. "They'll return the favor with a vote."

This sounded okay to me, and I worked hard at doing that. After all, the role that political machines played in helping poor immigrants in New York, Boston, and Chicago was well known. Helping them get settled, buying them some food necessities, steering them to a job—the benevolent kind of private welfare system perfected by big city machine politicians. I actually felt good being a part of this system—at first.

A few other precinct captains and workers were sitting around on folding chairs, talking about their fear that the ward was changing, that a few blacks were moving in.

"Won't be long before the Nineteenth is a plantation ward," one said pessimistically.

I gathered that this meant a ward where a white ward committeeman and alderman ruled a ward that was mostly black. Most of the guys, however, did not agree.

"It'll take years," said one.

"Besides, they really deliver the votes."[2]

---

[1] The Democratic powerhouse in Chicago really began with Tony Cermak. He was called a Bohunk—the term they used for people from Bohemia in those days—who rose to power and became mayor in the early 1930s. He began by firing three thousand city workers and replacing them with his own people. Cermak brought in a burly Irishman, Pat Nash, as Cook County chairman of the Democratic Party. A Florida assassin made history when, aiming at the vacationing Franklin Roosevelt, instead he hit and killed Cermak. Ed Kelly succeeded Cermak, and that was how the Kelly-Nash machine was born.

My concern over issues amused them. But from then on, if I asked any precinct worker about issues, such as the environment or education, they were contemptuous. "What's wrong with you?" they would ask. For Chicago voters, elections were all about personal interests, not issues.

When I next saw Al, I asked him about all the voters asking for favors. "What do you do?" I asked him.

He shrugged. "I go see the ward committeeman. He'll take care of it for you. Dan, it's all about exchanging favors for votes. Fixing tickets, killing DUIs, getting garbage picked up and street potholes repaired, having turkeys delivered at Christmas, making liquor or cash available for winos and bums on Election Day—even lowering real estate tax assessments or getting somebody into the overcrowded Cook County hospital."

In California, party precinct workers might get you a ride to the polls, but nothing else. Maybe the machine had the right approach after all. And yet, why should a county hospital be so overcrowded in the first place? Tax dollars should be going into improving and expanding it. You shouldn't have to bribe your precinct captain to get in.

But people accepted this. Even businessmen went to the ward committeeman and then the elected alderman to get zoning changes and driveway permits, to put pressure on the building department or the tax collectors.

Jobs, too, were important—indeed essential to the machine's operation. Patronage, it's called. Then, and for years thereafter, good precinct captains had as many as three hundred jobs to dispense. These were jobs he literally *owned*, ranging from street sweeper and sanitary worker up to assistant attorney general. These patronage jobs were not just in city government but also in the Chicago Transit Authority, at the racetracks, public utilities, and in numerous companies doing business with the city that needed favors from the machine. For example, in the machine-powerful Twenty-fourth Ward, even job applicants at Sears, Roebuck stores had to have a letter from the alderman or committeeman.

---

[2]For years, black Americans had voted solidly Republican as a carryover from the days of Abraham Lincoln. The Chicago African Americans came to the Democratic Party in the days of Franklin Delano Roosevelt's New Deal. In Chicago, the saying was "Lincoln's dead. You don't need no ghost from the grave to tell you what to do when you go to the polls." Another South Side Chicago slogan was "Let Jesus lead you and Roosevelt feed you." The number of blacks voting Democratic jumped from 32 percent when FDR was first elected to more than 80 percent after World War II, where it has remained ever since.

In addition to the carrot, there was the stick. Mike Royko once wrote in his column, "If a ward boss gets mad at you, building inspectors come to the house and tell you to put on a new roof or something." And everyone understood that the quid pro quo was votes to be delivered on Election Day.

Another stick involved money. Money was essential to the machine's operation, and to keep it going, each ward organization was charged an assessment. Patronage workers were forced to kick back about 2 percent of their salaries, sell tickets to ward dinners and golf outings, and on top of that, buy books of ward organization raffle tickets. If the worker could not sell the tickets, he was obliged to "eat them," bearing the cost himself. There were also the "ward books" featuring pictures of the alderman and ward committeeman and full of advertisements bought by local businessmen at the behest of both patronage workers and precinct captains. All this emphasis on extracting money from political workers really upset me. I wanted people to work in politics because they believed in candidates and issues. And I also wanted people to vote that way.

I finally did as Al suggested, though, and gave the list of favors the voters had requested to the ward committeeman. He delivered, and so did I, but this was certainly not my kind of politics.

I must admit though, that there was also something gratifying about the way this worked. I enjoyed the direct contact with people and a sense of being able to get immediate solutions to problems—more gratifying, perhaps, than getting programs started and legislation passed. There was an immediacy, a directness, a simple justice to it—a favor for a vote. Some would ask, "What's the difference between a precinct captain getting a vote by giving a turkey and a senator getting a vote by promising better food inspection?" Patronage wasn't my way, but it was a way that worked. And maybe there was an integrity to it in that no candidates proclaimed that a vote for their party was a vote for patriotism or morality. It was what it was and didn't pretend to be anything more.

When the old lady who had asked me why I hadn't brought her anything saw the basket of carrots, green onions, and radishes grown in my own vegetable garden that I brought her, she loved it. That feeling of personally helping someone "right now" was one I never forgot, but it did not persuade me that personal favors were better than finding ways to improve government for people like the old lady or the precinct worker needing a job.

Some people wonder what the difference is between a precinct worker wanting a job and my wanting the job of governor. Perhaps the difference is commitment to a position that can bring about real change. You can't change things without holding some kind of power.

Machine people worked with power the way potters work with clay, but I always felt there was so much more to politics and government. It kept coming back to the concept of really helping people.

What hit me hard was one evening when, at my friend Al's request, I was scheduled to visit a retirement home in the Nineteenth Ward. We took a stack of affidavits saying that the person signing was unable to physically get to the voting place.

"They know the routine, Dan; I've done it with them repeatedly. Just get them to sign these affidavits and I'll get them also signed by a physician friend of mine. Then, I'll take absentee ballots over to the home and they'll all vote the way we want."

I remonstrated. "Al, that's fraud, out and out fraud. Damn it, I won't be a part of that."

Al didn't push me. "Okay, Dan, I'll take care of it myself."

On the Saturday before the election, the alderman himself came into the ward meeting, announcing that he had plenty of free racetrack tickets to pass out on the last canvass of zeros and pluses. This canvass would yield a final list of the "plus voters" who would receive the free tickets. All other voters would be ignored.

I was leaving ward headquarters, and Pat, the old Irishman, approached me using a cane. "Dan, you're a big fella." He looked me up and down. "I'd like to have you help me next Tuesday, Election Day. Your captain said it was okay, that she could handle it with the other assistants for a few hours. Meet me here at headquarters at seven in the morning."

When I double-checked with my captain, she said, "Yeah, sure. Pat'll give you a lesson on what being a good precinct captain requires. By all means, help him."

I had a vague idea of what I might be in for, but I had to see for myself. On Sunday, Roberta said the Catholic priests were urging parishioners to vote for good Irish candidates approved by the machine.

When I reported to Pat on that cold Tuesday morning in November, he took me to his station wagon, and we drove to a rundown area of the ward where there were some old warehouses. We pulled up to a sizable group of disheveled men. I saw what was going to happen and also what could happen if Pat were there alone. So I stayed with him and pulled a case of wine out of the back of his station wagon. He passed out bottles of wine to eight of the men. Pat also gave each man a card with a name and address written on it. To the others who waited, Pat said, "We'll keep making runs until we get all of you. You'll all get your wine. Just be patient."

"Jump in," Pat said, and the eight men brought their bottles to the station wagon and piled in. Pat drove to a nearby building that had the sign out, "VOTING PLACE." No one said anything. Apparently, the men knew what they were supposed to do. They left their bottles in the station wagon and trooped into the voting place, card in hand. As they came out, Pat handed each man his bottle of wine and off the guy would wander, clutching his bottle. But there was something more here than simply handing out wine for votes and getting these men to the polls.

"What are we doing?" I asked. "What are those cards for?"

"It's called 'voting the graveyard,' Dan," Pat answered. "Each of those guys has a card containing the name of a guy who's long-gone dead, but whose name has never been taken off the list of registered voters. The poll workers don't ask any questions. They just look at the card, check off the dead guy's name on the list of registered voters, and give the wino a ballot. A bottle for a ballot; pretty good deal, I'd say. It's cheap rotgut wine, anyway."

Dear God in heaven. I was committing voter fraud.

One of our winos had loitered outside the voting place without going in. He was obviously in bad shape, hands shaking.

I watched as Pat took the guy's arm and led him into the voting place. When they came out, Pat gave him his bottle of wine and returned to the wagon.

"He's pretty far gone," Pat explained. "I had to walk him through the process all the way."

I frowned. "But he was shaking so hard, I don't see how he could have used the pencil to vote."

Pat scoffed. "Get with it, Dan. You've got a lot to learn. I walked into the booth with him and marked the ballot, okay? How else do ya think we could get that vote? I doubt that guy can even read."

I think I went a little pale. "What about the polling place judges? Don't they ever stop you?"

"All bought and paid for." He looked at me as if I were an especially slow learner.

I told Al about this later that day, and he just laughed. "'Ghost voting' and 'four-legged' voting! It's how we keep the Republican special interests out of Chicago. Good experience for you, Dan. Listen, the boss has really put the arm on the captains. Last night, he read off six wards that in the last election brought in margins of at least ten to one in our candidates' favor. We've been running about six to one, and that's not good enough. The boss threatened to take some jobs away if we don't do better."

I agreed to help get voters to the polls. Armed with his list of plus voters, the precinct captains would sit at the polls and check off those who had voted. When voters remained on the list with no checkmark, the captain sent a precinct worker to drag them in. Some were even rounded up in pickup trucks. Once I saw a worker pushing a voter to the polling place in a wheelchair.

The machine's total concentration on first identifying and then turning out plus voters has no equal in political groundwork. Interestingly, it was not—and still is not—used anywhere else in the state. The kind of organizational discipline it required simply did not exist outside Chicago, even in the Cook County suburbs.

We did well getting out the vote in the Irish Nineteenth Ward, and the committeeman said, "Great job, guys. We even beat a couple of the river wards." Our turnout was by no means as good as some of the Italian and Polish wards that produced ratios of up to fifteen or even twenty to one in favor of Democratic candidates. Paul Douglas was reelected as U.S. senator, and that pleased me.

I was beginning to understand how the Chicago political system worked. I learned about the major problems confronting the city, particularly on the heavily black South Side, which, in turn, affected the rest of the city: bad schools, street crime, organized crime, forced segregation, lack of civil rights. The machine derived huge voting power from the blacks, who got very little in return. The machine was totally absorbed in self-perpetuation and thrived on voter ignorance and dependency, so it kept the blacks and other poor people down. Without a dependent constituency, the machine would become irrelevant. So the party hacks had no interest in curtailing crime, making schools better, or fighting for civil rights. Why should the machine use its power to destroy itself? No wonder none of these issues were discussed by the politicians at ward meetings or raised by the captains when they canvassed the voters.

Its corrupt practices were contemptible, but perhaps even worse was the machine's refusal to deal with the real issues and problems confronting people. To the lady who wanted a little something from her precinct worker, I would ask, how is it that you sell your vote for a basket of vegetables? Your grandchildren don't have decent schools, but you settle for hacks who toss you favors every now and then. Men given a pint of cheap whiskey or a "free" racetrack ticket or fixed parking ticket imagine the party bosses are taking care of them.

I learned that those who have little hope take what they can get.

A true leader must not only give people something to hope for, then, but must be the person who inspires that hope. I saw that if I wanted to enter into state government, I would not—and could not—do it by rising through the ranks of machine politics. My only avenue would be as an independent Democrat. And I would have to find a way to convince voters that there was something to hope for beyond the tawdry bribes of the machine. I would have to convince other Democrats that the machine could not keep going unopposed.

And yet I had no idea that the campaign of 1954 was just a prelude to the all-powerful political machine that would develop under a man named Daley. Nor did I have a glimmer of how that Daley machine would dramatically affect my life.

# 4

## *The Underbelly of Machine Politics*

I am often lonely in prison and would have much to discuss with a former Chicago alderman, Dick Kelley, mainly concerning how to get Chicago blacks out of bondage to the machine. Kelly will not become a friend, however, despite the fact that he moves in both black circles and white. He seems to avoid me. The black inmates make it clear that integration is unwelcome. Outnumbering whites and all other minorities, they segregate themselves, scorning company outside their group—whites especially. Newcomers soon learn the danger of crossing them. There will be no witnesses reporting any violence. And the guards—always glad to pit one group against another as a method of keeping control of the prison populace—look the other way.

In the evening, inmates can watch television in the recreation rooms in each barracks building, but the blacks control all program selection. No white dares select a channel. Same goes for the athletic equipment available to inmates on Sundays and holidays. Another prison irony is the way that men ally themselves for protection—a microcosm of politics surpassing the intensity of ward machinations, only in reverse. Here, the blacks run things. And they have no knowledge of the ways in which I helped African Americans and possibly wouldn't have cared if they did know. I dread the looks they give me.

## UNDERBELLY

Several weeks after the November election of 1954, Roberta gave birth to our fifth child. One of our agreements before we married was that I would choose the names of our sons, and she would select our daughters' names. We had believed that Carol Sue would be our last baby. I was quite pleased, though, that number five was a boy. I wanted to name him after my grandfather, Charles Anderson Walker, but we finally settled on Richard as the middle name. Again I failed to be as supportive as I could have been and managed to get away for more ward meetings.

Adlai Stevenson had commended Richard J. Daley, who had taken over the most powerful spot in the party, chairman of the Cook County Democratic Central Committee, though in his official job, his title was Cook County Clerk. So, I was prepared to respect Daley. Maybe he was, like Adlai, above the fray, more independent. He was a favorite topic of conversation at the ward meetings. I still attended, hoping to keep connections alive and learn the inside scoop from these experienced men. There was talk Daley might be running for mayor of Chicago that year, 1955, an odd-numbered year chosen because it would not conflict with national elections.

"Cook County Clerk is a machine job," a ward committeeman said. "Leaves you plenty of time to do whatever you want to do. Like campaigning."

The men in the ward were talking about how Daley had moved into Arvey's political power shoes when Arvey had to step down because of the Tubbo Gilbert scandal.[1]

"Was choosing Daley as a replacement Arvey's idea?" I asked Al.

Al shrugged. "I don't know. 'Big Joe' McDonough used to be Daley's chinaman."

---

[1] I remembered the "Tubbo" Gilbert fiasco in 1950. Chicago police captain Daniel Gilbert ran for sheriff, but the Kefauver Committee, conducting crime hearings around the nation, exposed him as "the world's richest cop," so named by the newspapers because he had assembled at least $360,000 on a modest policeman's salary. The office he sought, Cook County Sheriff, was known throughout Illinois as a moneymaker. Because of graft and fees, common knowledge in Cook County held that if a sheriff didn't leave office after four years with a clear million dollars for himself, "he just wasn't trying." Tubbo lost the election, and this led to the ouster of Col. Jake Arvey as chairman of the Cook County Democratic Central Committee. I admired Arvey because of his 1948 backing of Paul Douglas and Adlai Stevenson.

I had picked up enough of the lingo to know that every jobholder had his sponsor, or "chinaman," the politico to whom he owed his job. McDonough was the Eleventh Ward alderman and committeeman.

"Daley's a good man," the ward committeeman said. "He kept his nose clean down in Springfield. Most legislators opt for 'girls, games, and graft,' but not Daley. Always straight-laced and never a heavy drinker. Devoted family man."

"Like I said before," Pat said. "How can you trust this guy?"

They all laughed.

"He's been a solid Kelly-Nash man ever since his Springfield days," the committeeman said. "Daley performed for the machine."

"I heard he was never on the take," I ventured, hoping to sound knowledgeable and defend Adlai's approval of Daley.

Al said, "Daley's no angel. I know he was a double-dipper, drawing government pay as both deputy county controller and state senator."

"That's standard practice," one of the precinct captains said.

Years later, columnist Mike Royko described the Daley commandment on taking money: "Thou shall not steal, but thou shalt not blow the whistle on anybody who does."

"Guy's smart," another captain said. "He coolly brings in money from places no one would ever think of. One bill he sponsored gave a $5 fee to the state's attorney's office for every divorce action filed in Cook County."

"At least he never tried any Mae West bills," the committeeman said.

I looked to Al, but he shrugged.

Grinning, the committeeman continued. "A come-up-and-see-me-sometime bill. Also called 'fetchers'—bills written to get the attention of some special interest that would pay good money to get them killed before they ever reached the floor."

"Daley's ducks may be lined up, but he's not a surefire winner by any stretch," another precinct captain said. "Lost his bid for Cook County sheriff."[2]

---

[2]The story came out about how the Cook County board decided to pay a $10 bounty to hunters killing wolves in the county's forest preserves. Some complained that entrepreneurial hunters were paid for dead police dogs. Daley, as deputy controller of Cook County, defended the county to reporters with a straight face. "Having served in the state legislature, I consider myself an authority on wolves." Daley did such a good job that the machine tapped him to run for sheriff, but he lost.

"I just wanna know how he's going to deal with the Mob and the blacks," Pat said.

My ward, the Nineteenth, was a good example of how the Chicago political system—run by mostly Irish whites—effectively wove together a strong organization of labor unions, the business community, the Catholic Church, and city government. Stories I heard about other wards—for example, those where the Chicago Mob, or "Syndicate," bubbled in the stew of ward politics—piqued my interest, challenging me to learn more about what some called the "underbelly of Chicago."

The men who ran the Nineteenth Ward were fearful that both the Mob and the blacks would move in, just as they had in other wards. The Chicago that I first encountered in the early 1950s was a thoroughly segregated, white-controlled city, with the machine helping to keep it that way. And another force that definitely wanted nothing to do with the blacks was the Mob.

I, like everyone else in America, had heard of Al Capone and the Valentine's Day massacre. Indeed, the world's view of Chicago centered on Al Capone's gangsters with their machine guns. But I never dreamed that the Mob still operated in rather wide-open fashion and was amazed to learn that there was a real working relationship between known mobsters and officials of the Democratic Party organization.

In addition to political patronage, kickbacks, and constant, mandatory support for political party fund-raisers, many local businessmen also paid protection money to the Mafia, which in turn paid off the cops. Some said that about 10 percent of gambling revenues went to city politicians. The Mob had a variety of moneymaking operations: prostitution, drug running, gambling, even jukeboxes the Mob placed in bars, restaurants, taverns, and other public places. "Juice money" meant the interest on Mob loans with rates ranging up to 100 percent per month. Mob collectors were unmerciful. One warning on a delinquent loan was all the borrower got. After that, failure to pay could bring "capping the knees" as a very painful reminder.

The Mobsters and the black hoodlums, whom the Italians running the Mob never liked anyway, came into conflict. The Mob guys tried to bribe the police to let their hoodlums take over the policy wheels run by the blacks. On the South Side alone, about 4,200 black-operated policy stations handled bets from up to 100,000 people each day.

The Mob couldn't get control of this operation; it was too enmeshed in the black community structure. For example, William Dawson, who ran Chicago's South Side, parlayed his Second Ward power all the way up the chain, becoming one of the most powerful black elected officials in the nation. The policy stations were rampant in Dawson's domain. His power was so great that he squelched the Mob's attempted takeover. He was largely instrumental in building what was called the "Black submachine," an essential part of the Chicago machine. Unfortunately, it never bothered Dawson that he was called a classic Uncle Tom politician practicing welfare politics. The Chicago machine regulars never ran into opposition from Dawson in their successful efforts to keep Chicago the most segregated city in the North. Dawson worked well with Richard J. Daley.

### MAYOR DALEY

The precinct workers proved right about Daley, and I continued to follow him closely. He reached for the brass ring and was elected mayor. He believed in centralizing power, and soon the mayor's office, "5th floor City Hall," became central, not just to the political system, but also to the Chicago business establishment. Daley, as chairman of the Cook County Central Committee—the powerful political job he continued to hold while mayor—inaugurated the slate-making procedure for picking Democratic candidates for statewide office. Those seeking office had to appear before the slate-making committee carefully picked by Daley from members of the county and state central committees. But even they did not have the power. Daley himself wielded it in secret meetings with a few committeemen who were his closest cohorts.

Those appearing before the slate-makers had to answer two critical questions: Will you run for whatever office the committee ordains? Will you support all those slated for all offices? This was rightly called the "Machine loyalty test." When guys claimed to be independent, they had to pass this test, and they came to a painful understanding of how that system worked. They came in the door as independents, and if they bowed, went out the door almost as bound to the system as were all the machine hacks.

Daley's well-earned national reputation for "knowing how to get things done, knowing how to make the city work" was born in those years. While the so-called gray wolves were still running the city council, and colorful hacks like saloon aldermen Paddy Bauler and "Botchy" Connors wielded substantial political power, all city politicos soon came to accept Richard J. Daley as boss. When Daley narrowly defeated a reform candidate in his bid for reelection, Paddy danced a jig in his saloon while yelling what became a nationally known machine refrain: "Chicago ain't ready for reform." He embellished it. "Those other fellas are gonna run nothin'. They ain't found it out yet, but Daley's the dog with the big nuts."

And he was right. In that city, anyone wanting favors knew that from driveway permits and zoning variances all the way up to building skyscrapers, the route to take went to "the Man on Five." Daley didn't mind passing out the moneymaking power. Businessmen throughout Chicago knew that it was wise to buy insurance from a firm owned by one of the machine aldermen. The best market was in the Loop, part of the First Ward, which was considered a gold mine of insurable property. The insurance firm in that ward was owned by Alderman John D'Arco, known as the "Mob voice" on the city council, mentioned earlier in connection with lotteries on the South Side.

A very comfortable (some called it "cozy") relationship developed between the Daley machine and the Mob. D'Arco delivered the votes on Election Day. For example, in the 1955 primary election, Daley beat his opponent in the First Ward by 13,275 to 1,961. When asked about the Mob, Daley denied publicly that it existed. But to insiders, he said, "Well, it may be there, but you know you can't get rid of it, so you have to live with it." (Some years later, mobster Murray "the Camel" Humphrey was wiretapped by the FBI as saying to D'Arco, "Daley has been good to us, and we've been good to him. One hand washes the other.") And John Johnson, head of a Chicago-based African American media empire, said a few years later, when Daley's control had become even more solidified, "It's impossible to do business in Chicago without dealing with Mayor Daley."

Those were also the years when illicit procedures for winning elections were refined. Daley himself summed up the prevailing attitude in his regular Election Day admonition to his minions. "Tell 'em to vote early and vote often." In addition to the practices I witnessed directly, other techniques were added, like throwing out Republican poll watchers and having police arrest them for disorderly conduct. Wherever an opponent was popular, the machine packed the line of waiting voters with people—anyone—to the point where folks anxious to get to work got tired of waiting and would leave before voting. When the "interlopers" got near the head of the line, they melted away.[3]

---

[3]Such machine machinations were not secret at the time and have since been widely publicized. These and others are detailed in *American Pharaoh*, by Adam Cohen and Elizabeth Taylor, published in 1991, and even more colorfully in Mike Royko's *Boss*. After Royko's book was published in 1971, it was pulled from the shelves of some two hundred bookstores in Chicago, a good demonstration of the business community's fear of Daley's political machine.

This, then, was the political system I encountered when I moved into Chicago and continued to observe over the years I worked there. Sometimes naive and too idealistic, I thought more and more about the possibility of entering politics and achieving a high office from which I could help change what I believed was a rotten system. Positioning myself to be an independent Democrat, however, would require too much time and more resources than I had. And I had five kids to support.

Even if I somehow started climbing that ladder, fulfilling the goal seemed so unlikely as to appear impossible. Yet I wanted nothing less and would one day be called "the Man of La Mancha" because I would, against the odds, take on the giant windmills of Daley's Chicago machine.

# 5

## *My Political Baptism*

A small group of black prisoners has begun to threaten me. Being among the older inmates, I cannot hope to defend myself physically. I want to look to the guards for protection, but that is useless. They are somehow not around when this gang attacks others. I had no idea minimum-security prisons would tolerate such practices.

The guards—the policemen of the prison—use brutally direct and psychological means to enforce the rules. They deliberately allow other prisoners to be the informal dominating force in day-to-day prison life. Besides this particular group of blacks, another group also has power: the old-timers, men serving out long sentences for violent crimes. Nearing the end of their sentences, they are often downgraded from high-security lockups to the minimum-security prisons because there is little fear that they will try to escape. If caught, they would again be serving long sentences in high-security prisons. So, these men are willing partners with the guards in seeing that discipline is sometimes brutally enforced. And who among the inmates would want to cross a man found guilty of violent murder?

On a subzero day with little needles of sleet blowing into me during the long wait in line in the prison yard to get into the cafeteria for lunch, three tough black guys cut in directly in front of me. I protest. "Why don't you guys go to the end of the line like everyone else?"

The response is quick. "Shut up, f——er white boy. Listen, you ain't no governor here. Some night, we're gonna put you in your f——n' place. We gonna kick your ass and teach you somethin'."

---

### WHITE FLIGHT

Our neighborhood of Morgan Park occupied the far South Side of Chicago. Eight blocks east of Longwood Drive, the street where we lived, Halsted Street ran north and south, unofficially dividing black and white neighborhoods as if it were a physical barrier. Roberta called me at the law office one morning, concerned about a Morgan Park mugging, an unknown in our neighborhood. Two black youths had attacked a white woman coming home from the store the previous evening.

"We've got to face the fact that Morgan Park is going to change, Dan," she said. "Maybe not next year, but within the next five or six years."

She expressed the same fear that precinct workers had shared with me, though I hadn't quite admitted it. Should we leave Morgan Park? The location suited my job and the family. Walking a mere two blocks from our rented house, I could board the Rock Island Railroad commuter train, which would take me to the Loop in less than a half-hour.

In our home on Longwood Drive, I had become much more of a family man. At McGowan's legal firm, I was given few assignments, and of those, few cases seemed to be of importance or interest. My light workload had enabled me to have a nine-to-five job. In the positive column, I had much more family time, and I really got to know my children again. To the amazement of my family recalling Morgan Park times in later years, I did handyman work around the house, actually tiling the kitchen and bathroom floors. The small yard accommodated my vegetable garden, a sizeable concrete fishpond that we turned into a "paddle around" swimming pool for the children, and a huge, built-in barbecue. I occasionally fixed breakfasts there, making pancakes on an iron griddle over the coals.

We did have our share of mishaps in that house: A preoccupied Roberta got into the car and backed right through the garage door. I loathed the coal furnace, a completely alien contraption that required regular filling from a truck through a basement side-window onto a conveyer belt that automatically (sometimes) carried coal to the furnace. We woke one morning to find the basement flooded. The water was over one foot deep in the basement, mixed with backed-up sewage, and black with greasy coal dust. And the damn furnace was dead in below-zero weather. So, despite the garden, pool, and barbecue, I wouldn't hate leaving the place.

Kathleen, Dan, Julie, and Carol Sue all got started in the nearby Catholic school and were doing very well. I hated uprooting them. Carol Sue decided that she wanted to be named after her mother and become Roberta Sue, so I prepared a faux certificate with lots of legalese and took it to her teacher. I knew, of course, that no legal steps need be taken to change a child's given name, but it made a good show. She was "Robbie" from then on. I was surprised at how much I enjoyed this time with the children. I played Shawnee Indians with them, shaking the beds and chasing them, making them scream and giggle.

"Dan!" Roberta would call in exasperation, "Don't get them so excited! They have to go to bed!" She was happy though, perhaps the happiest in her life.

On holidays, we drove north to visit grandparents in Kenosha, Wisconsin, as well as Aunt Gertrude and Uncle Dave in Wadsworth, Illinois, where Dave and I continued to talk Illinois politics. Our whole family loved Gertrude and Dave. They still lived 1800s-style in an old house that had no plumbing, no electricity, and no running water. In the fall, I would head out into the fields with my old L. C. Smith shotgun to hunt pheasants. With no dog to hunt them out, I didn't often get one. Thanksgiving with them was a ritual. After the meal, Dave and I would retire to the sitting room and talk politics while he smoked cigars. These times were so satisfying as to make one want to forget about ambition and just live the quiet family life.

My restlessness at the law office had finally unraveled the close-knit coziness of our lifestyle, however. Tom Mulroy had become lead trial lawyer in a major firm named Hopkins, Sutter, Owen, Mulroy & Wentz. He remembered me well from the time I had worked with him while in law school, and he chaired the legislative committee of the Chicago Crime Commission. Tom contacted me and persuaded me both to join the Crime Commission as a member and to work with him in the firm. Since I was focused on what is called "desk law," I had never given thought to becoming a civil trial lawyer, but I soon discovered that this was the legal practice for me. Hopkins, Sutter was known among young lawyers as a sweatshop, so the hours were long, but I found trial work engrossing, particularly when I became involved with Tom in what is called "major case litigation," such as legal battles between General Telephone Company and AT&T.

My transition to Hopkins, Sutter marked the end of my "normal" nine-to-five life and therefore drastically cut much of my family time. I not only wanted the new and better-paying position as a law firm associate, rather than law clerk, but the family needed it as well. With five children, we constantly had to buy things like a new refrigerator, a washer, or a new car. We were deeply in debt. This firm would enable me to become a partner sooner than the other firm, and with the changes in our neighborhood, we wanted the option of a new home. We considered becoming a part of the "white flight" into the suburbs. Experience had shown in Chicago that once a barrier was broken by a number of blacks moving in, predominantly white neighborhoods rapidly changed. I learned about this from the precinct captains at ward headquarters and from downtown lawyers who had experienced it firsthand. Roberta heard about it in the beauty shop and the local stores.

At dinner the night of the mugging, she said, "The sisters at school tell me that they, too, are fearful. It's the schools and crime. They say they can maintain high standards in the Catholic schools, but that teachers in the public schools just are not able to do that."

Despite my strong beliefs about the need for integration and my aversion to racist arguments, common sense told me she was right. The crime factor tipped the scales. I just couldn't raise my children close to areas of street violence, knowing that I would be working long hours downtown and that my wife and kids would be without me during those nighttime hours. I felt guilty but decided we had to make the move. We joined the exodus to the suburbs when I found in Deerfield a builder who would let us buy on contract since we had no money for a down payment. We moved to 1158 Wincanton Drive, Deerfield, in Lake County and enrolled the kids in the Holy Cross School, within easy walking distance of our home. Joining a swimming pool and tennis club gave us a place for pleasant family recreation. The Milwaukee Road commuter railroad station was also within easy walking distance, and the trip downtown was under an hour, just enough time to read the newspaper.

My parents came from faraway San Diego to see us in our new home. Profiting from the tomato fields Dad had been growing and improving since World War II, my brother Waco invested with Dad in the crops, and one year they did so well that they bought two matching red-and-white Pontiac sedans. Dad had acquired three or four racehorses and hired a trainer to work with the "claimers" he bought at Agua Caliente racetrack. "Claimers" were horses bought at a designated race where any buyer could claim a horse for the price listed. Dad and Mom had taken several of the horses on a tour of racetracks, including AkSarBen (that's *Nebraska* spelled backwards) and Sportsman's Park in Cicero near Chicago, winning barely enough to pay for the trip. They stayed with us in Deerfield, and Dad soon managed to find the Mob's poker game in the basement of a hotel in Cicero and won close to five thousand dollars. When he told me, I advised him strongly to close down his horse racing venture and leave town while he was ahead. An outsider winning substantial sums at poker with Chicago mobsters was dangerous business.

The kids had thoroughly enjoyed their grandparents, learning the Walker pie-eating tradition that ordained using a spoon, never a fork. "Otherwise," said Dad, "the pie flavor drops down between the tines." That was to be my mother's final visit and Dad's last until my inauguration came along.

Dad was a constant communicator, always a ready-and-willing talker. Not I. Those who knew me during my public years may be surprised to learn that, when not on stage or in a meeting or in the courtroom, I can be uncommonly uncommunicative.

### MAKING WAVES IN DEERFIELD

Deerfield had the second heaviest Republican registration in the state, but there was a Democratic club that tried to keep our spirits up in Lake County. I took a lead role in that organization and canvassed my precinct as a volunteer, just as I had in the Nineteenth Ward. Every two years, we worked hard to elect Democratic candidates, but the highest we ever achieved was a 42 percent vote for state's attorney. I did not, however, develop a close relationship with the Democratic county chairman. Like other chairmen of the regular party organizations throughout the state, he was more concerned with getting state jobs for his precinct workers than with building an issue-motivated organization. This was especially frustrating since people where I lived already had good jobs and would not work in campaigns just to get jobs. No wonder the Democratic Party lagged behind. We needed an issue-oriented campaign to impress voters in Deerfield. For example, teenagers of middle- and upper-income families were beginning to experiment with drugs, and people became frightened. We needed to talk with voters about this issue to get them excited about Democratic candidates who sought solutions, such as meaningful drug-education programs in the high schools. I couldn't get this concept through to the chairman and finally stopped going to meetings. My independent streak kept growing.

We lived the quiet family life typical of the times. Roberta, a devout Catholic, wanted to be active in her parish. I was Protestant, but inactive, and since I was so involved in my work and the local Democratic Club, I thought that this would be something we could do together. So we joined the Catholic lay organization called Confraternity of Christian Doctrine (CCD) and attended evening meetings for discussions on matters of controversy within the Catholic Church. For recreation, I took up tennis, which I have avidly played ever since. We briefly became members of a country club but didn't enjoy the social life. We were not really country club people.

A major controversy broke out in Deerfield when a developer named Morris Milgram announced plans for an integrated housing development for moderate- and lower-income families. Surprised at the virulent racist opposition that erupted throughout the village, I formed the Deerfield Constitutional Rights Committee to help rally the community on the civil rights side and try to bring the bigots to their senses. We had public meetings in our home, urging patience and acceptance, and tried to assuage our neighbors' fears of dropping property values. When the controversy heated up further, I made some radio and television appearances in an effort to help calm the growing hysteria.

Then, the village announced plans for a referendum to force condemnation of the developer's site as a public park. I took a highly unpopular stance against the referendum at village meetings and in the media. My public activities alienated a number of our neighborhood friends. We were openly labeled "nigger lovers," a term I had never expected to hear in Deerfield—though it was home to a founding member of the infamous John Birch Society, whose children, along with others, taunted our kids. People stopped speaking to me, and Roberta and I lost friends, including some of our neighbors. Not surprisingly, the referendum carried by an overwhelming margin. I hoped that many people at least respected me, even if they didn't like what I was doing. The integration controversy ended, but real scars remained in the community. This was the first time I paid a price for acting publicly on my idealism. It was a price I would pay again and again.

### WATCHDOGS AREN'T ENOUGH

Trial preparation often consumed my evenings, and I spent more and more time in downtown Chicago. Only breakfasts, lunches, and telephone-time were available for matters not directly related to law clients, such as becoming legislative chairman of the Crime Commission, a position I considered essential if I were to keep my quest for a government office alive. I worked up five tough anticrime laws—including one on antiracketeering aimed directly at the Mob—*and* we managed to get them passed by the state legislature. This required numerous trips to Springfield, which gave me opportunities to meet influential legislators and taught me more about state government, yet the traveling took more time away from my family.

I also launched a new political organization called the Committee on Illinois Government (CIG), designed to be a watchdog over the performance of Governor William Stratton, Stevenson's Republican successor. Serving as chairman, I brought together a number of young "good government" Democrats like Abner Mikva. Many were lawyers who had worked in politics or government with Adlai Stevenson. We were ambitious young Turks who thought that candidates should be elected on issues, not favors, and that good ideas and legislation could change people's lives for the better. We met in members' homes to clip newspapers from around the state and compile a record of the failures, scandals, and mistakes of the Stratton administration. Roberta, though unhappy about my ever-increasing absence from the family, went along with all this and even got involved with the clipping sessions in our home and the homes of the others.

What I really wanted, though, was to get more involved in actual campaigns. I watched from afar with nearly painful envy when, in 1956, Ab Mikva mounted a primary campaign against the regular Democratic organization's candidate in the University of Chicago area on the South Side for a seat in the state legislature. At the time, I believed Mikva would remain dedicated to continued opposition to the Chicago machine. He selected a sharp and energetic campaign manager named Victor De Grazia. I knew right away that there was something special about Vic. His ability to understand the flow of political power and knowledge of the players impressed me. I wanted to get to know him better. That primary fight against a Daley-backed machine candidate would be Vic's toughest challenge as Mikva's manager, and if he could pull that off, that would prove his genius and Mikva would be a shoe-in for election in the fall in his heavily Democratic district.

I couldn't run for office yet, but two separate political campaigns engaged me that same year, both involving candidates who wanted entrée into the Illinois community of lawyers who donated substantially to political campaigns. My standing in a major law firm, former association with Adlai Stevenson, and record with the Crime Commission prompted both Richard Stengel, a candidate for the U.S. Senate, and Joseph Lohman, running for Cook County sheriff, to ask me to become treasurer for each of their campaigns. I asked myself what I was doing, spending so much time on tactics and strategy with Lohman, since the office of sheriff was strictly local, but I hoped the man would climb further up the political ladder and become a leader who would help reform the Democratic Party. That sheriff's office had enabled many men to get rich, but Joe Lohman would not be one of those men. He held such strong views on justice that I often wondered how he ever earned the machine's endorsement. He was one of those men who could help shift the party away from patronage.

I wasn't running my own campaign, but I was in the arena and still working for change, helping to elect first-rate candidates. This took considerable time, but I still managed to stay active in our CIG watchdog group. By this time, Stengel, Lohman, and Mikva had won their primaries. Mikva no longer needed his campaign manager, Vic De Grazia. Vic was footloose, and—with the money CIG raised from our network of Adlai Stevenson supporters and our own contributions—we hired him part-time as executive director of CIG. We soon became close friends.

Vic was thought of as a true Renaissance man, and I agreed. He was a talented vocalist, choir conductor, jazz trumpeter, piano player, and composer who attended the Chicago Conservatory of Music. Yet, he decided to forsake music for politics, perhaps influenced by his older brothers who both held doctorates in political science. Sebastian De Grazia won a Pulitzer Prize for a biography of Machiavelli, with whom Vic was often unfairly compared. As an expert, Vic certainly used manipulative tactics, as would a Machiavellian politician, but never with venal intent or unethically.

Our CIG plan was to fully research all state government issues that could be involved in the governor's race. We compiled a campaign book full of detailed critical information, but the only ones elected were Mikva, as predicted, and Lohman, who won because the machine had turned out its Chicago voters, as it always did. To win statewide office, a Democratic candidate must win Chicago plus either downstate or the suburbs, and neither Stengel nor Dick Austen, the Democratic candidate for governor, was able to put together that combination. But this was a valuable lesson for both Vic and me.

After this election, I gradually drifted away from CIG, the organization I had helped to found, but two successful young lawyers—both my good friends who had earlier worked hard for Stevenson—took over the helm. I sought political action with direct impact, rather than working on issues through research: Enough talk, more results. And a lot of young people all over the state felt the way I did.

# 6

## *Becoming an Independent Democrat*

In prison, not all the blacks were hostile. Only three had threatened me. Many of the inmates, blacks as well as others, are addicts who have been convicted of no other crimes than drug offenses and are a completely different kind of prisoner from those who have committed violent crimes.

Initially, I thought it would be relatively easy to establish good relations with the black inmates. In my Deerfield days, I had "broken my lance," had been defeated in my first battle to improve race relations, but I never stopped trying. Now, I go out of my way to talk to as many blacks as I can, but they continue to prefer to stay to themselves. One I often encounter on my way to the prison's clothing store responds when I speak to him. His name is Jamal, and he has attended a community college.

Idealistically, a few of us want to try to integrate the two groups. It occurs to me that I could invite him to the Toastmasters Club, an organization that encourages public speaking, which I am surprised to find in the prison. Naturally, I'm attracted to it, and the men seem to like the way I use a critique session after the speeches to try to impart to them some of the lessons and tricks I've learned in speaking in the courtroom.

I stop Jamal on the tarmac and ask, "Hey, why don't you come to the Toastmaster's Club this evening?"

He looks puzzled. "What kind of club is this?"

"It's a kind of social club where men try to get comfortable giving speeches while standing in front of others. Bring some friends if you like."

He nods, though I gain no sense of whether he will come to the meeting or not.

I am surprised when he and two others attend that night—the first blacks to participate—and I'm even more delighted when he gives his first speech. Several weeks later, though, the retiring president nominates me as his successor, and a small group, led by a former president who wants to come back, opposes me.

A near shouting match erupts. "You think just because you were governor, you can just come in here and take over!" the former president yells, and a few others join in.

I try to calm things, pointing out that I don't really care whether I become president or not. "But I do want to try and change things a bit," I say. "Too many speeches revolve around the misery of prison life, but all of us have knowledge and experiences that, if shared in speeches, would allow each other to have a time where we escape the drudgery and horrors of this place."

Most of the men calm down, but I can't bring everyone together. The dissidents simply walk away from the club. Jamal and his friends leave also. I have no idea why. This truly disappoints me. I learn again that whether it's fighting a system or an ingrained practice, bringing about change can be extremely difficult, even with the best of motives.

The direct physical threats in prison are frightening, but even small failures erode my resolve. Trying to stay upbeat in a place I hate and not allowing myself to slip into despair where I quit trying are a continuous and difficult fight.

## STICKING MY BIG TOE INTO STATE POLITICS

The machine-run, patronage-oriented regular Democratic organization continually frustrated me. The statewide political system wanted no part of independent-thinking, issue-oriented activists. And I wasn't alone in my frustration. A number of us sought a vehicle for direct political action. The result was the Democratic Federation of Illinois (DFI), a statewide network of Democratic clubs completely independent of the regular Democratic organization.

We repeatedly turned to Vic's good friend David Green, an innovative businessman who proved to be an excellent political tactician, and I also got to know him well. Vic, Dave, and I became an enduring trio. We frequently discussed my desire personally to get involved as a statewide candidate, but all three of us knew that my growing family, my extreme distaste for machine politics, and my lack of financial independence made that extremely unlikely. We did think that somehow DFI might prove to be a stepping-stone.

We wanted to create statewide enthusiasm for bringing about a seismic shift in the closed Illinois political system that for many years had been totally obsessed with patronage and money. Our optimism for dramatic change continued as we sought campaign workers throughout the state who could be attracted to Democratic candidates because of their positions on issues that really mattered to people, not just on party loyalty.

Paul Simon—a young independent-minded activist who published a small downstate newspaper and was just beginning his long, successful political career—became DFI's temporary president. We attracted a strong supporter in Arnold Maremont, a wealthy, liberal Chicago Democrat, and convinced many young people to join us in our attempt to change the system. Once they learned how bad it was, they became as upset as we were. As a result, the new organization grew rapidly to about one hundred clubs with close to five thousand members statewide. This was amazing and exciting.

Vic, Dave, and I talked to as many of the leaders of these clubs as we could. It was well known that I had formed and led CIG, that I was a successful attorney, and that I was motivated to take on responsibility in a statewide organization. As a result, I was asked to chair DFI's convention. I should add that no one else wanted the job!

Our first aim with DFI was to establish a structure that would give us a seat at the table of Illinois Democratic power politics. Several hundred delegates from the individual clubs all over the state attended. Vic, Dave, and I decided the convention schedule, appointed committees, selected speakers, chose motions to make and who should make them, discussed which delegates I could call on and how to cut debate when necessary, and conferred on a myriad of other matters essential to running a convention. At the end of a tumultuous day with many procedural battles over bylaws and platform, it was apparent to everyone that I was the logical choice to be the first permanent president of the new organization. Arnold Maremont said publicly that he would underwrite Vic's salary as executive director for a year if I became president. I was duly elected, and Vic was hired. Arnold became DFI treasurer and brought with him Mort Kaplan, a talented public relations executive. This exciting time in my life was also the first time that Vic, Dave Green, and I worked together as a political team.

Dave really impressed me. Unassuming in appearance, he had a mind I would one day describe as half computer. Each of us felt our compatibility could be the beginning of something bigger than DFI.

I had hoped that Roberta would be happy about all this, but when I told her of my election as president, she had the opposite reaction. She thought only about the fact that I would be away from home more than ever, which I understood. She was pregnant with our sixth child, which happened after our second "No more diaper" celebration. As a devout Catholic, Roberta refused to practice effective birth control, and we were both frustrated. However, I certainly did not see abandoning my political aspirations as a solution.

"Maybe I should have married a gas station manager," she said. The remark really hurt me, and I remonstrated. She admitted she had gone too far. "Of course I want you to succeed."

Yet I could not easily forget the bitterness in her tone. My traditional thinking saw my wife's role as running the home with however many children came along, particularly since it was her religious preference that resulted in there being so many. But I could not have said this out loud at that time, and I also hasten to say that as time went by and the children grew, I not only loved them but realized it was their presence that in great measure made my life worthwhile.

About that same time, Vic's wife gave birth to a baby boy, and Vic named him Daniel, after me. I was extremely flattered and pleased.

The rebellion on the domestic front subsided, but the political rebellion escalated. DFI became a force to be reckoned with. The regular Democratic organization's reaction to us ranged from disdain to active opposition, particularly in Mayor Daley's domain of Chicago and Cook County. As president of DFI, I paid a formal call on him, hoping to encourage him to recognize that the time was right for reform, that there was a strong reform movement on the march, and that he would benefit by choosing to acknowledge it. Buddha-like, Daley listened politely as I described the organization and said exactly nothing. Not one word.

Not only did we seek statewide recognition as a legitimate organization of Democrats but Vic worked hard to gain recognition from the Democratic National Committee. Our big break came when the DNC sponsored—through local Democratic organizations—a series of national celebrations to honor Harry Truman and raise funds for the national party. Mayor Daley startlingly announced that Chicago would not participate. Vic, Dave, and I huddled, and I announced that the DFI would sponsor a Harry Truman jubilee in Chicago. Guests learned about the DFI, and our program featured an all-star cast of entertainers. The Truman event was a resounding success, filling the Civic Opera House with more than a thousand people at $25 a seat.

## MY FIRST TRY FOR STATEWIDE OFFICE

In late 1959, Vic, Dave, and I decided that I should make a try for the office of Illinois Attorney General—definitely a long-shot effort. I was filled with almost childlike excitement. Looking back, I wonder at our audacity. Although I had good legal standing in the community, I had no public following and clearly had little prospect for any support within the regular Democratic Party organization. The image of myself riding around in a black limousine as the top lawyer in the state of Illinois was a powerful daydream. I shared it with Roberta, hoping to entice her into sharing my enthusiasm, but also warning her that the ambition was virtually unattainable—unless I had the support of the regular Democratic Party—which meant Daley.

With mixed emotions, I appeared before the ever more powerful Daley slate-making committee on January 3, 1960. Mayor Daley was now nationally recognized as the political boss who not only ran Chicago but also the city *and* state Democratic Party organizations like a Caesar. He made a show of party democracy by inviting all candidates for statewide office to seek the committee's blessing, but in reality the choice would be Daley's alone. The committee would never choose me, but I thought there was an outside chance Daley would see me as a blue ribbon candidate in the way that Col. Jake Arvey had supported Stevenson and Douglas.

The committee convened in a suite at the Bismarck Hotel in Chicago. I stood around waiting in the hallway, hearing the drone and rise of men's voices, followed by bursts of laughter and a round of smokers' coughs. A party hack I recognized finally opened the door and said, "Okay, Walker."

The air wasn't actually thick with smoke, but breathing it wasn't pleasant. There were maybe a dozen men present, a couple holding stogies, and several dragging on cigarettes. Balding men with beer bellies and suspenders, a few in vests with shirtsleeves rolled up, ties loosened. Not a tennis player in the bunch. A diamond flashed on the pinkie ring of a guy with rumored Mob connections. Other than the ring, he blended in with the others. The only two men in the room who looked different were Daley and I. We both wore suits—mine gray, his the nondescript dark blue, three-piece suit he customarily wore. He attended Mass at least once a day and always dressed as if it were Sunday. He sat in the most comfortable chair in the center of the room, again the passive Buddha. The men regarded me arrogantly and yet managed to be sycophantic toward Daley at the same time, hanging on his every silence. He nodded at me.

I took a deep breath, made eye contact. "I feel that with your support, I could empower the office of attorney general in new and different ways. For instance, the ability to convene grand juries is vastly underutilized and untested. I would convene them to go after corruption . . ." I had to be very careful here and not mention political corruption. I didn't dare look at the guy with the pinkie ring. "I'd go after corruption in businesses." I gave a few examples.

Numb faces stared back at me. Ears had stopped working. Several men on the fringes conversed.

"How much money can you bring to the campaign?" a stogie smoker asked.

A few heads angled toward me.

"I'm good at fund-raising and served as treasurer on other campaigns. I would, of course, do my best to raise the money."

Muttered skepticism buzzed. Daley just watched me.

The guy sitting next to Daley was Jim Ronan, state Democratic Party chairman. He asked, "Will you pledge to support the decisions of the committee and run for whatever office it designates?"

The famous loyalty oath.

"Well," I hedged, "at this stage, I'm only interested in becoming attorney general and would not run for any other office."

Daley nodded at the guy who had let me in.

"Okay, Walker, wait outside," the man said.

I stepped outside, grateful at least for the fresh air. The committee was a waste of time. What was I thinking? Ronan soon came out of the room to throw his arm around my shoulders.

"Good presentation," he said. Then he lowered his voice conspiratorially, "Dan, you gotta be realistic. There's a bunch of Catholics on the ticket this year from Kennedy on down, and one more will be hard for Boss Daley to swing."

I was stunned at his reaction, but I spoke up. "Jim, I'm not a Catholic."

He didn't miss a beat. "Doesn't matter, Dan. With all those children, everyone'll think you are."

Politics!

That night I was with Roberta at the hospital where our little Margaret had just been born, our sixth child. The phone in the room rang and I answered.

"This is Findley, Dan. Vic told me where to reach you." Findley was a political columnist for the *Chicago American*, known to have close ties to the Daley machine.

I listened with amazement when he said, "Congratulations, General. I found a pay phone here at the Bismarck Hotel where I managed to get the inside dope. You've been tapped to be the Democratic candidate for attorney general. What's your comment?" (At both the state and federal level, those holding the office of attorney general are customarily addressed by others in the political-governmental world as "General.")

Flabbergasted, I muttered some kind of statement and quickly called Vic to arrange a meeting early the next morning. When we got together, I called Mayor Daley's secretary, and she confirmed that I had been slated to run for attorney general.

"I suggest you write an acceptance for the media," she said.

Thinking it was locked up, I called in Mary Parrilli, my legal secretary, to dictate a press release. Vic and I were ecstatic. But then Findley called again. "Sorry, Dan, at the last minute you were bounced in favor of Bill Clark."

I had to know why. One obvious explanation was contempt for my independent political activities, including my stand on integrated housing in Deerfield. But there was another reason involving inside politics. Bill Clark had been slated, against his will, to run for secretary of state against a popular Republican incumbent. So he sent his mother, a woman reputed to know "where the bodies were buried," to see Daley. She supposedly said, "You promised my husband on his deathbed that you would take care of my Billy, and he wants to be attorney general."

Daley placed great store on family matters. Her plea, together with the rebelling regulars, toppled me. Actually, I never did understand why Daley had accepted me as the party's candidate for attorney general in the first place. Yet in those few hours when I thought I stood a real chance, my world had changed. I saw myself in office.

The letdown was tremendous. Still, I hoped to work for change within the Democratic Party, and my name appeared on the primary ballot in 1960 for precinct committeeman of Deerfield Township, Lake County, Illinois. If I were ever going to hold state office, I really needed a win. With my stand on integration in Deerfield, even this low rung of the political ladder wasn't a sure thing, however. I had enemies in Deerfield. Remembering what I learned in the Nineteenth Ward, I knocked on every door and did my "plus, minus, zero" routine, determined to persuade voters the campaign had nothing to do with favors, and all to do with the candidates and issues.

And, of course, we all worked for Kennedy that year. I took charge of the Businessmen for Kennedy Committee in Illinois. The year was turbulent politically, and it challenged my own ideals versus my pragmatism. Sometimes clinging to ideals results in total defeat—a self-inflicted shot in the foot. The regular organization, controlled by Daley, decided to slate Otto Kerner—a widely respected county judge—for governor. I had no real objection to Kerner. However, an independent was contesting the party machine for the first time in many years—my old friend Joe Lohman. This seemed like a breakthrough for the DFI at last, and we were thrilled. He had progressed from Cook County sheriff to president of the Cook County Board of Supervisors and seemed reasonably independent of the machine.

And then we had too many good men. Steve Mitchell, who had managed Adlai Stevenson's presidential campaigns and gone on to become chairman of the Democratic Party nationally, also decided to make a run for governor. This precipitated a fight in the DFI between those who supported Lohman and those who wanted Mitchell. I knew both candidates well and finally decided that neither had a chance in this three-way race. Mitchell and Lohman would split the independent-minded voters, and the solid machine vote would win. Vic, Dave, and a few others in the DFI agreed.

We turned our attention to Kerner, our best hope of defeating a Republican. We concluded that there remained a real possibility that Kerner, once he got elected, would act on important matters independently of the machine. Backing Kerner was a tough decision, and I took some criticism. Kerner won the primary easily, but the DFI lost its steam after this. It had proved, however, that there were a substantial number of young Democrats throughout the state deeply dissatisfied with the Chicago machine and the downstate regular Democratic organizations. My hopes to lead the DFI, which I had helped build, into a credible political organization focused on independent-style politics were now dashed.

I was elected precinct committeeman in that primary, proudly receiving one more vote in my precinct than Jack Kennedy did on the Democratic ticket. Mayor Daley had dumped the Illinois favorite son Adlai Stevenson as presidential candidate in favor of Kennedy. In the general election, he was credited with electing Kennedy president by delivering enough votes in Chicago to hand him the critical state of Illinois. Daley was called a "king maker," and the media hailed him as one of the nation's most powerful politicians.

Reporters asked Daley about the charge that his Chicago organization had "stolen" the votes needed to put Kennedy over the top statewide. "Nah," he said. "I don't need to steal votes. Besides, we have to do something to match the Republican downstate vote stealing."

Though self-contradictory, there was merit to his argument. Sure, key Chicago machine wards used their usual tricks, but it was also true that Republicans downstate had their own tricks for invalidating votes for Democratic candidates.[1]

As precinct committeeman, I pulled in my share of votes for Kennedy as well as for Otto Kerner, who became governor, but the election was a personal turning point. Politically, where could I go from there? Additionally, my law career had stalled and, with six children, the family's debts were climbing.

---

[1] The tricks included, for example, counting a vote for every Republican on the ballot when a voter punched or wrote an X for a straight party vote but then crossed over to select one or more Democratic candidates. Legally, the individual selections should have overridden the straight party designation. In precincts where the Republican judges outnumbered the Democratic ones, or where (as in many precincts in heavily Republican areas downstate) there were no Democratic poll judges on Election Day, all those individual selections were not counted. Kennedy lost many votes downstate because of this maneuver.

# 7

## *Becoming Controversial in Chicago*

As another session of my law class in the prison chapel is about to begin, my inmate students harp on their favorite subject.

"That S.O.B. judge sent me up for a crime I flat out did not commit."

"My lawyer is an idiot. He sold me out."

"Habeas corpus," I say and wait for their silence. "Habeas corpus." I look each man in the eye. "Do any of you have any idea what this precious right could mean to you?"

I have their attention, but they stare blankly, or they frown.

"It can get me outta here?"

"It might. And that's what you'll learn. Hundreds of years ago, habeas corpus changed the legal system in England, and America copied the reform. Before the right to petition for a writ of habeas corpus existed, anyone could be jailed on a whim for whatever crime the king or his sheriff felt like charging them with, and they could rot in prison with no recourse. The writ of habeas corpus. It means literally, 'bring me the body.'"

"Dead?" an inmate asks. A few others laugh.

"Very much alive. The petition asks a judge to issue the writ and thereby command that a prisoner be brought physically into court where the judge can inquire into the legality of his or her incarceration."

I had learned a great deal about this writ when I served at the U.S. Supreme Court where the chief justice personally reviewed these petitions, often handwritten, sent in by prisoners from federal prisons all over the United States. Most of the petitions did not contain legally meritorious claims, though some did. My task with my students in the Duluth federal prison was to explain which claims could have any chance of succeeding and then teach them how to write such a petition.

After class sometimes, as many as a dozen men tell me their stories and ask for advice. Even more stop me on the tarmac, during meals, or in my room. The warden and the guards remain angry about my giving out legal advice, but I don't give a damn. I take a special interest in a farmer named Tim who grew a small patch of marijuana on his 360-acre farm. He pleaded guilty, expecting a light sentence because he never sold any, yet received a sentence of twelve years. I find his case so outrageous as to warrant relief and offer to help Tim draft a petition for filing in the local federal court. Tim chooses to contact his attorney. A petition is filed, and the judge dramatically reduces the sentence.

For myself, habeas corpus is not an alternative, since, although unfair, my sentence was still within the law. I do have the right to file a petition for parole, but under the law, I can't do that until I have been confined for a minimum of two years. Every time I slip into "poor little old me" thinking, I remind myself that this is a part of the whole legal system I so revere. But seven years?

I grow weary at the thought.

It is five in the morning and, while spring approaches, it is, in fact, still very cold. A freezing rain with sleet falls. I hear the rough sound of hacks and sneezes on top of the snores through the flimsy walls. The lights are never out, merely dimmed for sleep. For years I've suffered from chronic bronchitis that gets to my chest and leads to walking pneumonia, and I know by the familiar tightness in my chest, sore throat, and coughing that the head cold bothering me all week has worsened. I am probably running a fever.

My choices are to try to get a little more sleep, get up and get some breakfast, and then struggle through the day—or go stand in line at sick call right now. One of the guards serves as a paramedic, and for forty-five minutes he distributes over-the-counter remedies or fills doctors' prescriptions for inmates with established conditions like diabetes. I have no prescription for the antibiotics I need. There is never a doctor here, and the infirmary's lone paramedic can only hand out aspirins or chits that excuse prisoners from the daily work routine. These can be worth the wait.

The line for sick call is usually a long one, and the paramedic will see only one man at a time. Everyone else waits outside in the cold. And if he doesn't get to you, you will have suffered in the cold and missed breakfast for nothing.

This is my second onset of severe bronchitis. Or maybe the last one never really went away. I put in a request for a prison in a warmer climate. There are federal prisons in Texas, California, Florida, and West Virginia—all have milder climates than Duluth, which some consider the coldest city in the nation. I would not dispute that.

There is one other alternative, but I don't really consider it an option. Really sick inmates are transferred to Rochester, Minnesota. Nobody wants this if it can possibly be avoided. Transportation there and back is by a small Bureau of Prisons bus, referred to as the "bus from hell." It travels by a slow, circular route around the nation, moving people from one federal prison to another. Prisoners must wear leg irons and handcuffs and are always kept shackled to their seats, released by an armed guard only for necessary toilet stops and when they stop for the night. Nights are spent in county jails along the route, sometimes as many as fifteen, during the arduous round trip. These places, as inmates' stories tell it, are miserable: lousy meals on trays shoved into the prison cells shared with stinking winos. Deputy sheriffs despise the federal prisoners. And inmates of those jails, if they got a chance, would gladly take out their frustrations on "those fed guys." I have already helped one guy write a letter to a congressman about this deplorable procedure, but I don't have much hope that anything will come of it.

I decide to wait in front of sickbay. The line doesn't appear too long, but I'm still feverish and so damn cold. I think of my life during the high times when I had the finest medical attention available and all the creature comforts I wanted. I think of my beautiful wife who hasn't answered my letters and then quickly think of something else. I remember my lifestyle back in Oak Brook, and how—from the troubling vantage point of prison hindsight—my life then seemed nearly perfect.

### MIXING LAW AND POLITICS

Much to Roberta's consternation, I served along with Vic De Grazia in the new Otto Kerner administration. My position was in a voluntary capacity, so it meant no extra income, just more time away from home. Kerner had appointed Vic executive director of a new Board of Economic Development, a very prestigious appointment, and named me as a member of IPAC, the Illinois Public Aid Commission, which disbursed millions of dollars through various state welfare programs (including AFDC, Aid to Families with Dependent Children, a federal program). I was chosen to be secretary of the commission; the chairman named by Kerner was our friend Arnold Maremont, the financier. At the time, constant charges circulated about women on AFDC having more children just to get more public welfare money. Maremont proposed a highly controversial birth control program for AFDC mothers. The Catholic cardinal in Chicago quickly condemned the program, and the intense publicity that resulted greatly displeased Governor Kerner. Also, Roberta, ever the devout Catholic, became personally upset when I told her that I was working with Arnold on the program. After weeks of controversy and pressure, he resigned, and the program died. Arnold persuaded Vic to also resign from his state position and help set up a foundation to concentrate on rehabilitating housing for low- and moderate-income families. Vic stayed with this job throughout the 1960s. I then served as acting chairman of IPAC until a new Illinois Department of Public Aid took over.

During this time, both Vic and I watched with dismay as Kerner's independence waned and he became more obviously subservient to the Chicago machine. There had been high hopes when he won in 1960 that he would assert his independence from the Daley machine and bring change to Illinois. But he did not.

In those years, the system continued to tolerate legislators like Ralph "Babe" Serpico, who consorted regularly with mobster Tony Accardo; state senator Bernie Neistein, absentee boss of a ghetto ward who reputedly took orders from "Chuck" English of the crime syndicate; and Edward "Big Eddie" Quigley who was in charge of the city sewer system and ran the Twenty-seventh Ward, where his top precinct captain was sentenced to federal prison for violating federal election laws. Then there was the infamous Vito Marzullo in the Twenty-fifth Ward. He was a Mob-connected undertaker, and Mike Royko once cracked in a column, "Even in death, there is no escaping the Machine."

### MY LOVE AFFAIR WITH THE COURTROOM

In my early forties, busy as a trial lawyer, I kept myself politically involved. This didn't help our finances, which became a critical problem with seven children. So I pushed myself to move into the top echelon of Chicago trial lawyers, handling difficult, major business-related cases for corporate clients. I learned to love the courtroom. Nowhere in the practice of law did I ever find an equal to trial work. It was *mano a mano*, and at the end, you knew whether you had won or lost—considerably more exciting and personally satisfying than writing a will or contract, or advising a client about legal matters in the office.

This demanding work often required long trials with complicated factual issues, many witnesses, and hundreds of documents. At first, I was Tom Mulroy's top trial assistant, "second chair" as it is called, and he was a strong taskmaster and a bear on preparation. I learned to be meticulous in trial preparation, and finally I was moved to the "first chair." One of the earliest big cases came to me from Consolidated Foods Corporation, involving a merger alleged by the Federal Trade Commission, or FTC, to be in violation of the federal antitrust law.

I advised Consolidated that their case would almost certainly be a loser before the commission but could be won on appeal to the Seventh Circuit Court of Appeals, a very conservative court. However, the temper of the times was against winning *any* corporate merger case opposing the FTC. If the case went up to the Supreme Court, I predicted we would almost certainly lose since that Court was very progovernment in antitrust cases.

Nate Cummings, then CEO of Consolidated, decided to fight it all the way. "Hell," he told us, "the profits we'll get will be far greater than your legal bills. So delay the loss as long as you possibly can, and I'll gladly pay your fees."

So, delay I did, through a long series of intensive hearings around the nation. In city after city, I produced purchasing agent after purchasing agent to testify. Then, after calling the appropriate executives from Consolidated itself, I put a series of expert witnesses on the stand to discredit the government's economic theories.

As these trials went on for many months, Consolidated cheerfully paid the very substantial bills. The case followed precisely the path I had predicted. The FTC ruled against us, but the Seventh Circuit Court of Appeals reversed the decision. The FTC doggedly appealed, and I had my first case in the U.S. Supreme Court, where the odds were distinctly against me. I knew most of the justices from my time as law clerk for the former chief justice, but they still appeared very formidable when I faced them. After I finished, Justice Felix Frankfurter was kind enough to send me a handwritten note with the message, "Excellent job." That note was my only solace when, months later, the Court announced its decision: unanimous, nine to zero, against my client.

I lost, but the outcome wasn't a surprise, and the high-profile case did help me become a partner in the law firm. However, because of the firm's accounting system, it would be several years before partnership income exceeded my existing salary plus bonus. I was deeply in debt and destined to remain in the red for years. Eventually, with significantly more victories than losses and with business clients almost always willing and able to pay their bills, my income improved.

My various activities left precious little time for the family. By 1962, Kathleen was in high school, Dan and Julie were in junior high, Robbie was ten, Charles was eight. Margaret turned two, and our seventh and last child, Will, came along in September. When more income made it possible, we moved into a new and much larger home at 1152 Norman Lane, just one block away from the old one. What social life I had revolved around Roberta's Catholic friends, our neighbors in Deerfield, Little League, and ice hockey games. Rarely did our social life take us outside Deerfield. We had everything we needed, enjoyed good health, and felt blessed. Most men would have been happy with all this good fortune. A siren song still beckoned me, however.

## THE CONSTANT LURE OF POLITICS

I generally devoted my minimal spare time to promoting my standing in the legal community and to political work, rather than spending it with the family. I found time for Bar Association activities and continued working with the Crime Commission, becoming a member of the board of directors. I took time to support selected candidates for office whom I thought showed some promise of independence, yet I avoided the independent "Lake Shore liberals," who were simply too liberal for me. Illinois state politics—not national, not local, but state politics—remained my major fascination. Heart and soul, I still wanted to be a part of a movement that would cripple machine politics, open up the system, and make the Democratic Party in Illinois a statewide vehicle for sensible campaigns based on the issues—the kind of issues that, since the Great Depression, had made the Democratic Party the "party of the people."

While I would have loved to give it a try, our seven children and substantial debts kept me from running for any major office. As I watched the stranglehold that the Chicago machine had on the state's political system in the Democratic Party, my view hardened that only a governor could have any hope of making drastic changes in that system.

When the position of United States Attorney for the Northern District of

Illinois, a presidential appointment, opened up during the Kennedy administration, I decided to go for it. I could support the family on the salary and take a big step up the governmental ladder. Kennedy had let it be known that he was going to rely heavily on his attorney general (brother Bobby) in choosing the U.S. attorneys. Vic De Grazia, Dave Green, and I mustered all available contacts, including Sargent Shriver, who had married into the Kennedy family and ran the Chicago Merchandise Mart, owned by the Kennedy family. Mayor Daley had his own candidate.

We were, of course, delighted when the Department of Justice sent word that Bobby Kennedy, the attorney general, had decided to recommend me to his brother, and even more so when the department informed me that the papers were on their way to the White House for final presidential approval. On that fateful day in 1963, I was having lunch to celebrate the good news with Vic and Dave at the Mid-America Club in downtown Chicago. Suddenly, the news spread through the club like wildfire: "President Kennedy has been assassinated." Many more important causes than mine were killed along with the president that day.

In 1964, Vic, Dave, and I campaigned for Adlai Stevenson III, son of the former governor. His strong name recognition helped Adlai capture a seat in the legislature. Another winner was downstater Paul Simon, a popular independent and a rising star in the Democratic Party. I liked backing a winner, but I felt increasingly like a perpetual cheerleader, destined never to be a player. Any idea of having my own political campaign for a state office was beginning to seem like merely the dream of a man's youth, one that must die as immediate responsibilities took precedence.

### A "KEPT LAWYER"

In 1965, I received a surprising call from Tom Brooker, chairman and CEO of Montgomery Ward. I had never before met him.

"Dan," he said after introducing himself, "I want to hire you as vice president and general counsel. Don't automatically say no; please hear me out." He offered a very attractive financial package. The thought of higher salary that could pay off some of our debts plus stock options, retirement plan, health insurance, and expense account—none of which I had at the time—was very attractive. Brooker stressed that I would report directly to him and that he had no problem with my continued involvement in both political and community affairs. This job could keep me from abandoning political ambitions.

Though I loved the courtroom, life as a trial lawyer had definite downsides. With no secure client base of my own, I had to depend on referrals from my partners and my ability to attract new cases in competition with other leading trial attorneys. While I received cases from both of those sources, there was no guarantee it would continue. Another downside was the lifestyle of some successful trial attorneys in Chicago. Long trials often required staying with support staff in a downtown hotel, dining in restaurants every night. Heavy drinking and constant separation from family became a way of life for too many of these lawyers.

Yet I was strongly considering giving up something I loved: the drama of the courtroom and the constant duel of wits, the lay-it-on-the-line and win-or-lose life that made being a trial lawyer so exhilarating. Traditional lawyers are rather contemptuous of becoming a "kept lawyer" or "house counsel" and losing treasured independence. Further, I would become a desk lawyer, a paper shuffler, and I would definitely lose face with my professional litigator cohorts who would sneer at my "crossing the river," as it was called.

I agonized over the decision. Roberta hoped I would take the job, although she very carefully did not put any pressure on me. I was deeply troubled at our continually growing debt, the lack of a secure retirement plan, the impending burden of getting many children through college, and our inability to afford some of the nicer things of life like new cars and resort vacations for the family—all the material things that perhaps should not have, but definitely did, provide a powerful inducement. In the final analysis, though, the lure of very measurable security and a job enabling me to spend more time with my wife and children who were growing up so fast, as well as continued opportunities for political activities, tipped the scale. It never occurred to me that financial security might also better enable me to seek elective office.

I have never regretted the decision, and the job more than lived up to my expectations. Starting with going home at five every day from a handsome executive office, with lots of perks and a satisfying personal relationship with my boss and the other executives of Montgomery Ward, it blossomed to provide other benefits. Becoming more a legal executive manager than a frontline attorney, I supervised no less than forty-five lawyers: about twelve in the Chicago corporate office, one in the New York City buying headquarters, one in the Washington government office, and the remainder in the various regional headquarters in Chicago, Denver, and Oakland, California.

Professionally, the legal work at Montgomery Ward interested me and weighed less on me than trying lawsuits. Actually, my staff did the heavy paperwork. Labor relations had its own lawyers, and I provided only top-level policy oversight. Since Montgomery Ward was self-insured, we had hundreds of what were called "slip and fall" lawsuits brought by Ward's shoppers all over the nation, but my regional lawyers handled those. For the regional offices, my responsibilities were controlling both budgets and work product quality. Several higher-level lawsuits had to be handled at corporate headquarters, but I farmed them out to private law firms, providing only oversight. My prime personal responsibility was providing legal advice to the top executives and the board of directors and ensuring compliance with all formal filing and other regulatory requirements of federal and state government. The responsibilities were considerable, but I proved to be good at delegation.

I had even more hours and freedom to devote to outside activities than I had experienced at Hopkins, Sutter. Plus, with Kathleen, Dan, Julie, and Robbie considering attending colleges in California and Colorado, I would always be able to find a reason to visit my staff attorneys in Oakland and Denver and incidentally visit my kids. If I wanted to go to Washington, D.C., for any reason, I could work in my attorney's office there. Same for New York City. Supervising important litigation in Southern California and Florida frequently required conferences with outside attorneys handling the cases. For example, seeing trial lawyer Warren Christopher in Los Angeles allowed side trips to visit my parents in San Diego. Working on cases with Senator Lawton Chiles in Florida provided opportunities for fishing and quail hunting.

This was the best job I had ever had, and my drive to seek high office actually diminished somewhat, particularly since I worked on national issues and legislation that affected retailing and was constantly involved with regulatory agencies like the FTC and the SEC (Securities and Exchange Commission). At one point, I took the lead on behalf of Montgomery Ward in supporting the proposed truth-in-lending law. This placed us in opposition to other large retailers who didn't like the detailed consumer protection portions of the law. Only Tom Brooker's steadfast support for his sometimes-controversial general counsel enabled me to continue the fight.

There were other instances where I became involved in controversial matters of one type or another, some totally unrelated to the company's business. My boss Tom Brooker didn't remonstrate with me, although I know that other Wards executives often complained to him about the publicity that occasionally resulted.

Tom tried repeatedly to get me more involved on the business side of Montgomery Ward, inviting me to attend important executive committee meetings in Chicago and in the various regional headquarters. He confided a desire to train me to become an executive vice president, but I steadfastly resisted. I had absolutely no interest in pursuing such a path.

I still maintained some involvement in Illinois and Chicago governmental matters and frequently discussed Chicago politics and government with high- and medium-level business executives and professional leaders. To my disappointment, they applauded Mayor Daley's firm grip on the city's government almost unanimously. Over and over from the businessmen, I heard this or words to the same effect: "How Daley runs the city, I don't care. Things get done." Or: "Just so long as he runs it and makes it work." And: "If it ain't broke, don't fix it. I hate reformers."

Daley's reputation for capably running the city overcame—even among many liberals—a dislike for his autocratic ways, this despite what they perceived as disdain by both him and the Chicago machine for such areas as civil rights, police abuse, and the environment. The business and professional establishment in Chicago was decidedly stacked against anyone who tried to change the political/governmental system that made Chicago "the city that works."

At that time, as a mostly conservative Democrat, I had great misgivings, along with many other business executives, about President Johnson's Great Society. I thought it smacked too much of a liberal philosophy of just throwing huge sums of money at problems. But I differed with the others about Chicago. Despite the city's "it works" reputation, too many things weren't working for the people as they should have. Public schools were ranked among the lowest in the nation. Street crime was too high. Environmental issues were ignored. Daley's "benevolent boss" reputation obscured these failures, and the 1966 elections lay ahead. Race issues were demanding attention nationally, and it would only be a matter of time before they would erupt in Chicago.

My controversial activities were about to escalate.

# 8

## *Marching with Rev. King and Taking On the Mob*

My prison room is small, holding two double-tier bunks. There is no door, allowing the guards walking by to keep tabs on us. As a latecomer to the room, I am in a top bunk. I'm almost over my bronchitis, but I still have night sweats and a persistent, hacking cough often keeps me awake.

Late one night, a young man—white, upper class—sleeps in the lower bunk across the room from me. He is in for a drug conviction. Three black men slip silently into our room. I am awake and horrified at the intrusion of the heavily muscled guys in shorts and undershirts. Mean faces, hard eyes.

"Turn over, white boy," one says to the young man, pushing down hard on one of his shoulders.

Startled awake, he takes in the scene as they force him to turn his body back up. One of the guys pins him to the bunk while another drops his shorts, clambers over the young man, and sodomizes him while the other two watch. Then the other two take their turns. Out of the corner of my eye, I see a guard walk by, look in, and go on his way. I learn later that in sophisticated prisoner parlance, this is called "psychological regimentation of the population." Overlooking these degrading and even violent practices helps the guards maintain control over both black and white prisoners.

What could I do? Absolutely nothing. That becomes one of the hardest parts of prison life. And what I had just observed was not just violence; it was racial violence, crying out for punishment. Enforceable justice was a vital part of my lifelong respect for the majesty of the law in America. As I finally close my eyes and find badly needed sleep, I think back to my involvement with Dr. Martin Luther King Jr.—a man who would have abhorred the violence as much as I did—when I marched with him through racist crowds in Chicago.

---

## CIVIL RIGHTS, THE MOB, RIOTS, AND POLITICS

Civil rights finally became a top local issue, though certainly not brought on by the Chicago machine, which for many decades had been perfectly comfortable with the city's flagrant segregation. Daley was quoted repeatedly in the press saying, "We don't have any segregation in Chicago. There are no ghettos in my city." But the Chicago Urban League vehemently disagreed, stating that it was "the most residentially segregated city in the United States." There were boundaries that everyone acknowledged. For example, Daley insisted that the Dan Ryan Expressway be realigned, and it became a formidable racial barrier on the South Side. Concern then grew among white businessmen and political leaders when African Americans threatened to encroach on the Loop area. A businessman said in a meeting I attended, "The whole goddamn town is going to hell."

This shocked me. The wildly exaggerated fear of desegregation was not only ridiculous, it was a scare tactic of the times intended to intimidate the white population. Daley was surprised when his opponent, Benjamin Adamowski, won 51 percent of the white vote, which meant that, in effect, the African American vote elected Daley. At that time, as Mike Royko pointed out in his book *Boss*, the people who were trapped in the slums and nightmarish public housing projects had the worst school system, were the most degraded by police, and were the most ignored in campaign promises, yet they gave Daley his third term. Wrote Royko, "They did it quietly, asking for nothing in return. Exactly what they got."

### MARCHING WITH REV. MARTIN LUTHER KING JR.

Daley continued to do nothing with the city government to foster more integration—more open, nondiscriminatory housing programs in Chicago.

Finally, Rev. Martin Luther King's Southern Christian Leadership Council decided in 1965 to make Chicago a test case for attacking big city segregation as preventing housing opportunities for minorities. When the SCLC commenced demonstrations, Daley invoked the old cry, "Those protestors are communists." He dismissed King with the remark, "He only comes to Chicago to cause trouble." In what he thought were closed meetings, Daley went further, as Mike Royko reported in *Boss*: "Daley went into a wild rage, calling him a dirty sonofabitch, a bastard, a prick, a rabble-rouser, a trouble-maker." He preferred the black congressman William Dawson, whom he and the Chicago machine had supported for many years. Dawson was never a fighter for civil rights, even during these post-Kennedy and Johnson years. He had done his best as a congressman to dissuade the Kennedyites from offending his "good Southern friends" in the Congress.

When the highly publicized "open housing marches" began in Chicago, King led them personally, along with Al Raby of the SCLC, and Ralph Metcalfe, an African American alderman who courageously broke ranks with the machine on the open housing issue. I knew Al and had worked with Ralph on a new city charter. The media played up the first marches, and I watched television with disbelief at white people's reactions. I couldn't believe it. I knew it was bad in Selma, but surely not here—surely what I was seeing was media exaggeration. I had to go and see for myself. Yet I also thought of the courage of the Selma marchers, and I knew it was time for me to be courageous as well. Some liberal whites, a few other business executives, and I joined the marchers. Ralph and Al introduced me to King and his associates.

This was the first time I had ever done anything like this, and I didn't know what to anticipate. I did know, of course, that the marchers encountered at least a few hostile mobs assembled on the sidewalks, but I suspected that would be the exception, and not the rule. The protesters would be walking from Marquette Park in the city and then through Cicero, a totally white ethnic suburb on the edge of Chicago.

Someone called out, "Let's get started!"

And there I was, heading down the street, arm-in-arm with about ten others in the first rank. I would guess about twenty or thirty men and women, mostly black, but with a sprinkling of whites, followed. King was in the middle of the first rank. He seemed preoccupied, but it was obvious that his presence inspired those around him. All of us knew that we were a part of Chicago civil rights history. And we certainly knew that we were, by our presence, in effect, demonstrating against the all-white Chicago establishment as we walked at first hesitantly and then resolutely up the street. Bystanders initially watched in silence, glowering, but then a few catcalls erupted. Sometimes people clustered along the curbs, while other stretches of sidewalk were nearly empty. On some corners, crowds gathered. Soon the catcalls turned into curses and name-calling.

"Nigger lovers!"

"Get out of our town, you communists!"

Much of the yelling was indistinguishable. Admittedly, I got a little nervous. A black man on my left said, "We been through this at Selma and worse places than this. We can handle it. Just look straight ahead; try to ignore them and keep walking."

This behavior typified the people's conduct on the several occasions that I participated in the marches. I was not there on the day the mob decided to throw rocks and bricks at King and his associates. Once, a rock felled King while the crowd repeatedly shouted, "Kill the niggers!" King said publicly that he had seldom seen mobs as hostile and hate-filled as he marched through other white communities.

The marches with King were certainly among the most momentous experiences of my life. Mayor Daley himself called my boss, Tom Brooker, to protest my participation in the marches. Tom told me about the call but did nothing to dissuade me. I have often wondered if he derived some vicarious pleasure from my outside activities.

After days of intense publicity about the marches, Daley finally—and with obvious reluctance—agreed to negotiations and brought in Ben Heineman, CEO of the Northwestern Railroad, to chair the meetings. Participating to show the business community's support for open housing were other prominent CEOs, such as Robert Ingersoll of Borg Warner; C. Virgil Martin of retailer Carson, Pirie, Scott; Thomas Ayers of Commonwealth Edison; and a few other high-profile businessmen. I joined them, representing Montgomery Ward.

An agreement to halt the marches in exchange for open housing reforms, including action by the city council, was hammered out, but it was highly unpopular in many white neighborhoods of Chicago. Then came the 1966 election, and a white backlash became apparent, particularly in the ethnic neighborhoods where open housing was anathema. Many in Chicago voted in protest against Democratic candidates, enabling Republican Charles Percy to defeat U.S. Senator Paul Douglas. The patronage-powerful presidency of the Cook County Board went to Republican Richard Ogilvie. These defeats were an astonishing setback to the Democratic machine. Overall, it was a disaster for the Democrats. However, Vic, Dave, and I worked for Adlai Stevenson III again, and he was elected state treasurer.

Immediately after the white backlash election, the powerful alderman Thomas Keane, Mayor Daley's city council leader, proclaimed a repudiation of the carefully negotiated open housing agreement. Daley quickly agreed in a public statement. Mike Royko later wrote in his book *Boss* this about the ending of the open housing negotiations: "Dr. King went back home in the South, the marches faded into memory, and Daley hadn't rejected [Alderman] Keane's suggestion to 'f——k 'em.' He just did it slowly."

Throughout this controversy, Mayor Daley charged repeatedly that it was the realtors who were responsible for Chicago's deplorable housing segregation, but that didn't stop the dispute, and the media kept the issue alive. Negotiations resumed in which I again participated along with other business executives. The long-lasting controversy finally ended with another settlement agreement. The Leadership Council for Metropolitan Open Communities was created, and I was named chairman of its government relations committee. This led to the Metropolitan Housing Development Corporation, formed to fight racial bias in selling and renting housing throughout the metropolitan area. I was chosen as president of MHDC, and my staff went about persuading realtors to sign fair housing agreements pledging to show properties to any qualified buyer or renter regardless of race. They enlisted landlords to sign similar agreements. Through speeches and meetings, lenders were persuaded to make fair loans. These outreach programs proved reasonably effective.

Chicago had other major problems relating to reforms of the public schools, the city charter, and the police. Wanting to play a role by getting the business community involved, I organized a "Deputies' Committee" composed of officers of major Chicago corporations. There were about ten of us, all second-level executives. We represented our chiefs, the CEOs, on a number of these issues. We met regularly to review proposals and brief our bosses, and this gave me valuable education on some of Chicago's major problem areas and what state government could do to help local government.

### TAKEOVER

In 1966, I faced a crisis at work. Montgomery Ward became a possible takeover target, in great part because of its considerable cash reserves and the large balances of credit account customers. In many respects, the huge retailer was also a bank. The executives were understandably nervous about a takeover and gave me the job of preparing a defense strategy, working with Arthur Andersen, the auditors, and consulting with other major corporations similarly threatened.

In the final analysis, we determined that we needed to become bigger, to make the company too large a bite for a corporate pirate to swallow. So, we wooed and won Container Corporation of America, and the resulting holding company was called Marcor Incorporated. Montgomery Ward was the larger of the two, so our executives became the principal officers of Marcor, with Tom Brooker as CEO. The merger, rather unique in form, required a lot of work with the financial vice president, Gordon Worley, and the SEC. Throughout the merger, Worley and I were the working team, and we developed a very close business friendship.

The merger required that I spend more time on corporate legal matters. The Container Corporation had a history of rather cozy cooperation with its competitors, and a federal antitrust price-fixing case was launched against it. Because of my antitrust expertise, Brooker insisted that I become personally involved in the defense. Then Montgomery Ward organized its own bank and insurance company, and I became both general counsel and a director for those entities. This was a new challenge. Gordon Worley and I worked together on the bank, and in my involvement with the insurance company, I found a new lifetime friend in Howard Lamb.

### TAKING ON THE MOB

I continued to serve on the board of directors of the Chicago Crime Commission, chairing the legislative committee and then becoming president for three successive annual terms. The commission, supported by the business community with enough money for a large office and staff, was historically involved in keeping tabs on law enforcement regarding organized crime. Other police departments, congressional committees, and the U.S. Department of Justice often consulted with the nationally known executive director, Virgil Peterson, and used the commission's extensive files.

One of my ideas was publicizing the extent to which organized crime had infiltrated legitimate business in the Chicago area—a subject often discussed in general terms by the media, though the specific businesses involved were rarely identified by name. With the help of Harvey Johnson, whom I had brought in as a new executive director of the commission after Peterson retired, I persuaded the commission's board of directors to let me publish a report naming both the Mobsters and their businesses. Calling it *Spotlight on Organized Crime*, I identified by name 214 individuals and 102 businesses dealing with the public—restaurants, car dealerships, repair shops, appliance stores, and others.

Dubbed a "Hood's Who," the *Spotlight* received substantial media attention. *Chicago Daily News* headlined my report and even printed the names of all the individuals and businesses. Some suggested that I should be concerned about libel lawsuits and even personal retribution by the Mob. A *New York Times* editorial called me "gutsy," saying "Daniel Walker does not lose any sleep over it, but his name surely stands near the top of any list of candidates for elimination by the Chicago Mafia."

Actually, I did not lose sleep because, as I had earlier told both my wife and the Crime Commission board, there was no reason to worry. "The last thing the Mob guys want is the publicity and demands for prosecution that would result if I were harmed physically." None of them would risk the disclosure that would result from litigation permitting subpoenas for business files and depositions of the named individuals.

The Mob threats did come, unfortunately, at home when Roberta answered the phone. I had told her that if this did happen, she should try to write down on the handy pad as exactly as possible the words used. They were virtually the same in each call.

"Your husband's dead meat. I'd get the family out of town if I was you."

Roberta was frightened, naturally, and spoke in a stage whisper when she called to report the threat so the children would not hear. The calls rattled me, but I tried to stay calm. "This is simple intimidation, Roberta. They can't touch us, and they know it."

"Dan, I'm scared. When will it stop?"

I reassured her that the threats were empty, and she calmed down. I advised her not to tell her dad. He lived with us after Roberta's mother died; we had built an addition onto the house so he could have his own quarters.

The Mob filed two lawsuits against the commission and me. We immediately filed notices to take the depositions of the mobsters and issued subpoenas to produce sensitive documents that would disclose details of their operations. The results were as I had predicted. Patting Roberta's arm, I was glad to be able to report to her, "They've dropped the lawsuits."

Interestingly, Vic De Grazia reported to me that some liberals and the Italian community strongly disapproved of the *Spotlight*—the Italians for obvious reasons having to do with the names in it; and the liberals because they disliked on principle what they called "blacklisting." But I paid no attention, and in the following year published *Spotlight II*, adding the names of even more individuals and businesses. Some Mob-run companies failed, but there were never any statistics compiled.

Events such as these fed my pride, a tendency some of my detractors later called arrogance. I had tangled with the Mob openly. I took a continuing part in helping with racial integration. I had worked with major corporations on important legal and community problems. Through IPAC, I understood the limitations of the state welfare system. My legal skills had taken me to the Supreme Court. I had a reverence for law and democracy and a clear vision of the boundaries of government. I felt I was qualified to govern, and I had guts, energy, drive, and stamina. Perhaps I was pretentious and even a little cocky, but the political system was badly awry, and I felt certain I could help turn things around.

The world was about to change, though. On April 3, 1968, Rev. Martin Luther King Jr. delivered his famous last speech about his dream, "I Have Been to the Mountain Top." He was assassinated the next day. Chicago was about to face a serious crisis.

# 9

## *Reporting on Urban Riots and Dealing with Daley*

I smell lunch. Today's is a watery soup of lima beans with a little ham in it and dry cornbread on the side. I stand in the prison yard in my fatigues and rain poncho, coughing. The day is cold, gray, and damp. Just behind me in the lunch line is Joe DePeri, one of the few lasting friends I make in prison. Joe had been deputy chief commissioner of police in Philadelphia until he was convicted of taking favors from Mafia guys who treated him to expensive weekend gambling trips to Atlantic City. His sentence is twelve years. I want to talk to him, but I'm trying to keep my coughing fit under control.

Joe is a devout Catholic, and we often talk about a book I'm writing on early Christianity. For two years before prison, I had been doing research on this, trying to separate the message Jesus imparted while alive from that attributed to him after his death—a subject that fascinates me, and I'm trying to continue the research while in prison, using books my children send me.

I haven't heard anything from my second wife, and I try not to think about that too much. She's upset about the prison sentence, of course, but maybe she's more accepting by now. If she would just come up for a visit, I'd tell her that I'm going to do everything I can to get out early. Maybe she'll come up next weekend.

Roberta, my divorced first wife, had come to see me with one of our children, but it isn't what I most need. In any case, having someone interested in my project pleases me. And besides, Joe DePeri and a few others are good company.

The three black guys who often cut in front of me and had threatened me earlier cut in front of me again. "Move aside, white f———r!"

The words I most often hear—particularly from the black guys—are f———k, f———in', and f———er.

This time, Joe is with me and hears the threats. That evening, Joe goes to see one of the black guys. "You put a finger on the governor, and I'll see that the Mob gets you. I know some top Mafia guys, and they'll find you no matter where you are when you get out of this joint."

The three black fellows leave me alone after this, but the irony of prison life stuns me again. I marched with Martin Luther King Jr. to protect the rights of the three who persecute me, and then the Mob, whom I actively persecuted as president of the Chicago Crime Commission, is a force that ends up protecting me. And I'm grateful!

---

## THE BIG-CITY RIOTS

One hundred sixty-eight cities across the nation erupted in rioting, arson, and looting after the assassination of Martin Luther King Jr. Parts of Chicago and most particularly the near West Side went up in flames as both rioting and looting swept through neighborhoods. Worst hit was the Twenty-ninth Ward, one of the so-called plantation wards, ruled over by Bernie Neistein, often described as "a Mafia man who was both white and rich." That was when Mayor Daley made what has been called "the most famous utterance of his career," issuing an order widely reported as directing the police to "shoot to kill looters." While the written order actually read, "shoot to kill arsonists and shoot to maim or cripple looters," which was bad enough, it was widely understood by policemen as a license to use deadly force against law violators.

When the riots ended, Mayor Daley announced the formation of a riot study commission, naming me a member, undoubtedly because of my public reputation as president of the Chicago Crime Commission and my status as general counsel of a major national corporation. When the new commission assembled, about fifteen men and women as I recall, they elected me to chair the steering committee that directed the commission's work. I spent many hours with Charles Bane, the commission's executive director and a prominent member of Chicago's legal establishment, and the chairman, Alderman Ralph Metcalfe, to produce a unanimous report that condemned both the riots and some over-the-top law enforcement activities by the police. Despite our unanimity, the report was largely shelved and there was little follow-up. Nothing major came out of the report.

I developed great respect for Charles and Ralph. Although both were often aligned politically against me as the years went by, they often voiced privately their personal respect in some of my troublesome contests with the Chicago power structure. Metcalfe several times would take me aside when I was governor to say privately how much he regretted his inability to work more closely with me.

Despite the numerous meetings I participated in with Mayor Daley on the open housing issue, on the West Side riot investigation, and with our "deputies' committee" on major city issues, plus a few private meetings, we never established anything even approaching a personal rapport. To some degree, this was an obvious and natural result of my independent political activity. But it went deeper—much deeper. Richard J. Daley's life and outlook were as different from that of a Southern Californian with Texas in his blood as can possibly be imagined. To Daley, *reform* was a swear word, and I was disliked as a "do-gooder"—an even more loathsome category. Actually, the plain fact is that Daley and I never really learned how to communicate with each other.

While the independent columnist Mike Royko sometimes seemed to like Daley as being representative of "the city with broad shoulders," far removed from the New York kind of city that Royko disdained, he also frequently cited instances revealing Daley's toleration of corruption. In his book *Boss*, Royko wrote bluntly that Daley was "arrogant, crude, conniving, ruthless, suspicious, and intolerant." But then Daley could afford to ignore Royko while Democratic presidential candidates like Adlai Stevenson, George McGovern, and Fritz Mondale paid homage and lavished praise on the mayor. Also presidents like Lyndon Johnson and Jimmy Carter and even Richard Nixon often in speeches in the city called Daley's Chicago "one of the best managed and governed cities in the nation."

Daley ranked right up there with the best for memorable malapropisms. I always liked this one: "They have vilified me, they have crucified me; yes, they have even criticized me." Others include "exhilarated progress," "I resent insinuendoes," and "to higher and higher platitudes." He was a strong family man, and I respected him for that. However, he sometimes carried his family loyalty to extremes. His sons Richard, John, and William were frequent beneficiaries of the machine's outreach capabilities. When one was attacked for receiving a lucrative appointment and another with favoritism in obtaining insurance and real estate licenses, Daley reacted publicly and strongly to the critics. "If I can't help my sons, then anyone who doesn't like it can kiss my ass."

## MEANWHILE, THE FAMILY AND MY JOB

The family had grown rapidly while I was often away. While hopefully demonstrating that I was a caring parent, I clearly did not provide the constant presence that my father had when I was growing up. I tried hard to instill in all my children the beliefs in family loyalty, hard work, and self-discipline that I had acquired from my father, but I had nowhere near the time to devote to parenting that he had. Fortunately, Roberta shared my strong belief in what some would call "old-fashioned family values." I said and believed that a father could teach the kids what was necessary without spending as much time at home as other fathers did.

I missed my parents, and we were in touch perhaps once a month over the years, though I always felt I should have done better by them. We went out to San Diego to see them a couple of times, and Kathleen, Dan, and Charles had each spent a summer with my folks. While at Santa Clara University in Northern California, Kathleen and Dan occasionally drove down to San Diego for holidays. I often asked my parents to come visit us more often, but my dad facetiously claimed, "I cannot get a passport to cross the Mississippi River."

Roberta's Uncle Dave and Aunt Gertrude died in their midseventies, and Roberta had the responsibility to close out their affairs. I will never forget the day when she began cleaning out their old house. While we arranged lunch on the dining room table, a piece of silverware fell to the floor, and Roberta went down on her hands and knees and crawled under the table to retrieve it.

I still remember her yelling, "There's a hundred dollar bill!" And there were lots of them, stuffed into supports under the dining room table. It didn't take long for us to figure out that Gertrude and Dave had regularly cashed their pay and retirement checks and, like many old folks before them, decided to keep the money "under the mattress," rather than at a bank.

Painstakingly, we searched the house. Under mattresses, under tables, in corners of cabinets, in all kinds of hiding places, we found scores of hundred dollar bills. The culmination came when we cleaned all the trash out of the house and started a big fire in an open space. I was standing there with a rake to keep fire from spreading when suddenly, I saw some greenbacks and raked out of the flames a large, badly charred roll of hundred dollar bills. I submitted the charred roll to the U.S. Treasury Department and, to my surprise, got full payment in new bills. When we totaled it all up, we had managed to recover $18,000, and I have always suspected there was more we did not find.

Our social life continued to involve family, friends, and local community. Roberta and I never moved in Chicago social circles. We did little entertaining and rarely went downtown to attend social events, symphony, opera, or plays. Actually, I did not in those years feel comfortable with what is called "society." The old saying that you can get the boy out of the country, but you cannot get the country out of the boy had, perhaps, some applicability to me.

I paid a price when I became governor for not taking the opportunity when I was a corporate executive to create more friendships and contacts in the Chicago business world. Never did I pay enough attention to courting the establishment. I could have belonged, since many thought of me as part of the establishment when I was a La Salle Street lawyer and business executive. But although I was such in form, I never was in substance.

While at Montgomery Ward, I continued to be active politically. I was the corporate "house Democrat," since all other executives were hard-core Republicans. Here, too, CEO Tom Brooker gave me a great deal of latitude as I kept up my intense interest in state government.

Like Adlai Stevenson before him, Otto Kerner, as Democratic governor, gave Chicago's political boss a controlling voice on decisions involving governmental matters related to Chicago, thereby avoiding, I thought, an important part of the governor's responsibilities for the state as a whole. And, again following Adlai Stevenson, who sometimes gave the impression that he thought politics was beneath him, Kerner made no effort to open up the party to younger, independent, reform-minded men and women. He let Daley's people run the state legislature. It was after Kerner repeatedly kowtowed to Mayor Daley that I, along with other independent-minded Democrats, finally concluded that only a thoroughly independent Democrat capturing the governor's office could make any deep changes in the political system in Illinois.

Not only did Kerner let the independents down by yielding overmuch power to the Chicago machine, but he also got involved in a racetrack scandal. Marge Everett, owner of a racetrack, sold him stock in her company at a price far below market, and Kerner subsequently approved very favorable summertime racing dates for her track. Ted Isaacs, his administrative assistant, did not think politics and even machinations were beneath him and, in fact, reveled in what might be called Machiavellian politics. I believe that Kerner, who was often blind to the machinations of others, was probably unaware that there was any correlation between the stock and the racetrack dates. It may be, indeed, that it was Isaacs, not Kerner, who made the stock deal with Marge Everett. In any case, Kerner was indicted, tried, convicted, and jailed by U.S. Attorney James Thompson, a Republican, for bribery, conspiracy, and tax evasion. Obviously, the jury simply didn't believe him when he denied knowledge of any deal. "Big Jim" Thompson bagged a governor. I should have paid very keen attention.

In the 1960s, I began to change my political outlook by becoming more conservative on some national issues. I saw firsthand the failure of public housing in Chicago and had seen the problems in the Illinois welfare system, where it often seemed that the social workers were more interested in keeping people "on the dole" than in getting freeloaders "off the dole." I learned the meaning of the phrase "knee-jerk liberal" when I encountered those convinced that the best solution to social problems was to spend more government money.

### "POLICE RIOT"

The war in Vietnam became a decisive issue for me. I supported the war from the beginning. Toward the end, when many liberals were turning strongly against the war, I was swayed by the arguments of my brother who then served as the senior U.S. Navy officer on General Westmoreland's staff and was convinced that we could and should win the war. He visited me in Chicago, telling me in more detail what was going on in Vietnam. His views and my own thoughts (perhaps swayed by my navy background) kept me from joining the Chicago liberals who were all-out against the war. I became even more of a hawk. I felt strongly that some of the demonstration leaders and war opponents were getting close to providing aid and comfort to the enemy.

In 1968, I took no active part in the presidential primaries. I found Eugene McCarthy interesting and amusing, though never took him seriously as a presidential candidate. Along with everyone else, I watched the gathering storm as the Democratic Convention in Chicago convened and thousands of protesters against the Vietnam War streamed into Chicago. The announcement by President Johnson that he would not seek another term increased the controversy, as did the antiwar campaign waged by McCarthy.

Mayor Daley made it clear that protestors were not welcome in Chicago and that both marches and rallies would be curtailed severely. Wide publicity was given to the wild threats by Abbie Hoffman and Jerry Rubin, the Hippie-Yippie (Youth International Party) leaders that they would foster open nudity and female seduction of delegates, lace the water supply with LSD, and on and on and on.

Hoffman and Rubin called themselves "revolutionary artists" but added, "our concept of revolution is fun." While most viewed their repeated threats as "street theater" and did not take them seriously, Mayor Daley and the FBI did. Indeed, when Daley was interviewed by Walter Cronkite, he charged that "certain people planned to assassinate the three contenders [for the presidency] and myself" and argued that this justified extreme precautions in preparing for the convention demonstrations. No evidence was ever adduced to support those fears.

The arrival of thousands of protesters fed the fires of Mayor Daley's determination that order would be preserved at all costs in his beloved Chicago. Before the convention began, units of the National Guard were mobilized to assist the police department; a thousand Secret Service and FBI agents were deployed in the city; barbed wire was strung around strategic locations; and all manhole covers were sealed. Written petitions for permits for parades, rallies, and sequestered sites for demonstrations were repeatedly denied. The Chicago FBI office reported to Washington that it had infiltrated the Hippie-Yippie organizations and learned about "plans for massive disruptions in Chicago that would threaten orderly proceedings at the Democratic Convention." President Johnson passed this dire warning on to Mayor Daley, and both men were convinced that dangerous radicals led the demonstrations.

Predictably, with no place or means to blow off steam, the protesters congregated in the public parks near the lake front, where they were confronted by phalanxes of blue-uniformed Chicago policemen with pistols holstered and billy clubs at the ready. Often bearded, dirty, disheveled, and half-naked, the hippies taunted the policemen, whom they derisively called "pigs" and even worse names, screaming filthy epithets right into their faces. These Chicago policemen, largely Irish Catholics, abhorred what they saw and heard, knowing—as they constantly reminded themselves—that their beloved Mayor Daley disliked these obscene people as much as they did. These people were not "citizens" but "dirty, radical rioters," offensive to any decent, law-abiding Chicagoan. Soon, widespread club swinging, undeterred by superiors, answered demonstrators' taunts. As later reported, "police indiscriminately clubbed members of the press, clergymen, women, old, young, and anyone else who was within swinging distance."

The nation saw on television and read in newspapers full reports of the almost mindless police violence that occurred in the parks, streets, alleys, and byways of Chicago. There were pictures of police repeatedly swinging clubs at already downed and bloody male and female demonstrators, newsmen, photographers, and even innocent bystanders.

Mayor Daley was unperturbed at the reports of police violence, but the tough media questions clearly upset him. As sometimes happened when he became emotional, the mayor slipped into one of his frequent malapropisms. At a press conference, he stated, "Gentlemen, get this straight once and for all. The policeman isn't there to create disorder; the policeman is there to preserve disorder."

Widely watched on national television was the scene at the Democratic National Convention when Senator Abraham Ribicoff, the convention chairman, strode to the podium to deplore the breakdown of law and order in the streets. Daley, on the floor very near the rostrum and within the chairman's hearing range, cupped hands around his mouth and screamed at Ribicoff. Lip-readers transcribed his words as "F——k you, you Jew m—— f——r! Go home!"

Did the protestors' obscene provocations justify the savage police response that Daley certainly condoned, if he did not directly order? The immediate reaction by the media was overwhelmingly that it did not. All across the nation, from the *New York Times* on down, the media demanded an investigation, and I was about to land right in the middle of this controversy.

## 10

## *The Walker Report*

The prison psychiatrist has asked me to take an IQ test for a study he is conducting on the intelligence of prisoners. I'm happy to comply. It gets me out of work, and the test is interesting.

"Have you heard anything about my request for a transfer?" I ask.

"You're wasting your time, Dan," he says. "The warden kills all your requests."

I nod, but I'm extremely disappointed.

"I'm sorry."

"What about the petition for a congressional investigation into psychological mistreatment of prisoners?"

He just looks at me as if thinking that for a smart guy, I should know better.

Actually, I do. The Bureau of Prisons is anxious and wants to avoid a riot because of its dread of an ensuing investigation. No Washington bureaucrat wants an investigation. I've learned this lesson all too well. And those who commission investigations often don't really want to know the results, as I learned in Chicago.

"You have an amazing test score, Dan," he says. "Your IQ is at the genius level."

"Wonderful," I say, not really caring, and step out of his office and into the freezing rain, thinking that the shrink is right—a total waste of time.

### THE SPOTLIGHT

In response to earlier big-city riots, Lyndon Johnson established the President's National Commission on the Causes and Prevention of Violence. It held hearings and conducted studies with Lloyd Cutler, a prominent Washington attorney, as executive director.

When the president's commission decided to investigate the Chicago Convention riots, Cutler asked me to form a Chicago study team to investigate and prepare an exhaustive written report as soon as humanly possible. Money was made available for expenses, and we would use it up to the penny, but not for personal compensation to me or any member of the professional staff. Everyone who worked on the project, except for a few paid to do secretarial or clerical work, volunteered. My boss at Montgomery Ward, Tom Brooker, gave me his blessing when I reassured him that I would still work mornings in my office.

With Vic De Grazia working full-time as my assistant, we assembled the team and went to work immediately. He and I literally lived in hotel rooms downtown for many days. I arrived in early afternoon and often worked past midnight until the job was finished. I asked leading law and accounting firms to donate the time of men and women for my staff, and they complied.

From the beginning, many staff investigators reported excessive police violence. Vic and I were skeptical and decided that he would take a positive "pro-police" role with the staff, forcing thorough documentation of any allegations of police violence. Definitely not biased either way, the staff was totally dedicated to fact-finding. We even selected a classic Republican-establishment, three-piece-suit lawyer from a major law firm to interview hippie leader Abbie Hoffman.

The FBI's special agent in charge in Chicago refused to release its investigative reports on agent eyewitness interviews. I flew to Washington and personally appealed to Attorney General Ramsey Clark to obtain the thousands of necessary FBI reports. I also appealed publicly for eyewitness accounts of violence and asked newspapers all over the nation to submit photographs of confrontations and violence in Chicago. All television networks were asked to supply their film clips. I paid a formal call on Mayor Daley to obtain any input he wished to provide. He was very polite but had nothing in particular to offer.

After reviewing thousands of documents, photographs, film clips, and

FBI reports and interviewing hundreds of eyewitnesses, the volunteers got the job done. We used no newspaper or other media accounts in writing the final report, and I edited all staff submissions. In the introduction to what became known as the "Walker Report," I wrote: "The Chicago staff started on September 27, 1968, and only by disregarding both clock and families was it able to complete the report fifty-three days later." Eventually, it was named "Rights in Conflict," and I personally wrote the summary that would launch a national controversy. One phrase upset people.

Vic and I had spent considerable time discussing this phrase. We finally agreed the term was entirely appropriate. We termed the disturbances, in part, a "police riot."

The members of the president's commission read it, and Lloyd Cutler summoned me. "We don't like the summary, Dan. We're disappointed and request that you rewrite it or omit it entirely."

"I will do neither. It's accurate," I said.

I admired Lloyd Cutler, but he spoke for the commission, his employer. I felt certain the commission would water down the summary.

I had also sent the mayor a copy of my report before I released it to the public. He shared it with others, including Chief Judge Campbell of the U.S. District Court of Chicago. The judge, whom I knew from trial work, called me into his office.

"Dan, I agree with Mayor Daley. This report will hurt Chicago. I'm asking you not to publish the thing."

"I have to do what's right," I told him.

I summoned a news conference and faced a throng of TV cameras plus uncounted numbers of radio microphones and reporters. Major national newspapers and the weekly news magazines featured the report. Newsmen on national network programs read the entire summary.

The president of Bantam Books contacted me that night and offered a high-royalty contract for publication rights. I referred him to the Government Printing Office, explaining that the report was government property to which I had no personal property rights. I did not receive a cent except for actual and documented out-of-pocket expenses.

Next day, members of the president's commission were predictably upset, but the media generally praised the report as courageous.

Bantam obtained the copyright permission and published it. *Rights in Conflict: The Walker Report* (New York; Bantam Books and Regency Press,

1968) sold over one million copies and became a standard text in college classes across the nation studying the growing phenomenon of mobs demonstrating and disrupting cities in open conflict with the police.

The Walker Report capped off my relationship with Mayor Daley. Any small hope for personal rapport died. Along with Mayor Daley, the Chicago police (also predictably) hated the Walker Report. The business establishment fell into line. Within a matter of weeks after the convention riots, people who had recoiled from TV film clips of brutal police violence against demonstrators and innocent bystanders totally wiped those pictures from their minds. They adopted the "establishment" line that all the troubles were caused by the longhaired, obscene demonstrators.

Vic and I were dumbfounded.

"But you saw the actions on television!" we would say.

Shoulders would shrug. No argument. No justification. They didn't want to believe the report or even what they had seen with their own eyes.

U.S. Attorney Tom Foran prosecuted the "Chicago Seven" in a trial that made national news. I would turn to Tom one day in my own legal crisis.

Individual policemen I spoke to agreed with me that many of their brothers had engaged in undue violence, but that—as we had also reported—the majority of policemen were restrained. The department's number two man, who was in charge of all police work during the convention, told me privately that my conclusions were accurate.

I received several awards for the report, including the prestigious Harvard Club and Roger Baldwin (ACLU) Community Service awards, both conferred at formal black-tie dinners in Chicago, where I stated repeatedly that any praise should be given to the talented, hard-working staff. Naturally, I was flattered when the Society of Midland Authors gave me their annual award. I never regretted my decision to go public with "The Walker Report," though it would be used against me in the not too distant future.

### ADLAI STEVENSON III

While with Montgomery Ward, I continued a degree of political involvement, but considerably lost my appetite for someday, somehow running for high elective office. Doing interesting work, confronting repeated challenges, making good money and enjoying it all with reasonable working hours while highly profitable stock options accumulated—all this was extremely satisfying. I had made up my mind to concentrate on making money, enjoying life, getting all the kids through college, having good family vacations like the ones we had begun enjoying at Marcos Island, Florida, and looking forward to a pleasant retirement. My life would have been so very different if I had accepted this comfortable lifestyle.

I kept busy in a few causes, including fund-raising for Northwestern University School of Law. I was always grateful for the excellent legal education, the lifesaving scholarship I received in my last year, and the entrée to my legal career the law school provided.

In early 1970, I had the sense that if something didn't happen soon, it was just not ever going to happen. The Committee on Illinois Government (CIG) that I had founded years earlier was giving a Democratic fund-raising Sunday picnic on the grounds of the Adlai Stevenson home in Libertyville. The CIG still maintained its independence from machine politics. Perfunctorily, I attended, along with Vic De Grazia.

Adlai Stevenson III was speaking as state treasurer. In the middle of his speech, who should show up but Mayor Daley.

Someone next to Vic said, "What's *he* doing here?"

Adlai nearly stopped midsentence. He threw away his prepared speech about reform politics to speak graciously about the mayor.

My stomach turned. "Listen to this guy," I said to Vic.

He shrugged, implying, *so what else is new?*

Vic and I were both realists, though. Most candidates tried to maintain a certain diplomacy with Daley. We still believed that Adlai would act more independently than others the machine routinely backed.

Senator George McGovern came from Washington to speak at the event and told the crowd that Republican Everett Dirksen, the senior senator from Illinois, had died that morning. The seat would be filled at the general election in November 1970.

Vic looked at me. "We gotta jump on this."

He flew into action at the picnic, summoning a few of us involved in independent Democratic politics. We called Adlai over and gathered in a guest facility on the picnic grounds.

"Adlai," I said, "we want you to run for the seat in the senate."

Adlai beamed as applause broke out. Next day, he contacted regular Democratic Party organization leaders, including Mayor Daley, and received their support. It was reported at the time that Adlai, who had publicly prided himself on being in the ranks of the independent, reform-minded young Democrats, had repeatedly said Daley was a feudal boss. After getting Daley's support, he added, "But I didn't say he was a bad feudal boss."

Adlai asked that I become his campaign chairman, responsible for assembling and overseeing the staff and consulting on tactics and strategy. He reported that when he informed Daley that he had chosen me to be campaign chairman because of my organizing skills, "there was dead silence." Then Daley asked Adlai incredulously, "Do you mean to tell me that in a state of over ten million people, there's only one person you could find with the organizing ability to be chairman?"

Adlai kept me on, despite Daley's hostility. However, another issue came between us. Adlai made it clear that he did not care for Vic De Grazia. That didn't stop me. I thought the campaign needed Vic's advice and consulted him regularly, which led to difficulties. Vic and I, along with others on the campaign staff, felt strongly that Adlai was virtually assured of winning. He had a strong following in the state, obviously had great name recognition, could draw on the popularity of his famous father, and had a weak opponent in Ralph Smith—a colorless politician largely unknown in the state who had been appointed to fill the vacancy caused by Dirksen's death.

What was in it for us? Vic and I both felt that Adlai could afford to run an independent campaign, establishing himself nationally as a man who was elected on his own virtues and abilities, not just as a famous-name candidate ushered into office by the Daley machine.

Adlai disagreed with our advice, however, soon making it clear that he intended to stay close to Daley and the regular Democratic organization. At the beginning, though, he did leave it to me to select and organize the staff, and with his approval, we brought in some very talented people with excellent reputations. I also concentrated on building an organization of volunteers to supplement the work of the regular organization, particularly downstate, where Smith had his greatest strength. For the campaign headquarters' staff, with Adlai's approval, I brought in Norton Kay from the *Chicago American* newspaper as press secretary and Bill Holtzman to run scheduling/advance because of his substantial experience on presidential campaigns. The choice of these two would prove to be one of the main perks of the entire campaign for me personally and professionally. For many weeks thereafter, I worked closely with Bill and Norty and other key staff members in organizing and directing the campaign. I was on the phone repeatedly with them, ate sandwiches in the office with them, held meetings with them. They were damn good at what they did, and we became close friends.

About that time, Norty lost his wife, who had been a well-known columnist. Bill and I and others on the staff helped him survive this crisis in his life. He persevered with the campaign, and he and Bill established a close working relationship with Adlai as well. Norty, Bill, Vic, and I met frequently to discuss the relationship of the campaign with the regular organization. We agreed that Adlai was wedding himself too closely to the Daley machine.

"Adlai's numbers are good. Running very strong," Vic said. "Adlai at the head of the state ticket will bring in voters for all candidates running as Democrats."

I said, "Why can't Adlai see that Daley needs him more than he needs Daley?"

"Daley should be doing Adlai's bidding," Bill said, "not the other way around."

I pointed all this out to Adlai and more. "I have some figures here, Adlai. This year the Chicago Civil Service Commission reports that the number of patronage workers has gone up to a record 15,680. There were only 3,478 when Daley was first elected."

Adlai didn't want to hear it and muttered something good about the Daley organization's efficiency during the campaign. As the campaign progressed, he grew more and more defensive and sensitive about his relationship with us independents, about his liberal reputation, and about his father's ideals.

Adlai started working harder at being accepted personally by the members of the regular organization, like the ward committeemen in Chicago and the downstate county Democratic chairmen, almost all of whom were anything but liberal. Those were the days when antagonism toward hippies was rampant. Several of my organizers attracted Adlai's attention.

"They're too wide-eyed, longhaired liberal," he said to me. "They'll antagonize conservative members of the regular organization, maybe even Daley himself."

"But Adlai, these young people are the best source of campaign workers. We can easily recruit them, partly [actually, it was *mostly*] because of your father's fame among liberals. I want and need them to be active members of the team."

Liberals were not very popular right then, and he knew my stand on Vietnam. Adlai was quick to respond, "Dan, despite that riot report of yours, you're no liberal."

"But I cherish the First Amendment. The hippies and yippies were guilty of outrageous conduct, but I never questioned their right to protest, and you don't fire people for their beliefs."

He looked disgusted. "That guy Tony Dean with the really long hair has got to go," he insisted. He had just found out that Tony was a conscientious objector during Vietnam. Tony was an exceptionally good worker. I tried to persuade Adlai that he was overreacting, but he persisted in demanding that I get rid of Tony.

If I gave in on this, it wouldn't be long before I was giving in to the machine. "You, of course, have the final say on everything, Adlai, but if Tony is fired because of his longhaired liberal look, a large portion of this campaign staff will quit." I let that sink in and then added, "Including me."

Adlai backed down, and Tony performed admirably in the campaign. I had earned Tony's loyalty, which I wouldn't forget. My relationship with Adlai, however, was never quite the same.

Mayor Daley had continued to make clear his displeasure with my being in the highly visible chairman position, so Adlai assuaged him by appointing Tom Foran, prosecutor of the Chicago Seven, and Paul Simon as co-chairmen. I knew both Tom and Paul and had no objection. Tom desired a high political or governmental position but would inevitably cater to Daley's wishes, as he made very clear from the outset.

As the campaign wore on, Adlai increasingly became his own campaign manager, leaving me to handle day-to-day staff operations while he consulted Daley on a regular basis. I found I didn't mind being moved aside, especially since victory seemed almost certain at that point, and I couldn't be faulted if a reversal occurred. Adlai was always very sensitive about comparisons with his father, whose eloquent speeches garnered an international reputation.

Often, Adlai's lovely, talented wife Nancy and I teamed up at events Adlai couldn't attend, prompting some to say she was a better campaigner than Adlai. All in all, though, Adlai's overwhelming victory was mostly his own achievement. Unfortunately, we were much further apart personally by the end of the campaign.

Adlai and the campaign discouraged and disillusioned me. What was the use? Here was another guy who had a tremendous opportunity to lead us, and instead, he left us in the lurch, tailoring his campaign to the party regulars and largely ignoring the independents. My heart wasn't in the last part of that campaign at all. Vic had started referring to Adlai Stevenson III as "The T'ird."

On election night, there was the usual jam at headquarters. When Adlai had clenched the victory, national television wanted to cover the win. Bill

Holtzman and most of my handpicked staff was as disillusioned with Adlai as I was.

"This is going to be on national TV," Bill said to me. "I want your face in that picture. Stand on my back." Astonishingly, he knelt down on all fours. "Get on!"

With the help of a guy standing next to me, I stood on his back so that my face would appear near Adlai's on national TV. And it did. Holtzman bragged about this story to the staff, who thoroughly enjoyed it. I was told Adlai didn't appreciate any of it.

Bill was unaware that my life had changed dramatically that summer of 1970. During the thick of the campaign, I had thought, admittedly selfishly, *what's the point of this for me?* "I might as well crawl back into my legal cocoon," I told Vic De Grazia and Dave Green. And I did. I believed that I had finally abandoned my political ambitions.

That August, when my role in the campaign began winding down, Dave called to suggest we meet for lunch. We did, at the Mid-America Club, one of the most prestigious private clubs in Chicago, where I was a member. On the top floor of the Standard Oil Building, it looked out over Chicago, Lake Michigan, and Meigs Field, where the governor's plane routinely landed. We dined in elegance.

"Vic and I have been talking," Dave said before our food arrived. "We think you should run for either governor or senator in 1972."

I could only stare at him.

Then he added, "Starting your campaign right away."

With brother, Lewis W. "Waco" Walker Jr. (*right*), and maternal grandmother, 1934.
Author's collection

In U.S. Naval Academy full-dress
uniform, 1945. Author's collection

With Waco, as naval officers, 1946.
Author's collection

With mother, Virginia May, and father, Lewis W. Walker Sr.,
1960. Author's collection

Author's first wife, Roberta
D. Walker. Author's collection

Map of the campaign walk, created by Carol A. Manning. Author's collection

With sons Dan (*left*) and Charles, at the end of the first day of the campaign walk, in July 1971. Photo by Rich Block

On the walk, waving at a passing car. Photo by Rich Block

Campaign staff members (*from left*): Rich Block, Norty Kay, and Bill Holtzman.
Author's collection

Meeting Paul Simon in Springfield while on the walk. Photo by Rich Block

Son Dan in stocking feet for the last two miles before Harrisburg. Photo by Rich Block

Typical visit with a farmer during the walk. Photo by Rich Block

With sons Dan and Charles in Springfield at the exact spot of my
later inauguration, in front of a statue of Abraham Lincoln.
Photo by Rich Block

Walking across the Wisconsin line (*from left*): Dan, Margaret, Will, the author, wife Roberta, and Charles. Photo by Rich Block

Campaigning in southern Illinois with Secretary of Agriculture Robert J. "Pud" Williams (*in overalls*). Photo by Rich Block

Oath of office administered by Chief Justice Walter Schaefer in January 1973.
Author's collection

Speaking at an accountability session, 1974. Photo by Rich Block

With my blind father on Inauguration Day. Author's collection

Typical bill-signing ceremony with legislators, 1975. Photo by Rich Block

Office meeting with top four (*from left*): David Green, adviser; William Goldberg, counsel to the governor; Victor De Grazia, deputy to the governor; and Norton Kay, press secretary, 1975. Photo by Rich Block

With Mayor Richard J. Daley discussing the 1974 Regional Transportation Authority bill.
Author's collection

Greeting President Gerald Ford on his arrival in Illinois for a visit. Author's collection

Greeting Emperor Hirohito of Japan at O'Hare Field on an official visit to the United States.
Author's collection

Greeting presidential candidate Jimmy Carter in fall 1976. Author's collection

With former governors William G. Stratton and Samuel Shapiro, 1977. Author's collection

With second wife, Roberta Nelson Walker, Richard Burton, and Elizabeth Taylor, 1985.
Author's collection

Walker family in 1997: with former wife, Roberta D. Walker, seven children, and sixteen grandchildren. Author's collection

With third wife, Lillian M. Stewart, in 2001. Photo by Leslie Walker

With grandsons (*from left*) Jimmy Kollar, Kenny Okamoto, and Chris Vaught, carving Beef Wellington, 2004. Author's collection

With sons Dan and Charles, in 2005. Photo by Lillian Stewart

## II

## *Launching the Campaign for Governor*

I'm back at my job cleaning toilets in the prison's clothing center. The weather, my health, and my mood have improved. I hear someone snicker, though, and the word *governor* echoes in the stalls. I try to concentrate as though I haven't heard any comment and work harder.

"Make damn sure you always do a good job"—that was the message my dad drummed into me. "Whatever the job, work like you did when you shoveled the manure out of the mule's stall." That's part of what he would say to me now, if he were alive. Of course, there would be a lot more he'd say. Picturing the sadness I would see in his eyes about my being in prison makes me scrub the porcelain still more furiously. "What the hell are you doing here?" he would be asking me.

I again see in my mind the pride and delight he exuded at my inauguration. No father could ever have been prouder. Would this prison sentence cancel in his mind the achievements I made as governor? During many sleepless nights here, I have regretted not having involved him more, not discussing with him what it was that I wanted to achieve that would have made up for all the time I took away from my family. What keeps me awake at night more than any other thought are these questions: Where had I let him down? Which of his "breakfast sermons" had I forgotten?

One of them returns to me vividly. It is a lesson Dad had learned the hard way and one he desperately wanted Waco and me to learn to save us from a consequence as harsh as his. He and the whole family suffered for five years as a result of his mistake.

In 1933, Dad learned that his next navy duty would be a two-year tour in China on one of the navy's famous Yangtze River patrol boats. He was a chief radioman, and he and his fellow chiefs made up a tightly knit circle in those days. When the senior chief at the Navy Department informed Dad about the long China tour, Dad became very despondent. He loved his work and his shipmates, but two years away from his family was more than he could take. His current four-year enlistment term was expiring. He faced a difficult decision. As Mom explained to me, in many respects Dad lived primarily for his sons. We were his life, and he was absolutely determined to put my brother and me on the road to success. Two years away was more than he could bear.

So, he left the navy on January 1, 1934. His sixteen years of service only gave him a pension of $50 per month, but the poor pay didn't faze him since he was confident he could find a good job. He did not reckon with the depth of the Depression, the joblessness and soup lines from coast to coast.

Dad went to work as a cashier at the ships' service store (later called a commissary) at the Naval Air Station in San Diego. We eventually settled into a rented home in Encanto, six miles east of downtown San Diego. Waco was fourteen and I was nearly twelve.

On the job as a cashier, Dad had an unfortunate habit of rolling bills into $1000 rolls and then tossing them into the safe. Two turned up missing, and Dad was "allowed to quit." The job loss was a severe blow to the family. A later audit found the two rolls of bills behind the safe, but this was too late to matter. He became a butcher (I have no idea how he learned the trade) in a small grocery store in San Diego.

One day, he was told to deliver a large watermelon to a lady who had been an annoying customer, quibbling constantly about the calf's liver she ordered for her cat. This lady had been very demanding about the melon, wanting it "just perfect" for a luncheon party she was giving. Dad knocked on the door, and when it was opened, he walked inside and pitched the watermelon up in the air so it would land on the floor and break open in the midst of all the ladies.

"There's your damn watermelon, Mrs. Smith," he said.

That ended his butchering career, though Mom actually tried to run the butcher shop for a while, but it was just too much for her. This started five jobless Depression years in a variety of rented homes in the backcountry of San Diego County. That meager pension of $50 per month was our livelihood, and it was soon cut when President Roosevelt reduced all navy pay by 15 percent—which infuriated Dad. We survived by raising rabbits and chickens and growing a large home garden.

Difficulty in making rental payments, Mom said, caused us to move frequently from one small house to another. Dad kept trying to find work, but five years would pass before he had any luck—a harsh consequence for indulging his frustration.

"Never," he said to us after he related this story, "never let cockiness take over your decision making, boys. 'Pride comes before a fall.'" A cliché, but a powerful one.

Is this my failure? Had I been too bold, too aggressive, too cocky?

I pack several urinals with ice, the finishing touch for my unpleasant prison job, as I ponder these questions. I have to get my mind off of this humiliation in order to hang onto my sanity.

---

### THE DECISION TO LAUNCH

During that life-changing lunch at the Mid-America Club in August of 1970, Dave Green had said, "Dan, I'm telling you—we can win the governor's office without the backing of the Chicago machine."

I absolutely had to hear more about his strategy. The following Saturday, we arranged an all-day meeting at Pheasant Run, a resort on the far western edge of Cook County. Vic and Dave brought longtime friends Mort Kaplan and Rich Blakeley. All of us had participated in the "political wars" of the time, all had worked for Adlai Stevenson, father and son, as well as Paul Douglas, and all had worked with independent Democrats in their battles.

The incumbent Republican governor, Richard Ogilvie, was vulnerable. He had been the one to initiate a new state income tax—a necessary but highly unpopular step. Ogilvie took considerable heat. I agreed the tax was necessary and would never attack him on that basis, but we could take advantage of his unpopularity. However, the primary came first, and that meant confronting the Democratic candidate slated by the machine.

"We've got plenty of ammunition," Vic said. "The Kerner racetrack scandals, the investigation of Democratic supreme court justices, and Hanrahan's West Side apartment raid." He was referring to Edward Hanrahan, the state's attorney and close friend of Daley, who authorized a nighttime raid that resulted in killing two African American activists, members of the Black Panther organization. Black community leaders called it a "planned murder."

Dave used a mathematical model to demonstrate how we could win. "I've reviewed many years' primary results," Dave said. "The machine's top turnout was seven hundred thousand votes. Obviously, this amount would easily win as long as the total number of Democratic voters stays below one million. But," he continued, voice rising with enthusiasm, "if we could increase the turnout to one-and-a-half million, we could beat the machine's seven hundred thousand votes."

"That's a pretty big 'if,'" I said.

"We're not saying it'll be easy," Vic argued, "but it could be done with an effective candidate, an effective campaign, and a strong, statewide grassroots organization."

A heated discussion ensued, but everyone finally agreed that a winning primary campaign against the machine was doable. Interestingly, the subject of fund-raising for a tough campaign never came up that day. All of us just assumed in our naïveté that we could raise enough money.

"What about Adlai?" somebody asked. "Think he'd help?"

"I'd like to hope so. I still believe that deep down he cherishes independent politics," I said, "and he definitely owes me."

Vic shook his head. "Adlai will never openly split with the regular organization."

"However, he might be quietly supportive among his wealthy friends," someone said.

At the end of the day, everyone agreed we should take on the battle. I would run for governor, announcing my candidacy as soon as possible so we would have almost two years for what we all knew would be an extremely difficult, uphill fight all the way to the 1972 March primary. We were all totally convinced, though, that we could win. That "one-and-a-half million turnout" became our mantra.

It took me awhile to screw up my courage to tell Roberta. This would obviously tear our lives apart. Running for governor is a full-time job, and what would we live on? I decided not to tell her until I had talked to my boss, Tom Brooker, still CEO at Montgomery Ward.

Tom looked astounded. "What in the hell are you doing, Dan? Why would you want to give up a great job for a losing venture like this? You haven't got a chance of winning."

I explained Dave and Vic's plan and said I was convinced we could pull it off.

"I can tell your heart's in it, Dan, so there's no use my trying to talk you out of it," Tom finally said. I had hoped for this reaction. Tom had always conveyed warmth and concern for me, and he had never been a heavy-handed boss. "Okay, Dan, go for it. I'll try to maintain your pay as long as possible." He actually wrote out a personal check for $10,000 for my campaign fund and, heartwarmingly, several other top Ward executives followed suit.

That evening after the kids went to bed, Roberta said she could tell that I was excited about something. The whole story came out pell-mell, ending with a description of my meeting with Brooker and his promise to keep me on the payroll. This meant that we would have enough income for the immediate future.

"So I want to take this on, Honey. I really think it's doable."

She knew that this was my most cherished dream, but I still expected her to suggest a delay of several years or drill me with questions. However, she said nothing. I could tell, though, from the look in her eyes that she was far less than excited about this.

"I'm going to lose you," she said.

"No, Roberta," I assured her. "No. I won't let our family suffer. I can do both."

She was silent for what seemed a long time. Then she sighed.

"I know you see this as your big chance." Her expression subtly changed to one of resignation. Roberta knew me and realized that opposition would ultimately be pointless. "You're my man," she said quietly, "and I will do all I can to help you win."

### THE MAN OF LA MANCHA

We spent a great deal of time on the announcement of my candidacy, and Mort Kaplan scheduled a press conference for two days after Adlai Stevenson III was sworn in as U.S. senator, filling the seat of Everett Dirksen for the remainder of his unexpired term. Mort circulated the prepared statement, and I met the media, print, radio, and television, at the North Side's Water Tower Inn. My prepared statement was an all-out, frontal attack on the Daley machine.

"The Democratic party organization bossed by Mayor Daley is still controlled by an antiquated Machine dedicated to special privilege politics and performing a discredited function: the exchange of jobs for blocs of votes."

After decrying "political prostitution of the courts," the statement went on to say that I would fight for "a political system that will not permit use of party position to acquire personal wealth." Forswearing "the kingmakers of the party," I concluded that I would take my candidacy directly to residents of every one of the 102 counties in Illinois who had suffered from political exclusion.

About a dozen conscientious reporters showed up, which we considered a fair turnout. They didn't seem hostile, but the disbelief was palpable. *Who is this guy, and what does he think he's doing?*

One columnist compared me to Don Quixote, the Man from La Mancha, tilting at windmills—an image that caught on. I had hoped that popular Chicago columnist Mike Royko, an outspoken foe of the machine, would support my candidacy, but he did not. John Dreiske, the crusty *Chicago Sun-Times* political editor and usually a follower of the Daley party line, wrote a column headlined "Dan's the Man, Idealists." He said, "Young people are being shown a battlefield on which they may die gloriously, oblivious to all, but a belief that it's the battle for principle that counts—not victory." I normally shared this kind of realistic thinking, but this time I felt totally convinced that we could have both: a battle on principle and a victory. I didn't think anyone would die carrying my banner.

We later learned from friends that Stevenson's staff reacted with shock, anger, and finally amusement. Jim Bagley of the staff, whom we knew well, reported, "We decided Walker's running was a joke, that he had gone off the deep end." Adlai never forgave me for what he thought was a deliberate effort to publicly upstage his being sworn in as U.S. senator. My relationship with him, already strained by our differences during his campaign, had not improved. Adlai carefully kept his distance, immediately making it clear to Mayor Daley, the regulars throughout the state, and the public that he wanted no part whatsoever of my independent quest to be governor.

Nonetheless, I held on to my optimism and a hope that Adlai, after all that I had done for him and his father over the years—and recalling his earlier work for independent causes—would, if not openly, at least privately welcome my striking out for the kind of government and politics he and his father had often talked about.

## BEGGING

We started at ground zero. Absolutely nobody gave me a chance. Although we had expected it to be tough, we had thought that at least the media, the party, and those active in politics would see me as a realistic contender in view of my position and background.

They did not. Definitely not.

I had hoped that some members of the business and legal establishment who had been my friends would rally to my cause. But prominent lawyers and businessmen (except for those few Montgomery Ward executives) made it very clear that they wanted nothing to do with me. Even those I had worked with closely kept their distance—not just because they thought I could not win, but, as they openly admitted, they did not want to offend Mayor Richard J. Daley. The powerful grip that Daley had on the Chicago establishment soon became very evident.

Against these odds, Vic, Nancy Shlaes (who had worked hard for us at the DFI), and I leased a commercial space in the Loop that would include offices for each of us plus a generous work area. Walker campaign headquarters opened at 525 West Adams Street in Chicago. Vic worked full-time there, and Dave Green came in regularly—my campaign strategists. Vic focused on specific tactics, and, in an early gambit, we spent $20,000—a huge portion of our tiny war chest, on a full-page announcement of my candidacy in all major state newspapers, reasoning that people would then take the campaign seriously. It did not; the ads were mostly a waste of money.

My friend Norty Kay—a capable, experienced reporter with the *Chicago American*—who had served as Adlai's campaign press secretary, agreed to serve as mine. Bill Holtzman came over from the Stevenson staff as well to handle scheduling and advance work. Mary Parrilli, my legal secretary since the 1950s, and Al Raby, the leader in the African American community I had often worked with, also joined the campaign staff. Tony Dean, still wearing his hair long, showed up, and Vic put him to work organizing. Many young people flocked to the campaign, including Gloria Parseghian, the daughter of our Armenian landlords when I was in law school. Indeed, a motley crew, mostly young idealists, almost all unpaid. Nobody would ever mistake the staff for the pros who usually ran a governor's campaign. All these people reported directly to Vic, the campaign manager, so that I could concentrate on being the best possible candidate.

At the beginning of 1971, I was still viewed as an unknown. We had not realized that fund-raising was going to be so difficult, however, and we had thought that the state's liberals and independent-thinking men and women, many of whom were well situated financially, would flock to the campaign.

A few did, and I shall always be grateful to them, but most did not. They just did not think I had any chance of winning.

It was a constant and enervating struggle to keep the campaign office open and pay the telephone bills. I spent many hours essentially begging for money. Often, the few hired staff members worked without pay. And the campaign disappointingly generated no public excitement or even interest. Dave estimated in the spring of 1971 that my name recognition statewide was at best around 10 percent, no better than when we started. Political experts knew that that this figure needed to be at least 80 percent to win a statewide campaign. We had to do something bold to attract public attention, and all of us—Vic, Dave, Bill, Norty, Mort Kaplan, and I—wrestled constantly with this problem.

I was able to devote enough attention to business matters at Montgomery Ward to earn my pay until May that spring, and that had meant a great deal to my large family, but continuing the campaign would be a full-time job. At the same time, we were broke, out of campaign funds, had no money to pay any member of the staff, let alone myself, and precious few voters thought of me as a serious contender. I couldn't see a solution, but nothing was going to stop me.

## 12

## *The Long Walk*

There is a room at the prison headquarters building known as "the hole." It is where inmates singled out for special punishment are placed in solitary confinement. "Lockdown" it's called in the yard. Men in lockdown stay in solitude in the cell for twenty-three hours a day; one hour is allowed for walking around the yard, arms shackled, of course, with a guard in attendance. The inmates are allowed no reading material.

My young friend Evan currently suffers this punishment. He made a smart remark to one of the guards who is notoriously anti-Semitic, as indeed many of them are. These men seem to take particular delight in taunting young, well-educated Jewish men. Drug offenses were the most common reason for their sentences. Evan made the mistake of responding angrily to the taunt of "Jew boy" and ended up in lockdown.

On our many walks together in the prison yard, Evan and I had often talked about anti-Semitism and the role it plays in America. I told him about the big difference between the way Jews were treated in Chicago and in San Diego where I grew up and where they were less numerous at the time.

My father knew a man named Isaac—originally Itzak. He had been a tailor in the navy and ran a clothing store in San Diego. On the rare occasions when Waco and I needed to wear more than country clothes, Dad took us to that store. We always got a real bargain. We asked Dad about that, and he said, "Boys, Isaac is a Jew. When a Jew is a friend of yours, he's a friend all the way. And they're smart folks. Never met a dumb Jew." Dad returned to that subject one day when he and I were talking about my future. On this occasion, he brought up the subject of Jews.

"If you ever do get into politics, Dan, make sure you have a Jew right with you. They seem to know how to stay one step ahead of the other guy in their thinking."

I asked Dad, "How do you know all that? We don't have any Jews around here."

He responded, "Son, read the Old Testament. Got a lot of wisdom in it."

Those words stayed with me and played a role in my having Jewish men always on my staff. Dave Green was right at the top, advising me constantly, one of the most remarkable men I have ever met. It was Dave who conceived our main strategies. He had an uncanny ability to discern what people were really thinking—not so much the politicians, which was Vic's domain, but the voters.

I sit in the prison chapel after working with the chaplain, thinking about how much I appreciate my dad's wisdom, without which I might not have come to enjoy and profit from Dave's friendship. Evan comes into the room to help set up for the rabbi's services, looking depressed after his stint in the hole. Handsome and friendly, he prides himself on being a Renaissance man, and as such, doesn't often turn to the Old Testament, but I try to encourage him along these lines.

"I know this experience must have made you despondent," I say.

He nods, avoiding eye contact.

In prison, we help boost each other's morale by corny jokes, corny advice, the emotional cliché. It is the only language we have to help each other. On many prison exercise walks, I would talk with Evan about the Old Testament.

"I know this sounds a little corny, Evan," I say, "but think of the Israelites wandering in the wilderness, believing that God was with them. Believe that He is with you still."

This is the kind of thinking that helps sustain me here in prison. It also helped on my long, lonely stretches of road when I was walking the state of Illinois. Then I would often find myself remembering the words of both Old and New Testaments and the old hymns. *He walks in the garden alone, while the dew is still on the roses.*

I hope I cheered Evan. I think in doing so I cheered myself a bit. I begin to believe I just might get parole. That would reassure my wife and give us back a future together. Evan's companionship has helped immeasurably.

---

### THE WALK

In the summer of 1971—the campaign now more than eight months old—we were still unhappily stalled at the starting gate. With meager campaign contributions, the headquarters could barely stay open. I fell badly behind on personal bills. We desperately needed something both attention-getting and meaningful.

I knew my friend Lawton Chiles had walked portions of his state, Florida, when running for the Senate, and I called him to discuss it. He said it was a good campaigning venture but had no idea how it would be received in Illinois.

My team discarded lots of ideas before we finally reached a consensus: "Walk the entire state. Walk over a thousand miles. Walk from the Kentucky border to the Wisconsin border, from the Wabash River to the Mississippi River. Walk with two of my sons to make it a family enterprise."

Nobody had ever done this before. Vic presented the idea to a group of top-flight public relations experts, and they were unanimously appalled: "The worst idea we've ever heard." One said, "He'll be a laughing stock. A LaSalle Street, pinstripe-suit lawyer trying to look like a governor while walking through the cornfields of downstate Illinois. The cynical media'll kill him." But the idea stayed alive; it had no competition. Vic, Dave, and Norty joined me in a meeting to make a final decision about walking the state.

Norty Kay put it bluntly: "He'll be walking only if the media says he's walking. And if they dismiss it as a stunt or a gimmick, he'll walk to nowhere."

Vic said, "Some of the PR guys who watched Dan's initial efforts at campaigning said, 'Dan's so damn wooden and aloof, people downstate won't like him.'"

Dave took off his glasses, rubbed his head, and squeezed his eyes shut as if trying to concentrate. Each time he did this, we knew he had given a lot of thought to what he was about to say. He opened his eyes and looked at us. "Dan has to get over the wooden-ness, and I think he can. The real key here is not the fact of the walk, but the perception of the walk. In politics, it's people's perceptions that count. If people perceive Dan as just a guy out there walking the state, which is the fact, it won't mean a damn politically. If people perceive the walk as standing for something about Dan, then this risk could be worth it. The key is the public perceiving Dan as a fighter. It's as simple as this, guys. Will the walk dramatically portray Dan as a fighter?"

There was no way to test it, however. The statewide walk would have to be executed regardless of initial media reaction, or else I'd be labeled a quitter. Risky? For sure. The danger of commencing an already shaky campaign with a crippling stumble was very real. But nobody came up with anything better. I said, and both Vic and Dave agreed, "The entire campaign's a risk, so why not take another risk?"

When I told the family what I was planning, reactions were mixed. Roberta had anticipated that I would have to spend a large part of the summer campaigning and therefore be away from home a lot anyway, so this scheme didn't bother her too much. Dan, twenty-two and in his last year of college, thought it would be a great adventure and was eager to get started. Charles had just finished his junior year in high school and complained about having to give up his summer plans, but, of course, went along, as I knew he would. I had raised my children the same way I was raised: You obey your father, whose priorities come ahead of yours. I needed Dan and Charles, and frankly, I didn't think too much about interrupting their young lives—as my dad had done with me one summer during World War II.

It was after I graduated from Annapolis in 1945, before the war ended. I had become an ensign and was headed for a month of "flight indoctrination" in Jacksonville, Florida, or "Jax," as it is known in the navy. After that, I looked forward to a month leave before reporting for duty on board the USS *Compton* (DD 705) in "West Pac"—more navyese, referring to the ocean area west of Hawaii. Everyone knew that an invasion of Japan was being planned. The battle for Okinawa was already under way, and destroyers were being sunk by kamikaze suicide bombers. I just assumed that my destroyer would be participating in the invasion of Japan, along with most destroyers in the Pacific Fleet. This month of leave was my first real freedom in a long while, to be followed by possibly deadly combat at sea. I had a plan for that month.

I was going to spend a week with Roberta, my steady girl then, at her home in Kenosha, Wisconsin, and then three weeks with Mom and Dad. The week with Roberta was wonderful, and our relationship made considerable progress. On the train from Chicago to San Diego, though, I met a lovely girl named Justine, and we spent many hours together. Her father was a Marine colonel, and she confided that her mother hoped she could find a good naval officer to marry. She also told me at the outset that she was a proper girl, and I knew what that meant; but I was far from being ready for marriage, was facing combat, wasn't officially engaged, and knew a good opportunity when one came along. So I dated her when I got to San Diego and met her parents. Sure enough, they welcomed a naval officer as a suitor.

My dad had an idea far different from mine as to how his son should spend his last three weeks of freedom before going off to war. He didn't have enough Mexican workers for harvesting his five acres of string beans, so when I got there, he was desperate for help. There was no question as to what had to be done. Every day, I rose at dawn to work in those damn bean fields until dark. And every evening, I headed out for a date with the Marine colonel's daughter. I arrived at her house a little early for our second date.

Justine yelled from inside, "Come in and wait a sec; I'm all by myself." I was standing in the living room when I heard her again. "Come in the bedroom, Dan."

I did and there stood the "proper girl." Stark naked.

Dad had always taught me, "Don't ever ask anyone else to do something that you wouldn't do yourself." I had made a mental vow long before that night to remain a virgin until I was married. After all, I thought, if I expected my wife to be a virgin, then I should have the strength to be the same. So Justine and I were mightily tempted, and though we came awfully close, we never, as they say, "went all the way." We had great fun, with lots of light-but-steady lovemaking, and when I left, there were no hard feelings.

The experience proved exhausting: Every day, twelve hours of hard, stooping work in the bean fields. Almost every night with Justine. I grabbed maybe two to three hours of sleep. For years, I could not stand to look at a string bean, let alone eat one.

So, though I didn't consider my boys' plans that summer of 1971, Dan and Charles agreed to help me. I may not have ever conveyed my profound gratitude, but I would come to feel it keenly. My two sons and I spent long hours getting ready for the statewide walk.

The final plan came together rapidly: Start in Brookport at the state's southern border, about four hundred miles south of Chicago on the Ohio River, and zigzag up the state to end in Chicago, trying to come within fifty miles of every one of the eleven million people living in Illinois. Everyday attire would be blue work shirts, khaki trousers, white wool socks, and hiking boots. A young volunteer, Steve Senderowitz, would drive by at intervals in the RV a supporter had loaned us, service us on the road, and give my sons a place to sleep. I would spend nights with families along the way, arranged for by a hardworking volunteer. Norty Kay would usually hover around the area and work with the media, keeping me advised as we walked. One rule was absolutely essential: Walk in a forward direction, but never ride in a car in the forward direction of our journey. I could ride in a car to a host's house that was several miles out of the way, but for the benefit of cynical reporters, we would place a marker at the end of each day's walk and always start the next day's walk precisely at that point. Reporters could always learn from Norty Kay where to find us. I would dictate a daily diary, using a pocket Dictet, and the tapes, along with the names and addresses of people we met, were sent regularly to Mary Parrilli, still faithfully serving as secretary in the Chicago campaign headquarters.

### OMEN IN SOUTHERN ILLINOIS

The walk began in deep southern Illinois in Brookport, right across the Ohio River from Paducah, Kentucky. Southern Illinois, I soon learned, is a "land unto itself." It's not the southern half of the state, as most people think; to those who live there, it's only the counties south of Highway 50, running due east out of East St. Louis, a region that prides itself on its separate identity. Much of it is very hilly, not flat like most of Illinois, and was originally settled mostly by pioneers from Kentucky, Tennessee, and the Carolinas—often "hill country folks." Their descendants frequently talked like southerners, enjoyed southern-type food, and expressed personal feelings akin to people in the southern states.

We were anxious as we began with the kickoff press conference. In our blue shirts, khakis, and boots, I stood with my boys right under a large sign featuring the man I hoped ultimately to defeat: "GOVERNOR RICHARD G. OGILVIE WELCOMES YOU TO ILLINOIS." A few radio and newspaper reporters from southern Illinois turned out, plus, notably, a reporter-photographer team from the *Chicago Tribune*, Tom Seslar and Walter Neal. Their story could set the tone: gimmick or realistic campaign venture. The questioning was straightforward—not antagonistic, not cynical—so I had hope. We took long swigs from our canteens and set out, leaving the press behind. I shook hands through Brookport, and we soon found ourselves out in the countryside on the highway running northeast over toward the Wabash River. We were on our own until Steve would come by in the campaign RV and check on us in a couple of hours.

The day was hot, the concrete road hotter, and we were soon sweating heavily as the cars whizzed by. The first one to stop was a green Ford, driven by a man named William W. Walker.

"Heard about you on the radio," he called to us. "Would you like to cool off in my air-conditioned car?"

What if this were a reporter trying to trap us, intending to prove we weren't really walking all the way? "Sure," I said, "as long as we stay stopped."

As we enjoyed the cool air, the traveling salesman said, "I just wanted to wish you good luck and charge you to take good care of that Walker name."

I chatted gratefully with him, and we got back on the road. "That's sure a good omen for our beginning," I said to the boys.

As the miles passed, the road became hotter. I made up my mind to wave at the occupants of every car going by, although that, too, became a physical effort. People responded with blank stares. I could almost hear them saying, "Who the hell are those guys?" and I began to get a glimmer of what we were in for.

Our destination was the Davidson farm home in Bay City, twenty-two miles from Brookport. The same *Tribune* reporter and photographer from the press conference surprised us by finding us on the road and actually walking with us for a ways. They soon learned the lesson that many others did: Tennis shoes are not made for hot concrete. So, their stay was short, just enough time for the photographer to get what Seslar said were "damn good pictures of what you guys are up to." We began to hope for a favorable *Chicago Tribune* story.

After they left, a few cars stopped to ask if we could visit Rosebud, where some folks wanted to meet us. When our RV came out to bring us water and a toilet, I asked Steve to get hold of Norty Kay and tell him that we were going to take a little side trip off the main road to reach Rosebud. He met us in Rosebud and told me how excited he was.

"This could provide a dateline for a story evoking images of *Citizen Kane* and Orson Welles." And it did. Norty was a highly competent journalist and also the epitome of a loosened tie, bespectacled, sometimes disorganized, constantly on the telephone, rumpled-jacket reporter.

Rosebud lies on the edge of the Shawnee National Forest, which was particularly steamy and buggy in the summer. At mile fifteen of our walk, we were tired, hot, dusty, and foot weary. I grabbed the large dipper at an antique hand pump in front of the general store in Rosebud, and a bunch of people on the porch broke into applause as I poured the cold water over my hot head. That visit—we later learned from "stoppers" along the way—generated a good deal of talk, and I began to learn the importance of word of mouth in southern Illinois.

We finally reached the Bay City gravel road turnoff. Two more miles to go. The boys clambered into the van to go their way for the night, and it was almost dark when I could see my host and hostess waving from their front porch rocking chairs—Mr. Davidson in farmer's overalls, his wife in a shapeless cotton print dress. I was very glad to end the day's walk and must have downed numerous glasses of iced tea. Dinner, immediately served, was home-cured ham, potato salad, fresh corn, and coleslaw. Then, chess pie—a rich, creamy, tasty pie—for dessert. This was the first of many good home-cooked meals throughout the walk.

That chess pie was good for a mention when I talked with small groups. As I wended my way through downstate Illinois, it always brought head-nods and knowing smiles from old-timers. Same with the hedge apples that grew on the trees that often separated the fields of corn and soybeans common to almost every farm. Charles enjoyed picking them up on the roadside and throwing them at his brother Dan. I learned from a farmer that they're not useless, that they will keep varmints out of basements. Happily, this turned out to be another crowd-pleaser.

We talked a little after supper. Mr. Davidson quietly told me, "Dan, I've gotta say right up front that I can't vote for you. I'm a solid Republican and won't vote in the Democratic primary." But he added, "I'll talk it up for you, Dan, if I'm convinced you can do something about our lousy state government." I did my best to persuade him that I would give it a good try, and this was my first glimmer that, in southern Illinois, inspiring favorable talk was as good as a promised vote.

Next morning, I recorded my thought: "I looked out the window and saw that damn road; why didn't I run for governor of Rhode Island?" After a hearty farm breakfast, Mr. Davidson taught me how to "jug" for catfish and told me in detail about the differences he and his neighbors had with the state Department of Agriculture. He also complained about having to buy both Illinois and Kentucky fishing licenses since the border was out in the river. If elected, I was determined to remember this conversation.

I joined my sons on the road, and we agreed that twenty-two miles was too much, particularly when we wanted to take time to talk with people along the way. Dan was charged with getting names and addresses, if possible, which went up to Mary Parrilli, who prepared letters that were brought down to me for my signature. These personal contacts, amounting to several thousand by the end of the walk, proved invaluable for recruiting workers.

We encountered barking dogs running out into the road for the first—and far from the last—time. Fortunately, I had learned from Lawton Chiles's campaign walk down in Florida, where he became both senator and governor, how to deal with hostile dogs. "Turn your pockets inside out so they look like two long white rags. Lean forward and wave your hands so it looks like you have four arms. At the same time, yell loudly, 'Get outta here; scat, dog.'" Lawton was right; they turned tail and ran. Strangely, we thought, Charles did not need this technique. The dogs loved him, trailed along behind him, and we often had the devil of a time getting rid of them.

That day, the blisters began. Nobody had told us not to break them open, that we should prick them with a needle and leave the skin intact. We stupidly tore off the skin and soon had blisters forming on top of blisters. Not Charles, though. Amazingly, he never had any blisters. Dan and I got lots of advice on how to treat the blisters: Dab them with Jack Daniels, piss on them, walk barefoot for an hour or so—the home remedies went on and on. None worked.

Next day, Norty brought good news. Walter Neal's pictures of us walking were on the front page of the *Chicago Tribune* along with a good, long story that described realistically how rough the hot road could be. The *Chicago Sun Times* sent a reporter-photographer down the next day, and then television cameras from Chicago showed up. All treated the walk as legitimate campaigning, and our fears of it being dismissed as a gimmick were largely, but not totally, behind us. There were a few downstate newspapers like the *Alton Telegraph* that persisted. Even weeks later when I visited the skeptical city editor, Elmer Broz, they called it a gimmick. To him, as I did regularly to other media unbelievers, I said, "Just walk twenty miles with me on hot concrete when the temperature's in the nineties, and see if you'll still call it a gimmick."

The next day's walk took us along the Ohio River through the town of Golconda, with Elizabethtown ("E-Town" it's called) our destination for the evening. The roads were hard on blistered feet. Sometimes a car passing us from behind would see an oncoming car and move to the right, barely missing us and forcing us to jump off the concrete onto the rough shoulder. We also learned to get off the concrete when an eighteen-wheel rig roared by since its draft could knock us over. To our dismay, some kids got perverse pleasure out of swerving their cars to make us jump out of the way. Traffic sometimes kept us on the rough shoulders. We heard complaints constantly about those shoulders from farmers: "Why doesn't the state spend more road money down here?" I resolved to make downstate road improvement an important talking point in my campaign.

One thing that irritated me before I became well-known was the frequent response after I said, "Hi, I'm Dan Walker, running for governor."

"What state? Kentucky?"

If it was the end of a hot, tiring day, I would sometimes snap, "Why do ya think I'd be walking in Illinois if I were running for governor of Kentucky?"

Mostly, though, I bit back that response and turned it into a kidding exchange. Gradually, I learned the art of one-on-one campaigning. And I liked it when I noticed that people started calling me "Dan."

I should have known from the beginning that we needed to drink more liquids than usual. My favorite soon became the iced tea that was the drink most often brought to us on the road by thoughtful women hearing about us on the radio. Lemonade and cola drinks were too sweet for me. Copious amounts of iced tea brought by too many "stoppers" sometimes caused a problem. To be polite, we had to drink it every time it was offered. With no bathroom facilities, we had to squirm through a long conversation until we could get an opportunity to duck into the bushes.

The walk to E-Town proved one of the worst days of the whole trek. It seemed like we had been walking a week. The day was the hottest yet, and we covered twenty miles. My journal reads: "My feet were really killing me and I had four or five good-sized blisters. Dan also had some tough ones." We finally walked through E-Town to reach the home of Ken and Harriet Jones. Ken covered Pope and Hardin counties for the University of Illinois Agricultural Extension Service. He was bragging about his prize hog when the sheriff called to ask him if he had heard anything about a bunch of longhaired hippies in the neighborhood. Vietnam War protestors still made nightly television news, and the conservative folks in southern Illinois did not take kindly to hippies. Ken asked me, and I said I'd better take the phone. I told the sheriff that just possibly there was talk about seeing my sons on the road; they did have rather long hair. The sheriff asked how long, and I responded defensively, somewhere between short and long, not too long.

"Next day, we'll all get haircuts," I told the boys.

Harriet took pity on my blistered feet, recognizing that I was having a hard time being a proper guest. She made me soak my feet in hot water into which she sprinkled a lot of Epsom salts. This brought back memories of my mother, who often used Epsom salts as a home remedy. I wondered what she would think about me sitting there in a stranger's living room with my feet in that tub for over an hour.

Next morning, it was a painful task getting my feet into white socks (two pair, Harriet insisted) and then into the damn boots. This morning task continued day after day as my feet got worse. Norty looked at them during one road break and saw some places where the skin had cracked and blood oozed out. When he reached Chicago a few days later, he told Vic (exaggerating somewhat for emphasis, he told me later), "Dan's bleeding all over his shoes, the blisters are that bad. We've got to call this off." Vic said, "Norty, we can't do that. Somehow, he's got to keep walking."

That I did, right after our haircuts. Heading for Old Shawneetown, we walked through an area ravaged by strip mining for coal. My journal records, "We walked over a bridge and the river underneath was opaque and a most unnatural shade of green." I learned later this was caused by some of the chemical wastes.

As I talked with folks, I heard about the problems associated with strip mining. Not far from a creek, which also flowed with the ugly green water, a farmer stood by the roadside near his tractor, taking off his straw hat and wiping the sweat from his face with the huge handkerchief he pulled out of his overalls. I grabbed the opportunity to ask him what he thought about the huge black piles of detritus from the strip mines that were scattered among the green hills. Expecting a vociferous complaint, I was taken aback at his reply.

"Naw, those miners ain't all that bad. They can help us folks out."

"What do you mean? In what way?"

"They buy stuff from our stores. Lots of times during storms we need their heavy equipment. And they've got jobs that're hard to come by down here."

The boys saw that this was going to be a conversation. Dan sat down to rest his feet in the shade under a tree across the road, and Charles went off for some of his skylarking.

"We need help down here," the farmer said, "and we sure don't get it from the state. Peabody and the other coal companies hire our young folks."

I glanced over at the ugly green creek to see Charles skipping stones on it. "Don't you hate what strip mining did to this beautiful countryside and rolling hills?" I asked.

"Yes, sir, I do. It's terrible what they do to God's country." The farmer spoke with the slow cadence typical of southern Illinois. "Why doesn't the government make these guys restore what they ruined? Or at least clean it up?"

So, I learned that the folks in this hardscrabble country had mixed feelings. Here was another issue a governor should deal with, and I vowed to dig into the land reclamation problem when I got the chance.

We walked into Old Shawneetown for an experience I'll never forget. My hostess, Jessann Logsden, met me at the door to her home. She was more dressed up than most of the women I had encountered on the road and shushed me immediately.

"Dan, come right in. Your room's down this hall and your bathroom's right next to it. There's a pitcher of cold martinis on the bedside table. You go clean up and relax, and we'll see you in an hour or so."

God bless that lady. Not just the martinis; I never expected and did not want cocktails, but I did crave a little privacy, time to wash, relax, and sip something cold before shifting gears for the conviviality I would need to get through the rest of the evening. That was rarely offered during the walk. I used the chance to place a collect call home to report to Roberta.

The hour of respite passed quickly. After dinner, Jessann had arranged a reception. The mayors of both Old Shawneetown and New Shawneetown were coming to the party to meet us. This was highly unusual; most often, mayors were conveniently out of town when I arrived, wanting little to do with this "antiestablishment" candidate. Since I opposed machine politics, the press had given me this label despite my respectable career in the legal establishment. I didn't really disagree though. I'm a rebel at heart.

It turned out that Norty had really outdone himself. Much to our surprised delight, television cameras from the Chicago CBS station arrived at our host's home; more evidence that the media didn't see the walk as a mere gimmick. I had to laugh when the Democratic county chairman shied away from me when he saw the camera guy focusing on us. The camera instead caught Charles sitting at the piano playing "Lara's Theme" from *Dr. Zhivago,* surrounded by more people than I was.

Norty had announced a press conference the next morning in Old Shawneetown. We walked to the large, brick, Doric-columned bank—part of the history of this once-thriving Ohio River town. We hoped for television cameras, radio mikes, and newspaper reporters from around southern Illinois. But only one person showed up, carrying a camera. I asked what newspaper he represented.

"None," he responded, "I'm getting a picture for our college annual."

That was the least-attended press conference I ever held as candidate or governor. We were very discouraged, Norty especially. He felt he had personally let me down.

### THE RED BANDANNA

Next day, I talked to Mary Parrilli in Chicago, and my journal reads, "Mary reports they're getting calls that some disc jockeys are dedicating songs to us and our feet." And it wasn't just my feet that were troubling me. I have vitiligo, lack of pigment in the skin on my hands, so the backs of my hands started blistering. To shield them, I wrapped my hands with the large, red cowboy bandanna-handkerchief I carried. Then, when not needed, I wrapped it around my neck. At one of the prearranged nightly gatherings of friends and neighbors, a lady asked, "Where's the bandanna I saw you wearing on the road today? That's a red badge of courage for you." So, I wore it every day, and that bandanna became a walk trademark.

We had large signs mounted on tripods reading "DAN WALKER AHEAD: HONK AND WAVE" and placed about a mile or two ahead and behind us. When we reached one, we simply turned it around to be the one behind us. It was the job of the guy in the van to move the other one up ahead of us. I diligently waved at every car, trying to make eye contact. At the beginning, people had no idea who I was, but that gradually changed as the days went by. One of my daily diversions was counting the cars that responded to my wave, sometimes just by lifting a finger off the steering wheel. It happened, but very rarely, that a driver would "give me the finger."

Those honks and waves paid off in a way I never anticipated. Long after the walk, people would say, "Dan, I met you once when you were walking the state." Often, though, the "meeting" was only that eye contact on the road. But it became a real personal meeting to that individual, and many said, "That was the first time I ever met a governor." When the number of honks and waves picked up on the walk, it really lifted our spirits.

After Shawneetown, we were on a road headed almost due west to Harrisburg, now two weeks into the walk. Before we got there, Dan gave out. He sat down beside the road, took off his boots, and said, "Dad, I can't stand these boots any longer; the pain's just too damn much." So, carrying the boots, he walked in his stocking feet for the last two miles into Harrisburg.

Fortunately, we found a podiatrist right away, and he was shocked when he saw our feet. Except for blisterless Charles, of course. The doctor was amazed when he learned that we knew nothing about the tincture of benzene used as a foot toughener by athletes.

Harrisburg was my first television studio show, *Jim Cox in the Afternoon.* He ended the show by picking up his guitar and singing about the walk to the tune of "Danny Boy." I was nonplussed. What kind of expression should I have on my face for the television camera when a guy's singing a song about my feet?

The doctor had taken Dan off the walk for several days, and this made him very unhappy. I was able to stay with it, wearing soft shoes for a few days, and the benzene helped. But for many days, the morning ritual remained hard to take: rubbing on the benzene, pulling on two layers of white socks, and then gradually easing painful feet into the boots and lacing them up tight. In this way, Charles and I made slow progress toward Carbondale, and Dan rejoined us on the road.

The blister situation had improved, but the boys soon started complaining about itching. I finally figured out they had picked up some ticks while lolling on the grass by the roadside, and it took a while to get them out of their hair.

An eighteen-wheeler roared up behind us, and I hastily stepped off the concrete, twisting my ankle. It was sore, but not bad enough to stop me. The next day, I again jumped off the road too quickly and turned my other ankle. That night, the journal reads,

> The plans for an overnight stay fell through, and I was just as glad because both my hands and my ankles were in terrible shape. We found a motel where the owners, Mary and Duke, were just wonderful. Mary brought containers of ice to my room so I could pack my ankles. She told me to rub my hands with vinegar and water to get the swelling down, and I remembered my grandmother teaching that vinegar was the best sunburn cure. Next morning, the swellings were gone, my ankles felt better, and I was ready to hit the road again.

We brightened that morning when a Wonder bakery truck slowed down, and the driver leaned out to toss a half-dozen Twinkies at us. Dan and Charles scrambled for them. We finally neared Carbondale, home of Southern Illinois University and the largest town we had walked into. That was the day the rest of the family first joined us. The journal describes it:

> Before our wondrous eyes appeared . . . count 'em, Kathleen, Robbie, Julie, Will, Margaret, and, of course, Roberta. Here, out in the boondocks, along-

side the highway deafened by the thunderous passing of the 18-wheelers, were all the kids and my beloved wife. The swelling in my feet suddenly relocated to my chest. Roberta had brought her special deep-dish cherry pie cooked in a large baking pan. Like hungry kids, Dan and I each took a big spoon and dived into that pie while the UPI photographer took pictures. We then proceeded, all nine of us, to walk into town.

Roberta had wanted to come out and walk more on the road. This was just not feasible. Vic felt very strongly about this. Her presence would detract from the image. I had to be viewed as being engaged in a lonely battle. My sons did not detract from that image—Vic, Norty, and David agreed—but a wife would. It was all bound up in the hard work, endurance, loneliness, Don Quixote, uphill-fight imagery of the walk.

Actually, walking significant distances wasn't feasible for Roberta in any case because of physical problems. However, I'm convinced that she realized how the campaign, my preoccupation with it, and particularly the long absence caused by the walk were creating a gulf between us. I'm also convinced that she increasingly resented the power that Vic had over my life. This wasn't a case of simple jealously. Vic was a bit gruff and came across as a big-city political operator in a way that Roberta, brought up in Kenosha, Wisconsin, simply couldn't fathom. She would have agreed with those who considered Vic to be Machiavellian. I did love her, and her visit cheered me, yet the long separation certainly strained our relationship.

Next day, the family left, and the boys and I walked to the beach and rolled up our trousers to enjoy Crab Orchard Lake. I recorded,

> The lifeguard came over and told us the lake was polluted. I pulled Dan out because of the open sores on his feet and the same condition beached me. I felt a little silly, but why take a chance with many miles of walking ahead of us. Charles, though, had no fear and gaily cavorted in the lake like a young porpoise while we jealously sat on the beach glaring at him.

After Carbondale, we finally began to feel comfortable with the venture, finally hitting our stride. The number of honks-and-waves was high. To pass the time, I counted them once or twice a day. And I heard for the first time a memorable yell from the driver of a big rig going by.

"Keep fightin', Dan!"

The "fighting" theme picked up as more and more people found out that I was running as a decided underdog against the Chicago machine they had heard so much about. In different ways, we heard this over and over: "You're workin' hard, Dan. If you've got the guts to do what you're doing, fighting that machine and walking the state, I'll vote for you."

Perhaps too optimistic, I told Vic on the phone, "Something's happening out here on the road."

# 13

## The Good People of Southern Illinois

Springtime has brought a false optimism in the Duluth prison. The season can be cruel. You think the bone-chilling cold is past, and then you get a blizzard around Easter. Such is the day's weather as I stand in line waiting to get into the mess hall for lunch. I stiffen as I see the new warden move closer, inspecting the line of prisoners. I fear I'm in for a rough time.

Since graduation from the U.S. Naval Academy at Annapolis, I have always proudly worn my large, gold class ring on my left-hand ring finger. The warden is a graduate of the Military Academy at West Point. Walking by, he spots my ring.

"Come over here, Walker," he says loudly.

When I come close, he speaks loudly again. "Take off that ring, Walker. No rings are worn in my prison."

I look at him and say, "Warden, I've never taken off this ring."

"You will this time," he snarls.

"I will not," I say firmly.

The warden motions to the guards accompanying him. "Take it off."

They force me to my knees, and when they can't get the ring off, one guard runs to the washroom to get some soap. When he returns, they tell me to stand, and pinioning my arms behind my back, soap my fingers and strip off the ring.

"You'll learn to take orders here, Walker. You're not a governor in my prison," says the warden. He faces one of the guards. "Search him."

I earned that ring and wore it proudly every day for forty-five years. How could a minimum-security warden demand this as part of my punishment?

I have learned to go elsewhere in my mind and think back to my days at the Naval Academy when I earned that ring. How fortunate I was to have been accepted and to have made it through.

In high school, being in the Naval Reserve, I served summers as an apprentice seaman aboard a World War I destroyer known as a "four piper" because of its trademark four smokestacks. I did my share of cleaning the heads (navyese for *toilets*), chipping paint, and swabbing decks. One day, while scrubbing soot high up on one of the smoke stacks, I slipped sideways in the bosun's chair on which I was perched. Reaching for support, I mistakenly grabbed the steam line to the ship's whistle, burning all the skin off my right hand. I learned how hard a sailor's life was and envied Waco his acceptance to the Naval Academy.

Though I had been named class valedictorian in high school and had been accepted at San Diego State College, I had to quit when my Naval Reserve unit was mobilized to active duty. I went through boot camp and then reported aboard a small minesweeper that was conveniently docked near Point Loma. Dad had also been recalled for active duty and assigned to become head chief radioman at the Point Loma Naval Radio Station with comfortable quarters for the family—much to my mother's delight.

Aboard the minesweeper, I was given the job of "captain's yeoman" (secretary) since I could type and take shorthand. Dad, with his customary foresight, had insisted that I take those courses in high school. I soon made the rank of third-class petty officer, and it was a proud day when Mom sewed that "crow" (eagle insignia with one red V-stripe) on my sailor's uniform sleeve.

Tired of being constantly told what to do and tired of the enlisted navy routine, I took the competitive examinations for entry "from the fleet," as they called it, to the Naval Academy. More than three thousand sailors took the exams. I was fortunate enough to finish in the top five and was sent to the Naval Academy Preparatory School in Norfolk, Virginia.

While I was at Norfolk, the Japanese struck at Pearl Harbor, and the navy stepped up all its priorities. Though some thought this would be a short war, I knew that wasn't true. My dad had predicted a long war with Japan for years.

I passed the final exams, reported to the Naval Academy in June, and was soon sworn in as a midshipman. Entering midshipmen endured a very thorough physical examination, and the dentists initially rejected me for what was called "marked malocclusion." My front teeth were crooked and off-center. Dad went to the "old boy circle," the chiefs, and reached a senior chief pharmacist mate. Somehow I got by, but I don't think I would have made it into Annapolis without Dad's last-minute help.

Hazing of "plebes," or first-year midshipmen, went by easily. After Dad's disciplinary routine, those upper classmen seemed like amateurs. Their hazing "antics" were sophomoric to those of us who had come from the fleet. We just couldn't take it seriously. When we were forced to walk to the center of a corridor and make a square right turn, or walk next to the wall while going upstairs, or bark like a dog upon demand, we found it ridiculous. The former sailors frequently failed to earn good conduct grades from supervising officers as a result. We knew the navy wasn't really like that.

The academic year didn't go well either. The engineering courses bored me. Based on my entrance exam, I started out with a star rating in the top one hundred of our fifteen-hundred-man class. Yet I lost my star when I almost failed some of the engineering courses. I learned how to just barely get passing grades with a minimum of studying and a maximum of goofing off.

A sport was required for every midshipman, so I signed up for crew, rowing in a twelve-man shell where I barely managed to stay in synch with the other oarsmen. After classes, I would head for the boathouse to practice in a one-man shell. I had kept my sailor's uniform hidden away, and out of boredom and frustration, I stuffed it into the shell and rowed up the Severn River a few times to find a quiet spot where I could beach the boat, don the uniform, and have a few beers at a nearby tavern.

What an idiot I was. If caught, I would have been shipped out the next day to join the fleet somewhere in the Pacific. Yet I became bolder. A few times in my second and third years, I went "over the wall" for a night on the town—even more idiotic. One night, I escaped Bancroft Hall, where all the midshipmen lived, by climbing through a first-floor window and then running across the yard to climb over the wall and going into town. Returning, I skipped the wall-climb and walked right up to the gate where the potbellied "Jimmy Legs," as we called the gate guards, stood on duty, armed with .45s.

Approaching the guards, I broke into a fast run right through the gate, confident they would never shoot me. I could run very fast in those days and entered Bancroft Hall through that window, raced down the hall into my room, and dived under the covers in my bunk in a very short time. When the duty officers did a room check, they never uncovered me. I was stupid to take such risks, but risk was a basic instinct to me.

My few good grades in social science courses and Japanese did little to help my overall GPA. Too often, I played cards at midnight in a hideaway place in the basement: "Walker's elbow-bending society." Until we were caught, that is.

I was assigned to a new roommate, Don Iselin. Don, who would later achieve a brilliant naval career, becoming the top admiral in charge of the navy's engineering corps, led our class and was named to edit the annual, called the *Lucky Bag*. Standing in class is all-important to a naval officer; the class number, which becomes final on graduation, has a major career effect, particularly on promotions. My class ranking wasn't looking too good, but because I volunteered to be an assistant editor, we were placed in the same room.

I did win several oratory contests, enjoyed the academy debate team, wrote for the midshipmen's weekly paper, and made some lifelong friends. In addition to Don, I became friends with the guy in the next room, Wally Schirra, who would go on to become one of the most famous of the astronauts. Despite my dislike for the Naval Academy curriculum and the fact that my number on graduation was 1,325—quite a comedown from my initial rank in the top one hundred—I did develop a strong attachment to the academy and to my class. The camaraderie was intense for all three years. Annapolis deliberately instilled a strong feeling of loyalty and pride.

One of the most prominent dances just before becoming a first-classman is the "ring dance" where the midshipman's ring is dipped into a container full of water from all the seven seas before placing it on the midshipman's finger. Graduates often clink rings when they meet another alumnus. I am proud of my class ring.

A common form of greeting among naval officers is "Beat Army," referring to the annual Army-Navy football game. I am tempted to say "Beat Army" when the warden strips my cherished ring from my finger, but I think better of it. Such insolence could place me in the hole. I hate it that this West Point Napoleon wannabe has stripped me of my ring. I wouldn't put it past him to somehow misplace it.

### FINDING THE MEDIA

Vic De Grazia once told an interviewer that I was a very private person. He described my upbringing and the Naval Academy:

> Annapolis took this kid and turned him into a polished version of a human being, put that Annapolis veneer on a poor country kid from California. Then he got used to wearing a lawyer's pinstripe suit. After several weeks on the walk, he somehow got rid of all that; the veneer disappeared, not just on the surface, but deep down. He could walk into a grain elevator and feel right at home. That downstate comfort stuck; he never after that became the person he was before.

Even while on the walk, I began to think that I was becoming a different person, but it took a long while for that realization to sink in.

After Carbondale, we doubled back northeast across the state through a number of small towns. We learned that mostly the media would not come to us; we had to go to them. So Norty Kay would drive to a local newspaper or radio station to tell them I was nearby and then come back to find me. When we reached a roadside place with a pay phone, I would call his contact.

For Norty, *peripatetic* was the word—always back and forth, attempting to get recognition of the walk into newspapers and onto radio programs. He also made frequent trips to the campaign headquarters in Chicago and issued press releases. Sometimes we would get a break and just walk into a town with a radio station. I welcomed the respite and learned the value of radio talk shows.

Then as now, country folks and working folks tended to open up on the radio talk shows—encouraged, of course, by a popular host who had a knack for stimulating controversial talk. On these programs throughout downstate Illinois, I would get very direct, tough questions on a wide variety of subjects. I learned to turn a variety of these questions into an attack on the Chicago machine. On gun control, for example: "Those machine politicians up in Chicago can't control the gang killing on the South Side. You guys know how to handle guns; they don't." I spoke their language.

Once, I said, "Why not just declare martial law in those gang-run areas of the city and go in and confiscate all the handguns, particularly those Saturday Night Specials?" I was surprised at the strong favorable reception this evoked from people I met on the road. When the inevitable question came, I got to describe the cheap, easily made handguns that bore the name and why the state should outlaw them. This brought no back talk from gun-owners downstate. I could always tell if I did well on the program when I heard about it repeatedly from people I encountered on the road. "Heard you talkin' about guns the other day on the radio," folks would say for days after I appeared on the talk show.

People like that often commented that they had never before met a candidate for governor and talked about how important this was to them. One old guy said to me, "Dan, I like to meet my candidate. I like to talk to my candidate; I like to listen to my candidate. Hell, Dan, I like to smell my candidate!"

## MEDIA ATTENTION INCREASES

Sometimes, not as often as we had hoped, a news guy would drive out to join me on the walk. Mostly, though, they stayed only long enough to ask a few questions, just enough to make a short story. One exception was Taylor Pensoneau of the *St. Louis Post-Dispatch*, who walked with me for the better part of two days and would in later years write my biography with another reporter, Bob Ellis. Actually, Taylor held the record for journalists: nineteen miles. Two others who stayed with me weeks later and sweated for several hours were Burnell Heinecke of the *Chicago Sun-Times* and Frank Leeming of the *Decatur Herald Review,* both well-informed reporters who kept me on my mental toes. But I never slowed the walking pace for them or any other reporters. If they wanted a story, they had to keep pace with me on the road. I wanted them to fully experience and hopefully report that this was no cakewalk, pardon the pun.

One hot afternoon, we learned that the walk was getting national attention when Ike Pappas, a famous CBS television reporter, showed up. His presence was highly unusual in a primary contest like mine, particularly long before the election, and the possibility of national television exposure was exciting.

Ike shot a lot of footage and then decided to get one last picture of us as the sun was setting. He wanted us walking over the crest of a hill, revealing first our heads, then our bodies, and then the boots. A perfectionist, he had the cameraman shoot us three times, and each time we had to go down that hill and walk up again—a very trying experience at the end of a long, hot day. We never saw it on television, but Norty said it was great.

One day Norty came out to tell us that the radio was broadcasting a story about three escaped convicts, describing them as being dressed in blue shirts and khaki trousers, just like us. Next day, I saw a police car park on the shoulder across from us, and I walked over to talk with the officer, leaning toward the car window. The officer seemed tense, but after I introduced myself, he relaxed and told me that his concealed right hand gripped his gun, ready to shoot me if I made a move. He had thought we were the escaped convicts.

Back in Chicago, both Vic and Dave were anxious to get a better feel for the walk's impact on voters. They didn't tell me at the time, but they polled one county before I arrived and again after I left. The difference, Vic later told me, was stunning in both name recognition and favorable evaluation. Although unaware of this at the time, I began to feel that there was a growing awareness, at least in southern Illinois, where word spread rapidly of what I was about, what my mission was, and that I was a fighter.

When we neared the end of the third week, I recorded, "This damn heat wave goes on and on. We should have walked the state at night. We'd have been much cooler and in the bargain would have grabbed the burglar vote." The boys and I called this "road humor." Indeed, sometimes we really had to reach for a laugh. Next day, I recorded, "I was nearly hit by cars twice. Thus far the score on close encounters is: Walker nine, cars nothing. Of course, I can lose only once." But again I brightened that day when I counted an unusually high number of honks and waves. I recorded, "Something special is unfolding. We can feel a stark difference out here on the road."

This was borne out in Johnston City, on Illinois Highway 37. The tempo of recognition in the middle of town really picked up, causing a traffic jam. One lady got so excited when I yelled, "Hi" that her car ran into a television truck from Harrisburg. Dan quickly found her jack and managed to untangle her car from the truck. A few miles later, as we neared West Frankfort, the reception again surprised us. The managing editor of the newspaper (and later coauthor of my 1993 biography), Bob Ellis, called it "something to behold."

People came out into their front yards to greet us, cars stopped, drivers honked, and the boys and I got excited as crowds built up. For the first time in the campaign, people reached out to touch me, and I felt the kind of crowd magic Jack Kennedy had evoked in 1960. I knew then, deep in my gut, that I could win this campaign because it was becoming a highly personalized dramatic quest independent of specific issues.

It was in Johnston City that I met the lady who turned out to be one of our most indefatigable and long-lasting downstate volunteers in both 1972 campaigns, Dorothy Hughes. She assembled a large crowd at the post office at nine in the morning and later fixed a lunch for more curious residents.

Tireless worker that she was, nobody has a count of how many folks from southern Illinois she signed up for the campaign.

Also in Johnston City, Charles somehow found a world-class violinmaker, and that encounter dramatically improved his view of southern Illinois. He did sometimes jump to conclusions, such as when he met Tony Costellano in his steak house in Marion, an experience that proved to be a total contrast with the southern Illinois we had been experiencing. From our evening stop in Johnston City, we drove back down to Marion and had dinner in a private room, complete with big steaks and lots of red wine. This and Tony's Italian looks convinced Charles that we had found the Mafia in southern Illinois.

The next day on the walk, Charles said, "Dad, how come you want the Mafia working with us? You've always been an enemy of the Mafia."

"Tony is Italian," I said to Charles. "He looks Italian. He eats and drinks like an Italian. Italian doesn't mean Mafia. Tony happens to be an active and influential local independent Democrat. It would be great if we could get him to join us."

### STAYING WITH FOLKS EVERY NIGHT

My supporters came in all varieties. Among my hosts and hostesses in the evenings were factory workers, a mailman, farmers, a sharecropper, schoolteachers, retail store clerks, a carpenter, an auto mechanic, ministers, a postmistress in a small town, a policeman, a fireman, an unemployed farm worker, and several other unemployed people. I had very few hosts who could be considered "establishment" people—I can recall only attorneys in Jacksonville and Carlinville and a retired newspaper editor in Collinsville.

In West Frankfort, I stayed with Agnes and George Michalic, a wonderful couple who took us to their hearts. George sold insurance, and Agnes worked for the local government. They invited my boys to join them for the after-dinner gathering that turned almost into a party. After Dan and Charles joined us for breakfast the next morning, Agnes actually cried when we left. They were so typical of the many hosts and hostesses on the walk who, after supper, would often invite friends and relatives to join us. I got to know many of what I call the wonderful, ordinary folks of downstate Illinois.

These gatherings gave me a chance to talk casually about my campaign mission and were great learning experiences. Not only did I learn how to relate better to people individually and in small groups, picking up valuable campaigning techniques, but also I learned firsthand about my state—its geography, its people, its problems—in a way that is rare for politicians. And

I learned how to talk with people, how to bring out their deepest feelings. Even at the start, down in southern Illinois, I was comfortable with the way they talked, perhaps because of my southern parents. Unconsciously, I found myself changing my manner of speech, talking slower and more countrified: "I'm beginnin' to like this country."

A constant theme when people relaxed with me in their homes was the "left out" feeling. One farmer's wife put it this way: "Me and my family—folks like us down here—don't mean anything up there. They don't really care about us folks. We're forsaken folks by those guys in Springfield and Chicago."

Her husband chimed in. "Yeah, they're all alike. They take care of each other, those guys. Both parties—don't make a damn whether they're Democrats or Republicans. Who always gets left out? Us."

Over and over, people told me about feeling forsaken by state government. It took me a while to appreciate the depth of their "left out" feeling. And I was surprised as I walked through the rest of the state how often that theme was repeated. It became a litany I heard over and over as I walked day after long day and met with residents in the evening.

"Government ain't workin' for us. It may be for some folks we hear about, like those on welfare. But it ain't workin' for us." The words often changed when better-educated people dropped the *ain't*, but the message remained the same. It took me a while to learn that this was something different and deeper than the traditional American cynicism about government. Actually, as I thought about it, the feeling was not much different than the discontent of their older children over the divisive Vietnam War, which caused many kids to protest against the government. I couldn't persuade the parents, could not get them to understand the similarity, but both they and their kids were upset about the same thing: a government that was not listening to its people.

# 14

## Blister Pains Balanced by Personal Pleasures

I have always believed that intelligent communication is the best way to resolve differences. I want to continue to hold onto that belief in an attempt to work things out with Roberta Nelson Walker, my second wife. Since her first name is the same as my first wife's, my children often call her "R2," or, after the *Star Wars* film, "R2D2." I want so much to talk with her. I live for the day we will be together again. Without that hope, life seems bleak.

An inmate named Alger has just delivered the mail, dumping it from the sack onto a table. Some inmates rush to the table, confident a letter will arrive for them. Others feign marginal interest, knowing the odds are against anything arriving with their name on it. I steel myself against disappointment as I look for a letter from R2. I've written many letters to her, but she has responded to none of them. I do, however, receive a letter from one of my children. They write me often, as do friends from the campaign and others. One such letter arrives, telling me that my wife is bad-mouthing me back in Oak Brook, where she is blaming me for everything and selling our lovely home.

She has the legal right to do so because I've given her a general power of attorney, but I had hoped, and still hope, it wouldn't come to that. The fact that she has taken this step without telling me is a blow. I resolve to try to call her again. I also fill out the forms, submitting an immediate request for a twenty-four-hour pass, the kind that Alger seems to get frequently. If I could just get one and persuade Roberta to join me for a weekend, maybe I could turn things around.

I dream of going back to our home—a split-level, four-bedroom house in the suburbs on an acre of land, with a generous patio and swimming pool. You can see the diving board from the glass doors in the kitchen-dining area. Twisted Japanese pines grow in back of the pool, while other unusual trees, like Japanese maple and perfectly shaped blue spruce, form scattered clusters around the property up to the wood fences. Across the road, a large pond attracts ducks and geese. Every spring, we try to protect the trains of goslings and ducklings that waddle across our front yard.

I especially love the flower borders that edge the lawns, front and back. Each spring, I plant them myself. The image of one particular flowerbed is painful. I built a heart-shaped flower garden in the front lawn, edging it with angled half-bricks to form a low border, and then planted a large cluster of red salvia in the center, surrounded by blue petunias that mingled into multicolored ones along the outer edges, like trim on a valentine. We celebrated with champagne when I finished it. Roberta loved that flowerbed. *How can she sell our home?*

The next morning, I have a visitor. I hurry over to the visitor center, endure a strip-and-spread body-cavity search, and learn that my first Roberta, Julie, and Margaret have come to see me. Not Roberta Nelson. I actually discourage my family from coming up because I don't want them to see me in prison surroundings. It's just too painful. In the lounge area, they wait, clustered around a small table. I sit down with them, look at Roberta directly across from me, trying unsuccessfully to focus on our past together. I try to be grateful they've come, but their presence just reminds me of the life I left, and I'm miserable. I keep thinking about Roberta Nelson, R2. All I can talk about with the mother of my children is our kids.

Afterwards, while I'm at work spearing cigarette butts, I learn that Alger has another twenty-four-hour pass. Alger holds one of the most sought-after prison jobs, cleaning only the public places in the barracks building. This gives him a lot of free time, and he's on good terms with the prison guards. Other inmates often say they think that Alger checks our lockers, which are never locked, to see if he can find anything that might interest the guards. We have to stay on good terms with this wiry little man because he can make life quite difficult by doing things like messing up a room just before a barracks inspection, causing the inmates to get the blame. I dislike Alger, but I can't blame him too much. If I could just get a pass, I might kiss the damn warden's backside too.

That evening, I leave supper early to stand in a line of about twenty inmates waiting to use the phone. This consumes most of the hour allotted to phone use. My wife probably won't even be home. She has rarely been at home on the few other occasions when I was able to place an outside call. Still, I have to try. With less than ten minutes left in the hour, I finally get into the phone room and find a free phone. I place a collect call, and after several rings, Roberta picks up and accepts the call.

I want to pour out the love I feel for her, but instead I say, "Why haven't you been home when I called the last few times, dear?"

"I've got so much stuff to do to get this house closed out."

The chill in her voice fills me with dread. "I miss you, dear."

"This is all your fault, you know."

*All?* I'm stunned that she is saying this. "We did everything together. Don't you remember? You were as involved as I was."

"No, I wasn't."

"Listen, I might be able to get a twenty-four-hour pass. I could get a hotel room in Duluth. Please come up here, darling, and we can talk. They monitor our calls, and I don't feel comfortable discussing anything."

"I'm not coming up there. That's final."

---

### HEARTLAND

Visitors would break the long monotony of the road one day in the fourth week of the walk. Driving his RV, our trusty Steve Senderowitz[1] led Roberta and my youngest son, Will, along with Norty Kay, out to meet me on the road at Ina, a small town approximately twenty miles south of Mt. Vernon in southern Illinois. I was, naturally, glad to see Roberta and Will, but I was especially anxious to find out what was going on with the campaign in

---

[1] Every day, right from the beginning, Steve Senderowitz drove the van to bring our lunch. I always had a liverwurst sandwich; I never got tired of the taste. Steve made up a menu offering six different ways to make that liverwurst sandwich, and I chose from that menu. Many years later, I would call the firm where Steve was working as a lawyer, and though I hadn't seen him in years, his first words when he came on the line were "How do you want your liverwurst sandwich today, Governor?"

our Chicago headquarters. Were we getting any press in Chicago? Was the grassroots organization growing? To get our million-and-a-half voters, we had to enlist and train volunteer organizers all over the state.

On a grassy triangular island formed by the intersection of three roads, we all sat down at a picnic table in the shade of a tall oak to talk and eat the sandwiches Roberta had fixed for us that day. Norty and I were intent on our conversation. As anxious as I was to get campaign news, nine-year-old Will was even more anxious to get going on the walk.

"We're getting lots of young volunteers who want to join us," Norty said. "They genuinely want to fight machine politics, but as to the press, you know how it is, Dan . . ." Norty shook his head. "Politics is dead in the summertime, as far as the Chicago media is concerned."

Will quickly finished his lunch. "Dad, when are we going to walk?"

"In just a minute, son."

Roberta had to leave to attend, on my behalf, a women's political event. Steve and the boys diverted Will by playing catch with him.

Norty was talking about his public relations efforts. "We try to get mentions of the walk in columns or on talk shows and news programs." He named some contacts that hadn't responded.

All this pounding of the pavement, the heat, the hardships of the road, and so little to show for it. "I'd hoped for at least some mention up there in Chicago, so I'm a little disappointed, Norty." *Depressed beyond words* was more like it, but I would never have said that.

"Well, what did you expect?" Norty asked. "What little the columns do mention about the governor's race is mostly speculation about Foran and Simon. Right now they think Tom Foran has the 'in' because he's Irish." Knowing how partial Daley was to Irish politicians, Vic and Norty were also guessing that he would favor Foran. Daley had no personal love for Simon, who was a bow-tie Protestant.

Will's ball rolled nearby, and he ran over to get it. "Dad!" he called. "Can we go now? Let's go."

"Just a minute, son. So, what about the money, Norty? Is any coming in?"

"Damn little." Norty's white shirt revealed circles of wetness at the armpits.

I sighed. "Well, at least I'm getting a good response out here in the heartland. Tell Vic that the increasing honk-and-waves are keeping my spirits up."

"Daa-aad!" said Will.

With that, we ended our break, set off walking, and in a short time reached the little hub of buildings that made up the town of Ina, a place where time seemed to have stopped a century earlier. Several men, all "country-dressed" in clothing that either came from the small general store or perhaps from a Sears, Roebuck catalog, sat on a bench in front of the store. Others stood around a post at the entry. The merchant had taped a poster advertising Camels and Winston cigarettes onto the cracked storefront window. The men sized us up. Most were dour, but a few grins appeared. A dog belonging to a farmer in overalls walked over to greet us, wagging his tail. We struck up a conversation with these men.

They kidded my boys. "Your old man make you do this, spend your summer with him?"

Dan piped up right away. "Yeah, he sure did. But I don't mind. I've learned a lot more than I do in school."

I started to pick up on this, but one of the guys, a grizzled man, probably in his sixties, broke in. "Well, I dunno what you'd learn here in this godforsaken little town that God left behind."

"You a farmer?" Dan asked. When the guy nodded, Dan said, "Bet you couldn't teach me how to drive a tractor."

Charles spoke up, "Me too."

I was delighted when the guy said, "Come on boys, I'll show you a thing or two."

And off all three of my sons went with this farmer to get their first experience in handling a Caterpillar. When they returned, full of talk about their tractor experience, I thanked the farmer, and we continued walking through the long, hot afternoon.

I recorded in my journal, "We walked and talked through a valley area surrounded by low hills, lots of trees, just a few farmhouses with the usual fields of corn and beans. A picturesque countryside."

### BEAUTIES OF THE COUNTRYSIDE

We stopped to watch fish in a stream and exchanged greetings with a fisherman. I tried to identify the trees and flowers we passed but could name only a few and mentioned that I wished we knew more. The tranquility of the countryside worked a kind of magic on us. Strangely, it seemed to cast a spell that somehow fostered a sense of individual freedom while at the same time connecting us to each other, our fellow human beings, and our country.

We reached Bonnie, another small town about ten miles north of Ina. Roberta joined us for dinner in a flyspecked café, sharing with us the best blackberry cobbler I have ever tasted in my life. Roberta then left to drive home with Will, and I settled in with my host of the evening, pondering this remarkable day with my boys and how the afternoon with them had erased the disappointment I had felt about Norty's news. I continued to draw strength from the feeling that people we encountered really liked us and were responding, even though some stressed that they were committed to voting Republican. I recorded all this in my journal that evening, pondering one line in particular: "You see so many more flowers by the roadside when you walk than you do when you drive."

That last line would give me a little lift and inspiration, standing as a metaphor for both the beauty of the countryside and the friendliness of the people I experienced. I would use this line often in speeches later on.

The last entry in the journal that night read, "All three of my boys were with me today, and it's good, very good, for a father to have this quality time with his sons."

### REACHING THE MISSISSIPPI

We walked north from Mt. Vernon to Centralia and then reached Sandoval on Highway 50, which divides central from southern Illinois, and from there turned due west, passing through Ferrin, Huey, Carlyle, Breese, Trenton, Lebanon, O'Fallon, and Fairview Heights. Although it didn't seem that way at the time, we had completed our first month on the road by the time we reached East St. Louis and the home of Mr. and Mrs. Leonard Long, both black schoolteachers. Photographers from the *St. Louis Post-Dispatch* and UPI showed up that evening, having been alerted by Norty Kay. We always perked up when a wire service photographer took pictures. This could reach newspapers all over the state. Mrs. Long wanted the boys to stay for supper.

During our walk through what is called the "Metro East area," lasting several days, the media coverage exceeded expectation: four television stations, several major daily newspapers, six radio stations. They often mentioned my campaign theme about bringing government and politics back to the people, opening up the system.

One day, I went up onto the Eads Bridge over the Mississippi River to meet Joe Teasdale, Democratic candidate for governor of Missouri. The television cameras focused on us as we shook hands, and he bragged about walking parts of Missouri that summer. (I was shocked when I saw that he was wearing pancake makeup.) Cameramen recorded this milestone, but

I couldn't get Dan to even stick his foot into the Mississippi River for the photographers' shots. He was still afraid of the pollution.

My hosts in the East St. Louis area, all fans of Mark Twain, loved to impart the lore about the Mississippi River, most of which they obtained from Twain's writings. Sometimes in the pleasant evenings after supper, the menfolk would have a drink or two of bourbon. We would sit on the front porch, watch the fireflies, chat with passersby, and eventually a small crowd would gather. The stories and recollections would flow.

"Folks up in Chicago don't know that it was the Mississippi steamboat captains that caused the transcontinental railroads to go through Chicago instead of St. Louis," one of my hosts said.

His wife was a teacher. "That's right," she added. "Mark Twain wrote that for many years the steamboat captains prevented the building of a railroad bridge across the river because it would stop the tall-stack steamboats that carried goods and people up and down the Mississippi River."

"So that ruled out St. Louis," a neighbor said.

In another home, the evening stories turned to violence long since passed into the history of Nauvoo, a town in Illinois on the Mississippi where prejudiced residents had formed a hostile mob opposed to the polygamous Mormons who had moved into the area. Angry townsfolk stormed the local jail, killing the Mormon leaders, the Smith brothers.

Was I accomplishing anything on this walk? I didn't know. There were no polls, and I had to simply trust that we weren't wasting our time, but sometimes getting up in the morning and facing the road seemed like a mine-not-to-reason-why, mine-just-to-do-or-die situation.

We took a most welcome break from the walk in St. Louis since I had to fly to Des Moines, Iowa, for a much-needed fund-raising dinner hosted by an old law school friend of mine. This was the only such stop on the walk. The boys really enjoyed themselves in St. Louis. Charles told me later (years later), "Dad, I attended my first rock concert, smoked my first dope, got a little drunk, and tried to chat up a twenty-two-year-old nursing student six years my senior. Dan gave me lots of breathing room that night, but kept a close eye on me. I learned a lot about his patience and understanding."

When the walk resumed in Edwardsville, Roberta, Kathleen, Robbie, and Julie came down for a visit. We stayed at a motel that night and had a great time.

Kathleen said, "When are your daughters going to get a chance to walk with you?"

I said, "Let's do it tomorrow."

Next day, the three girls walked with me for about five miles to Wood River, but the shoes worn by two of them proved inadequate. Kathleen, though, lasted the whole day.

When we left the St. Louis area, we headed northeast toward the capital in Springfield. The overall plan was to continue to Champaign, in the eastern part of central Illinois, and then double back northwest through Peoria to the Quad Cities area (East Moline, Moline, Rock Island, and Davenport, Iowa—the latter because all the television stations were there), and then head northeast through northern Illinois to the Wisconsin border, and finally walk down to Chicago.

When my birthday month of August arrived, the terrain remained the same: flat, with lots of rich farmland. Here, as in southern Illinois, most farmers wore bib overalls, though increasingly the younger men preferred just jeans. On long days walking past innumerable cornfields, I had many occasions to practice what I had learned about talking with farmers. Often, seeing me as he plowed a field, a sweating farmer would stop his tractor at the end of a cornrow and walk over to the fence and hail me to join him.

"Just wanted to talk a little, Dan. Saw your bandanna on TV and heard on the radio you were out here. My sister down in Hardin County wrote last week that she met you and hoped I would."

I said, "Yeah, I'm Walkin' Dan Walker. What's your name and what's on your mind?" Then I reminded myself: Slow down, Dan; talk slow. I used the toe of my shoe to scuff the dirt a little, pull my ear, look up at the sky, and venture a comment about the weather. Or about the price of beans and corn. Compliment the guy.

"That big tractor looks mighty powerful to this city guy." Only gradually, very gradually, I had learned, bring the subject around to government. I had finally acquired the art of a pause, not to be concerned if a quiet time comes and sometimes seems painfully long. I would never talk about the economics of farming and never met a farmer who was making money. "Tough for a man to make a livin'—price o' corn bein' what it is." I would commiserate about this and also about taxes and often hear complaints about people on welfare.

"Ever hear 'bout those Welfare Queens? They got fancy cars, and I got this old Ford I've had for years. Lemme tell ya 'bout that woman in front of me at the store over in town. Know what she used her food stamps for? Whiskey."

I learned never to ask a direct issue question like, "Where do ya stand on this abortion issue?" Got me nowhere. I had to say, as I did to this farmer, "Met a guy back down the road a piece. Know what he told me? Said folks were upset about these darn abortions; too darn many of them." Then I asked casually, "What're folks 'round here sayin' about that?"

This opened the conversation door, and the farmer told me that his friends were more concerned about their daughters. Mostly, he said, they wondered how the issue would be faced if one of them got pregnant before marriage. We discussed whether parental consent should be required if they were under age. When he said, "Dan, gotta get back to plowin'. God bless you and your family," another useful encounter ended.

On the road and at the after-dinner home gatherings, I learned how to talk with people in a relaxed way about their beliefs and what are now called "values." About "God and family," about "down-home country values," about "loving our country," and how to say, "Ain't America great?" I found that I could say, "Growin' up, I heard a good deal about 'family and God' from my parents, and I've heard that talk a lot when I visit with folks in downstate Illinois. Made me feel right at home. You folks feel that way?" Or I might ask, "I haven't been to church much while on this long walk around the state. Folks around here go to church regular?" This could often get people talking about their religious feelings, and I learned that to many of them, churchgoing was as much a social event as a religious experience. They also stressed how important it was to be able to rely on neighbors at family crisis times and how helpful church members could be at such times.

I had to learn how to really listen. When relaxed and comfortable, people would open up and talk about their problems with government, and it took me a long while to learn that most often they were not expecting to hear any solutions. They just wanted to feel that "somebody important" was listening. "First time I ever talked to somebody like you," they would tell me. And I learned not to be afraid to disagree. On hunting, for example. If any downstater asked me how I felt about guns, I said that I liked them and had always owned a gun. But I didn't hesitate to add that I favored laws requiring gun registration. "Guns can be dangerous, just like cars. If we register our cars, what's wrong with registering our guns?" I may have lost some votes with that frank statement, but I doubt there were many.

One-issue folks were a challenge. For example, it was useless to discuss abortion with either a strong pro-life or pro-choice advocate. I took a simple position: "I do not personally favor abortions and would advise my daughter against getting one, but the Supreme Court has ruled on the issue, and in our system, that's controlling."

### LEARNING ABOUT VALUES

I met many so-called evangelists and fundamentalists and stayed sometimes in their homes. Those I encountered in the Bible belt were not rabid about their beliefs, not about evolution versus creationism, or any other issue. None matched the images pictured by some liberal political commentators. Opposed to abortion and believed in creation rather than evolution, yes; but never with emotion, never with an attitude—more often in a puzzled way. As one farmer put it, "Dan, why do those folks I see on TV get so upset about this? It's just our way of livin' down here."

I learned that what some today call "values" is—to the "ordinary people" I met on the walk—a mixture of many strongly held beliefs about family, relatives, church, honesty, relying on neighbors, raising kids right, taking care of grandma and grandpa, "God Bless America," "Amazing Grace," "Battle Hymn of the Republic," strong respect for men and women in the armed forces, working hard for a living, not being bashful to talk about patriotism, keeping a clean house, knowing what tough times are like, showing respect for the minister and for elders, disliking a lot of what Hollywood stands for, disliking dirty-talk music, dressing properly on Sunday to go to church, solid meals on the table at dinnertime, good manners, not telling dirty jokes or using bad four-letter words in front of women, and perhaps more—all of this is what American heartland folks mean by the word "values." Those folks deserved a better hearing in political circles.

While walking through this part of the state, I met an old and dear friend from law school, John Russell, in Carlinville.

"You're really making progress here in Macoupin County, Dan. The locals are talking about you in the coffee shops, and this is high praise from guys who normally ignore politics."

I welcomed his words like a drink of cool water. John's ten children crowded into the old house, but he wanted my boys to stay with him. So he asked a neighbor to accommodate me for the night. John later worked actively in the campaign. I learned to say the *c* in *Macoupin* like a very subtle *g*, "Ma-GOO-pin." *Gillespie* was "Gill-ISS-pee."

In neighboring Sangamon County, we walked into a country café on the main street of a small town. Its plainness along with its aroma of freshly baked apple pie typified rural America. I walked among the twenty or so customers, greeted them, and spoke to people.

"It's great to be here in New Berlin," I said, pronouncing it "Ber-LIN."

An old guy pulled me aside and said, "Dan, you've got to learn to call it 'New BURR-lin' if you want to get any votes here." One might think I would have learned back in Gillespie to be careful about how I pronounced town names. Miles further north was Bourbonnais, near Kankakee (Kanka-KEE). The junior chamber of commerce was leading a campaign to pronounce the town's name in the proper French, but old-timers persisted in calling their town "Burr-BO-nis." Natives of San Jose, in central Illinois, persisted in calling it "San Joe's."

We neared Springfield. I remembered my history: Vandalia, much further south, was the original capital of the state. And that got me to thinking about the other "capitals." Springfield itself was known at one time as the "Illinois Chili Capital" because of all its chili parlors. We enjoyed a bowl before leaving town. Then there was Taylorville, called the "Rose Capital" because its greenhouses supplied roses to florists all over the state. A little further east was Decatur, the "Soy Bean Capital of the World." West of Springfield, Pike and Henry counties vied for the title "Hog Capital of the United States."

I didn't spend much time in Springfield. This was a voyage to "the folks out there," not to those involved in state government. Needless to say, Governor Richard Ogilvie didn't invite me to visit him either at the state house or at his office in the Executive Mansion,[2] which was then being remodeled. Illinois had the nation's only remaining governor's residence built specifically for that purpose. I dared to dream of living there.

We headed east out of Springfield. A big, weathered barn alongside the road in Rochester bore the message "Vote Dan Walker," painted in large, red letters. I stayed there with a teacher who introduced me to the Chicago Teacher's Union leader and his wife. All three became loyal supporters.

Then came Illiopolis, Niantic, and the sad day in Decatur, about halfway through the twelve-hundred-mile trek, when Dan and Charles left me. They had been constant companions for two months. Dan left to begin Northwestern University School of Law and Charles to finish high school at

---

[2]Years later, when Rod Blagojevich became governor, he became, to my amazement, the first chief executive to refuse to live in the Executive Mansion. To the dismay of downstaters, he preferred Chicago.

Loyola Academy in Wilmette, a Chicago suburb. Saying good-bye to them was tough. The walk never felt the same after that. I hadn't realized how important the boys were to me until they left. Every hour became lonelier. I had taken their camaraderie for granted. Even though we went for miles without talking sometimes, their presence brought reassurance. The boys left separately, each later claiming with true sibling rivalry to have walked the furthest. Charles won that argument by citing the miles he walked with me while Dan's blisters kept him off the road.

When the boys left, it felt like being alone in a cavernous house. The days were long and empty, save for Steve Senderowitz bringing lunch. I felt isolated and marveled at how the pioneers could trudge on day after day, in their westward migrations, with no conveniences whatsoever. I tramped by myself down long stretches of road with few cars and nothing around me but farmland. Cornfield followed cornfield. I still had another six hundred miles to go. Why had I simply assumed I would be able to complete such a venture? What if all of this was for nothing?

At this point, I wanted to simply walk directly up to Chicago and get it over with.

## 15

## *Stories of the Walk*

An icy wind cuts through the inadequate prison jacket I'm wearing as I walk around the quarter-mile track for my daily exercise regimen. The prison is built on an old airfield, and there is nothing, not even a tree, to buffer the frigid sheets of air that blow in from a dagger-shaped arm of Lake Superior. The cold is relentless. I am thinking, thinking, thinking about Roberta Nelson. I do not interpret her refusal to come up to Duluth as meaning we are through, and I imagine ways I might reach her. I can't give up on our marriage.

Cussed determination is something that runs through my very being the way blood runs through my body. This is one rationale I often ponder. How much did that Walker DNA contribute to both my rise and my fall?

My young friend Evan walks alongside me, and I need the distraction of conversation. I know Evan does, too. His friendship is unexpected and most welcome, one of the very few spots of warmth in this bleak place. I don't want to talk to him about my wife, though, or even think about her right now. A prisoner's thoughts often turn homeward and especially toward the parent that had the most impact on an inmate's life. Evan's been talking about his dad recently.

In the middle of our first lap, I say to him, "Your father seems essentially to have been pretty much a calm guy, kind of taking life as it comes. My dad was quite different, a hell-for-leather kind of Texan."

Evan perks up, interested. He likes my stories, bless him.

"Dad's name was Lewis, and he was a world-class troublemaker growing up and a practical jokester all his life. As a kid, he and his ally Brian were lucky to have escaped jail time themselves. Hell, they were lucky they didn't get shot. Brian's mother said she could have raised a perfect son if it hadn't been for that little devil, Lewis Walker."

Evan nods, unsmiling. He still feels depressed over his experience in the hole.

"They lived in east Texas. 'Deep in the piney woods,' my dad used to say. One night, they walked a neighbor's mule onto a wooden platform, which they somehow managed to hoist about four feet off the ground, using ropes tossed over a tree branch. They got up early to hide in the trees and watch as the neighbor came out in the morning and found his mule up in the air."

Evan laughs. "I bet the guy was royally pissed."

"He was, indeed. He swore that he would give a real switch-beatin' to those blankety-blank youngsters up to their damn-fool nonsense again." I shake my head. "He usually got away with his stunts, like the time the boys raided Cousin Bill Ault's watermelon patch and then sold fifteen of 'em to Bill himself at his store for a dime each."

Evan chuckles at this. "And got away with it."

"Well, Bill was suspicious. 'I shay, I shay, Lewis' (that's Dad's mimicry of Bill Ault's speech impediment), 'those look mighty like my melons, and if I'd been in my patch, I'd a' kilt you, sure as shootin'.'"

Evan doesn't seem amused by this story. He pulls his collar tighter against a strong gust. "This guy would kill two boys over fifteen watermelons. And probably never go to jail. 'Course, I guess he was just mouthing off."

"Oh, no. This was no idle threat. In fact, this 'Cousin Bill' once went into the storeroom in the back of his store and caught a boy red-handed, fondling and kissing his daughter. Cursing him roundly, Bill physically kicked the boy out of the store. The boy ran quickly over to my grandfather's house and related what had happened. Charles Anderson Walker gave an order. 'You better go right back to Bill Ault's store and apologize.'

"My dad secretly followed the boy, watching from afar as the boy dutifully went back into the little store. Bill gave him no chance to say a word. Reaching under the counter, he pulled out a double-barrel shotgun and killed the boy."

"Oh, my God!" Evan said. "UN-believable! So, what happened?"

"A customer who saw the killing ran to tell my grandfather—my dad right behind him. Charles took his shotgun down from the pegs over the door and said to his wife as he walked out the door, 'Sally, I guess I'm gonna have to go kill Bill Ault.' By now it was evening, and Charles went to the Ault home. Staying out of sight, my dad tagged along. Charles brushed aside Bill's wife at the door and searched the house until he found Bill cowardly hiding under his bed, whimpering for mercy.

"Charles yelled, 'Cousin Bill, come out and take it like a man. I'm a-gonna shoot you like someone should've done long ago.' Bill Ault kept begging, 'I shay, Cousin Charles, I shay, I shay, Cousin Charles, please don't you kill me.'

"Meanwhile, Lewis's older brother, Boss, had come home to find his mother in tears. When she managed between sobs to tell him what had happened, he ran to the Ault home to dissuade his father from killing Cousin Bill. After hearing his son's arguments and more of Bill's begging, Charles finally calmed down and decided to leave Bill to the law. Bill Ault was tried three times for the killing, and each time, his lawyer got him off with hung juries."

"But there were witnesses. People saw him kill the kid. How'd he get off?" Evan slipped on a patch of ice but regained his balance. Another inmate ahead of us did the same thing. We had reached an area of the track where the mud and puddles still iced over at night.

"My dad said that in those days in east Texas, juries just would not convict a father for killing someone who had 'wronged his daughter.' The times were tough, very tough, and the men were hard, accustomed to violence and killing in a way that's hard for us today to imagine. My dad grew up with those kind of people."

"Must have been some father you had."

I gave this some thought. "*Tough love* describes it. One story captures his Texas way of thinking. I was home on leave from the navy and went to visit with my dad at a shed about a mile from our home. He farmed tomatoes then, and the Mexican workers were sizing the tomatoes before boxing and trucking them into town.

"The phone connected with the house rang, and he answered, 'Yes, Virginia,' and then just listened a while. Saying nothing, he hung up the phone and pulled his pocketknife out of his pocket and hunkered down, sitting on his heels as backcountry folks often do. We watched him take out his little whetstone and commence spitting on the stone for the moisture needed for sharpening.

"The soft swish-swish of the knife blade was the only sound in the shed. Then came a loud knock and there at the open doorway stood a border patrol officer in a neatly pressed khaki uniform with a large, holstered .45-caliber pistol strapped around his waist.

"'Walker!' Silence. Then louder, 'Walker! I know you're here, so speak up!' At this point, Dad stood up, and without a word, swiftly stepped over until he was eye to eye with the officer. Raising his hand quickly, he laid the sharp edge of the knife blade right up against the officer's jugular vein. I could see a tiny trickle of blood."

"Holy sh———!" Evan said.

"I remember Dad's words vividly. Soft, but with deadly menace. 'Young man,' he said, 'you ever seen a man's throat get cut?' Silence. 'Lots of blood goes everywhere.' Silence. Then he said in a harsh whisper, 'Are you listenin'? You hear me?' The two men were almost belly to belly, and neither moved. Then the officer nodded slightly.

"Dad spoke firmly then. 'You better run right quick back up to my house and apologize to my wife. Where I come from down in east Texas, callin' a man's wife a liar is cause for killin'. And if you don't apologize to my wife right now, I'll find you. I'll find you, and I'll kill you. I'll kill you sure as shootin'.' With that, Dad snapped his knife shut, turned his back on the armed officer, and walked slowly over to talk with the Mexican workers who had all backed off but were staring with eyes opened big as quarters."

Evan gave me a skeptical look. "I think this is one of your tales, Gov."

"I was there, Evan. Those are facts. I was stunned. I kept thinking any minute the officer would simply jerk back and then shoot my dad, but that could have been suicide if his throat got cut before he could even get his gun out of the holster. He just turned and left without saying a word. He went back to the house and apologized to Mom. Anyway, we later learned that the officer had accused Mom of concealing 'wetbacks,' as they were called then.

"Mom had insisted there were no illegal workers—in fact, they were all properly green-carded, but the officer had said, 'You're not telling the truth,' and left the house to find my father. That's when Mom phoned Dad."

"So your father took it personally," Evan said.

"No, you're missing the point. It's hard for us to understand today, but years ago, a man just did not tolerate an insult to his wife. Other men would ridicule him if he didn't react strongly. Remember, those men were only a generation removed from the days of dueling, when a man would be called out if he insulted another man's wife.

"Dad wasn't afraid of anyone, but I did see him back down real quick on the few occasions when Mom went on a rampage. She picked her battles, but when she drew a line, such as over cleaning some of Dad's bloody ducks, well, that was that. 'Lewis!' she called out one time when he threw the ducks onto the kitchen sink, expecting her to take care of them. Mom almost never swore, but she did then. 'Lewis, if you want to eat those ducks, you can damn well clean them yourself.' To which Dad replied, 'Yes, Virginia.' Of course, my brother and I wound up cleaning them."

Evan laughs, and it brings a measure of cheer, so I tell more duck-hunting stories, one of how Dad shot seven mallards in flight with only seven shots fired. "He was a force of nature," I say. "He often said, 'Don't get in my way when I'm goin' somewhere.' And he certainly had more than his share of spunk."

"Sometimes, I guess a man has to survive on guts alone," Evan says.

I look at him and nod. "Times like now."

As men often do, we pat each other's shoulder as we part. I head back to resume my job of cleaning toilets. At least it will be warm inside.

---

### NOT SCARING THE MACHINE

Although depressed over the loneliness and boredom of the walk, I could not cut it short. I had to go all the way, no matter how I felt. The cynical reporters would never have let me forget that. Besides, as I thought about it, I reminded myself that the Old Man would never have stood for quitting on a job. So, I kept walking.

Oreana, Cisco, Argenta, Monticello, White Heath.

I finally reached the campus of the University of Illinois in Urbana-Champaign. All along the walk, I made a point of visiting every college I could reach. The campaign had a strong appeal to younger voters, because they naturally hearkened to my rebellion against a political machine, and also because they liked many of my positions on the environment and fair housing. Champaign wasn't very exciting, though, since the fall term hadn't yet begun to bring thousands of students. I walked through Champaign and turned back to zigzag west across the state.

Mansfield, Farmer City, LeRoy, Bloomington.

As September wore on, and I trekked through central Illinois, there was more talk that my opponent chosen by Mayor Daley's slate-makers would be Paul Simon, the incumbent lieutenant governor. I had heard much about him in southern Illinois, where he published a small weekly newspaper and was known at the beginning of his career in the state legislature as an independent Democrat. I had met men and women who were staunch supporters, as well as detractors who predicted he would "toady" to Mayor Daley to get his nod to run for governor with machine support.

My position never varied. A reporter from the *Bloomington Pantograph*—a paper founded by Governor Adlai Stevenson's family—caught up with me in Morton, ten miles west of Peoria. When he asked me whom I would rather have as my opponent in the primary contest, I told him what I told all reporters: "I don't care who they pick. One name on the primary ballot will be Dan Walker. The other will be Daley's boy."

This was the way we played it throughout those months. The "other guy" did not really count as a person. He was just a puppet of the machine. My opponent was always Daley.

Norty Kay showed up with Rich Block, a photographer who often shared RV duty with Steve Senderowitz, and we stopped along the road to talk about the current political situation. Rich said he wanted to get some background shots and then drove off while we stood alongside the millionth corn and soybean field of the trip. Norty took off his glasses and cleaned them with his handkerchief: a sure sign he was thinking of a way to tell me something I didn't want to hear.

"Out with it, Norty," I said.

"Adlai gave an interview yesterday. He stated emphatically that he not only refuses to support you but is openly allying himself with Simon."

I stood there, speechless for a moment, remembering all the work I had done for Adlai and his father. "Well," I finally said. "We always knew his support would be a long shot."

"Yeah," Norty said, "we definitely weren't counting on it, but it sure would have helped."

"Well, we'll just have to win without him."

Rich Block returned, excited about a place he had found for good pictures. When we walked to the site, it turned out to be a vast pumpkin field with great heaps of pumpkins waiting to be trucked away. Rich pointed to a pile well over ten feet in height, stacked with ripe orange pumpkins, some as big as washtubs.

"Climb up on the pile, Dan," Rich said. I obliged as his camera clicked. The picture of me lying lazily on the pile of pumpkins became a part of my permanent collection.

Shortly after that, I spent the night in a bedroom where a big picture of Paul Simon hung over the head of the bed. My hostess apologized for it at breakfast, saying she had somehow forgotten it was there. Then she added, "Dan, we wanted to see what you were like, but I'm sure you'll understand we'll have to vote for Paul if he's the Democratic candidate."

In talking with her, I realized for the first time the confusion that existed over the selection of the Democratic candidate for governor. Some Democrats thought the slate-making to be done in December of 1971 meant picking the Democratic candidates for statewide office, whereas what it really meant was selecting those who would get the support of the regular Democratic organization. The Democratic candidate for governor, I often had to explain, would be the winner of the primary election in March 1972.

Many people could not understand how I could still be a Democratic candidate for governor after the slate-making. That misunderstanding continued for months. And to make matters worse, after Paul Simon was finally picked by the slate-makers, reporters and commentators often referred to him long before the Democratic primary election as "the Democratic candidate for governor." I always wanted to shout, "Hey, what about me?"

Some of the stops in private homes provided good stories for later use while campaigning. Tina was a hostess wearing one of those silver Playboy Bunny pendants around her neck when she met me at her front door and showed me into her very small home that quite obviously had only one bedroom.

"I'll show you your bedroom so you can freshen up. My Jim will be along from the iron foundry in a few minutes."

I remonstrated, "Tina, I can't take your bedroom. I'll just sleep on the couch."

Back and forth we went, until finally she said, "Dan, you must sleep here. I will always want to say that a governor slept in my bed."

That stopped me. She closed the door. The room was barely big enough to hold a double bed and a large dresser. And there on the wall facing the bed hung a collection of prints of half-naked Playboy Bunnies. As I often said when telling this story, after weeks of lonely nights on the road, I didn't sleep a wink that night.

Onward through Chillicothe (pronounced "Chilly-cawthy"), and a round trip across the Illinois River to Lacon and back. The Illinois River was especially beautiful to me, sometimes wide and placid, sometimes narrower and flowing more swiftly. I watched mallard ducks and a few redheads flying back to the river in noisy flocks after going out into the fields, fattening themselves on corn. At a wide span south of Hennepin, I frequently saw fishermen casting for bass near the bank. Men from all over the state came to the Illinois River to fish and hunt ducks and geese.

This river is replete with Illinois history. There's the suicide leap of the Indians at Starved Rock a little to the northeast, Abraham Lincoln riding circuit in the area to argue cases, and illegal gambling flourishing in the area until Adlai Stevenson Sr. and the state police cleaned it out in 1949.

Some of the most interesting people on the river were known as "River Rats." Many of them lived right on the river and were forced to flee in the springtime when the river rose to flood stage, yet they refused to give up their homes. This happened nearly every year. Hunting and fishing seasons were meaningless to these men. They killed what they wanted when they wanted to eat it, and the game wardens pretty much left them alone.

One day while walking alone, I noticed a pickup truck drive by several times. The guy was driving back and forth, looking directly at me each time he went by. The rifle mounted over the rear window of his cab made me nervous, and I turned off at the next side road to walk into a small town. Suddenly, I saw this guy's truck on the other side of the road, and there he was, walking directly toward me with one hand in his pocket. I was scared for the first time on the walk.

The man stuck out his hand when he got near, saying, "Dan, I've been trying for hours to get the nerve to stop and meet you. I've followed your walk all over the state, and you're my candidate, Dan."

The road was full of surprises, this one especially gratifying. I plodded on, approaching La Salle. Vic rarely talked to me on the telephone, but he decided to relieve my boredom and asked Norty to have me call him from La Salle. When I did so, he confided that I was finally being considered a contender—very much an underdog, though, and barely a blip on the political radar screen. I was flattered when I read in a downstate newspaper article, "Walker has an outdoors-rugged look. A corporate Marlboro Man. A political Randolph Scott." And another piece in the *Chicago Daily News* headlined, "Has Walker Scared the Machine?"

"Listen to this," Vic said. "I'm reading from the article. 'Money, lots of it, is rolling in to Walker from limousine liberals throughout the country,' and 'Kennedy people themselves are starting to join up.'"

"Huh! Where are they getting this? Don't these reporters have some slight interest in facts?"

"Actually," Vic said, "a few young people from Robert Kennedy's campaign came over to work on organization and advance."

"Certainly not his movers and shakers, as the article implies. Tell me, has even one liberal in a limo come by dumping money?"

Vic laughed and then grew quiet a moment; then he hit me with the bottom line. "You're getting recognition downstate, but most folks think we have no realistic chance of winning. You're pursuing a quixotic thousand-mile march into political oblivion and, in fact, scaring exactly nobody."

I didn't like this conclusion but obviously couldn't say anything.

Vic went on. "Dave agrees. But this is not bad news, Dan."

"No? Tell me how it could get worse."

"We're laying low," Vic said. "We want those guys to think we can't win. That way, we can sneak up on them, and they won't know what's coming. We've got to blindside 'em."

"Sure. Right. Send me a bucket of ointment, will you? I think I'll just lie down for a month with my feet up."

"Just keep walking, Dan."

### THE QUIXOTIC QUEST

In the La Salle–Peru area, I stayed with the Marders, who, like many other people I met on the walk, would later join the campaign. For some, their lives would change dramatically as a result. Sid and Natalie Marder lived in a small town; he was a plant manager, and she was a housewife with little kids. We had a great evening talking about government and politics. Sid's intelligence and leadership potential impressed me. I made a note to remember him as being useful to me in office if I won the election. I entered Sid after Don Johnson. Don headed a small tradesmen's labor union downstate, and I wanted a savvy labor man who was absolutely not tied to the Chicago labor leaders, all beholden to Mayor Daley.

Out of La Salle–Peru, I headed straight west, passing through Princeton, Sheffield, and Geneseo. Nearing the Quad Cities (Rock Island, Davenport, Moline, and East Moline) back on the Mississippi River, I stayed in a home in a small town and found myself in a bedroom with my hosts' bedroom in between the bathroom and me. I was too embarrassed to walk through, fearing that I would awaken them. I had been drinking a lot of iced tea that day, so I woke up in the middle of the night. What's a guy to do? I looked around the room and found nothing I could use. Finally, I found some little

Dixie cups stacked on the dresser. Well, it took about eight of those cups. Next morning, I wondered how was I going to get rid of the cups, since I also had to go through the kitchen where my hostess was waiting to greet me? So, I sidled through the kitchen on my way to the bathroom with one cup held behind my back.

"Hi! How're you this morning?"

It took eight trips and it was not until the last one that she said, "Dan, what in the world are you doing?"

All I could do was mumble, "Nothing, ma'am. Be right with you." God knows what she thought. (The things a candidate does.)

I left the Quad Cities area and headed up into northern Illinois, roughly along the Rock River, through Hillsdale, Eerie, Lyndon, and Rock Falls. In late September, I first experienced that chilly north wind in the morning hours. Once along a lonely country road through this rich farming country, a farmer pulled his big, green Deere tractor over to the side of the road to let the cars get by, and I walked up to talk with him.

"Hi, I'm Dan Walker, running for governor. Hope you've heard about me."

"Yeah, but I'm not much on this politics stuff."

"Lots of folks don't think I am, either," I responded.

He smiled. "Yeah, so I hear. Them big shots in Chicago don't think much of you. But I kinda' like what you're doin', Dan. Glad you're out here. You sound like a real fighter."

"Mind if I ask a question?"

"Shoot."

"I saw a lot of Caterpillar tractors—'Cats' the farmers called them—down near Peoria, where they've got that huge factory. Guys I talked to at the factory gates really rave about the Cat tractors. What's better 'bout this Deere tractor you're using?"

"I guess loyalty's a big reason I'm using Deere." When he saw the puzzled look on my face, he opened up to talk readily. "My chance to teach somethin' to a politician." He went on. "Back when this was all prairie land," he said, referring to the 1800s, "all over the state 'cept down in southern Illinois was sod. Hard sod. Them settlers found out you couldn't break that sod like they did the land back East. Took strong horses and a steel plow. A guy named Deere invented that plow. Right near here. That plow opened up the Illinois prairie land for farmin'." If I hadn't realized it already, this story taught me about the loyalty of downstaters. If they bestowed on me the honor of their votes, I would also have their loyalty.

In Dixon, Ronald Reagan's hometown, I visited the home of Sherwood Dixon and his son. I had become friends with Sherwood back when I worked for Adlai Stevenson and Sherwood was his lieutenant governor. One small town not too far from Dixon that I loved in northern Illinois was Pecatonica, where for some reason the residents, mostly strong Republicans, took a very strong liking to me. When I walked into town, the greeting surprised me; it was more than heartwarming, it was exciting to me. And then came more excitement.

Several towns back, Norty had told me that the staff talked to my old friend Senator Lawton Chiles in Florida, asking him if he could possibly come to Illinois to give my campaign a boost. Lawton knew, because I had told him, that the pundits gave me very little chance of winning, and yet he agreed to come. I was extremely grateful.

I had said to Norty, "This should be newsworthy, that a sitting U.S. senator would travel a thousand miles to help a guy who is running what people are saying is a losing race. Only a real friend would do that."

And Lawton was a real friend. We had hunted and fished together many times over a period of years. He had shared with me his difficulties in climbing the political ladder in Florida to become a senator, and I had often shared with him my dream of defeating the Daley machine in a campaign for the office of governor that would change the face of politics and government in Illinois. His willingness to join a fellow "walker" in what many saw as a lost cause moved me intensely. Yet we had to scrub the planned press conference, and I personally called Lawton from a roadside phone to tell him that he need not come, that there would be no publicity in it for him. Lawton didn't hesitate.

"I'm coming to see you and encourage you to keep up the fight, Dan," he said, "and if you get some publicity out of it, that's icing on the cake."

On the road from Pecatonica to South Beloit, Lawton caught up with me and joined me for the walk to the Wisconsin border. My sons Dan and Charles also rejoined me that day, much to my delight. And we even got a little press out of it after all. When Lawton and Charles left, I turned south and headed for Rockford, on the home stretch.

Back at headquarters in Chicago, Vic and the rest of the team had frantically been trying to capitalize on the walk, using it to attract volunteers to work in the campaign. Starting virtually from scratch, creating the essential campaign organization was a massive job in a state of this size. Vic had fortunately found just the right man in David Cleverdon, a veteran of the 1964 civil rights movement in Mississippi, who learned organizing with Vic on Chicago's South Side in a congressional campaign. Vic persuaded "Clev" to take charge of organizing my campaign.

Clev later told me, "I knew how to organize a South Side district, but a state with eleven million people?" Yet he jumped right in. "Often, unexpected help came," he said. "I would get a call from someone who would say something like, 'I've got thirty names. Now what do I do?' Bingo! I had a new Walker Coordinator. And I would get the person to meet Dan on the walk." Clev later reported in a letter to me how he and David Caravella launched an instant campaign in Rockford:

> We had eight names, a roll of dimes, and a bunch of index cards. He took the phone in our motel room, I used the pay phone in the lobby, and we split the leads. Each of us called, got more leads, and phoned, phoned, phoned. That night, we spread out the cards on the bed, splitting the names. Next day, [we] were back on the phones with more calling, more visiting, more talking. After three days, surprisingly, we were both getting the same leads and figured we'd about exhausted the independent Democratic universe in Rockford.

So Caravella then took over in Rockford, and an organization was, amazingly, in place when I reached Rockford on the walk. The Rockford newspaper ran a front-page picture of me holding up one of my boots to celebrate the completion of a thousand miles, and the story described the group of volunteers that Clev and Caravella had put together. As I met with all these people, their enthusiasm rejuvenated me. And they loved my stories.

Said Clev, "That's how it went, county by county, city by city, town by town."

After Rockford, a national television crew showed up in Belvidere, home of the huge Chrysler factory. We walked into a coffee shop to see my picture prominently displayed on the wall. The guy who owned the shop, Doc Knapp, was a real fan.

Naturally, I guess, I reminisced as I walked by myself during the long fall days with the leaves turning gold and red, the state a varied and beautiful tapestry. Illinois is not just another farmland state with a big city stuck in it; the land of Lincoln has its own special kind of beauty. Northern Illinois, like the southern part of the state, is hillier—the scenery more varied, with more streams and trees and less flatland. God knows, I learned there are far more hills in Illinois than most of its residents realize.

Illinois politicians who merely fly over downstate Illinois—as all of the state outside the Chicago Metropolitan Area is called—or occasionally visit county fairs or give a local speech and leave, just don't appreciate the state. Sure, they occasionally get to Springfield, Peoria, Rock Island, Champaign, even sometimes to Decatur, Bloomington, and Mt. Vernon, but they get in and get out fast in a plane, or they speed along on the interstates. How do these candidates learn about downstate Illinois? The answer is that, by and large, they really don't.

As I came into Cook County, *Newsweek* magazine's National Affairs section took note of my candidacy, much to my surprise and pleasure, describing my "journey of 1,000 miles" as "Illinois's most energetic gubernatorial candidate in memory." En route, the magazine said, "Walker sampled a stupefying array of home cooking while campaigning against a rotten, sordid system." They quoted me as saying, "If we get a million and a half turnout in the primary, I can't lose."

John Dreiske of the *Chicago Sun-Times* wrote that I had "taken a 1,200-plus mile foot-weary trek to spread a message that 'the Democratic Party in Illinois is a cynical dictatorship.'" He added, "Walker's slashing strokes at the Daley image of cruel bossism" attracted people who admire a man with guts, and that "people love a fight, and Walker is going to give them one that will be absolutely uninhibited."

## 16

## *The End of the 1,197-Mile Walk*

Here I am, walking alone again.

My young friend Evan has joined several other prisoners who appear to be his own age out on the exercise track. We're still friends, but he needs the companionship of other young people. My friend the ex-cop was transferred to another facility, and except for the chaplain's inmate secretary, Jess Kraft, who became a close friend and ally, I have little in common with the other inmates. Most of the guys, I'm sure, feel uncertain about me because I am, after all, a former governor and one of those disdained politicians. In any case, they are standoffish. My loneliness is acute.

I hadn't expected this sense of isolation to descend upon me as an almost palpable fog, even though I have never socialized easily with other people. Sure, I became an expert at one-on-one campaigning, relating to people through handshakes and a few quick words. But that's a far cry from social-izing. I have never been either comfortable with or adept at small talk, nor have I been one to engage in emotionally charged deep conversations.

So, in the prison yard, I stay pretty much apart from the other guys, and they from me. I'm sure they see me as a loner, and that's the way I feel most of the time. This shouldn't seem new to me. I grew up in the backcountry in a family that lived to itself. Except at school, I had little contact with other young people and very few friends except for my brother Waco. I always knew he was there if I really needed company. On beautiful days with blue skies and the warm sun beating down, I often walked the hillsides around Encanto with only my Irish setter Fritz to keep me company. On weekends, I often took my .410 gauge shotgun and went hunting with Fritz, rarely interrupting my reveries only to take a shot at a dove or a rabbit. I occasionally heard a warning rattle and would immediately freeze until I located the rattlesnake, knowing that a sudden move would provoke a strike. Actually, I grew to love solitude.

Yet what I am experiencing now cannot be so described. It is far deeper and more troubling. I am not in the hole, but I am nonetheless in a kind of solitary confinement that exists only for me. Others may experience my same feeling, but the notion of anything like a prison support group for loneliness is beyond ludicrous.

I have never been this lonely before. There has always been someone I could reach out to, like members of my family. Here, there is practically no one. The prison chaplain is not an alternative; he is too close to the guys running the prison.

Mostly, though, despite the loneliness, I could keep at bay an idea that has begun to torment me. I'm beginning to believe that my friends and family were right about Roberta Nelson Walker. I haven't gotten over my shock at her saying everything was my fault, implying that she is innocent of all wrongdoing.

"She's bad news for you, Dan," Vic had told me when I first got involved with her. "What you do with women is your business, but this one's going to hurt you."

My son Dan said, "She's not your kind of woman, Dad."

Even my father had had an almost eerie premonition that was apparently proving true. "Women will be your downfall, Dan. It's in your blood."

Yet to me, R2 is a wonderful person. It can't be she who led me into trouble. We were so happy together. Surely we can somehow iron things out. My mind swarms.

I keep slamming up against a wall with the question, How could things have turned out so badly? I have lost weight, am constantly tired, and suffer from insomnia in the glow of nighttime prison lights. I can't ever stay warm enough, and my chronic bronchitis is back. And I'm so damn lonely.

The only spot of color out in the prison yard looms before me: a tall water tower painted red and white. Its brightness doesn't pierce the gloom of the place. Quite the contrary. Its ladder extends some five stories to the top of the tower and is easily accessible. It offers an alternative to my misery. I could, if things get any worse, climb it and jump before anyone could stop me. But I can't get up the nerve and constantly think that I have got to get control of my thinking. I just cannot resort to that tower.

I turn toward thoughts of Jesus and find companionship. This is no foxhole conversion, though, and involves no sudden epiphany. About a year before going to prison, I had started reading about the beginnings of Christianity in the first century. I learned that, according to many highly placed scholars, much of what I was taught as biblical wisdom was actually myth. I have read all the books written by the noted Catholic scholar Raymond Brown and many others and have decided to write a book about the way pastors in most mainstream Christian churches ignore modern New Testament scholarship. I continue my work on this book while in prison, utilizing research materials sent to me by my children.

The life of Jesus fascinates me. For example, I relate to Jesus's last trip to Jerusalem. He walked those many miles a very lonely and extremely courageous man, facing almost certain death—not, I believe, because he knew God ordained it but because human common sense told him that his persistent troublemaking and constant expression of seditious views were more than the Roman authorities could possibly tolerate.

My experience, of course, pales by comparison. But I, too, had walked with courage in what was called a hopeless quest, anxious to make trouble for the prevailing powers. Also, in my present prison situation, I need reassurance from some source. I cannot find it in the yard. I think Jesus must have been devastatingly lonely, more so than I. Thinking about him gives me solace. I don't compare myself to Jesus. I simply draw strength from thinking about how he summoned courage, confronted adversity, conquered loneliness.

I must not give up.

---

### SOLDIERS IN THE UNINHIBITED FIGHT

I was pleased when, near O'Hare Airport, a wire-service photographer who had taken that famous picture of General MacArthur wading ashore on his return to the Philippines near the end of World War II came out to photograph me. I posed for him as I pointed up to the huge sign at O'Hare saying, "Mayor Daley welcomes you to Chicago."

Next day, Bob Novak, the nationally syndicated conservative columnist, came out from Washington for a brief interview and concluded that I was wasting my time. "Nobody," he wrote, "could beat the Daley Machine by walking along cornfields in downstate Illinois." To the professionals and the political commentators—and opponents as well—I was some kind of dim figure out there walking around the state, proving little or nothing. But for the moment, I wouldn't think about any of that.

Such a good feeling, walking at last into Cook County and then the city of Chicago, knowing that the long physical ordeal was about to end, finally. Not sure how these cityfolk Chicagoans would take to me, however, I was pleasantly surprised at the reaction of people in their cars and on the sidewalk. I had not expected honks and waves on Chicago's La Salle Street in the heart of the financial-legal district, but there they were. Their instant recognition pumped me up. One reporter said people recognized the red bandanna, khaki trousers, wind-blown hair, and deep suntanned face. It was all wonderfully satisfying.

Not only was the long, physical ordeal ending, so was the forced separation from ordinary life with family and friends. I was on a high all that momentous day, and my family's presence lifted me even higher. Amazingly, the last day of the walk was Roberta's birthday, October 31. I couldn't have timed it better. Except for two brief visits on the road, we had been apart for a hundred and eighteen days and nights. A long kiss on the sidewalk was all we could manage as people and photographers watched. Applause broke out during the kiss, embarrassing Roberta. As we headed down La Salle Street to the rally that waited, we walked hand in hand, flanked by Dan and Charles, plus two of our daughters. Roberta had wanted to walk with me as soon as we came into Cook County and neared Chicago, just as she had wanted to come out and walk more on the road. Vic remained adamant that now of all times, and with media coverage more intense than ever before, the image of the solitary candidate returning at last from the long and winding road was critical. Unfortunately, this had hurt Roberta.

We entered the Midland Hotel in the Loop and proceeded to the ballroom. I was expecting an ordinary campaign rally and instead walked into organized pandemonium. Many hundreds of shouting, screaming people had assembled, waving handmade painted signs and throwing confetti. I had never experienced anything like this. There had been no rallies before I commenced the walk, and during the walk, twenty bodies or so was the most I had faced in a home gathering. This was fantastic. I could only think that Cleverdon had done a hell of a job getting this many people to greet me. As I scanned the crowd, I could tell that they were from all over the state. It took me a while to compose myself enough to give them what I hoped would be the rousing speech they expected. I have absolutely no recollection of what I said; my mind was too full of the excitement of the moment.

An intense political campaign for high office often "develops a life of its own." Emotionally, I had—in some sense—separated from Roberta and married the campaign. To varying degrees, this happens to most candidates involved in difficult campaigns that command all of their thoughts and all of their energies for many months. Perhaps it was the uncertainty that made it more all-consuming, being engaged in what was almost a physical fight while totally unsure of the outcome. The campaign would use up all my remaining stores of energy and exhaust my vigor. I had already lost weight and actually lost my sexual drive for the duration of the walk, as sometimes happens to marathon runners and other endurance athletes. I found no way to help Roberta understand what I was going through. I do know that other men in public life have found that their marriages were almost never the same after they commenced politicking seriously.

Still, I felt thrilled to be home. During the one hundred eighteen days on the road, I had walked precisely 1,197 miles, according to the count meticulously recorded by Norty Kay. A staff mathematician computed it at 2,540,000 steps. I had met individually more than ten thousand people— many more than Gallup reaches in a national poll.

Politicians who think they know their constituents by giving speeches, answering questions after speeches, and holding town hall meetings often do not have a clue as to what those folks are really thinking. The government-doesn't-work-for-me feeling shared by so many people is not the same as the populist thinking of many politicians that pits little people against the powerful establishment. That largely misses the point. People don't want a joust with the biggies; they want a leader who they feel can find solutions to real problems. They want to feel that the officials they elect are thinking about them and fashioning a government that works for real people with diverse needs, not some hypothetical voter from a demographic profile or special interest group. They want a candidate who fights for them.

Columnist Mike Royko often made fun of my walk through the state and my frequent emphasis on the people of Illinois. "Walker with his phony red bandanna constantly prates about the pee-pul," he wrote, sarcastically emphasizing that word in a demeaning way. Mike prided himself on being a political liberal, but he never really understood how the people of Illinois felt about their government beyond Chicagoans' feelings about their aldermen.

Mike understood Chicago, but he never understood Illinois, often writing about downstaters as "ignorant hicks." "Rubes" he repeatedly called them in his columns.

I often wondered if I could have extended the walk into the neighborhoods of Chicago, particularly the ethnic areas of the city, learning from them and perhaps giving people there a better feel for what I was all about—a feeling that I cared about them, which was the feeling I generated downstate. But perhaps not. Television coverage of the downstate walk conveyed visually a unique, hardworking candidate, which came through dramatically. This critical image couldn't have been replicated in Chicago. A picture of a wind-blown man wearing khaki trousers and boots, striding day after day down a country road to reach people in small towns, is entirely different from a picture of a man in proper clothes walking down a city street to shake hands with people.

Vic commented years later in a formal "oral history" interview by Sangamon State University about the political significance of the walk:

> I viewed it as most of the media did, as an event to get Dan Walker's name known. I had no idea that it would have such an emotional impact on the voters. It struck some chord I cannot define. Something strange happened, but what it was I did not know. And the mystical, emotional reaction that people had to the walk was mirrored in Dan Walker. . . . in a sense, I think people watched him and said, "That guy's willing to suffer for me. . . ." Dan became almost totally a downstate person. So much that we had difficulty getting him into Chicago because he really felt more comfortable with people downstate.

At the time, though, I seldom thought about the subliminal impact of the walk. The physical impact was often all-consuming. Those who have not undertaken this kind of ordeal don't appreciate the constant, draining physical effort involved in walking, walking, walking all day long under a hot sun, day after day, for four long months.

I encountered a woman some years later who told me that she had a strong recollection of watching from a second-story window in a small town in southern Illinois as my sons and I walked by. I was puzzled because I had not walked in that town. But then I realized that she had somehow made that mental transformation after seeing us on television. Another strange transformation involved the word *work*. My image apparently became associated with this word and was a big part of the walk's impact. A waitress told me, "Dan, I can relate to you. You're out there working. I know what it's like to be on my feet for many hours. . . . I felt you were working for me." And people perceived that I sincerely believed I was, in fact, working for them. My son Dan later wrote a good evaluation of the walk, responding to my request for his retrospective view to be included in this book.

> None of us dreamed at the time it would have such a lasting impact. Over thirty years later, people still approach me to talk about it, often to tell how they came out to meet Dad on the road or waved at him as they drove by, remembering exactly where it happened. Many turned drive-by eye contact and a hand wave into an actual meeting.
>
> One thing and one thing only did it: hard work with constant determination. Dad was always confident this would be rewarded. I watched him learn daily how to listen and how to communicate with folks. With him for many days on the road, I saw that walk become a part of my Dad. Walking fifteen miles or more a day, he had lots of time to digest what he heard and use it as a basis for his thinking.
>
> Then there was the symbolism that I never anticipated, never thought about at the beginning. But I watched it develop as I listened to folks who talked with me after they met Dad. They often repeated what he said about the evils of Chicago Machine politics and what it was doing to downstaters. They saw him as a symbol of hope, that just maybe "hard-workin', walkin' Dan" could make things better for us folks down here.

There was a waitress I met over breakfast at a Holiday Inn when I neared the end of the walk. The marquee had posted "Welcome Walking Walker" on one side and on the reverse side, "Open 24 hours." The waitress described how she felt, how her feet hurt when her long day came to an end. And then she paused and added revealingly, "Now Dan, you take care of your feet, honey."

Soon after concluding the walk, I flew around the state to appear on radio and television with a "thank-you" message to all the people who had received me so graciously. I never let an opportunity pass to couple these thank-yous with repeated onslaughts aimed at the Daley machine. I didn't hesitate to use strong language. "I'm not going to let Daley run the Democratic Party or this state. His cruel bossism has already gone too far. What Illinois needs is people participation, not bosses." I never let up on this theme.

The publicity surrounding the walk tapered off all too soon, which reminded Vic of the absolute necessity of enrolling workers all over the state, his constant theme.

"We have to concentrate on building a statewide organization of volunteers. The captains and committeemen of the regular organization vastly outnumber our current recruits." He faced me. "You should be much more directly involved. You could enroll hundreds more to our corps of volunteers."

### JEWISH ARITHMETIC

Always keeping Dave Green's irrefutable arithmetic in mind—that the machine's maximum turnout was seven hundred thousand, and if one-and-a-half million voted in the Democratic primary election, we could beat the machine—Vic preached constantly that only organization could do it. There was nothing new about this. The key to many a successful campaign is organization. There have to be hundreds and hundreds of warm bodies getting people out of their homes and to the voting places.

Vic's mantra was "To win, we gotta have a candidate with a cause who turns 'em on and an organization that turns 'em out." Our antimachine cause and my walk helped take care of the first; now we needed the second. David Cleverdon—from his minuscule beginning using his handful of index cards—began to build a statewide army. Paid staff, the backbone of the campaign, never numbered more than twenty, and even they missed paydays when funds ran short. Nobody talked about fancy titles since there were none at any time in the campaign; the word from the beginning was plain and simple: *organizing*. Clev's notion was basic: "I want an army of campaign ruffians, hardworking, slightly disreputable, eminently practical, sometimes ruthless young workers who are totally result-oriented."

He quickly discarded the standard plan calling for organization by congressional districts. He began by poring over statewide election returns, population statistics, and registered voter lists, talked with some old-timers, and then used all this to lay out territories based primarily on the highway system and population centers—the centers to find the organizers and the highways to move them around.

Then, he needed money to prime the organizing pump. Beverly Addante set up a silk-screening operation in a vacant loft on the northwest side of Chicago that churned out DAN WALKER FOR GOVERNOR posters. The middle of the poster was a silhouette of the state with my walk route superimposed over it. These were sold to raise funds, and for a while the campaign became a sign manufacturing and distribution business.

Vic sent Clev to see Dave Green. To Clev's surprise, Dave knew the downstate numbers by heart. More important, he knew the anomalies—the places where, for example, a Democratic candidate had not received the votes that the numbers indicated he should have.

Dave said, "You gotta understand something. There's numbers and then there's reality. The way you get reality is with Jewish arithmetic: You take the numbers and then based on what else you know, you add a little here and take away a little there . . . and you get to reality."

Clev learned well from Dave Green, and Jewish Arithmetic also became part of the "Clev M.O."

The original staff members were only Vic, Norty Kay, Nancy Shlaes, and Bill Holtzman—with Dave Green hovering over all (and David Cleverdon soon joining on)—but the staff grew steadily in both numbers and efficiency, even though we rarely had the money to pay them. There were nominating petitions to be signed and filed in December 1971, and formal committees to be set up in each of one hundred counties. To achieve all this, it was Tony Dean—my longhaired assistant in Stevenson's senate race—who came up with the organizers' slogan: "The little campaign inside the big campaign."

The field organizers developed their own identity, esprit, and discipline and prided themselves on generating whatever they needed, from cars to printing to telephones. They rarely gave a damn about conventional wisdom; they wrote their own book.

Clev never let anyone forget that the key to the entire "little campaign" was quantification and accountability. Numbers, numbers, numbers. Establishing individual goals and then rigorously demanding specific, quantified results. Clev laid out the foundation for the statewide organization and built it from scratch in the summer and fall of 1971.

Downstate, some of the Democratic county chairmen—the regulars who looked askance on my campaign—often worked both sides of the street, helping me surreptitiously. As one chairman told Clev, "We aren't supposed to help you, but here's some leads in my county. I don't want to totally piss off Vic. He may someday control the state jobs. You never can tell in this game."

Mostly, though, it was just plain hard work tracking down leads, talking to people, getting more leads, talking to more people, until idealistic or disgruntled Democrats who wanted to make a difference could finally be found.[1]

By late 1971, the "little campaign" was ready for the training phase. A business expert, Beryl Michaels, produced training programs; topflight organizers armed with them, such as Barbara O'Connor, could train a roomful of volunteers into workers as good as the old-fashioned Chicago precinct captains. Clev developed a system of weekly report nights and periodic area and statewide meetings. These sessions were "kick-ass times" when he had to remind organizers that X had damn well better get done within Y days, openly condemning and praising workers. He often acted as a father confessor, but he never hesitated to point out when necessary, "You're just not cut out for this tough contact sport."

David Vaught, later my son-in-law, often flew a plane with my daughter Kathleen from White County in southern Illinois up to Chicago, picking up area coordinators on the way. Somehow, some way, the dedicated workers came from all around the state at regular intervals. Despite Clev's pleadings, Vic was exceedingly reluctant to take me off the campaign trail to attend these meetings. I did attend a few, however, and was each time inspired by the roaring enthusiasm.

As the campaign grew, the printing and distribution of materials (posters, bumper stickers, brochures, cards) became a huge bottleneck. Lori, a young daughter of Lou Silverman, one of our top campaign executives, took over and amazingly solved the problem. She found a motivated trucker, Jerry Cosentino, who donated the services of his fast freight semis to move material all over the state. (Years later, Cosentino would be elected state treasurer.) She also figured out a just-in-time inventory management system long before that concept became well known in the business world. Tens of thousands of Walker Workers all over the state would meet on the same weekend to prepare for canvassing, each needing two to five hundred pieces of literature.

A driver called Clev at 2:00 A.M. "Lake County's all over the road," the driver bawled. Heading for a Lake County workers' meeting with his van full of campaign material, he entered a railroad underpass. The top of his van didn't clear it, and the campaign material was all over the road. Somehow, Lori got the needed materials to the meeting before it ended.

---

[1]Regrettably, I cannot list all those who were leaders, let alone the thousands of spear-carriers, but I must acknowledge a few at the top not yet mentioned. Among the early starters who became leaders as the ranks grew were David Robinson in the middle of the state who later ran for Congress, and Pat Quinn who, as I did, fell in love with southern Illinois and, along with Dorothy Hughes and Pud Williams, covered all those counties. Bob Lehrman managed to find many workers in that Republican bastion called DuPage County. Jeff Diver worked my home county of Lake, another Republican stronghold. Jim Gitz and Mary Brady focused on eastern Illinois, and on the other side of the state, Mike Curran found organizers in what is called "Forgotonnia" by the folks in the western counties along the Mississippi River who felt deserted by state government.

The working day for top volunteers commenced late in the morning and usually lasted until midnight. In a report he later prepared for me, Clev described the whole campaign volunteer experience:

> It usually took just one success, like raising enough money to put phones in the office . . . to get a worker hooked on being effective. One by one, they began to believe in themselves. Improvising new ways to recruit . . . riffs on basic organizing . . . drives to get Walker signs up in windows, designating volunteers as . . . Walker Walkers, Walker Talkers, and Walker Workers, raising "Dollars for Dan." There were . . . weekend phalanxes of college kids to blanket an area like locusts, setting up mini phone banks and local rallies, making local mailings, opening offices. . . .
>
> Sometimes they excited me by achieving results going far beyond their assigned goals, doing things I had never heard of. They fought each other for even an hour of Dan's time, since his presence in their area meant more workers. . . . They fought for and hoarded campaign materials. Their energy was palpable, ever present. . . . They had only one thing on their mind and it wasn't "pro choice," the environment or education or any other issues like that. Or even being nice to each other. It was winning. I remember a week before the primary election, looking at the big map of Illinois on my office wall and realizing that nowhere in the state was there any group wanting Paul Simon to win in the extremely intense way that my organizers wanted Dan to win. Our "little campaign inside the big campaign" had succeeded beyond my dreams.

Because of his dedication and even his toughness, Clev's army of volunteers grew to 105,000, mostly young and all dedicated to the cause. Our poster person, Beverly Addante, sent Clev a heartfelt compliment: "For all the times you 'kept the faith' even when there was no money and no hope . . . thank you. For all your passion in the process of creating something bigger than all of us . . . thank you."

While I didn't come into contact with the organizers much because I was busy doing personal campaigning, Vic told me about them to keep my spirits up.

"The excitement exceeds anything I've experienced in other campaigns," he said. "There is a euphoria out there among the workers."

I was filled with hope at our progress, yet the primary election was just months away, and we were still far down in the polls, though Vic and Dave made a point of shielding me from the specifics. Even with Dave's Jewish arithmetic, I knew our battle was still uphill.

## 17

## *Shaking a Million Hands*

As much as I have other rogue elements "in my blood," as my dad would say, I also possess the saving grace of optimism always stirring around in my soul. At least, I hope it will save me. I actually slept well in my prison bed last night and am feeling better today. I am expecting a visitor.

It isn't my wife, yet I'm looking forward to this meeting. I shower and groom with care, steeling myself against the inevitable strip search. When I approach the guard in the visitors' building as he's slipping his hand into a white rubber glove, I decide to mentally visit with my dad as a way of distracting myself. What pops into my mind, though, is the story I often used on the walk when people asked how I got the guts to tackle the Daley machine in a campaign to become governor against such overwhelming odds.

The guard gives me a bad time, but I can almost ignore him as I remember my constant reply to the "guts" question: Risk-taking, going against the odds, had been ingrained in me by my father—usually through the stories he told about his involvement in outlandish adventures, such as his brief stint with Pancho Villa, the notorious Mexican bandit and revolutionary in the World War I years. A supporter of Pancho enlisted my father's help in Juarez, across the border from El Paso where Dad had left a job telegraphing for the railroad. Pancho needed a telegrapher who could lull the Mexican army's trainmaster in Juarez with reassuring messages about a movement of empty railroad cars when the cars were really loaded with Pancho's soldiers. The cars with the hidden soldiers were backed into Juarez in the middle of the night. Dad had helped perform the Trojan Horse mission, and Pancho's men captured Juarez while the Mexican army slept.

In his book *Intervention*, John S. D. Eisenhower, son of the famous Ike, corroborated the role of a telegrapher from El Paso in Pancho's escapade. I always ended the story by saying, "If Dad could risk fighting with that bandit Pancho Villa against the Mexican army, why can't I take on Richard Daley?"

The strip search is over, and I'm putting on my clothes, telling myself the experience wasn't much worse than a visit to the proctologist. The visitor for whom I have willingly endured the search is Mary Bucaro, one of those fantastic organizers who joined our team in Springfield. I'm amazed and grateful that she has come; I'm happy to see her. She has driven all the way up from Chicago to Duluth and submitted to the visitor screening process, surrendering her purse and anything the guards found the least bit suspicious, such as jewelry or anything metal. We hug each other in greeting, and I see the tiny sparkle of a tear in one eye.

We sit at a table, and she hands me papers, which the guards have no doubt examined carefully. I had managed to call Vic from prison to request help with a petition for parole after listening avidly to the talk among inmates sentenced under the old law about their experiences with the parole board. Old-timers agree that a lot depends on your lawyer. And there are a few in the nation who have built a reputation for parole board success. One in particular appeals to me because he knows the members of the parole board in Kansas City that would act on my petition, but it would mean a $10,000 retainer plus $200 an hour if his time went over fifty hours.

I needed some fund-raising to pay the legal fees. Such petitions aren't normally considered until a prisoner has served two years, but I am told that exceptions are occasionally made. I have decided to give it a try since I have nothing to lose.

"Your friends still love you, Dan," Mary says, smiling.

"The funding came through?"

"It did, indeed. Your reliable supporters are going to pay the legal fees needed to file this petition."

I hug her again, picturing the faces of those generous souls. "Well, this is wonderful news itself, no matter what else happens."

"We're engaging the lawyer you picked, but we can cut expenses if we draft the petition carefully ourselves." She points to a section. "The only problem area is here, Dan. Are you willing to detail your wife's culpable activities that contributed to your conviction?"

Now here is a tempting thought, if only for a brief moment. I picture my second Roberta's lovely face. I am furious with her and disillusioned, but I cannot bring myself to make her suffer the torments of a possible indictment.

"No."

Mary looks up at me, concern in her mild brown eyes. "You realize that playing up such participation could possibly minimize your own responsibility."

"It also smacks of just pointing the finger at someone else," I say.

She nods, sighing.

I pat her hand, and we chat a little longer. A buzzer indicates that visiting period has ended, and Mary leaves. I endure another strip search before reentering the prison grounds, but it doesn't bring me down. I'm not wildly optimistic, but I'm still thinking of my dad and Pancho Villa tricking the Mexican army. This story of his outlandish spirit helped me on the walk, and it can help me now. I walk back to my job and, though a bitter late spring wind is blowing and my hands are a bit blue with cold, I hum "La Cucaracha" as I stab cigarette butts.

"What are *you* so happy about?" my least favorite guard asks me.

---

### SHOOTING FOR THE MOON

Vic decided we needed more volunteers from the Chicago area. "Home gatherings!" he announced. "Or call them 'coffees,' whatever. This will be the best way to recruit workers. Through these coffees, we'll excite volunteers to become activists. Coffees in the morning, coffees in the afternoon, coffees in the evening, coffees as long into the night as possible."

Every day, except for the few days involving media events or trips to headquarters to solicit campaign contributions, I attended coffees. Just as the walk had absorbed all my time for four months, these gatherings monopolized my time throughout November and December of 1971.

Fortunately, four months of walking had totally changed me as a campaigner. I was confident with both one-on-one campaigning and motivating people in small meetings with brief but warm, intense talk that would reach both minds and hearts. I had to convince them that I was not just an unrealistic Man from La Mancha—which to my way of thinking, I never was in the first place—and that we had a practical program.

The routine was the same for up to eight to ten coffees a day from 9:00 A.M. until close to midnight. Organizers prepped people, so when I arrived, I immediately went from person to person, greeting each with a warm smile and memorizing names. I had already learned on the walk how to work the room, how to always remember where I started. Then, I would sit down for my informal pitch, building to a quietly impassioned conclusion about the need for people's involvement.

Answering questions was often the best part of the program. One of the most frequent was, "How will you, as an independent guy, be able to work with the legislature?"

I answered, "For twenty-five years, I've heard about the need for a governor who can play the game. Well, pardon me, but where the hell has it gotten us?"

The organizer was prepped to interrupt, saying that another meeting was waiting. I then stood up and worked the group again, repeated names, thanked the host, and left. Immediately, the organizer took over to make an impassioned pitch for workers. I did more than three hundred of these coffees before the holidays. Vic and Dave Cleverdon figured that we had signed up over three thousand new workers. It was hard work, but absolutely essential. At the same time, we knew that we had to have a constant theme, or "mission statement," as it is now called. Mine was, indisputably, "Change the System."

In December 1971, Mayor Daley's slate-makers almost seemed to prove our point about the secretive power of the machine leaders. They met in a secret session to pick candidates for statewide office. Paul Simon for governor, Neil Hartigan for lieutenant governor, Roman Pucinski for U.S. senator, and Thomas Lyons for attorney general. The last three were all Chicago ward committeemen.

I immediately stated to the press, "Never before has the Machine dared to ask the voters of Illinois to promote three ward bosses into high office." I immediately challenged Simon to debate the issues and join me in making full disclosure of all personal income and all campaign contributions. Simon refused.

I spelled out again my distaste for what I called "the club system of politics" that controlled both parties. The Republicans may have had a few different ground rules, but the game was essentially the same. The elected officials and their associates were the club members, the insiders, and the public was on the outside. Patronage jobs and political contributions permeated and controlled the system. "Pay to play" was the name of the game. Issues counted hardly at all. Until I came along, every governor including Adlai Stevenson had a patronage assistant who wielded power at the state capital.

How could voters tolerate such a system?

A critical part of the Illinois system is party registration. When a person votes in the primary, that involves party registration, and both name and party choice are recorded in the county clerk's office—a standard practice. In 1971, party registration bound the voter to only vote in that party's primary for two full years, even if there was another intervening election. Party registration was public knowledge, and this inhibited changing parties. For example, registered Republicans I met on the walk who might want to vote for me would have to face the fact that their asking for a Democratic ballot would label them publicly as a registered Democrat. This could be troublesome or even job-jeopardizing in heavily Republican territory downstate. For reasons like these, many people downstate do not vote in the primaries, thereby avoiding party registration.

With the "regulars" though, party binding was essential. This party-bound, patronage-oriented, pay-to-play system was strongly entrenched in 1971 and particularly strong in the office of the secretary of state because it handled all drivers' licensing and motor vehicle registration functions and thus had an abundance of patronage jobs all over the state. And it was strong, too, in all the agencies under the governor, operating fully under Democratic governors Adlai Stevenson and Otto Kerner. Neither Adlai Stevenson III nor Paul Simon as legislators and state officials challenged this system.

Neither did any of these men ever try seriously to upset the Chicago machine's apple cart. Bowing to Daley was a part of their approach to Illinois politics. In government, they also never challenged the system's custom that Democratic county chairmen "owned" certain state jobs, picking the men or women who would fill them. And none of these men ever spoke out against that most odious part of the club system of politics: the forced use of state employees to raise money for political campaigns.

I hasten to say that Kerner, Simon, and the Stevensons—father and son— were never venal, never dishonest. And, to their credit, each generated his own image, his own issues, seeking to improve government. Nor did they turn their heads while others around them "made out"—a practice zealously followed in the Chicago machine. But when the chips were down at critical junctures, each managed to give Daley and his machine the power they wanted, and each allowed the venal practices described above to continue. They were unusually adept practitioners of the club system of Illinois politics because they managed to be a part of that system while appearing to be above it. I found it depressing over the years that these men often bragged of their independence as they began the fight for political office, but once secure in office, soon joined the "kowtow to Daley" chorus line to preserve their tenure.

I was determined not only to become governor, but to become a governor who would break the mold. Just before 1971 ended, I had dinner one night with Wally Schirra, the famous astronaut and a Naval Academy friend. Wally, with his well-known sense of humor, cracked that he, too, knew what it was like to shoot for the moon.

### IGNORE ME AT YOUR PERIL

Obviously, campaigns cannot be won without large sums of money—although we came close to trying to prove that they could be. Fund-raising was constantly in a crisis mode. Big contributions were impossible, so we resorted to a statewide "Two Dollars for Dan" campaign that didn't bring in much money. We never solved the fund-raising problem.

Immediately after the holidays, I rose before the cold dawn to greet workers at factory gates because those blue-collar votes were so essential and then repeated the ritual when they streamed through the gates going home. Many candidates viewed this as a chore, but not me. I loved it and established an easy rapport with the workers, kidding with them as they came through the gates.

"Hi, I'm Dan Walker, running for governor, and I need your help."

"I know what workin' on the line means. My feet still hurt from that walk."

"Your bosses are for the Republicans, so I need your help."

If there was a bar nearby, I would work the bar after I finished handshaking at the gate, continuing a stream of patter with the workers and occasionally tossing back a beer, to their cheers.

When the United Auto Workers (UAW) endorsed my opponent Paul Simon, we determined to take the membership away from the UAW officials. And we did. At UAW plants in Decatur, Peoria, Danville, and Chicago, I bonded with the workers—mostly men, but there were some women. They responded over and over as they streamed through the gates, showing their feelings in different ways: a hand salute by a man walking by, shaking a fist with an arm raised while saying nothing.

Or, more vocally, "Go get 'em, Dan!" Or, "I'm with you, Dan!" Even, "F—— the bosses, Dan! I'm with you!"

Shopping centers during the day and evening. Shaking hands constantly, asking for votes and keeping up the patter. Then I visited a bowling alley one day, and the advance man reported excitedly back to Vic.

"They're Dan's kinda folks. He really turned them on."

So, Vic put bowling alleys, bowling alleys, and more bowling alleys on my schedule. I quickly learned to avoid walking on the hardwood area in the lanes, carefully making my way to the seats where players watched their teammates bowl.

"Hi, I'm Dan Walker, running for governor. May I visit? What's your name? Mary, how's your game tonight? I promise to bring you good luck; after shaking my hand, you'll get a strike."

Or, "Sure glad my name's Walker, not Runner. Let me watch your form, Jim."

They always liked it when I'd say, "This sure is hot work. How about a sip of your beer?"

It was hard work, hour after hour, day after day, but I enjoyed the camaraderie—up to a point. After working five or six bowling alleys as the nighttime hours went by, I would be hugely relieved when I saw on the marquee that the next stop had only four or six lanes. On the other hand, I'd quail when, around 10:00 or 11:00 at night, the sign advertised "32 lanes." Or worse, 64.

We finally enlisted the help of a consultant from Washington to seek dollars outside Illinois. Learning of this, some reporters proclaimed that I was raising big money from wealthy "limousine liberals"—a phrase they evidently considered wickedly witty enough to reuse. The *Chicago Tribune* even ran editorials attacking us for outside fund-raising, condemning us for nonexistent contributions, although I do remember a fun trip out to Hollywood, where I stayed and played tennis with Paul Newman. Back home, it was rumored and reported that I reaped big returns. If only that were true; I came home with pledges totaling less than $10,000.

My actual campaigning was almost completely ignored by the media. Only in the last couple of weeks did reporters make an attempt to come out to cover me, and their photographers rarely came along with them. Even when they did, they would stay only long enough to ask a couple of quick questions and perhaps get a picture. No interviews of consequence with me or the people with whom I was campaigning. No one tried to get a feel for what was happening with the voters. But Vic, Dave, and Norty were convinced that somehow the message was getting through that I was working hard day and night, carrying my message directly to people, just as I had during the walk. Bypassing the system, ignoring the establishment.

I knew I had succeeded one morning at an El train station platform on the near South Side where I shook hands with people going to work. A *Chicago Daily News* reporter showed up and was watching when one of those magic moments happened, just as it had months earlier down on Route 37 outside West Frankfort in southern Illinois when people swarmed around me and wanted to make personal contact. Suddenly, people—lots of them—began coming over to me, not waiting for me to go to them. They wanted to touch me, shake hands, clap me on the back. Some went on their way without stopping and just yelled, "Go get 'em, Dan!" or "Keep fightin', Dan!" over their shoulders as they headed for their trains.

In this strong Daley machine territory on the South Side, I was really taken aback at the unusual crowd response. A few days later, I encountered the same reporter and asked him about the incident.

"You saw that crowd reaction right in the middle of Daley machine territory, Jim. Why didn't you describe it in your article the next day?" I will never forget his words.

"Dan, by the time I got back to the newsroom, I persuaded myself that it couldn't have happened."

The reporter's obliviousness deeply disappointed me. But I had personally received a much-needed shot of adrenaline that helped me get through those tough Chicago winter days. I felt, just as I had on that day down in southern Illinois, that I was really getting somewhere.

I reported enthusiastically to the team. "The crowd's reaction at the El station was amazing. It's keeping me going. I think we're on the way to winning."

Vic promptly said, "You gotta cool it, Dan."

Dave said, "Remember that we want Daley, Simon, and all the establishment folks to continue with their comfortable feeling that you are tilting at windmills."

"I know," I said.

Norty chimed in. "Our game plan is to sneak up on 'em."

Again, I said, "I know."

Vic said, "I pray every day that they won't realize the depth of our support until it's too late."

We had conversations like this over and over.

We did get some breaks. One morning, I was riding in a car with Norty when I heard a news report on the radio. "Paul Simon announced today a proposal to substantially shift the state's financial support for elementary and secondary education from the property tax to the income tax."

Excited, we found a telephone and reached Bo Cutter who was then in charge of research on campaign issues and would later become a high-level budgeteer for Jimmy Carter. Bo talked to Vic, who immediately jumped at the opportunity. Armed with huge charts showing the dramatic income tax increase that would result from the Simon proposal, I boarded a small plane early next morning, flying to press conferences in every television market in the state. This made both evening television news and next-day newspapers all over the state.

The proposal to increase income taxes at that point was a bad mistake by Paul Simon. Many people from that day forward associated him with the hated income tax that Richard Ogilvie had worked hard to impose on the state just a few years earlier. I was able to take the high road: "Nobody likes the income tax, but we had to have it to keep the state solvent. However, I am solidly against increasing that tax. I will fight every day as governor to keep from raising taxes." Paul became the "raise-taxes liberal," and I became the "hold-the-line-on-taxes conservative."

We broke new ground in political campaigning. With no money for television commercials, we had to try for what is called "free TV" by generating news ourselves. I would do a "media availability" at an outdoor site that I could use for a campaign statement. For example, I would appear at a polluted river, a decrepit highway bridge, or a fire-destroyed building that I could link to machine politics at a time that allowed the film to reach the editors putting together the evening news.

Making the 6:00 news was good, but hitting the nightly 10:00 news was much better. A thirty-second spot there proved to be better than a commercial costing over a thousand dollars. At that time, most political reporters and commentators were preoccupied with what appeared in the newspapers, not aware that television was becoming a primary force in political campaigns—another feature of our "sneaky" campaign.

Physically, the hardest campaigning after the walk was handshaking at the commuter train stations in downtown Chicago. Mobs of people are moving rapidly from trains in the morning and to trains in the evening. A worker stood behind me holding high a sign that read, "Meet Dan Walker." As people streamed by, I tried to make eye contact as I shook hands with as many as possible, grabbing for hands and repeating constantly, "I'm Dan Walker and I need your help." The constant effort to make eye contact with people streaming by on both sides soon made me dizzy. Losing my balance, I would have to take a brief break before resuming the arduous campaigning.

I'm confident that I shook well over a million hands. Vic, Dave, and I are convinced that it reinforced the "hardworking" theme. Exhaustion dragged at me, but then something would come up to give me a lift, like surprisingly good responses or the unusual letter I received from the officials of downstate Clinton County.

For several years, the letter said, they had been fighting for improvement of crowded, dangerous, two-lane Route 50 that ran east from St. Louis across the state. The governor had not kept promises for a new four-lane highway, and I had met with a group of Clinton County citizens on the issue. Soon thereafter, in apparent response to what they saw as my intervention, the director of transportation came to Clinton and announced that work would soon start on a four-lane highway. The letter concluded, "Dan, it was you who got those guys to take action." Actually, neither the writer nor I knew whether the Ogilvie administration worked on the highway because of my campaigning or whether it was a coincidence, but I didn't hesitate to take advantage of it. In any case, the folks down in Clinton County were convinced I was their champion.

Roberta and all the kids, when not working or in school, played major roles in both campaigns. The boys spent two summers campaigning with me, and Roberta was all over the state. Kathleen was most often in southern Illinois, where she had met her future husband, David Vaught, a full-time organizer for the campaign. Julie, Robbie, and Margaret helped out mostly in the Chicago area. Statewide, it was truly a family affair.

As the end of the primary campaign drew near, Vic and Dave would only tell me that it was close. We desperately needed television commercials, but we had no money. I finally decided to gamble. I exercised my options to buy Montgomery Ward stock at a previously set price and then sold the stock for the market price, netting about $350,000. I couldn't hold the stock for the requisite period, though, and would have to pay a stiff tax on the profit at income tax rates instead of lower capital gains rate—a tremendous difference that would hit me hard at tax time. Incidentally, I had publicly disclosed my tax returns and listed all assets at the time I resigned my positions at Montgomery Ward—the first candidate for governor who had ever made such a complete personal financial disclosure. My opponent, Paul Simon, made no such disclosure.

I loaned all the stock option proceeds to the campaign, and every cent went into television commercials. Vic and Dave persuaded the highly rated New York television specialist David Garth to produce commercials featuring the walk. Soon, I could gleefully report to Dave Green that the commercials were biting.

"Dave, the people I meet use phrases they could only have picked up from the commercials."

Dave Green also loaned substantial sums to the campaign, and we occasionally commiserated about what would happen if we lost. We joked that we would have to find some place where nobody could find us. The prospect for me would include no assets, no job, nothing saved for retirement, nothing for college education for the kids, and an overwhelming debt. To make matters worse, I had not told my wife that all our savings and all of those stock option profits we had counted on for our nest egg had been invested in the campaign. There's an old Western saying: "Only a damn fool bets his ranch." Well, that's exactly what I did.

# 18

## *Election Night*

Five guys are playing Texas Hold 'Em in their regular high-stakes poker game in the rec room. While inmates aren't allowed to have any money in their possession, some have bank accounts on which they write checks, and some—including convicted drug dealers who have lots of money—use IOUs.

I have never backed away from risk-taking and would like to join the game, but the betting is way beyond my means. One of my father's constant teachings was, "Don't ever play poker for money you cannot afford to lose." However, walking by, I stop to watch the game, as I often do. I overhear one player say to the guy next to him, "There's a floating craps game in the john in Barracks 102 at 1:00 A.M. tomorrow night." This is exactly the kind of thing I do not want to hear. I want to be able to say, if asked, *"I don't know anything about it."*

That same player continues, "Winner on big bets can get a whore or a bottle." This brings low whistles and excited comments.

"What about the guards?" a new inmate asks.

"They mostly ignore it. Who knows? Maybe there's a payoff."

My curiosity overcomes my caution, and I break my rule against asking questions about things like this. "I can't help but wonder how in the hell they get a bottle, let alone a woman, into this place?"

A couple of the men eye me a little suspiciously, but obviously I already know about the craps game, so a few details won't make any difference. One man almost my age answers me. "Easy. Some guys take a chance and go over the fence to buy liquor at a bar near the prison or get it from a pal who waits somewhere. For the woman, someone on the outside brings her to the fence. There's a couple of places where it's real dark. Somebody keeps an eye out for the guards, and when the moment's right, over she comes."

*Over the fence. How dumb can they be?* I say, "You guys hear what happened to those two fellows I played bridge with?"

They hadn't heard the story. "They went over the fence, one because his wife was divorcing him, and he couldn't get a twenty-four-hour pass. He didn't come back on his own, and they caught him."

"They usually do," the player says, executing a fancy shuffle of the deck.

"They gave him an additional five years," I say, "and a transfer to maximum security. The other guy was an alcoholic, and he used to make regular trips over the fence. His girlfriend would meet him at a liquor store, and then he'd come back with liquor. The guards caught him, of course, so he got three more years and a transfer to maximum."

"Probably worse than the original sentence," another player says.

"The Bureau of Prisons wants us to get their message," I say.

I know what it is to want something bad enough to take crazy risks. After all, I had gambled my family's financial security because I wanted to become governor.

And what I want now is to see my wife. Badly.

---

## WHAT'LL YOU DO WHEN YOU LOSE, DAN?

I repeatedly challenged Paul Simon to a debate, but he ignored me. Once, we made a side-by-side talk-show appearance on a television program hosted by Irving Kupcinet (the *Chicago Sun-Times* columnist who wrote under the name "Kup").

Vic and Dave lined up by telephone a group of people, chosen at random, to watch the program and make before-and-after choices. We were all amazed at the results. The watchers were two-to-one against me before the show and two-to-one for me after. Although I had thought I was too soft, viewers thought I had clobbered Simon. That taught us a lesson about television appearances: Be careful not to appear too hard, too tough.

Anyway, when Simon continued to refuse debates, we set up a faux debate layout with Paul's picture displayed on a chair and his voice coming out of a recorder, stating a position to which I responded. This ploy got lots of attention all over the state. I continued to hit hard on the scandals that followed the exposure of "Shoe Box" Paul Powell, the secretary of state who hoarded hundreds of thousands of dollars found stuffed into shoe boxes in his hotel apartment after his death, and the two justices of the Illinois Supreme Court who were scandalized for conflicts of interest. Our message: the corruption had to stop.

Our attorney, Bill Goldberg, then came through with a strategic legal challenge. He had been working with the campaign part-time as a volunteer but joined the staff full-time. I knew Bill from when I brought him into the Hopkins, Sutter law firm because of his brilliantly analytical mind—over the opposition of a senior partner who didn't want any Jews in his law firm. I had threatened to quit if a lawyer of Bill's credentials couldn't be hired. Begrudgingly, the senior partner finally backed down, and Bill was hired.

Bill did his homework and came up with a lawsuit that would score an important legal victory. Working with fellow lawyer Andy Leahy, Bill persuaded the federal court to hold unconstitutional the Illinois law locking in party registration for two full years, with the result that people who had registered Republican in 1970 could now vote in the Democratic primary in 1972. This decision was handed down just twelve days before the election, and we devoutly hoped this would permit us to persuade thousands of former Republican voters to "switch this time and vote for Dan."

Campaign emotions ride a greased roller coaster. Our rush of pleasure over the legal ruling was a real high, but disappointments soon tumbled down on us. Every newspaper in the state endorsed Paul Simon. The fervor of the staunchly conservative *Chicago Tribune* surprised me. After all, Paul was a strong liberal, and I was more conservative and had been a prominent member of the Chicago business and legal establishment. No matter. Daley was sacrosanct, and Daley was for Simon. Downstate, the media kept up the mantra: "Dan may be a decent guy, but he can't win."

"Your job," Vic stressed to me, "is to maintain constant optimism."

This was especially difficult when reporters repeatedly pressed for an admission that I could lose.

"What'll you do if you lose, Dan?"

"What'll you do when you lose, Dan?"

That made me mad, but I held my temper until one day when I lost my cool and said to a *Chicago Daily News* reporter, "Oh, all right. To put an end to this tiresome line of questioning, I'd undoubtedly go back to the practice of law."

I'll never forget the next-day headline, "Walker Concedes Defeat."

Six days before the election, I walked into the pressroom in the Springfield state capitol building to emphasize my optimism to the assembled reporters. This was hostile territory since former small-town newspaper publisher Paul Simon was a decided favorite of theirs. Most not only expected but also wanted me to lose. One went so far as to say to my face, "Paul's entitled to win this primary and then take on Ogilvie. You shouldn't be trying to take this away from him. He's entitled."

I had heard this illogical, even absurd, entitlement notion many times. If Daley had endorsed Tom Foran and not Simon, no one would be talking about how unfair it was of Daley to take away Simon's entitlement. So, I ignored it and them and announced with bravado, "This will be the biggest upset in recent Illinois political history. I can sense it at every factory gate, every shopping center, every bowling alley. My candidacy has taken hold, and we're going to win."

They didn't laugh, but disbelief registered on many faces—cynical disbelief accompanied by more than a whiff of personal dislike.

We had taken no polls, because we weren't able to afford them, and consoled ourselves that in any event, polls are largely meaningless in a primary election largely controlled by turnout. I was told, depressingly, that many independent liberals on Chicago's North Side and in the University of Chicago area on the South Side where we had hoped for support were talking about going strongly for Paul Simon. The Independent Voters of Illinois endorsed him. This large independent liberal organization in Chicago and the newspapers kept up their barrage of support. Many continued to berate me for having dared to challenge the popular lieutenant governor for a position he had earned.

Shortly before the election, we read that Simon's campaign manager had personally polled the important downstate Democratic county chairmen. They confidently predicted Simon victories in their counties, and Simon's manager, Gene Callahan, quoted them as promising, "We'll carry our counties by a margin of seven to one or eight to one." And, of course, Mayor Daley assured Simon publicly that he had Chicago and all of Cook County in his pocket.

### PRIMARY ELECTION EVE

No candidate had beaten the Chicago machine since 1934, and Daley had immeasurably strengthened the Cook County organization since that time. I was personally exhausted and very nervous when we assembled on election evening at the Allerton Hotel on Chicago's near North Side. I stayed with my family in one suite, knowing I would only be in the way in the hotel conference and meeting rooms where Vic De Grazia, Dave Green, Bill Goldberg, Norty Kay, Dave Cleverdon, Nancy Shlaes, Mary Parrilli, and others were busy on the telephones. Hundreds of workers assembled in a hotel ballroom downstairs, with more continually streaming in as polls closed.

Anticipation increased as the hours passed, and the television returns were slow and sporadic. Finally, about midnight, I went over to huddle with the staff.

"Vic," I said, "we need to report something to the workers waiting down in the ballroom." They were exhausted but keenly excited and anxious.

Vic shook his head. "No." He was always in touch with workers in critical precincts, getting counts that would help predict what was happening statewide. "We're ahead, but not by much. It's very close, so we just can't express any optimism yet. If our poll watchers in Chicago think we've won, they might leave their posts, and the Machine'll steal us blind." It was a given that the actual poll workers were machine people perfectly capable of "miscounting" votes if our people left.

Another hour went by, and the tension grew unbearable. "Vic, I gotta know. The volunteers are going to give up and go home. We have to tell them something one way or the other."

Vic turned to Dave. "What do you think?"

Dave took off his glasses and rubbed his eyes. "I need privacy." He took his key precinct tabulations into the bathroom. "I'm going to sit on the throne and use my Jewish arithmetic."

It seemed a long time before Dave emerged, expression unreadable. "Tell 'em we've won," he said. The news jolted me like an electric shock. Vic nodded his agreement, and I left the suite, heading for the ballroom with Roberta and all the kids, plus key staff people. Before a riotous, screaming, jumping crowd, I took the mike. When they calmed down, I stood silently for a moment to build anticipation and then said, simply, "You won; you did it. We've done the impossible. We beat the Machine."

Bedlam.

It was an astonishing, spectacular victory, totally unexpected by the Daley machine, Paul Simon, all the regular Democrats, all the commentators, and all the pundits. And the next morning, Daley announced publicly on television, without enthusiasm, that he and the entire Democratic organization would support my candidacy.

In my family's suite—among the litter of Styrofoam coffee cups, soda cans, beer bottles, pizza leftovers, paper plates with chicken bones and limp coleslaw, ashtrays filled to overflowing, and thick smoke from way too many cigarettes—I gathered with my family and closest staff members for the glorious private moments of celebration. Magic was in our bloodshot eyes and shared triumph in our bear hugs.

"I'm proud of you, my darling," Roberta said.

No one would sleep that night, but things settled down a bit, and Dave, Vic, Norty, and I took a hard look at the election results. The final count showed how breathtakingly close the election was: a plurality of just over 40,000 votes out of a total of over 1,400,000—very close to Dave Green's original and constantly repeated conclusion that we would win if the total primary vote reached 1,500,000.

The big numbers were the main story, but other stories emerged from some of the smaller statistics. We looked at a precinct-by-precinct count in southern Illinois. I pointed to the heavily Republican precinct that included the town of Ina, where locals gave my boys tractor lessons and the restaurant had served world-class blackberry pie.

"Those old guys gave me 100 percent of the vote!"

It was Dave Green who did his homework and reported, to my delight, "Except for Daley's Cook County, Dan carried every single county that he walked through."

"Looks like a lot of Republicans crossed over after Bill Goldberg and Andy Leahy got the law changed," Vic said.

"I hate to rain on this party," Norty said, "but how are we going to handle the morning press conference? Are we going to talk about immediately joining hands with Daley and the regulars after months of mangling them?"

Conversation stopped and expressions turned thoughtful.

"Because that's the first question they're going to ask," Norty continued.

Fatigue seemed to descend on all of us at once, and we flopped onto chairs and sofas.

Someone said the obvious. "We've been so busy fighting that we gave no thought as to what we would do if we won!"

After much discussion, I spoke up. "There's only one alternative: Surprise everyone. As they say, let's get outta Dodge. Go away for a rest and come back with a game plan. Then hold the press conference."

"Good," Dave said. "Surely we can come up with something."

"Whatever it is, it's got to be good," Norty said.

# 19

## Victory despite Nixon's Republican Landslide

I am walking to the chapel after cleaning floors and toilets at the clothing store. The guard who manages to demand more strip searches of me than any of the others accosts me.

"Hey, Walker, you're supposed to be working over at the clothing store. Whaddya doing out here in the yard? You got permission to be out here this time of day?"

"Yes," I reply firmly, trying to keep my contempt for the guy out of my voice.

"You mean, 'Yes, *sir*,' don't you? Better say it, Walker. Told you before, you're no governor here at this prison. I don't say 'sir' to you; you say 'sir' to me."

I feel the bile rising. Having lost all that I have lost—and perhaps continue to lose—is damn near unbearable. Having to endure this idiot on top of it all is torture. Before I left for prison, Vic had talked to me about my response on occasions such as this. We had spent some time reminiscing, and then he said, "Dan, I know this is going to be very tough for you. You're a proud man. And you've done lots to be proud of. But in that place up in Duluth, the only way you'll survive is to kiss ass. Kiss every ass they point you to. It'll be hard to handle, but believe me, it's going to be the price of survival for you."

Most of the time, I heed Vic's advice. Right at this moment, however, it escapes my mind. "I don't say 'sir' to jerks like you." I instantly regret my words.

He moves toward me, and I know I'm in for trouble, but then a harsh, yet wonderful sound stops him. Luckily, the siren signals time for a prisoner count—a procedure that occurs randomly several times a week. Everyone, inmates and guards alike, is required to report to his workstation immediately. Only when the count reaches the correct total number of inmates is the warden told, "All prisoners present or accounted for." Then we are released to go on with the day's activities.

I walk away from this guard and head back toward the clothing store.

He yells, "You'll pay for this, Walker!"

After the prisoner count, I live in dread of encountering this guard for four days and then learn that he was transferred to another prison over the weekend. Relief floods me, and I vow never to be so stupid again. Evan has rejoined me on our afternoon exercise sessions, and I happily tell him the story.

"Wow. Sounds like your prayers were answered."

Evan tends to ponder the things we talk about, so I give him an honest answer. "Not exactly, Evan."

He turns to look at me. "You didn't pray? I thought you were really into that."

"I am, but I never ask God or Jesus to intervene in personal problems, especially ones I've created myself."

"You told me you pray every day." His earnest blue-gray eyes seek answers. "If you don't pray for personal help, what do you pray for?"

"I ask Jesus for strength. Strength to cope with adversity. I feel strongly that we are given free will. God doesn't move people around to solve individual problems. I've been praying for the strength to be humble." I shake my head. "Havin' a hard time with that one, though, Evan, a hard time."

---

## DIPLOMACY WITH THE DEVIL AND NO COATTAILS TO RIDE

To avoid the inevitable press conference question about how I could accept Daley's backing after publicly attacking him for months, we left for an immediate getaway to rest, recoup, and strategize over our response. I had called a supporter who owned a small Florida resort. Luckily, he agreed to provide rooms. Bill Holtzman, our wizard at scheduling, pulled strings to get us on a plane right away. After a fast packing job, we left for Florida, just the five of us. Vic, Dave, Bill Goldberg, Norty, and I. Exhausted and thirsty for a cool drink after reaching the resort, we immediately headed for the palm-shrouded bar near the swimming pool.

The bartender greeted us. "Gentlemen, you're lucky. Today you have a choice of orange juice, lime juice, and pineapple juice." We had arrived at a "fat farm." Apprehensively, I looked at a menu and saw to my dismay no steaks, no potatoes, nothing except vegetable dishes, salads, and lots of fruit.

"You gotta do something, Dan," said Vic. "Get us some decent food and drinks."

Easy to ask, but we had little money, and no credit cards with usable balances. I called my friend, and our luck held. I not only reached him, but he laughed and apologized.

"Give 'em an hour or so, Dan."

So we took our time unpacking, showering, and changing into beach wear. Then, back to the lobby, where a formally attired maître d'hôtel awaited.

"The bartender's ready to fix any drink you wish, Governor. And for you and your friends, we've typed this special dinner menu featuring steaks and seafood."

*Governor*, the man said. Gosh, that sounded good.

We hoisted a drink (several in fact) to Dave for his marvelous prediction accuracy and campaign strategy, then to Vic for a wonderful job of managing, then Bill for his legal savvy, and then Norty for his PR talents. We ate big steaks and had a good night's sleep.

Next day, we went to work. We needed a plan to show independence, while at the same time seeking unity and party campaign funds to defeat the incumbent, Dick Ogilvie.

"I've been pacing the floors, walls, and ceilings," Vic began. "Here's what I came up with. We have three men who won nominations for statewide office in the primary who hold Chicago ward committeeman party posts: Neil Hartigan for lieutenant governor, Roman Pucinski for U.S. senator, and Thomas Lyons for attorney general. Dan, you say this constitutes a conflict of interest, and you demand they resign as ward committeemen. You say, when they do, we will all join hands and march to victory."

I'm certain my jaw must have dropped. This was a bold and daring stroke. "No one has ever suggested such a conflict of interest," Bill said. "I think I could make a legal case with a lot of technicalities, but it will be tough to spell out publicly."

"Who cares?" Norty said. "It sounds good and it flaunts your independence."

Bill said, "I think it would stand up legally—at least to a credible degree."

"This slap at the regular Democratic organization will make them damn mad," Dave said, "but what can they do? Daley's already announced publicly that he and the entire organization will support your candidacy. They have no realistic choice."

"I hate to sound naive," Bill said, "but what's to stop them from ignoring Dan and letting voters split the ticket?"

Vic said, "Oh, no. They can't do that. They'd lose the power of the straight ticket box." Illinois ballots had a box that allowed voters to simply make an X to vote a straight party ticket and save themselves the time of marking each name. "To subvert the party candidate for governor could endanger the entire Democratic ticket," Vic went on. "This is especially critical for lesser-known candidates like assessor and treasurer. And these offices are absolutely essential to the machine's power in Cook County."

"Of course, there's no chance Hartigan, Pucinski, and Lyons will ever resign their party positions," Norty said, "so won't that make Dan have to fight them in the campaign?"

Vic scoffed. "What little controversy there will be over this will soon die down. It's just a face-saver."

Vic had found a brilliant solution to a very real dilemma. Then, surprisingly, we received some good news. Privately hostile or not, the Cook County organization contributed $50,000—one of the largest donations the Cook County organization had ever given to a statewide campaign. There was plenty of grumbling down the line, though, among the committeemen and captains.

Early polls gave me a small lead over Ogilvie. However, in a national election, the power of straight ticket voting could also work against us. Though it ensured lip service support from party regulars, it also relied on the name at the top in a presidential contest. If other Democrats would be riding on my coattails, I should be riding, in principle, on the Democratic presidential candidate's coattails. Senator George McGovern was the Democratic presidential frontrunner in the primaries, and Nixon soon labeled him as a tax-and-spend, soft-on-crime liberal.

"McGovern," Dave said, "has no coattail power, either in the suburbs or downstate."

"Democratic votes for the rest of the ticket will depend on you," Vic said.

### FIGHTING THE BATTLE ON TWO FRONTS

My opponent, Republican incumbent Richard Ogilvie, was an experienced adversary. In the previous election, he waged a well-financed, hard-hitting campaign. After the primary, he opened with a strong series of television and radio commercials trumpeting his record as a "good governor." And he had some real accomplishments. The influx of funds from the income tax had given him millions to spend on popular programs both in Chicago and downstate. Although his somewhat colorless image worked against him, Ogilvie played skillfully on the theme, "It's Walker's good looks against my good record. I've been a good, hardworking governor. I may not have that guy's charisma, but you don't govern with charisma." Also, Ogilvie was building a very substantial war chest that we could not hope to match.

Many Democratic regulars continued to feel that I was not "one of them." It didn't help when I declined to follow the age-old Illinois practice of team campaigning with all the other Democratic candidates for statewide office. I went my own way with my kind of personal, one-on-one campaigning.

I had hoped that Adlai Stevenson III, at least, would finally take a supportive stance toward me, but he remained hostile. Indeed, I learned to my dismay that in speaking to individuals outside Illinois, Adlai frequently disparaged both me personally and my campaign, reportedly commenting that I was both a "disloyal supporter" and "an opportunist who would stop at little to become governor."

The Democratic National Convention was about to begin with a dramatic fight. A requirement that came out of the chaotic 1968 convention was that future delegations must proportionately reflect women and minorities in a given district. Daley's response was typical. He ignored it and selected his own delegates for the primary ballot: mostly men, mostly white, all part of the machine. These delegates were not tied to the McGovern win in the primary and so were technically uncommitted, but they were actually committed to vote however Daley "the kingmaker" wanted.

Two of my volunteers—lawyers Mary Lee and her husband Andy Leahy, our assistant legal counsel—joined in challenging Daley, initially through local party caucuses to select delegates that more fairly represented Chicago districts. Daley people attended these caucuses in busloads. At one, a speaker was pulled down from a pulpit in a church in South Shore and kicked. Mary Lee was pinned to the wall. However, the caucuses were courageously reconvened despite a repeated skirmish, and eventually Jesse Jackson led an alternative delegation known as the Singer-Jackson Delegation. Mary Lee helped fight courtroom battles over this issue, all the way to the Supreme Court.

On July 10 at the Miami Beach national convention, the Credentials Committee seated the Singer-Jackson slate over the regular organization slate. Kicking Daley and his delegates out of the convention was an insult that infuriated him. He wasn't about to forget Mary Lee's role in it either.

I was impressed and proud of her. Meanwhile, instead of going to Miami, I gave priority to my own campaign and took my sons, Dan, Charles, and Will, on a tour in a very visible red, white, and blue jeep—on loan from a dealer—for some hard, personal, one-on-one campaigning; "retail campaigning" it's called. All over the state, we hit small towns where I could work the square, visiting every retail shop I could find. Vic and Dave checked the downstate areas where I hadn't received a majority of votes in the primary and found that they were in portions of the state where I had not walked. So the jeep tour concentrated on those areas. I avoided the county fairs that the other statewide candidates visited regularly.

My problem with the fairs was that each Democratic county chairman would inevitably meet me with a few of his cohorts, sticking with me throughout the fair, harping on the patronage jobs they needed. There's nothing basically wrong with giving a job to a person who worked for you, *if* that person is qualified. What these people were asking for, however, was the automatic granting of jobs that would be controlled by the county chairman, not by the state's personnel department. Handing out jobs without ascertaining qualifications was a patronage practice I fundamentally opposed. Hadn't they been paying attention? These fellows, whose support I needed, thought my speeches about ending patronage system abuse were just campaign rhetoric. They didn't think I actually meant it.

I avoided these people for an even more important reason. They kept me from doing my preferred kind of campaigning: shaking hands with every person I could reach. Also, at county fairs, the picture for the local newspaper would include the county chairman, which would not generate votes. Actually, a picture of me kissing a donkey or even a hog would be more likely to produce votes downstate than one with a Democratic Party chairman's arm around my shoulders. I wanted pictures with regular folks.

I wanted pictures showing me jumping out of the jeep with my sons and a caption such as the one that said, "Walking Dan Walker and his boys hit Main Street like a whirlwind."

I could cover the squares in four or five small towns in a county in the time it would take to work the county fair. And in those stores, when I shook hands and chatted a little with the women shopping, you could be pretty sure that after getting home, they would call up friends and relatives to brag about meeting that "walkin' guy who's now an official candidate for governor." Generating talk like this is what downstate campaigning should be all about. I also tried to reach every possible radio talk show. And, unlike all the other major Democratic candidates, I gave few speeches and avoided long party meetings.

As I moved around the state, I learned repeatedly the importance of my advance staff—young men and women who scouted each stop well before I got there, making all the necessary arrangements. Sometimes they had to improvise, such as the time I was scheduled to appear at a university campus. The band was all set, but other arrangements were totally inadequate and the students unlikely to show up. So, in walkie-talkie contact, the advance man radioed my assistant, "Let me know when you're ten minutes away." Then he called the nearest fire station, warned them that a campus prankster was planning a false fire alarm, and then waited near a fire alarm box. When word came that I was near, he broke the glass, and the alarm sounded loudly all over the campus. Students came running out of their dormitories, and a crowd was ready-made when I arrived. The advance man struck up the band and announced that the alarm was false, but the music kept most of the students to hear me speak.

Occasionally, an advance man caused problems. One longhaired, hippie-looking young man persisted in taking all kinds of pills and vitamin powders into a restaurant, ordering a bowl of milk, and then making a meal with the vitamins. This was certain to create animosity. However, these were minor obstacles compared to the continuing battle with both the regular Democrats and the Republicans.

### CUTTING

Back in Chicago, I tried to stay clear of the strong machine wards. My entire campaign involved careful avoidance of the fact that the machine I had attacked so hard in the primary was now supporting my candidacy. But as a practical fact of life, I knew that I would need the votes from those wards—desperately. Disappointing polls showed Ogilvie with a strong lead, and I was losing the liberals who continued to be angry with me for defeating Paul Simon. Persuaded by repeated Ogilvie television commercials proclaiming, "He's been a good governor," too many liberal voters in both city and suburbs appeared to be going with Ogilvie. The machine's ability to produce masses of Democratic votes would definitely help. Vic was hearing rumors, however, that couldn't be ignored. Machine ward committeemen were getting ready to cut me. "Cutting" me meant that the committeemen were telling their precinct captains that in canvassing voters, they could depart from straight-ticket instruction and split their ballot by voting for the Republican for governor—and president, since McGovern did not look strong.

I had no choice but to start speaking at the ward meetings of the precinct captains. When I was introduced in each ward, the hostility was as thick as their cigarette and cigar smoke. At meeting after meeting, I encountered rows of glaring, grim-faced captains who had worked hard to defeat me in the primary. When applause time came, too many of them sat on their hands. At one meeting, a heckler called out, "F—— you, Walker!" and a small ripple of applause followed. This insult made it even harder for me to seem to be begging for these people's support.

Afterwards, Vic tried to cheer me up. "This is all for show. If they do cut you, they risk other Democratic votes as well on the local 'meat and potatoes' offices. The ward committeemen will whip these captains into line. They know Boss Daley will be looking hard at the figures, ward by ward, to see who delivered and who did not." His comments helped, though I knew he was overstating the case.

Dave felt, I guess, that he could not in good conscience remain silent. "You're overstating the case, Vic. You and I both know that Vito Marzullo will probably take his ward over to Ogilvie. You yourself told me the rumor that Ogilvie's people are trying to buy off some of the Democratic ward committeemen."

Vic looked hard at Dave, as if trying to silence him.

"We all know the saying that Daley would rather have a Republican governor he can deal with than a Democrat he can't deal with," I said.

Vic frowned. "I also have the sense that the Republicans have something up their sleeve. An October surprise. We just gotta get even tougher."

What my two loyal comrades weren't telling me was that they were deeply concerned about the polls that showed Ogilvie's lead growing steadily, week-by-week, statewide. They feared that this bad news would adversely affect my campaigning. So they kept the polls from me to help me come across as an optimistic candidate.

### MONEY, MONEY, MONEY, MONEY

In September, with the election less than two months away, we hit severe problems. We had assumed that the individuals and businesses regularly supportive of Democrats for statewide office would fall in line after the primary to fill our campaign coffers. They definitely did not, even though we worked hard to solicit contributions. Some said it was because I was too antiestablishment. Others said I was too goody-goody, that they could not expect a return on investment. Whatever the reason, it was extremely troublesome. We raised about two million dollars, while Ogilvie raised and spent three times that much.

Just as we had done in the primary, we challenged my opponent to a mutual disclosure of all campaign contributions: I would if he would. Simon had refused to disclose, and so did Ogilvie. There was a negative side to such disclosures since many people simply do not like to have their contributions made public. Downstate, giving to a Democrat could be very troublesome for a Republican. In Chicago, giving to an opponent of the machine could invite retribution. To make it fair and doable, there must be a level playing field. Both competing candidates must make the disclosures, and my opponents refused to do so. That time around, I didn't either.

We ended the campaign substantially in debt. I had no hope that my large personal loan to the campaign would be repaid. For lack of money, we were constantly hand-to-mouth, and only intense loyalty kept the staff going. We were all deeply concerned about the national picture, where it looked more and more like Richard Nixon would win by a large margin. Polls showed Nixon with a 60–34 lead over McGovern. In short, McGovern was proving to be a real drag on the state ticket.

I visited campaign headquarters only to make fund-raising calls from a list handed to me by staff. Vic and Clev kept up their emphasis on organization. Bill Goldberg generated issue papers, helped draft press releases, and prepped me for speeches and debates, and Norty Kay was seemingly everywhere with the media. There were very few formal speeches. I maintained the practice of trying to "make news" in the morning that would appear on evening television news programs.

### ISSUES SMISHUES

Our strategy in dealing with Ogilvie's steady gains in the polls created a campaign carried out on two different levels, but with only one theme. The media focused on the presidential battles between Nixon and McGovern, so fights for state offices rated little attention, unless something dramatic occurred. At one level, our campaign had to concentrate on issues that had statewide impact. Norty liked these because all the reporters stressed them. The second level of the campaign stressed intense personal campaigning, reaching as many people as possible.

"Vic," Norty often complained, "we've got to get more issue stuff."

"Issues-smishues," Vic would reply. "People, most of them, do not vote based on general issue positions. Only the die-hard activists pay attention to issues. They vote for the candidate they're attracted to. They see Dan as a fighter. People like fighters. That's what will win their support."

"Okay, a fighter. Good. What's he fighting for, Vic?"

"He's a fighter for good government, obviously."

"Too general. What does that mean? He's not attacking Daley anymore. He has to attack Ogilvie. We need issues."

The team would argue a bit, but Norty and Bill Goldberg cranked out press releases that articulated how I would deal with specific issues. Often I would bring general issues like environment and education down to the local level. For example, the crosstown expressway that I continued to oppose, because it uprooted thousands of people, was outrageously expensive and unnecessary. And the flood control dam in the western part of the county, requiring no state tax money, I strongly favored. I continued to harp on the substandard schools in the poorer areas of the state. Taxation remained a constant issue. I would fight to avoid adding or increasing taxes, fight for a balanced budget, fight to cut the state payroll, and fight to control spending. Over and over at press conferences, I hit Ogilvie for excessive spending of the revenues from his new income tax.

The overall theme of both the issues campaign and the personal campaign was fighting, especially attacking the abuses resulting from the patronage system—a subject I had harped on during the primary. Ogilvie, like Daley with Democrats, hired people just because they were Republicans and allowed political county chairmen to "own jobs." My personal crusade continued against the reprehensible practice of requiring state employees to raise money for candidates, a bipartisan sin that was part of the "club system" of politics.

Near the end of the campaign, there was a debate scheduled by the IVI, the liberal-minded Independent Voters of Illinois. During the debate, I came out strongly against forced busing to achieve school integration. Jim Hoge—the *Sun-Times* managing editor very active for liberal causes and candidates—personally called in the story that led to a headline, "Walker booed by liberals, comes out against forced busing." Initially, I had widespread liberal support, based on my vociferous opposition to machine politics, but this publicity greatly intensified their disaffection with me over running against Paul Simon. Polls continued to show both liberal unhappiness and a positive reaction to my opponent's television commercials proclaiming, "Ogilvie's been a good governor."

There were three televised debates—Springfield, Chicago, and St. Louis. We enjoyed one picture on the front page of the Springfield paper. It was actually two pictures: One taken from the front showed Ogilvie and me on each side of the rostrum and appearing to be about the same height; the other, taken from the back, showed that Ogilvie was standing on a box. A little thing, but a good human-interest item for the campaign.

I should have remembered the lesson I had learned earlier about television appearances: Be careful not to appear too hard, too tough. In the debate in St. Louis, Vic told me, "Go get him, Dan." So I did. And polling showed that numerous watchers felt so sorry for my opponent that he got their votes.

Vic and Dave, after reviewing private polling results, said that overall, I won two of the three debates. That St. Louis debate was most widely shown in southern Illinois where the walk had earned me strong support, so we felt that my heavy-handedness hadn't hurt me much.

My main job was to keep up the intense retail campaigning, day after tiring day, seven days a week. Sure, I did some wholesale campaigning by appearing on television and radio talk shows, but mostly I was out with the people, still hitting the bowling alleys, factory gates, and every shopping center in the Chicago metropolitan area. I even hit, with permission, a few restaurants. Over and over again, I was reminded that Americans are usually open, decent, polite, and anxious to feel a part of the electoral process by meeting a real live candidate, particularly one running for high office.

We finally had enough money, much of it borrowed, to pay for television commercials in the fall. By early October, I could feel that those ads based on the walk were "biting." People would comment, "I saw you on TV with your boys and didn't know you were still out there walking the state." I reported this to Dave Green, and he informed me that the polls were now showing me closing the gap with Ogilvie, but still behind.

There is a degree of unreality about campaigning. There were three different campaign worlds: the headquarters staff, the workers in the field, and the candidate. Although those at the top knew the most, I was deliberately among the least informed. Isolation became more severe as October days flew by.

One bit I overheard dampened my optimism. Vic said to Dave, "My sources tell me that hostility remains bitter toward Dan in parts of the Chicago Democratic organization, a mix of regulars and independent liberals." I held back so Vic and Dave wouldn't know I had heard, but I started worrying. Could my party actually sell me out? And then Vic turned on the small campaign headquarters television. "It's here," he said. "The October Surprise."

## THE REPUBLICAN SWEEP

In addition to the problem of defecting Democrats, Republicans were powering up for October. Nixon's lead indicated that a national Republican landslide based on his "law and order" campaign could swamp me. Then, Ogilvie launched a new statewide negative television commercial, attacking me for the Walker Report that had described a police riot at the 1968 Democratic National Convention. People had moved to the right on law enforcement issues, and the concept of a police riot had become ever more unpopular. I could no longer be shielded from the bad news.

"This commercial looks pretty compelling," Bill Goldberg said.

"Maybe it'll bring the liberals back," Norty said.

"If that was significant, Norty, McGovern would be ahead in the polls," Vic answered a bit sarcastically.

"Okay, guys," I said, "so how should we counter Ogilvie's commercials? Nixon's constant law-and-order theme only adds to their impact. Law-and-order is clearly catching on, both nationally and in Illinois. Newspapers all across the state are editorializing heavily in Ogilvie's favor. I'm sick of hearing it."

Vic said, "I heard from my informants in the Ogilvie camp that they are openly bragging, 'Walker has run out of steam.'"

Vic, Dave, Bill, and Norty all seemed especially lethargic and gloomy.

"Is there something you haven't told me?" I asked.

Dave took off his glasses, squeezed his eyes shut, and massaged his temples. "Surveys are showing that Ogilvie is running ahead of his 1968 pace in Chicago and Cook County." The news hit me hard. This was our darkest hour of the fall campaign, but Vic, Dave, Norty, and Bill hunkered down to an intense strategy session. After several hours, they presented their ideas.

"Our polling has shown that people are fed up with criminals being out on bail, committing other crimes while their trial on the first offense is being delayed, sometimes up to a year," Vic announced.

Bill said, "If you agree, Dan, we want you to announce support for a sixty-day trial law. All felony criminal trials must be held within sixty days after arraignment." We discussed the legal ramifications a while before Dave said, "Personally, I think that the sixty-day trial law idea should be featured on TV commercials for the rest of the campaign."

"And," Vic said, "Dave and I are going to be using a technique that—so far as we know—hasn't been used before in political campaigns, only in commercial advertising: focus groups."

All this proved once again that I had chosen my team well. Vic and Dave had tested the commercial featuring the sixty-day trial law with focus groups and were surprised at its effectiveness. The idea easily condensed into a thirty-second television commercial and hit a chord statewide. Liberals wanted to remedy long trial delays, and conservatives were all in favor of rapid conviction of criminals.

Those were anxious times, and I was grateful that dawn-to-midnight campaigning left me little time to worry. On the weekend before the election, Vic made some sampling telephone calls in normally Republican territory in the Chicago suburbs, and the results were so positive that he decided to go all out. Volunteers using home phones and all available lines at headquarters called every home they could reach in those suburbs. A simple message was repeated over and over: "The election's close, please be sure to vote." No pitch, no mention of candidate. Just get out and vote.

Finally, November 7, 1972, Election Day. We desperately hoped for extensive ticket-splitting since Nixon was poised to blow away McGovern, and Republican Charles Percy, who would head the ballot as candidate for the U.S. Senate, was running way ahead of his Democrat opponent. A national and state Republican landslide loomed.

The day was long. To keep busy, I visited polls in tough machine wards, hoping my presence might help squelch efforts by some still-hostile regulars to cut me. A good example was First Ward Democratic boss Vito Marzullo, who had not only brazenly and publicly refused to support me but also made it clear that he personally detested me. No surprise, since his Mob connections were well known, and he would not have forgotten my Chicago Crime Commission fights against organized crime. I stood there watching voters until several of Vito's beefy poll workers approached. After a brief argument, I moved on.

Depressingly, it rained all day, and I feared this would cut down the large Democratic turnout so essential for our victory. Finally in late afternoon, I dejectedly drove downtown to the Allerton Hotel to watch the returns. In the family's suite, separate from the rooms where the staff was hard at work, I saw the results reported on national news as polls closed, beginning with the eastern states. Soon it became apparent that the national Nixon landslide we greatly feared was in the making. I watched with despair as in state after state, east to west, like falling dominoes, Democratic candidates for both U.S. Senate and governor went down to dismal defeat.

I gathered my wife, sons, and daughters and fought for emotional control. "I'm afraid it's all over. I won't be able to survive the national Republican sweep." They tried to cheer me up, but nothing they could say had any effect.

Glumly, I went over to talk with Vic and Dave.

"Cheer up," Vic said.

"We're still in the ball game," Dave said.

Good reports began coming in from our downstate poll watchers, even though I was not doing as well in Chicago as we had hoped. While I was there, the phones continued ringing. One was a poll watcher calling to turn in the first results from one of the Chicago "bellwether precincts" Dave had selected. Dave took the call and turned white as he listened. He turned to us and said, "It's a lopsided victory for Ogilvie."

Both he and Vic went into shock, a complete tailspin, until ten minutes later a call came in saying that the worker had misreported his tally. We sighed collectively and loudly but could in no way relax. The itchy, antsy minutes and hours crawled over us as if they were caterpillars with the power to drag time, prolonging torture.

"Still too close to call" was Dave's judgment in the wee hours of the morning.

An image of our ballroom sixteen stories below appeared on the television screen, showing the supporters not only still wide-eyed and hopeful but cheering when downstate results indicated I might beat Ogilvie in some normally Republican counties.

This cheered Dave as well, but we continued to worry that my vote in

Chicago was weak. And the East St. Louis vote, where Ogilvie had gotten the sympathy vote after I had come on too strong in the debate, also aroused concern. A call came in for Vic. He answered and then covered the phone with his palm.

"It's Ogilvie's manager," he said, rolling his eyes. Then into the receiver, "Yeah, well, don't be too sure," Vic said into the phone and hung up. "Guy's bragging that they've got it in the bag because they're carrying East St. Louis. He says our average Democrats over there have seen the light, or some such. The jerk." He paced. "I'll tell you what's really bothering me: Where are the results from the suburban counties? They're not in. Are they playing games with the ballots?"

After torturous hours of delay, the final vote count came in. The numbers were disappointingly close, yet I had won. I stepped into the ballroom of the Allerton Hotel where supporters had been waiting. They began screaming when they saw me. I shouted enthusiastically over the din, "This victory belongs to you and the people of Illinois."

After a few exhausted moments of glory, I retired with my family and close staff. Deliriously happy, I said to my sons who had been with me on that wearying walk through the state, "We've come a long, long way from that hot day down near the Ohio River when—with blistered, sometimes bloody, feet—we listened to those who questioned our sanity." And I thanked my other children who had worked so intensively and embraced my wife, Roberta, who had campaigned so hard for me. Raising my voice so all of the staff could hear also, I said, "Our underdog victory proves that dreams can come true. No longer can they say I'm tilting at windmills."

We had stormed the walls and conquered the castle. Biographers Penso-neau and Ellis later described me as "the fellow who turned political implausibility into reality, who had shown the underdogs of life that dreams—as far out as they may seem—still came true."

Dave Green told me later that he had been scared to death in the closing days. "Ogilvie had the momentum, and we just barely caught him. If the election had been held just one day earlier, we would have lost."

I squeaked by with a 77,494-vote lead, just 50.7 percent of the 4,665,112 votes cast. It couldn't get much closer than that. The critical vote was outside Cook County, in the suburbs and downstate areas that a Republican normally swamps. A good example was Republican Winnebago County, which I took 52,566–40,922. So, even though I did not do as well in some Chicago precincts as other Democrats had in prior years, I made up for that elsewhere. In deep southern Illinois, I walked away from Ogilvie, further cementing my love for that part of the state. As in the primary, I ran most strongly in the counties where I had walked.

In an interview the next day, Vic said, "It wasn't until two in the morning that I thought we had a fifty-fifty chance of winning." He reminisced about the days when everyone thought he was crazy for dedicating his life to my campaign. He talked about the fact that we had been friends since the late 1950s, that his son was named Daniel in my honor. When asked to comment on major turning points, Vic talked about the statewide organization he and Clev had built and my walk through the state. "It was the big thing that put us on the political map. I don't know anyone but Dan who had the discipline and the drive to do it."

In a television interview late that night after the results were announced, when I was asked what I would do as governor with this surprising victory, I responded with my usual message: Open up the system to broader people participation in the Democratic Party and throughout state government. And put a stop to the "pay to play" system.

Insanely, the reporter asked, "Will you now consider the presidency?"

I said, "Absolutely not!" My love—my true love—was state government.

The sixty days between election and inauguration were exciting, with no possibility of taking days off to catch my breath. We all needed a rest, but putting a governing team together and starting the arduous task of building a budget that would be due a few weeks after taking office were daunting, time-consuming tasks.

Vic, Dave, Norty, Bill, and I had carefully worked out the overall game plan, including the goal of opening up party politics to build a truly statewide party that would place more downstate Democrats in higher positions. In state government, we would decisively reduce the political power of Chicago's mayor, concentrate on ethics, and introduce modern business practices for controlling expenditures. When we gathered to discuss the plan, Bill cleared his throat. "Let's talk about my proposal for a series of really tough executive orders on a code of ethics for all state employees under the governor. You all have my list of the orders I'm proposing."

"Hell," Vic said. "It's never been done before. Executive orders are a red flag to the legislature. They think this kind of stuff is their turf."

"Sure," I said, "their turf to kill it."

Vic lifted a copy of Bill's proposal. "This list is dynamite. We're going to get hammered."

"Fine," I said. "Let 'em try. Voters know I'm a fighter. They'll love it."

Norty spoke up. "It's the same as the walk, Dan. You're only a walker or a fighter if the media says you are. You really think you'll get credit for this tough stuff?"

"Absolutely! It's revolutionary. And it's the only way anything will change."

Norty shrugged, cynically.

Vic shrugged also. "Just so we all know what we're up against. I agree though. Without such a drastic step, nothing will change."

I was happy to have my team's help in executing the overall game plan, with emphasis on the executive orders. Vic would be primarily in charge of the political part. Norty would be my press secretary. Bill would be my legal counsel. But—as the ever-practical David Green, who planned to stay in the business world, constantly reminded us—implementation of the game plan would require constant close collaboration between Vic and me, with Dave advising from outside. That we would do.

Dave said, "You and Vic are like brothers who need few signals to put a game plan into operation."

This was quite true. However, behind the scenes, Vic and I argued over cabinet and staff selection.

"Dan, you're going to really piss everyone off if you bring in so many people from outside the state." Vic raised his voice. "You just can't do it. You're going to be fighting every day in office as it is. We gotta bring in more state people."

"I want the best, Vic. A successful business would never restrict itself like that. A business would collapse under the competition."

"Competition! Who are we competing with? The State of Ohio? No. This is one area where we need to be savvy. The right people will get along better and—"

"I'm not doing things the machine way. And we'll get people who can get along."

Vic and I had many intense sessions, and I came to depend on him as never before. Then, suddenly, he was struck down by a heart attack. Pete Wilkes, my newly assigned state trooper, rushed Vic to the hospital.

## 20

## *The New, Tough Executive Orders*

I still help the chaplain or simply visit with him when I get a chance, although clerking for him has not been my official work for some time. The deteriorating situation with Roberta Nelson makes the denigrating prison work increasingly difficult to take, however, and I feel like I've got to do something or I'll lose my mind.

I hurry over to the chaplain's office as soon as I'm finished with the toilets and the floors and enter a mundane little room with its crucifix, religious images, and photos related to his career. We chat a bit, and then I ask my important question.

"You said you thought the work I did for you was excellent, correct?"

He agreed.

"Then how about helping me get the job back? Couldn't you make a case to the warden on my behalf?"

"Oh, I'm afraid not, Dan. I don't dare cross the man. I've only got a couple of years before I get my retirement, and I don't want to be sent to some god-awful job in a maximum security prison far away from my home."

"You mean just for trying to help me by simply talking to him? The guy'd do that to a prison chaplain?"

"Absolutely. He's got a reputation for that." He leans back in his chair, ready to drop this line of conversation. "How are things with your wife? Any better?"

I stand up to leave. "Oh, I'm still hoping." Actually, things with my second Roberta couldn't get much worse, but I need to stay positive.

I check the mail back in the barracks. Nothing from her, nothing from the new parole board lawyer, nothing from Mary Bucaro. No one else speaks to me.

I eat dinner alone that night, and the minutes pass slowly. Later, in the sick light of the huge night-dimmed lamps, I decide I must do something. I have to take some kind of positive step to try to make things better. I decide to write a letter to my congressman about the warden. If a congressman gets involved, surely the warden won't dare take it out on the chaplain. I write the letter and send it off in the prison mail.

Several days pass, and the warden sends for me. This can't be about the congressman's letter because the congressman would have only just received my request. I enter the warden's office, and he keeps me standing, glaring at me. He tosses a folded paper onto the edge of his desk. It is my letter, removed from its envelope. I had known the letter was a long shot, but I never imagined my mail would be taken, and seeing my slim hope of relief from the bleakness of my life lying there exposed on the warden's desk blindsides me.

"That's my letter . . ." I waver a bit and must steady myself. "You can't do that. It's against regulations. A letter to a congressman can't be tampered with. It's part of the prison code."

He makes a whinnying sound like a laugh, only there is no smile on his face. "Try to tell me what I can and can't do one more time, Walker, and you're going right into the hole. And you'll stay there until you learn your lesson. And you damn well better stop trying to subvert me here at this prison with your damn classes. I run this place the way I want to run it. Now, f—— off, Walker. Go pick up those cigarette butts I see out there."

"Today's Sunday, Warden."

"I don't give a damn what day it is. Get your ass out of here and get to work. *Governor!*" He makes the laughing sound again.

My powerlessness leaves a cold, gnawing rage inside me.

---

### BEGINNINGS AND ENDINGS

Vic's condition remained critical, and I went to see him in intensive care as soon as he could have visitors. His son, my namesake, was there, along with a doctor and a nurse. I asked if I could have a few minutes alone with him.

They obliged, and I approached Vic, who lay still with his eyes closed, IVs attached, tubes up his nose, digital monitors registering his vitals.

"Hello, Vic," I said quietly.

He opened his eyes and looked at me.

I was never good at giving reassuring messages, and Vic understood me completely. So I just said my piece.

"I don't want you to try to talk, my friend." My feelings welled up in me, and I couldn't speak for a few seconds. An emotional display would only embarrass us both, though, so I cleared my throat and took a deep breath. "Victor, I can't do the job ahead of me without you. You just have to get well."

He managed a smile. "I'll be there, Dan," he said, voice raspy, "one way or another."

After several days, Vic seemed to be recovering, but he needed a month's rest. During this time, I enlisted my friend Jack Foster to help assemble my cabinet. I still firmly believed a governor's cabinet should be a mix of qualified supporters who have earned positions in a new administration and "outsiders" chosen solely on the basis of experience and ability, even if it meant going out of state. Jack was more than qualified to assist me in this challenging task. He had been the chief personnel executive for several years at the Port of New York, one of the most highly respected governmental agencies in the nation, and then served as vice president for personnel (now called human resources) at Montgomery Ward when I was vice president and general counsel. Retired from Monkey Ward (as it used to be called), Jack had developed a national reputation with a new executive search firm.

Jack conducted a nationwide search for the heads of departments ("code departments" they are called in Illinois, because they are codified by state law) dealing with transportation, public aid, public health, mental health, corrections (prisons), law enforcement, child welfare, and a few others. It did not bother me (although some legislators complained) that some were from outside Illinois. I wanted talent plus experience, and that was hard to find inside the state.

I also turned to my trusted ally Bill Goldberg. Bill was also my tennis-playing companion in the early morning hours before going to work. One December morning in a "tennis barn," I spoke to him after a second set of tennis.

"Bill, I need you to be my constant conscience on all governmental matters while I'm in office."

Smiling, he agreed. With our handshake, Bill became counsel to the governor. He would be my strong legal right arm, and we would work together constantly, developing the bold executive direction we were envisioning. I wanted to hit the ground running, and Bill would help me do it.

I also spent considerable time with Vic and others selecting the "Walker Workers" I would bring into the administration. Three women who worked especially hard in the campaign became key cabinet nominees: Beverly Addante, Mary Lee Leahy, and Nancy Phillippi. Like these three, the other campaign workers I brought into the cabinet were well qualified. One stellar example was Robert J. "Pud" Williams from Carmi, in deep southern Illinois. With Pud, I got exactly what I wanted: a loyal supporter and a southern Illinois dirt farmer who understood family farming from years of practical experience. Another was Don Prince, who gave up a top business job to chair the Board of Higher Education. Then there were Nolan Jones and Frank Kirk in administration, Russell Dawe in mines and minerals, Joe Piscotti in local governmental affairs, Anthony "Tony" Dean—who finally cut his hair—in conservation, Roland Burris in general services, and Donald Page Moore to head the Law Enforcement Commission. On the whole, the cabinet, as finally assembled, had far fewer political figures than usual and contained more minorities and women than ever before.

I felt excited and ready to get to work. Ogilvie's staff, though, had been distinctly uncooperative during the transitional phase. We assembled transition teams for each important government agency, but Ogilvie's people did not cooperate. His extreme disappointment at his unexpected loss of the election was reflected in a stubborn unwillingness of both him and his people to work on the mechanics of transition.

At the newly elected governors' conference in Annapolis, Chairman Marvin Mandel of Maryland told me that a governor rarely gets credit for reform measures, in great part because cynics simply refuse to take them seriously. With my zealous dedication and my wonderful team, I believed I would be taken seriously, yet his warning registered.

While in Annapolis, I decided to pay a courtesy call on the superintendent of the Naval Academy. After the necessary staff arrangements, I arrived at his impressive residence for a very formal meeting. He received me in his medal-bedecked uniform with a senior aide standing at his side.

After the handshake, he opened with polite small talk. "Governor, have you ever been in Annapolis before?"

I responded with a simple, "Yes, Admiral."

He came right back. "Was it on business or pleasure?"

I hesitated. "That's a tough question, Admiral."

"What's so tough?" he asked a little testily, I thought.

"Well, Admiral, I'm a graduate of the Naval Academy."

Silence. Then he turned to his aide and chastised him, sotto voce, "You son of a bitch."

Obviously, the aide had not done his homework, and his admiral was embarrassed in front of a governor. However, we went on to have a nice visit. Sometime later, I received a package from the admiral. Inside was a photograph of a red-framed window in Bancroft Hall. Underneath was printed in large letters "Governor Dan Walker's Naval Academy Escape Hatch." It was the window I had used for my outlandish over-the-wall nighttime jaunts. He must have learned about it from one of my classmates. The admiral's signed note under the picture read, "Governor, I did my homework this time."

A successful transition also required the diplomacy of establishing connections with various agencies and dignitaries. Still prior to my inauguration, I paid a courtesy call on Cardinal Cody, the pontiff's emissary to Chicagoland's millions of Catholics. I arrived on time at the cardinal's splendid residence and found him awaiting me in the foyer, brilliantly garbed in red cap and cape. I almost froze with the thought: How do I address a cardinal?

"Good morning, Your Excellency," I said, arm extended for a handshake.

Silently, the cardinal stepped toward me, rustling his scarlet robes. Taking my outstretched hand softly between his two, he gently pulled me closer and whispered into my ear, "Governor, you're excellent. I'm eminent."

Never have I ever been corrected so diplomatically. "Thank you, Your Eminence," I said.

A cheering crowd of thousands watched the inauguration ceremony on a subfreezing day in January 1973 at the foot of the Lincoln statue on the capitol grounds, the first "open to all" outdoor inauguration in the state's history. The other elected state officials chose to have their own separate "tickets only" ceremony in the heated Illinois State Armory Building. Had they been present, those officials might not have been among those applauding when I said, "Too many in government do not believe in the American credo that people are the best judges of what they want and need. They believe that only politicians and bureaucrats and those with wealth or power can tell people what to do."

Adrenaline kept me warm, so I disdained sweater, topcoat, and overcoat. After I was sworn in by an old friend, Illinois Supreme Court Chief Judge Walter Schaefer, I delivered a speech aimed right at my core constituency.

During my walk and for months thereafter, I listened and spoke personally to those who had lost faith in government. Those of you in small communities, on farms, and in big city communities. Those of you all over Illinois who work—with your hands and with your minds—not just those with coats and ties, but also those in overalls, blue-collars, and hard hats. What you told me about government was disturbingly similar. You simply did not believe government was worthy of your trust. There was a pervasive cynicism. You told me you simply do not believe that government understands how you live, how you work, and what you want for your families.

I carefully explained my plan to use executive orders as the quickest and most effective way to bring about accountability and "restore faith in state government." In conclusion, I said,

> The central belief of our founding fathers is still sound. The people, not the politicians, are the best judge of what they want and need. The best answer to the cynicism about the Illinois governmental system . . . is quite simple. Let politicians and politics take a back seat. Let government step back; let people step forward.

The crowd cheered and applauded. My brother Waco had come over from Virginia Beach, Virginia, with his family. Listening, but not really seeing me, my seventy-nine-year-old father endured the cold. My mother had passed away the preceding year, and he had made the long trip to Illinois with the help of Al Walkoe, a law school friend. The Old Man was then almost blind. Al told me that on the flight from San Diego to Chicago, soon after the seatbelt sign had been turned off, virtually every stewardess on the plane had clustered around Dad, listening to his stories and enjoying his flirting. He told Al, "Nice thing about being old—I can flirt all I want, and nobody takes me seriously."

Just before he left Springfield, he gripped my hand. "Now that I've seen my son inaugurated as governor, I consider my life over."

We hugged good-bye for one final time. He returned to his home in San Diego, and shortly thereafter, while resting on the living room couch, he died quietly.

### THE SMALL OFFICE

The family settled into the newly rebuilt Executive Mansion, the only one in the nation that was originally built for the governor; all the others were converted private homes. The third floor provided our living quarters, and it was only a short walk to the capitol building. These were happy family days as Roberta set up her office, hired a social secretary, and set about being a busy First Lady. The two youngest—Margaret, still in middle school, and Will, entering sixth grade—were happily enrolled for their first day of school.

Getting down to state business proved an immediate challenge, however. The first floor of the Executive Mansion was the state level floor, and governors used an office there as well as the main office in the State House—what the capitol building is called in Springfield. The spacious mansion office with its high ceiling, wainscoted walls, and elegant furnishings looked out onto the parklike grounds that occupied a square city block. I was organizing my files at the desk in that office when Bill Goldberg called from the State House.

"All the file cabinets in the governor's office are empty!"

I sighed, imagining the useful records I would never see. "Well, I guess that's to be expected. Ogilvie wouldn't want to leave anything helpful behind."

"You don't understand, Dan," Bill said. "All the files. All. All the information about the many boards and commissions that report to the governor are gone. We can't even ascertain existing vacancies. Hell, we don't even know who's serving in those agencies. And some are critical. It's going to be tough to maintain the orderly operation of state government."

I was more than a little irritated. "Bill, you must not be looking in the right place. Even Ogilvie wouldn't do something that low. I'll be over—"

"No, Dan," Bill said. "I didn't believe it either when a couple of office workers came to tell me. We've already done a thorough search. There's nothing."

The truth finally sank in like a slug to the gut. "That petty bastard. Damn it all to hell. I've got maybe twenty people waiting to know what their new job is going to be. I've promised them."

"Well, I've rounded up as many of our people as I can and started getting all the information possible on these agencies out of the state Blue Book. It's not nearly enough, but that's all we can get. We'll have to start contacting people at each of the agencies individually, so it's going to take a while."

Instant headache. "I'll be right over."

I walked over to the State House, grumbling, and once inside, bypassed the immense, ornate office used by my predecessors and went straight to the small office that I had used when working for Adlai Stevenson twenty years earlier. Naturally, I had fantasized about a grand governor's office, but the reality of such spacious elegance made me feel as if I were trying to be an emperor or something. I wanted nothing more than to get down to the business of changing this place into a no-nonsense environment conducive to reform. I gave Bill the office across from me, also larger and grander than the manageable space I had chosen for myself.

"I feel a little strange in an office that's nicer than the governor's office," Bill said.

"You're right where I need you to be," I said.

He shrugged and went to work.

Lieutenant Governor Neil Hartigan knocked on my office door and wanted to talk. Neil had been chosen by Daley and defeated my candidate, Neal Eckert, in the primary election. Before 1972, the lieutenant governor ran separately from the governor in the general election. In 1972, they ran together as a team, as the president and vice president do under the federal system. I had demanded that Neil resign from his ward committee post if elected, but of course, he had not. We shook hands. I asked him to sit down.

"Why," Neil began, "is Bill Goldberg moving into the office last used by Ogilvie's lieutenant governor? I very much want and need that office."

*As if I were going to have Daley's puppet near me in a bigger office than mine!*

*As if a lieutenant governor actually had to do much of anything!*

"Bill is the official counsel to the governor," I answered, "and as such, I need him close to me. Neil, he's quite indispensable . . ." I looked at him pointedly, hoping he could finish the sentence: *in a way that a lieutenant governor is not.* "But there's another terrific office right down the hall that should serve you well—quite close to the office reserved for the new deputy to the governor. You remember Vic De Grazia." *A man who actually helps the governor.* "I do look forward to working with you and hope I can count on your support for my programs and legislation. Can I count on you, Neil?" I held my gaze, knowing that realistically, I could never count on a Daley guy, but I wanted it out in the open between us.

He stood. "I pride myself on my personal loyalty to Mayor Daley, and I'm, of course, close to him. Dan, you couldn't have won without his endorsement, but you've shown no reciprocity toward him."

"I'm happy to show reciprocity to Daley when there's real merit. But he wants blind reciprocity, and I won't do it. Besides, we're talking about the relationship between you and me. I admire loyalty, Neil, but if I can't count on your support, then involving you on policy matters would pose severe practical problems. If, for example, Daley opposed me on an important issue, I simply could not assume that *I* would have *your* undivided loyalty, or even that you would keep critical matters confidential."

He left in a huff. I tried to shrug off the prospect of the adversarial relationship ahead of us and immediately returned to the difficult task of naming individuals to fill critical positions for which we had no records but could not leave unfilled.

The regulars in both parties definitely did not like some of my choices. An example was Tony Scariano, who, before retiring, had been a colorful, controversial state legislator with a penchant for introducing bills reforming the scandal-plagued horseracing industry. I named him to chair the Illinois Racing Board, and one reporter gave the reaction of those close to the industry: "Bejesus, *anybody* but Tony Scariano."

One of my real staff treasures was Pete Wilkes, a state trooper assigned to me for security after the November 1972 victory. Right away, I placed him in charge of the entire state police security detail for all statewide elected officials. When things looked difficult, Pete sometimes took over as my driver. And even when not with me, he always—and I do mean *always*—knew exactly where I was at all times, night and day, so that instantaneous communication by radio could be established through him if a crisis arose. Pete and I became, and remain, very good friends. (President Nixon later appointed him U.S. marshal for Northern Illinois, supervising a large professional staff.)

Insisting that the number of troopers assigned to handle my security be substantially reduced, I eliminated the customary "tail cars" following my car and reduced from two to one (the driver) the number of troopers in my car. Unless I specifically directed otherwise, I wanted no trooper to walk with me, particularly when entering and leaving public events. I also substituted a Chevrolet sedan for the grand limousine, directed that my picture not be displayed in state offices, and eliminated my name from state documents such as hunting and fishing licenses. Similarly, I ordered that the large signs at highway entry points to the state customarily featuring the governor's name should instead simply read, "THE PEOPLE OF ILLINOIS WELCOME YOU."

My administration would not be business as usual. I was about to employ a formidable use of executive power, but I wanted to be clear that my strategies were not about personal glory.

In my first "state of the state" message delivered to the assembled legislators, I spoke of a progressive government requiring mutual respect between the legislative and executive branches and my desire for a working partner-ship to achieve programs in the best interests of all the people of Illinois. I concluded, "We cannot have war between branches of government."

It was apparent from the tepid, polite applause on both sides of the aisle that my words were spoken in vain. And this was soon confirmed by the legislature. The honeymoon usually given to a new governor was not to be. Very quickly, we glimpsed the rough ride we had feared. None of us had expected it to be so rough so soon.

Almost immediately, I commenced weekly breakfast meetings with the Democratic legislative leaders, reminding them of my "state of the state" message that had called for a working partnership on legislation. I held these at the Executive Mansion family dining room around a table that would seat as many as twelve. The formal dining room upstairs featured a huge formal dining table that would accommodate thirty Louis XIV chairs. I hoped the more casual setting for these breakfasts would encourage candor and coop-eration. The first few were cordial, and I became optimistic.

Not for long.

During an Executive Mansion breakfast in February 1973, Vic and I routinely turned to the Democratic leaders of both house and senate.

"So, what do we have coming up today?" I asked.

"Any potential legislative surprises?" Vic asked.

"None," they assured us.

"Absolutely none," Cecil Partee, Democratic leader in the senate, assured us.

Then pending before the senate executive committee for the traditional "advise and consent" of the senate required by the constitution were a num-ber of my cabinet nominees. Traditionally, it was the practice in the senate to give substantial recognition to a new governor's right to select his own cabinet and, in accordance with that tradition, we expected routine approval of fully qualified nominees.

What happened instead was the opening gun in an intermittent war with a combination of Daley Democrats and equally hostile Republicans. Added to their shared dislike for my independent style was the feeling of many legislators that they knew much more about state government than I did. In this first outbreak of open warfare, leaders of my own party led the way in defeating some key cabinet nominees, three of whom had been strong "Walker Workers": Beverly Addante, Mary Lee Leahy, and Nancy Phillippi. Of course, the Republicans were delighted to join in this unheard-of action.

"Sending them down the tube" it was called. Installing qualified loyal people and getting more women into top positions in state government were two of my priorities. Beverly, Mary Lee, and Nancy absolutely filled the bill. The issue of their confirmation never got to the floor but was killed behind closed doors, no reasons given. I thought the press might scream in protest about unfairness to women, but it was silent. Mary Lee felt that her rejection was related in part to her opposition to Daley's delegation at the Democratic Nominating Convention the previous summer.

The cabinet fight did not stop with those three, and it was a traumatic and turbulent three months before I managed to put my cabinet in place. Without question, though, it was one of the best Illinois had ever seen, and we held on to most of our minority and women nominees, still leaving us with a higher count than in any previous administration. Many were highly qualified experts who had not worked in my campaign and had no political background whatsoever, including Leroy Levitt for mental health, Joyce Lashof for public health, Joel Edelman for public aid, Jerry Miller for children and family services, Allen Sielaff for corrections, Langhorne Bond for transportation, Robert Alphin for revenue, Harvey Johnson (from the Chicago Crime Commission) for law enforcement, Wayne Kerstetter to head the "little FBI" (the Illinois Bureau of Investigation), and Dwight Pittman as superintendent of the state police. I named Jack Foster chairman of the Illinois Civil Service Commission, a responsibility he fulfilled to considerable acclaim.

Regrettably, we failed to completely vet one choice named Anthony Angelos whom I named to the Department of Insurance, anxious to obtain an attorney who was not politically connected. After some unsavory facts about his background surfaced, I hastily withdrew his name, but not before an avalanche of unfavorable publicity buried all other issues.

After Vic's recuperation, I named him officially as deputy to the governor—a new title I created that has continued in subsequent administrations. The media soon shortened it to "deputy governor," which is actually a different title. As chief of staff, Vic would become a hard taskmaster. "If I'd been here during the vetting, the Angelos mess never would've happened," Vic said. Everyone understood our working relationship, that it would place him in charge of most political matters and dealings with the legislature. Vic had a master's grasp on the trench warfare of practical politics that I never really learned.

My battle with Mayor Daley's forces in the legislature didn't stop with the cabinet battle. Their war against me raged on in other matters. In the early weeks, his leaders proposed a broadened state subsidy for the Chicago Transit Authority (CTA) that provides mass public transportation—both elevated and subway system—for Chicago. Instead of the one-to-one match, one state dollar for every city dollar—the ratio customarily applied to state subsidies for municipal programs—Daley brazenly sought for the CTA two state dollars for every Chicago dollar, a match ratio unheard of in state-city relationships.

This was my first governmental confrontation with Daley, and the media portrayed it as a political battle. In one sense, it was, but it also had serious governmental overtones. I was fully aware of Daley's remarkable record in obtaining state subsidies for Chicago programs. City colleges and relief/welfare aid were two prominent examples of Daley's success in shifting burdens to state taxpayers that Chicagoans themselves would normally have assumed. I refused to go along. The additional millions of dollars would not only severely impact my tight budget but the two-for-one match would discriminate in favor of Chicago as compared to downstate cities.

This was a perfect example of my break with past tradition on relations between a Democratic governor and the mayor of Chicago. I was determined to show that Chicago would not be given exceptional favoritism in the mode of my Democratic predecessors. In the ensuing floor fight, the Daley forces pulled out all the stops.

One unexpected Daley ally was Robert Gibson—a labor union official whom I had nominated to become chairman of the Capitol Development Board, a prestigious, well-paid position that controlled many major state construction jobs. Gibson openly worked the floor against me, using as political weaponry his many union contacts. Vic warned him to desist, but he persisted. So, I simply withdrew his job nomination. Gibson never forgave me for this and worked hard with labor unions to defeat me in all future campaigns.

On the state subsidy battle, I threatened a veto, and Daley knew he couldn't gain enough Republican support to override it, so in the end I won. However, Vic told me that this only made the Daley people more determined to defeat us in the legislature.

### BECAUSE I SAID SO

Today's governmental "buzz word" is *transparency*—making it easier for taxpayers to see how their government is working. Or not working. Transparency can limit opportunities for corruption and persuade the bureaucrats that they had better mend their ways because someone is watching—forcing good behavior, if you will—and helping to make public servants accountable for their action—or inaction, as the case may be. Transparency is the modern extension of the old "sunshine laws"—lifting the blinds to let the sunshine in, to let the public see what's happening. Illinois state government needed a whole lot of sunshine.

From day one, ethics, transparency, and accountability were our operational priorities. I insisted on immediate action to deliver on campaign promises for openness and honesty in government, feeling strongly (and Vic agreed) that we had to take the initiative and keep it. Control the agenda, as the political experts say. Our best immediate tool was the use of executive orders, as I had promised in my inaugural address.

Bill Goldberg had immediately set about drafting for my signature our proposed series of executive orders, and I began to issue them. The first and unprecedented step was my plan to eliminate politics from the state police. I had picked the superintendent from a list submitted by a blue-ribbon panel. Fortunately, I did not have to go outside the state since Dwight Pittman, an outstanding candidate from Illinois, was on the panel's list.

I chose Dwight, and he came in for his first appointment. "Dwight," I said firmly, "if anyone—even a legislator with power over your budget, even a high official in my administration, or a member of my staff asks you to reassign or promote a state policeman or do anything with the highway patrol—I want you to pick up your phone and call me. I will tell him to keep his hands off the state police." I followed up with an executive order stating this in formal legal language. Dwight obeyed my instructions, did an excellent job, and we ended the age-old Illinois practice of political control over the state police force, including the highway patrol.

Next, we had to tackle the state payroll, which had grown substantially in recent years. I issued an executive order freezing all hiring, except for essential positions, and directing that the number of employees be cut back severely. I announced, "I am determined to bring state spending under control, starting with the payroll."

I worked out specific, detailed employee cuts with each agency head. At the end of the process, I succeeded in reducing the number of state employees by about 10 percent. Hal Hovey, director of the Bureau of the Budget, estimated the savings at ten million dollars annually. This initiative raised howls of protest from the AFSCME (American Federation of State, County, and Municipal Employees), the state employees' union that had supported me during the 1972 campaigns. I hated endangering their support, but I was determined to eliminate unnecessary jobs, and I was saving taxpayers money. Yet, here was another place where I received no credit in the media.

The media and the Republicans charged that I was firing Republicans to create jobs for Democrats. True, some of those cut were, in fact, Republican patronage workers hired by former governors, but that was inevitable. When any enterprise, public or private, cuts employees, the most recently hired quite naturally get the ax first; seniority plays a role. Obviously, in the state agencies, those most junior had been hired during the immediately preceding years under my Republican predecessors. The proof of the pudding on this issue was whether the jobs remained unfilled. And they did. Of course, no reporter went back the next year to check and then retract the previous charges of patronage-motivated firing. I sometimes wanted to just throw up my hands, but on this one, I was satisfied. The payroll reductions stuck.

Next came an executive order requiring Democratic county chairmen as well as ward and township Democratic committeemen to resign their party posts before taking any state job. As with all executive orders, this one could apply only to jobs under the domain of the governor and not to independently elected officials. I followed this new order up with a formal announcement that there would be no traditional "patronage chief" in the governor's office and declared officially that no jobs in state government should be regarded as "belonging" to any political official, such as a county party chairman. This, too, was a first since, historically, county chairmen had "owned" certain state jobs they could fill with whomever they wished.

The directive prohibited department heads and agency chiefs from checking with political party officials or requiring an applicant to have a letter from his local party official. These actions not only departed dramatically from prior practices but cut to the heart of the patronage abuse in Illinois government personnel practices that for decades had made political activity superior to individual merit. Needless to say, these steps created considerable enmity in regular organization ranks throughout the state and also further exacerbated my relations with the Daley Democrats in the legislature.

Then came the executive order most upsetting to established politicos: the prohibition of any state employee from requiring or even asking other state employees to make or seek political contributions, including purchasing tickets for fund-raising events and selling ads in political event programs. These practices had for many years been a way of life in state government, regularly used to fill campaign chests.

One of the most far-reaching orders established a formal state ethics board to administer all the reforms. Also, higher-paid state employees were required to file with the board a complete and detailed financial disclosure statement accompanied by federal income tax returns, a measure greatly increasing "transparency and honesty" that was unprecedented in Illinois and, for that matter, anywhere else in the nation, so far as I knew.

There were other controversial executive orders covering government operations. I created an Office of Special Investigations (OSI) and placed in charge a former FBI agent and attorney named Donald Page Moore, a tough and incorruptible Irishman. I charged him with rooting out corruption by investigating each and every charge of malfeasance by employees in the departments and agencies under the governor. And I informed my cabinet that I would brook no interference with his investigations, no matter who was being pursued. Because the hostile legislature refused to appropriate enough funds for the OSI, I sometimes had to ask operating departments for staff personnel. The media jumped on this and labeled OSI a "pet agency of the governor." No credit for this being a positive step toward good government was given.

Another order broke entirely new ground, requiring all businesses dealing with the state to report all campaign contributions made by their owners, directors, and principal officers. It was, and still is, a regular practice for a business CEO to tell his subordinates to make personal contributions to a favored candidate, and there was no way to track down and accumulate all such contributions. For the first time in state history, a reporter might easily total all political contributions emanating from a corporation doing business with the state. Unfortunately, the Illinois Supreme Court killed this executive order and concluded that this time, I had gone too far. I still like the order.

Bill Goldberg had drafted all these orders, and all were challenged in the courts. Bill handled the litigation and won all but one of the cases. Significantly, no other elected state official in Illinois has ever adopted these reforms. A good example is the secretary of state, which controlled more than five thousand jobs in offices spread throughout the state and was blatantly in need of such reform—particularly the one prohibiting the prevalent strong-arm practices forcing state employees to engage in political fund-raising.

The spate of executive orders predictably upset the legislators, then in session in Springfield. Not just those who had no desire to see good government, but those who resented being bypassed by governing through orders rather than legislation. I had been warned, but everyone knew that the Illinois legislature would never have enacted these reforms into law.

Understandably, a degree of conflict between the executive and legislative branches is inevitable. However, the media preoccupation with the executive-legislative disputes is sometimes overdone and constantly fraught with fights over a president's or governor's programs. Unless there is a scandal or conflict arising out of the "oversight" responsibilities of the legislature over existing laws, reporters pay little attention to day-to-day governmental operations. Evaluation of success in governing is too frequently based on the fate of programs in the legislature rather than on how governmental agencies work. But the latter is where most Americans come into contact with their government, where, to use the current saying, "the rubber meets the road." This negative attention lies at the heart of public cynicism about government, which, in turn, unfortunately makes some elected officials themselves more cynical about voters.

I became more and more concerned about the state legislature. The difficulty of finding legislative allies and the unwillingness of the media to take up the cudgel on these reforms bothered me greatly. Our agenda for good government was first-rate, but we were going to have to fight every day to make it happen.

Other governors had warned me that one of the most frustrating aspects of a governor's life is dealing with the legislature. If the founding fathers intended this result, they certainly succeeded. Even Lyndon Johnson, one of the most successful legislative leaders of our time, found after he became president that he had to spend much of his time fighting with Congress. As one governor summed it up, "The only enjoyable time a governor has is when the legislature goes home."

## 21

## *Fighting with Daley's Legislators*

If there is a benefit to being in prison, it is that there is time to think. But this is also a curse. You damn near go crazy just from your own thoughts. Yet, eventually you work your way through at least some of your demons. I still have a long way to go, and I know it. I stab cigarette butts as if each one had a name on it. I've jabbed the warden so often I'm bored with him. I can't quite bring myself to jab my wife, but I'm jabbing the qualities I see in her that infuriate me.

*She used me.* Jab. Jab. Jab. Jab. Of course, I've known this one all along.
*She's completely self-centered.* Jab. Jab. Jab. But maybe I am too.
*She's a liar.* Jab. Jab. Jab. Jab, jab, jab-jab-jab-jab-jab.
"Aah!" I say aloud in disgust.
"You losin' it, man," a passing inmate yells.

I ignore him, yet I depersonalize the butts as I inevitably compare my first Roberta to the second Roberta. My first wife disappointed me and irritated me in many ways, perhaps in retaliation for all the times I disappointed and irritated her, but she was never guilty of R2's particular sins. And she still cares about me, despite the way I hurt her by the divorce. The truth is, I would not be in this situation if I had stuck it out with my first Roberta; that divorce decision was perhaps the worst I ever made in my life. Maybe that was the first step toward my downfall.

I think of the pretty and sweet-natured Roberta I met during my final "first class" year—which corresponds to senior year—at Annapolis. I was assigned to live with my new roommate, Don Iselin, as earlier related. Don took me home with him to Winnetka, outside Chicago, for our short holiday leave that year, and his girlfriend Jackie introduced me to her best friend, Roberta Marie Dowse.

It's beyond odd, bordering on spooky, how one prescient conversation will stand out in the memory after so many years. One evening, Don and I were talking about our girlfriends. Don smiled at me confidently. "Jackie's the one for me," he said. "I'm going to marry her, Dan."

I'm sure I congratulated him, but I think the thought was too daunting for me to add anything else.

"So, how do you feel about Roberta?" he asked.

"Well . . . we've had some great times together." This sounded like an appropriate thing to say. But actually, I enjoyed Roberta most because she was quiet and I could be perfectly comfortable in her presence. I was quiet too, and I realized that we clicked in a way I couldn't explain.

Then Don surprised me by asking, "Could you get serious about Roberta? Could she be your wife?"

After a moment I finally said, "Motherhood would be a major consideration for me." And then I said something to which I had given no prior thought whatsoever and that was as out-of-the-blue as his question. I responded, "Don, I just know Roberta would make a great mother. I'd like to have a lot of kids with her." Little did I know.

Should I have stayed with my first Roberta?

Despite my reverie, I seem to have picked up all the cigarette butts. The guard nods, and I leave the area, wondering if I were given a chance to change one thing in my past, should this be it?

---

## ACCOUNTABILITY AND SABOTAGE

Setting the standards in state government was not enough; communicating my administration's progress was also essential. Since the media could not be expected to print details about state governmental operations, I established the practice of holding monthly "accountability sessions" in different parts of the state; similar sessions are now often called "town hall" meetings. I would sit on a stool and take questions at random from the audience. This was not a popular practice with the legislature in session; they definitely did not like my going into their districts in this fashion.

This step in making government more transparent and accessible was followed by another designed to make it easier for people to get action on problems. First, I set up a Governor's Action Office in the lobby of the state office building in Chicago, right inside the entrance to be highly visible, and staffed it with knowledgeable individuals capable of directing each person precisely where he or she should go to get a problem handled. Then, I opened Governor's Action Offices in various parts of the state, and we publicly encouraged citizens to come in for help with their problems, including particularly those for which they had already tried but failed to get solutions. If my assistant in the office could not solve the problem by contacting the agency involved, his next step was to call my office. (I often took the calls personally.) This caused ripples of discontent in the agencies, but I could deal with that.

To staff these offices, I frequently used people in positions that had been allocated to various departments and agencies. I could not do otherwise since my office budget was simply not big enough. Both legislators and reporters jumped on this, calling these men and women "ghost employees" because their positions were not in my office budget. The "payroll padding" implication bothered me greatly. "Ghost employees" meant people being paid for not working. In fact, these people worked hard at their jobs. The practice of staff in the chief executive's office sometimes being paid by the operational departments is an age-old and fully accepted process in both state and federal government.

Regrettably, the "action office" concept designed to help confused taxpayers cope with governmental bureaucracy was not only marred by the "ghost payroll" controversy but also further crippled by media stories labeling these offices "Walker's political outposts." Hostile legislators—Daley Democrats and Republicans alike—jumped on these stories as an excuse to destroy the program, and they ultimately succeeded by denying funding. No governor since has followed this practice. I thought at the time—and still think—it was a "good government" initiative.

### THE EXECUTIVE MANSION

I did find pleasure in some things during those difficult days. Kathleen, my eldest, and her sister Julie both decided to get married. Kathleen married David Vaught, who had worked hard for me during the campaigns in southern Illinois. Julie married Jim Kollar, whom she had met while attending college in Denver, Colorado. Both had church weddings in Springfield and beautiful receptions in the formal "state" rooms at the mansion. The grand staircase seemed to be made for throwing bridal bouquets.

The fourth floor of the Executive Mansion housed the ballroom floor. A stage occupied one end, beautifully draped windows ran along the side, and there was a bar at the other end. Generous round tables seating eight could be set up for dinners. Vic and I wanted to host events there, especially dinner dances for potential supporters.

Vic entered my small office one afternoon. Outside of Mary Parilli, he, Bill Goldberg, and Norty Kay were the only ones who had free access to me. "I talked to Roberta's social secretary this morning, asking her to get Roberta to set up a dinner ball. Know what the woman said?"

I slumped, having a pretty good idea.

"She said it would make Roberta *mad*. Hell, Dan, you gotta talk to your wife. It's like she can't be bothered with being First Lady. She does realize that's who she is, doesn't she? God almighty."

I agreed to broach the subject with Roberta, dread building up inside me. I faced hostile encounters in my work all day. I wanted to be able to come home and engage my wife in relaxing conversation, but that wouldn't be likely on a matter like this. Admittedly, I was also resentful that for a long time she had made clear her dislike for Vic. Actually, this is not unusual in political marriages where the husband has a very close attachment to a campaign manager or chief of staff. But given the stress and needs of a job like this, I had hoped she would let go of that.

I called from my office and reached Roberta's secretary, who arranged for her to call me. We finally talked, and she agreed to have dinner with me that evening in the mansion. Very often, I had to be away in the evening so we seldom had dinner together. But this was important and had to be resolved.

That evening, Margaret and Will had their dinner sent up on the dumbwaiter and ate in their rooms, as they often did. The butler set the table in the family dining room for two. Roberta and I sat down, attempting chitchat until the butler finished carving the pot roast.

He returned to the kitchen, and I said, "Roberta, I'd like to invite some people to the mansion who have been—or could be—political contributors. You know, I've told you that our campaign committee is still deeply in debt."

"Oh, we can't do that," Roberta replied quickly. "It's just not possible."

My knife clattered loudly against the white china plate as I set it down. "Of course it is, Dear."

The butler entered with steaming hot rolls and set them on the table. I waited until he finished serving. I didn't need the mansion staff tattling to the press that the Walkers fought and argued.

Roberta said, "Dan, I enjoy greatly the position I have running the whole Executive Mansion. You know it's actually controlled by the State Historical Society." An SHS committee met regularly to make decisions regarding its function and maintenance. "They've made it very clear that there are to be no political gatherings here."

"That's ridiculous!" I blurted. "We're not talking about a political meeting, and I don't need their approval for my guest lists!"

Roberta was ready to argue, but the butler came in to replenish the salad. I waved him on.

It was a conjugal standoff. Technically, Roberta was right, but both Vic and I thought it could be handled circumspectly. There would be no funds raised at the event, though people would know that they were invited because they either had made—or would make—contributions. It's done often at the White House in Washington. However, I saw little point in making a big fight out of it.

The weather warmed up, and I really enjoyed monthly weekends at our doublewide mobile home on the little lake at Taylorville. Roberta did not particularly enjoy it since solitude, fishing, and eating were my main occupations while there. We were losing some vital connection with each other. Roberta didn't like the turbulence that went with my involvement in government and politics. I not only accepted it, I actually enjoyed the fight for good government. I felt that while surely I needed some quiet time, I was really—at long last—where I belonged.

### BLOOD SPORT

House Speaker Blair and senate president Harris, both Republicans dedicated to my downfall, regularly joined the Daley Democrats in opposition to my legislative initiatives. Harris led a group of senators facetiously called "the Bourbons," conservatives who detested both me and my "good government" causes. For example, when I proposed a statewide, uniform, professional probation system, Bourbon senator Graham led the floor fight that killed this forward-looking legislation.

"Why aren't there Republican state senators of the stature and statesmanship of the highly respected former Republican W. Russell Arrington?" I complained to Vic.

"From the sixties?" Vic asked.

"Yeah. Arrington laid party fights and political partisanship aside to support good legislation. These guys today fight over matters both large and small if they think it's something I have anything to do with." The Daley machine carried on an incessant, behind-the-scenes warfare—the constant, everyday playing of hardball politics in committees and on the floor.

"Politics ain't beanbag," Vic said, as he often did.

"I just didn't expect it to become a blood sport on the smallest matters," I growled.

In the senate, we also ran into the Republican caucus system. Think *solid wall*. Votes were taken on pending legislation, and all Republicans were locked in, required to vote in accordance with the caucus majority, regardless of their personal views.

A newly elected senator arrived in Springfield, Mayor Daley's son, Richard M. Daley—"Richie." Our problems intensified as Richie took on an informal leadership role over the Chicago Democrats. He was implacable in his opposition (*hostility* would be a better word) to all of our legislative programs. For example, the sixty-day trial law, which voters clearly endorsed, and on which I campaigned so vehemently, went down in defeat.

I had little contact with the Democratic leaders other than at our breakfast meetings, but I did learn to listen carefully in our mansion sessions to Gerald Shea, Daley's floor leader in the House who always knew the details of pending legislation. He did his homework regularly. Shea has since become a very powerful and highly paid Springfield lobbyist. He encountered David "Clev" Cleverdon long after we left office and made a very revealing comment. "You know, you Walker people—Vic and Dan and all the rest—were the smartest people I ever met in politics. You only had one problem: You thought it was all for real." That kind of thinking was what we were up against.

Often, we could only prevail by mounting a public fight. We held press conferences in the original grand executive office in the State House, seating as many as fifty reporters.

One reporter called me by one of their favorite pejoratives: "a confrontationist."

I responded, as I had on other occasions, "Why don't you ask Daley why he doesn't accommodate me, instead of always asking why I don't accommodate him? Isn't he really the confrontationist?"

But logical though this was, it got me nowhere. The label *confrontationist* stuck in the media. I was also called "controversial," and this I could not deny. It was true that over the years I consistently evoked strong feelings, but voters had elected a fighter. What's wrong with confronting a problem and fighting for the right solution? Why couldn't the press see this as a plus rather than a minus? Grossly misleading headlines like this in the *Chicago Daily News* upset me: STATE PURCHASES FROM WALKER CONTRIBUTORS. The article adduced as proof some sporadic purchases of tools from Montgomery Ward stores by employees at state institutions and linked this to the personal contributions of Montgomery Ward executives to my campaign. This was simply ludicrous. I wondered why the media didn't zealously pursue Daley's money trails.

I felt strongly—and still do—that good government requires an adversarial relationship between government officials and the press. However, in effectuating this belief, I may have gone too far. For example, I left day-to-day media relations entirely to Norty, and some reporters called me "cold" and even "arrogant." I readily concede that in those early years, I could have done more to establish a better working rapport with the Springfield press corps, and I place considerable blame on myself for the rocky relationship that unfortunately developed with those reporters.

Our differences came to the fore with the submission of the first budget that I had carefully fashioned with Hal Hovey, the talented and experienced professional budget director I had imported from Ohio. I wanted this budget to send a message, agency by agency, on how personally dedicated I was to holding the line on both spending and taxes. Ogilvie had become mesmerized by the revenues brought by the new income tax, which was making millions available for new initiatives as well as for the expansion of existing programs. I wanted to dramatically apply the spending brakes.

In the past, governors had disseminated their proposed budgets to the Springfield reporters several days in advance of release, giving them time to digest the mass of text and figures and prepare their stories. However, this meant that the Springfield reporters would control the budget message given to the public. All over the state, media outlets would look to the Springfield stories for guidance on evaluating the proposed budget. This could cause misapprehensions from the get-go.

This time, at my direction, Norty supplied no advance copies of the budget to the Springfield reporters, knowing that this departure from tradition would upset them. These reporters had not particularly liked me from the beginning, and I had won office despite them. If they continued to be critical, it would be nothing new.

I had mastered all the details of the budget and personally took over the presentation to the media. Twenty or so Springfield reporters took their places around the large conference table in the grand executive office for this important news event. For three hours, I explained the budget, agency by agency, and answered a myriad of questions. In the process, I forced attention on the portions of the budget that I wanted highlighted. "Message control" it is called today in politics and government.

My approach infuriated the Springfield press corps at the time, as Norty had predicted, with continuing negative repercussions. They became and remained highly critical.

The result is documented in *Dan Walker: The Glory and the Tragedy*, authored by Taylor Pensoneau, a respected reporter for the *St. Louis Post Dispatch*—the one who had joined me for two days on the walk—and Bob Ellis, writer and editor of a downstate newspaper whom I had also met and impressed on the walk. These two men described the inimical attitude of the Springfield press corps toward me during those years when Pensoneau was one of them. They summed it up as "emotional hostility amounting to disdain," reporting that their pet name for me was "the werewolf."

Pensoneau and Ellis concluded that the dislike stemmed from several factors in addition to the budget fiasco and the standard, to-be-expected cynicism about government officials. They said these Springfield-based reporters "never forgave [Walker] for beating Paul Simon whom they idolized." Then they added, "Walker's style did not include drinking, backslapping, pleading his case, or fraternizing with members of the Capitol press." Finally, they noted that most of the reporters had regularly accepted "the liquor and other gifts that officials (but never Walker) heaped on the Statehouse reporters every Christmas." The two reporters contrasted me with my predecessor, Richard Ogilvie, and my successor, Jim Thompson, both of whom "worked the press beautifully."

I adopted the practice of using "fly arounds," flying to press conferences in major media markets throughout the state to release state government news personally. The anger of the Springfield press corps intensified. Reporters correctly saw this as "going over their heads" and breaking their monopoly on coverage of news out of the state capital.

Like many others from president down to governor and mayor (and many business executives), I grumbled privately about the press coverage from time to time. But I tried to keep my perspective. Historians remind us that from the beginning of our republic, chief executives have complained about the media. Near the end of his eight years in office, George Washington wrote that he was tired of being "buffeted in the public print." Thomas Jefferson criticized newspapers severely during his second term. Woodrow Wilson often complained that the media misrepresented his policies. I never copied these comments and did my best to swallow my feelings, but the digestion of these reporters' caustic resentment of me certainly fueled a case of "heart" burn.

### PASSION FOR MANAGEMENT

In the way that a sexy romance is sometimes followed by a rocky marriage, the struggle to win power is exciting, but the daily grind of government doesn't make any headlines. Yet, I dearly loved taking control and working long days trying to make government work better. I believed that good people working hard under strong management could make people's lives better. I studied business and governmental managerial techniques, debated managerial systems endlessly, and experimented fearlessly—perhaps a little too fearlessly—trying to find the right combination that would make government work better for people. Naturally, I hoped the public would learn what I was doing and appreciate the results. Perhaps I was a dreamer, but I remain so in some respects. This is part of the essence of who Dan Walker was and is.

One of the most difficult management problems is what I call the "we-they" syndrome. A department head moves into his office, and civil servants who have held their jobs for years surround him or her. They resent what they call "interference" from above. The "we" in the we-they syndrome are the department heads with their coterie of aides, and the "they" is the governor's office. This we-they way of thinking has often developed into a reluctance to implement directives from the chief executive and resulted in departmental failures to implement policy.

To cope with this problem, I wanted strong, capable liaisons to my office who could raise a red flag if necessary. Ogilvie had used this system, but he made the mistake of giving these assistants, mostly younger men and women, power to tell department heads what they could or could not do, thereby creating resentment. Directives on meaningful matters must come from the governor. This meant, of course, that I had to be willing and able to devote considerable time to management—which would be normal in the private sector, but, alas, is rarely seen in state government and almost nonexistent in the federal government. I built an excellent liaison staff and met with them regularly. At the same time, Vic and Bill Goldberg helped considerably on troubleshooting.

Naturally, I had hoped that my dedication to good management would not only get governmental results, but would also attract some favorable publicity. But I could rarely interest the media in these governmental initiatives. The only newspaper in the state that did so was *Decatur Herald Review,* and I remember my delight in reading their long articles on the operations of various departments and agencies.

There were some early successes, like Bob Alphin's dramatic shake-up in the Department of Revenue. I had brought Bob in from outside because he'd attracted attention as head of the Kentucky revenue department. But there were also failures, and one was the Department of Children and Family Services. This department dealing with child abuse and wayward youngsters had always tended to generate controversy and publicity. To head it, I chose Jerry Miller, an innovative young government executive from Massachusetts. I wanted to try out some of his new ideas.

Unfortunately, we stumbled badly. The first red flag came when Jerry and I decided to force a major Catholic institution to accept more wayward children. To cut staff costs, they had been refusing difficult-to-handle youngsters. My efforts to change this would increase their costs, and influential board members criticized me severely to the media, resulting in negative press coverage in Chicago. We also embarked on a major effort to trim the layers of excessive, expensive middle management and then embarked on a much-needed program to de-institutionalize troubled youngsters and give them a home environment since the institutions merely exposed them to other troublemakers.

We had other innovations, but we were attempting too many initiatives in an organization much larger than Jerry had been accustomed to and were upsetting too many apple carts, earning more unfavorable publicity. Reluctantly—since much of the uproar was my own doing—I replaced Jerry with my "Walker Worker," Mary Lee Leahy, and this time we finally got her confirmed by the senate. She did an excellent job, running a tight ship while implementing reforms gradually, keeping her department out of the headlines.

The Department of Public Aid was a constant headache and consumed more dollars than anything else, except education. The social workers, I felt, were more concerned about keeping welfare recipients on the rolls than in job placement. My welfare department director allowed himself to be co-opted by the career bureaucrats who often called Washington for directives that would stop or cripple my initiatives.

At one point, I seriously threatened to run the department from the governor's office, but Vic quickly talked me out of that. Finally, I brought in a new director. Jim Trainor—a West Point graduate who had starred in Michigan, acquiring a reputation for being a tough, results-oriented administrator—was just what I needed. Jim ran the department capably for the rest of my administration. We learned the hard way that instituting welfare reform at the state level was exceedingly difficult so long as the Washington bureaucrats had undue control over both policy and purse strings.

Our first cabinet meeting had proved too large and inefficient, so we dealt with the inevitable "turf wars" by working directly with the individual agencies. I tended to leave the smaller agencies to what is called "exception management," where agency heads are left alone *except* when critical problems require the governor's involvement.

I needed a vacation, which I hadn't had in well over a year, and took the family down to a grand resort on Marcos Island, Florida. I was enjoying playing tennis when an attendant stepped onto the court and approached me.

"There's an urgent phone call for you, Governor."

I took the call immediately. The Illinois River had flooded, displacing hundreds of people and flooding thousands of acres in the region where I had walked and talked with many of the so-called river rats. By phone, I established communication links with the appropriate state and local officials. Vic, Norty, and Bill all assured me that my presence wasn't needed, that everything was under control. However, Lieutenant Governor Neil Hartigan decided to take charge at the scene, calling himself "acting governor."

"We have a problem," Bill told me over the phone. "Legally, there is no 'acting governor' in Illinois." He explained that because modern communications permit exercising control from any location, the 1970 constitution—enacted under the Ogilvie administration—"requires that the governor be in charge all the time, even when traveling outside the state."

National television broadcast news of the disaster. There was Hartigan on the scene. I immediately called Harvey Johnson, director of law enforcement, and Dwight Pittman, superintendent of the state police. I told them both the same thing: "Under no circumstances are you to obey any order issued by Hartigan." I continued to get reports from the scene and took the necessary steps to see that the state police, Environmental Protection

Agency, and Department of Public Health were fully involved. There were no casualties, and people soon returned to their homes.

Later, I assigned particular responsibilities to Neil, such as asking him to take responsibility for overseeing the effects of state programs on the elderly, and Neil did a fine job that led to a separate department of the aged.

My relations with the other elected officials were not always the best. Attorney General Bill Scott was a constant problem, wanting departments and agencies that used attorneys on a day-to-day basis to report to him. This was not done in other states or in the federal government. Bill Goldberg finally won a court decision for us on the issue.

The controller, Republican George Lindberg, was also a problem-maker, repeatedly issuing dire partisan statements that the state was on the verge of bankruptcy. I ran a tight fiscal ship and the state was never even close to insolvency. I called George privately and asked him to stop playing politics with the state's bond ratings, explaining that his fiscal exaggerations (I avoided the term "lies") could cause national credit agencies to lower our bond ratings, thereby increasing interest payments on state debt. Regrettably, it didn't do much good. George had his sights set on running for governor and wanted the publicity, though his false accusations never did him any good.

Administering the state prisons was a constant headache. A key senate committee heeded one irascible member who viewed corrections as "his child." I will simply call this individual "Senator X." The rumors were strong that he had used his influence to have young boys brought to him from state institutions. I shuddered at these stories but couldn't prove anything. We had to leave it alone. Senator X torpedoed my first choice for director of the department of corrections, David Fogel, forcing me to move Fogel to head the commission on Illinois law enforcement and install Allen Sielaff as director. Alan had done a very capable job supervising prisons in Wisconsin, so a senate committee veto of him would not have played well.

Not long after he took office, Allen called me directly from Joliet state prison one afternoon. "We've got a serious situation, Governor. A riot."

## 22

## *A Prison Riot and Midterm Election Victories*

My least favorite prison guard has left us, but unfortunately, two other guards seem to be in competition to fill his mean-guy shoes. More insults, mocking, baiting. There was a gang rape a couple of nights ago. No consequences for the perpetrators. The guards still look the other way and work with the same stool pigeons.

I know the inmates can do very little about such injustices. I've already experienced how ineffective complaints can be, even to a congressman. The irony of the situation hits me. I had once decided the fate of prisoners who rebelled against prison practices, and now I am essentially in their same boat—or at least one very similar. Irony rises up and really socks it to me every now and then. How can such a turnabout possibly be my fate? Not that I believe in fate, but if I did, mine would sail off the irony charts, a roller coaster with corkscrew turns.

I plan to teach my class tonight on prisoners' legal rights, but I wonder where I'll find the energy. The men have been asking if they can do any-thing legally about the guards, asking if this legal system I love so much can help them here in Duluth. I make a few notes about what I can tell them and then summon my courage to check the mail at the barracks. Nothing from my wife, but there are two bits of good news. Mary Bucaro and my new lawyer are coming, and we will be meeting in the administration building—meaning I won't have to endure strip searches, and they won't be limited to Sunday afternoons and holidays.

A bulky package has come, and my spirits rise like warm steam as I unwrap a book from my dear sweetheart of a daughter, Robbie. This book is on the life of Jesus, the man, and it details how he came to be considered "the Christ" only after his death. This book's author will be my new companion, and the research will fill me with a much-needed purpose as I work on my own book about Jesus.

Later in my class, some of the men become especially agitated over the guards' behavior. I tell them that the only recourse I know is to try through correspondence to get outsiders to somehow pressure the Bureau of Prisons in the Department of Justice to commence an investigation, though I held out little hope of success.

One young man says, "My uncle was in Attica during that famous riot back in the seventies. You know, that real bad one in New York?" He looks around at the others in the class. "My uncle told me how terrible they treated the prisoners there. Much, much worse than here. So even though they rioted, the governor came in and gave 'em amnesty."

"Governor Rockefeller," I say.

"Yeah, him. I think he did the right thing, don't you, Dan?"

I consider my answer, but another inmate interrupts with a memory of his own. "Didn't you have to deal with a prison riot when you were governor?" the man asks. "Down at Joliet?"

"I did, indeed," I say. I tell them my story, and disapproving murmurs circulate throughout the room.

"Well, at least you're honest about it," the man with the good memory says.

---

**PRISON RIOT**

Prisoners were rioting at Joliet, and I was very glad that I had previously studied Governor Rockefeller's disastrous handling of the infamous Attica prison riot in New York when he granted amnesty to revolting prisoners. I knew that if I mishandled this one, the adverse publicity could severely hurt my administration.

At Joliet, prisoners barricaded themselves in a cellblock and held a number of guards as hostages. Some of the convicts' complaints involving prison practices seemed to be open to reasonable negotiation, but two were presented as nonnegotiable demands: personal meetings with the governor, and eventual amnesty for the rioters.

I sent a message of willingness to take a hard look at prison practices but stated firmly that there would be no personal meetings with me and no amnesty. I immediately set up a command control room, summoned Bill Goldberg and Vic De Grazia to meet with me, and established direct communication with the prison warden, along with the corrections director, Allen Sielaff, who had himself been involved in riot situations in Wisconsin, and with the superintendent of state police, Dwight Pittman. I included Dwight because I had decided to use armed state police rather than National Guard soldiers for any necessary control measures.

The crisis continued for several days. Allen conducted onsite negotiations, and we made some progress. I continued my refusal to meet with the convicts because this would establish a bad precedent. Future prisoners wanting attention would always demand to meet with the governor. When the barricaded convicts finally understood this as final, all issues were resolved, except amnesty for the rioters.

I was adamant: No amnesty under any circumstances. The rioters would have to face punishment.

The rioters then issued a time ultimatum, after which they would commence killing hostages.

I conferred with my crisis team and finally made the decision to use force. I instructed Dwight to select a cadre of experienced state troopers, volunteers only, and arm them with soft-trigger, sawed-off shotguns loaded with hard ammunition. At the least movement of a trigger finger, these guns would blast away.

Dwight assembled his force in plain sight of the rebelling convicts and awaited my command. I sent a personal message to the convicts by loudspeaker:

"This is Governor Dan Walker. The state police are coming in with loaded sawed-off shotguns. If there is any opposition whatsoever, they should immediately shoot to kill all convicts involved in this insurrection. Repeat: Kill all convicts immediately if there is any opposition by anyone." I gave the order to charge. In went the state troopers, shotguns at the ready. Fortunately, the convicts immediately dropped their weapons and surrendered. The hostages were freed. I breathed a huge sigh of relief.

I had made a very risky decision, but there were no more prison riots. I did learn a lesson, and that was to improve communications. I had to rely too much on relayed messages to get essential facts, and I had the same experience when sudden floods or tornadoes caused extensive damage around the state. Piercing the fog that surrounds every crisis is extremely difficult, particularly if several command layers relay situation assessment. So, I had the state police train one individual who, with necessary communication equipment, could immediately go to any crisis site and establish direct communication with me. That way, I had a trained representative at the center of action who could keep me constantly informed and also be positioned to get quick answers to critical questions and instantaneously relay important commands.

### THE DAILY DALEY BATTLES
### IN THE ONGOING WAR

Emperor Hirohito was to stop in Illinois during a state visit in 1974. Mayor Daley informed the State Department that he would officially meet the emperor's plane from Tokyo at Chicago's O'Hare field. I challenged this, saying that the governor, as the state's ranking official, should give the official welcome. The State Department agreed, and I prepared a very formal speech in what is called Imperial Japanese, drawing on what I had learned about the language in the navy.

The day arrived, and a large group of officials met at a "holding room" to await the emperor. Roberta and I stood across the room from Daley. One of those lulls in conversation occurred, so that the mayor's loud voice carried across the room.

"Governor," Daley called out, "you have not responded to my invitation to the formal dinner tonight for the emperor."

Stunned, I responded equally as loud. "Mayor, I have received no invitation to any such dinner."

Undaunted, Daley went right on, as he often did, just as though I had not spoken, saying loudly, "My mother taught me to respond to all invitations. It's the polite thing to do."

At that moment, the loudspeaker directed us to take places for the arrival ceremony, so I was unable to undo the damage done by the mayor's outburst.

At the ceremony, I delivered my short welcoming speech in what I hoped was acceptable Japanese. At its conclusion, the emperor stood silent.

Absolutely silent.

Had I mispronounced some important word? Had I somehow offended him?

The empress then spoke up and said very graciously, in plain English, "The Emperor and I are delighted to be here in the Land of Abraham Lincoln."

Beautiful. The emperor later told me in private conversation that the reason for his surprising silence was that, astounded at my speaking fluent Japanese, he could not figure out whether protocol required that he answer in Japanese or English.

That evening, we were not impromptu guests at the dinner.

Next morning, my phone rang at 7:00 A.M. "It's Mayor Daley," the operator said.

Before I could say a word, Daley went right ahead. "Governor, I had my staff check the records. An invitation to last night's formal dinner for the emperor was sent to you several days ago at 1152 Norman Lane, Deerfield, and I received no response."

I said, "Mayor, I have not lived at that address for a long time. I live at the Executive Mansion in Springfield."

Clearly taken aback, he paused but recovered. "No matter. You should have responded to my invitation, Governor, like my mother taught me to do." Then he hung up.

How do you deal with that?

The general assembly organizes in January and aims to finish by early summer. Usually, bills take their time working through the process, and the great majority is passed in the closing weeks of the session. Then, the governor must either sign or veto within sixty days after each bill's passage date. A governor's annual bill review process is intensive, working constantly against those sixty-day deadlines, and it includes several choices: signing, of course, and an impressive array of veto options. Under the unusually broad Illinois constitutional provisions adopted in 1970, a governor can veto outright, use the line-item or reduction veto on appropriation bills, or use the amendatory veto that gives him power to actually rewrite a bill. All vetoes can be overridden by the legislature in the fall veto session. A straight veto takes two-thirds, line item and reduction require three-fifths, and for the amendatory veto, a simple majority overrides.

No other state's constitution had given its governor such broad veto powers. Bill Goldberg reviewed all legislation for me, preparing analytical memos on each bill. Then, he and I would meet to discuss my action. This was an extremely long and arduous task involving hundreds of bills each year.

Because I used it very sparingly, I had little trouble with the amendatory veto. Most often, this was done in cooperation with the bill's sponsor who

wanted changes made for a variety of reasons. But the veto actions on appropriation bills caused severe problems in the spring of 1974. Since the budget
was extremely tight, I had asked for just what was needed. I most definitely
didn't factor in an increase to make room for legislators to show off to their
constituents by making cuts. So, the legislature delighted in appropriating
more than I had budgeted. My reaction? I didn't just make a few scissor
snips. I honed the machete and slashed.

Daley Democrats were especially furious, and I dreaded the fall veto
session, which was sure to override me. An override would make the legislators appear to defeat the mean governor who was cutting seemingly worthy
projects while at the same time make me the one on whose watch the budget
got so out of hand. A veto override would create a no-win dilemma.

I had also proposed legislation dear to my heart: to require disclosure
of all campaign contributions by those running for statewide office. Once
again, a combination of Chicago Democrats—led by dear Richie, the mayor's
son—and Republicans doomed the bill to defeat. But I had another dandy
weapon in my gubernatorial arsenal: the special session. So, after adjourn-
ment, and to many smoldering groans, I called the legislature back to reconsider the measure.

Vic's legislative aides, Douglas Kane and Mike Duncan in the house and
Ron Messina and David Caravella in the senate, had their work cut out for
them. Vic told them to go all out, persuading and twisting arms to obtain
the necessary votes. He told them to emphasize what everyone knew: The
public supported this legislation overwhelmingly and they, as legislators,
could not dare vote against it.

The legislature closed ranks again in both houses and bottled it up in
committees. Angry as I was, I could not, of course, go onto the floor of either
house myself, but I had another message to deliver. Vic's liaison staff would
hammer it home to each individual legislator, and while they were doing so,
I summoned a press conference, going public with the same message: The
public wants and needs this law, and I promised I would call special session
after special session until the bill came out of committees and there was an
up-or-down vote.

This time it passed, and Illinois had for the first time its historical mandatory disclosure of campaign contributions—a major reform to add to my list
of ethics reforms, most of which had been achieved by executive order.

We had barely caught our breath from the special session when it came
time for the veto session that would consider my budget cuts. Once again,

Daley Democrats enthusiastically picked up enough Republican help to override my vetoes. The result was substantial spending excesses that I had to constantly fight to control.

One small victory came out of that veto session. Daley's forces managed to get an absurd bill through the state legislature that gerrymandered one congressional district in a way that would make it impossible for Abner Mikva, the incumbent congressman, to be reelected. Abner was my old friend, and an independent Democrat. Ab and I had been friends since the early days when Adlai Stevenson was governor and Paul Douglas was senator. Vic was his campaign manager when Ab, then hailed as an independent, defeated Daley's candidate for the Illinois legislature. This connection was, of course, how I first met Vic, who also had helped Ab in his congressional campaign. For years, Ab had developed a strong reputation as an independent liberal.

I vetoed Daley's bill, saving Abner's congressional seat.

### MANO A MANO

Clearly, our government reform efforts continued to be in danger. If we had any prayer at all of making headway in the legislature in the next two years, we needed new legislators who would be more responsive to my programs, and so we initiated some selective fights in the 1974 elections—not only downstate, but also in Chicago—trying to elect friendly candidates. Mistakenly thinking it would help, I sought a meeting with Daley to explain what we were doing, since some of our fights would be against regular Democrats in Chicago.

I had, of course, met with Daley numerous times when I was a corporate executive in Chicago, as president of the Chicago Crime Commission during the King riot studies, during the open housing fights, and concerning the 1969 Democratic convention disorders. Daley was never a particularly good listener. He knew what he wanted to say, he said it, and that was that. He was accustomed to obeisance, not differences of opinion. Vic De Grazia put it very well in his oral history given to a Sangamon State University interlocutor: "Accommodation was not in Daley's vocabulary. Or, to put it differently, accommodation to him meant lying down and letting Daley run right over you."

The staff maneuvering to set up the meeting was almost humorous. Daley refused to come to Springfield, and after this refusal, I could not meekly agree to a publicly observable meeting in his Chicago office.

We settled on a private meeting in a hotel suite. Daley made the reservation and had a uniformed Chicago policeman stationed at the door, reminding me of the time I had pitched my reasons for wanting to be attorney general. This time, there were no sycophantic regulars around. I entered and sat on the sofa; he sat in an overstuffed chair. Just the two of us, we asked about each other's families, as previous experience had shown to be one of our very few common grounds.

I said, "We need to campaign in Cook County, Your Honor, to seek support for some independent candidates for the legislature. I know there are rumors that we are sponsoring candidates against your people for Cook County offices: assessor, treasurer, sheriff, president of the Cook County board—for the primary election." These were all jealously guarded machine offices, and I knew that such a campaign on our part was one of Daley's greatest fears. "I want to reassure you that this is not our intent. Our support is simply for legislative candidates."

He looked at me without saying anything or showing any sign of human response, but he hadn't raised any objection whatsoever.

"Cook County offices are unimportant to us," I stressed. "Walker people will leave them alone. But we will, naturally, support our independent Democrats running for the legislature."

His response was totally deadpan, and we parted. I felt comfortable that our intentions had been clearly established, and I conveyed this to Vic and Dave Green.

The 1974 legislative election battles were toughly fought. Vic took a leave of absence to concentrate on helping our candidates, and Dave Green joined him in planning their campaigns to the extent that they wanted help. Most did. And I went out and worked hard, spending many hours on intensive retail campaigning with individual candidates. "Hi, I'm Dan Walker, here to help Vince de Muzio. Please shake hands with Vince. We need him in the senate." This kind of campaigning in districts all over the state, including Chicago, went on for several months. We created a new Illinois Democratic Fund headed by Dave Cleverdon to raise funds for the candidates.

One evening in Chicago, Norty and I were looking for a place to campaign with a candidate for the legislature. Norty spotted a sign advertising a church bingo game. I found the man in charge and asked if I could "call a card" and introduce my candidate. He said, "Sure, Governor, go right ahead." We then paid the customary door fee and went in. It was a good show for the candidate, and I left satisfied, joining Norty Kay for the drive back downtown. The car radio was on, and Mayor Daley was making an announcement.

"That guy Walker," Daley said, "not only lied about walking the state, but is ignorant about the courtesies of Chicago neighborhood church bingo games. Tonight, he came barging with his guys into a bingo game at a Catholic church, refused to pay any admission fee, interrupted the game, and demanded to give a speech. Walker should go back to Springfield and stay out of Chicago until he learns the courtesies of church bingo games. And he promised me he wouldn't oppose *any* of our candidates in the primary, and here he is doing it. "

Talk about the big lie technique! Norty and I sat in the back of the Chevrolet, yelping in outrage.

"Let's blast him for the lies," I said hotly.

"I'd love to, but of course we won't be doing that," Norty said. "Daley's a master at this stuff. He knows there's no way you can effectively respond to an attack like this."

Mind-boggled, still shaking my head, I said, "I know. If I try to correct the record, I give greater publicity to the lie. And he damn well knows I made it clear that I would be opposing his candidates for the legislature, but nothing else. Norty, these lies are below the belt."

"And, as calculated, it's sure to hurt us in Catholic precincts all over Chicago."

We were staying at a hotel downtown, and after I arrived in my room, various family members called. They had heard Daley's slander. My sons Dan and Charles were particularly outraged.

"How can this be allowed?" Dan said. "Can't we do something about this?"

"How can he deny the walk?" Charles was almost yelling. "What does he think all the people who saw the walk are going to think of *him*? Doesn't he get it that everyone can see he's a liar?"

I had to semiseriously convince the boys that going downtown and personally accosting Daley would serve no purpose.

### TRUCE?

Nervously, we watched the 1974 fall election results. All our hard campaigning paid off. Despite Daley's lies, we scored. Not only did Democrats take control of the senate and the house, a significant number of state senators and representatives—including some in Chicago, but many more downstate—knew we had helped elect them. But Daley and his hard-core machine legislators from Cook County were all the more determined against me, and they found eager allies among the Republicans. So, in a better position, but far from being in control of the legislature, we faced the next two years.

Our most vital task was the budget. This was our chance to make significant progress with the new legislature. We got busy during the end-of-the-year recess and put in weeks of BOB work—Bureau of the Budget. I personally put in many hours reviewing every agency's budget request. If passed, this budget would allow real transparency in government, enabling the public for the first time in Illinois history to actually measure progress made throughout the year in spending the taxpayers' money.

We employed two procedures successfully used in private business: zero-base budgeting (ZBB), and management by objective (MBO). ZBB works this way: Instead of following the usual budgeting practice of taking current-year expenditure by the agency and adding a negotiated increase for the next year, all programs for each agency are listed, with the most important at the bottom and the least important on top. The CEO can then assess programs from the top down, spreading available funds intelligently, depending on program importance.

Using the technique of MBO, I directed that each agency expenditure request be accompanied by quantified commitments on results to be achieved. For example, the Department of Public Health had to state precisely how many inoculations public health nurses would make with the money allotted. The Department of Transportation had to make specific commitments for accomplishment of road improvements throughout the state. The Department of Public Aid had to commit to how many welfare recipients would be placed in private employment. In conservation, how many park picnic tables would be replaced with the dollars allowed. In the Environmental Protection Agency, how many miles of a river would be cleaned up. True, some programs were hard to quantify, but skeptics were surprised at how effective specific goals could be worked out in almost all instances.

Not only would every agency have to make commitments to specific results, but I would also personally review each and every commitment and, whenever possible, negotiate them upward with the agency head. In short, accountability would be achieved, and the public could see it all. All commitments were reduced to quarterly numbers, and the result was a budget such as had never been seen before that would enable anyone to easily check throughout the year whether each agency was meeting its commitments.

We were still working on the budget at Christmastime, and I was riding alone in the elevator in the State Office Building in Chicago—that's *Chicago,* not Springfield. The operator spoke up.

"Governor, you've really changed things around here."

I had, but I didn't know it showed. "What do you mean?"

He answered, "We're all amazed. There's practically nobody riding the elevators to deliver presents and bottles of liquor and boxes of cigars to the government offices."

"That's one of the nicest compliments I ever received as governor," I said.

This was really a Christmas to celebrate. Back in Springfield, Roberta had helped Margaret McCollum decorate the staterooms in the mansion, and the kids who had come home pitched in to help with their sister Margaret and brother Will. The mansion was all done up beautifully, yet still with a homey touch here and there. Handmade ornaments only hung on one of the trees, but there were several throughout the mansion. Greenery and lights hung everywhere. We held a large staff party, a black-tie affair at the mansion.

In a quiet moment on the stairs with Norty, I told him the story of the elevator operator in the State Office Building in Chicago.

Norty looked thoughtful a moment. "You know I don't butter you up, Dan," he said, "but I want to say this: One man made this happen."

More than ready, we faced the January legislative session of 1975. Yet before submitting the budget, we faced another battle: the election of a new Speaker of the House. A Speaker sympathetic to our causes would be a powerful advantage, but a major fight broke out. Seeking the office with Mayor Daley's support was Clyde Choate, a southern Illinois legislator with whom we had many conflicts because he persisted in cutting deals with Chicagoans and Republicans to defeat my legislative programs. Through intermediaries, we informed Mayor Daley that we could not support Choate.

The voting was extremely close, and the election process entailed seemingly endless ballots. If our supportive legislators left the floor at any time during this arduous procedure, Daley people would pounce, call for an immediate vote, and we would be stuck with Choate. Vic's liaison team watched the legislators closely, and so did the Daley people. A dramatization would qualify as high slapstick comedy, if the stakes weren't so high. Legislators took frequent breaks, often going out drinking. Vic's team had the responsibility of knowing where our supporters had gone and dragging them in, even from the bars, no matter how intoxicated. The team often had to improvise stalling measures from the floor to keep the Speaker Pro Tem from calling for the vote before our guys could be found. Vic's team worked many nights doing this, literally carrying a legislator in on several occasions. The fight in the house was a long one, running through ninety-two ballots and requiring constant work to keep the vote against Choate solid.

Then, early one morning, Daley called me. "Guv," he said. He had never called me that before. "You're right."

"Right about what, Your Honor?"

"You said Choate could not be trusted, and you're right. He promised repeatedly he could deliver some Republican votes, and he lied. So I cannot support him." He added, "Guv, who will now be our candidate for Speaker?"

Recovering from my shock, I unhesitatingly replied, "Bill Redmond."

"Redmond it is," responded the mayor, and that ended that.

Redmond was a friendly suburban Chicago legislator, and we thought his astonishing election was one of our greatest victories. This momentary rapport with Daley apparently held as I presented to the new general assembly my innovative "accountability budget." This time, I gave the press advance copies, and the legislators even applauded at the end.

During all this time, I was able to keep campaign promises by blocking funding in Congress for the Crosstown Expressway—one of Mayor Daley's pet projects. Daley called it a "main street for Chicago," tying the Dan Ryan Expressway to the Kennedy Expressway. I called it (as I had while campaigning) "the world's most expensive highway, one billion dollars just so individual drivers can get from the North to the South Side of Chicago fifteen minutes faster." And I stressed that it would displace up to ten thousand people in 3,000 homes and apartments, 370 businesses, and 37 factories, an exceedingly high cost in residences and workplaces. That billion dollars, I said, could be better spent on public transportation, enabling people to move more quickly and less expensively from home to jobs.

I did have an opportunity to show that I could work with Mayor Daley when legislation was introduced to establish the RTA, the Regional Transportation Authority for the Chicago metropolitan area. RTA made perfect sense. Those who labeled me a confrontationist, preferring to fight rather than compromise, had to do a double take when the RTA came along and I took a lead role in the successful negotiations.

This didn't evolve into an era of good feeling between Mayor Daley and me. We had hoped that when the new legislature began work in 1975 with Democrats in the majority in both houses and our friend Redmond as Speaker, we would be able to map out and advance a significant legislative program. After all, I had helped a meaningful number of the new legislators win their seats. But Daley, despite attending Mass every single day, was a cynical man who believed that everyone had his price. He was certain he could find ways to get to people. Vic and I underestimated the continued hostility of the Daley Democrats and their willingness to cut deals with the minority Republicans. And, regrettably, Redmond sometimes sided with Daley.

### RECESSION AND HEAD BANGING

A very deep recession was hurting the state badly, the worst one in decades. Revenue from state sales and income taxes plummeted in 1975. The dramatic shrinkage hit hard right after I had filed my annual budget in March. Obviously, drastic action was necessary.

I would not ask for any tax increases, so the only alternative was sharp budget reductions. Almost gleefully, though, legislative leaders from Chicago joined with Republicans in passing excessive appropriations. Excessive. They knew exactly what they were up to, and it had nothing to do with good government, nor with serving their constituents, and especially not with addressing the problems of the recession. They were forcing me to veto their legislation. Then, they led the fight to override my vetoes, picking up support, naturally, from a variety of powerful special interest groups.

They struck at me where any governor's budget is most vulnerable: state aid to public education. I had made some across-the-board budget reductions, but in education, the reductions were less than those applied elsewhere. It was *in no way* a cut in spending: Even with the reductions, the education budget was still more than 10 percent *higher* than the previous year's. The reductions were nonetheless painful but necessary, since education, as the largest recipient of state expenditures, simply had to contribute something to budget reductions.

Disregarding the facts, Chicago Democrats, the Republicans, the education lobby, and the media labeled my action a cut in education spending—no matter that there was actually an increase in both state appropriations and spending. "Walker Cuts Education Spending" was unfortunately the headline that stuck.

The legislature took up the veto override attempt. Daley came to Springfield, and the Democrats took the highly unusual step of inviting him to speak before the General Assembly. He personally spoke from the floor against me but ultimately failed to muster enough votes to override. Yet, his message reached millions of people, particularly in Chicago: Walker cut money for education. Devastating in its simplicity.

Raising contributions from friendly sources, we prepared television commercials setting forth the facts that I had not proposed any reduction in actual educational spending, but in fact asked for a substantial increase. This was unheard of, running television commercials on a governmental, as opposed to a political, campaign issue. But we did, and the commercials appeared everywhere—except in the Chicago area.

The Chicago network stations (NBC, ABC, CBS) flatly refused to carry the commercials. Downstate, television stations are mostly privately owned. In Chicago, the networks own them, and the decision was made in New York to refuse the commercials. My message got through downstate, but not in Chicago. This would really hurt me later.

In response to the recession, we developed a multimillion-dollar "accelerated building program" designed to expedite statewide public building projects that would create jobs and stimulate the depressed economy. Daley and other Democrats had over the years applauded major federal public works programs designed to create much-needed jobs, and they had worked with the unions to put these programs into effect. Naively, I guess, we thought my initiative would be so essential and so in line with the ideals of the Democratic Party that they would go along with it.

No way. Daley fought me in the legislature, even getting help from the major Chicago union leaders. The union members would have been among those who benefited most directly from my program, but their leaders, essentially in bed with machine politicians, paid no attention to that fact. The whole state economy would have benefited. Didn't matter. Daley managed to kill my program. The broad stimulation to the state economy that I had hoped for was never realized. It was head-banging time.

### MANAGEMENT CAMELOT

We didn't lose all the fights. One of my longtime crusades as well as campaign issues had been mental health reform. I had worked with Sam Shapiro's commission and made detailed recommendations to the legislature. We managed to persuade the legislators to adopt a new, modernized mental health code for Illinois—a model for the nation.

It was in this context that I first met Roberta Nelson. In the spring of 1975, she was lobbying the legislature on behalf of an organization for developmentally disabled children up in her home county of DuPage. I saw her name on my daily schedule and called Vic.

"Who is this Nelson woman? Why am I seeing her?"

"Because Pate Phillips asked me to get her an appointment," Vic said.

I understood. Senator Pate Phillips from DuPage County was the Republican power in the state senate, and this was the kind of "favor" that Vic would normally grant if he thought it would help him in his legislative maneuverings.

So she came to my office. Very attractive, with long black hair and large, expressive eyes. A very sensual woman. Her personality was pleasant and outgoing. She came right to the point and made an impressive presentation.

"I understand you've been quite active in Republican politics up in DuPage County," I began with a smile.

She returned it. "I have. They even wanted me to run for county treasurer. In fact, my sons and I worked for Ogilvie and against you in 1972, but . . . ," her smile widened, "I'm happy to say, our efforts were unsuccessful."

So, a charmer as well. I heard her intelligent, effective pitch on behalf of the children. Since this was a subject I had continually been interested in, I told her I would help her in any way I could—naturally. I would remember her, but didn't really expect to see her again. I had important legislation coming up.

We managed to win legislation prohibiting the use of "redlining" by financial institutions to discriminate against minorities in mortgage lending, a first in the nation. African American leaders were jubilant. Redlining had kept many middle-class blacks from obtaining home mortgages.

Working with my chairman of the Board of Higher Education, Don Prince, we brought community colleges into full higher-education partnership with the four-year universities. Working with Don, I also named professional men and women with no political obligations to the various university and college governing boards. (Years later, I was both pleased and proud when the *Chicago Tribune* editorially commended my Republican successor for breaking political history by reappointing Don Prince, mentioning particularly his professionalism.)

Vic was also working on the party apparatus. One goal was to name a downstater chairman of the state Democratic Party, and Vic won this one, beating Daley's candidate, after intense negotiations with Democratic leaders all over the state. No longer was it taken for granted that the entire Illinois Democratic Party would be run out of the hip pocket of the mayor of Chicago. Downstate Democrats finally had a credible, statewide party voice.

I was pleased with all of the above, but it was the nitty-gritty management, taming the less-than-effective bureaucracy, that delighted me most. The work-division system I had with Vic enabled me to spend maximum time on both specific critical problems—such as the urgent mental health care situation—and initiating new management systems, such as the aforementioned zero-base budgeting and management by objective. Also, as implied, these procedures required intensive follow-up. I might say, "Jim, you committed to deliver eight thousand inoculations of kids in the first quarter if I gave you that money, yet you delivered only sixty-five hundred. What happened?"

Face-to-face, boss-to-subordinate, first in negotiating the goals, and then in confronting failure to meet commitments—this approach was the heart of the system and absolutely essential to success. Quantification of commitments requires negotiation with constant pressure by the governor to raise the bar. Assessing performance and demanding personal explanations for failure to deliver results can be done only by the governor.

MBO cannot work when turned over to the budgeteers to implement, as other governors and President Nixon learned. The chain of command referred to as "staff-on-line" does not work because staff personnel simply do not have the power to force agency heads to make difficult commitments and then hold feet to the fire when the agreed-upon commitments are not achieved. "Line-on-line"—meaning the boss working with a subordinate—is essential, a fact of life regularly recognized in the business world.

Obviously, MBO, ZBB, and line-on-line follow-up meetings require substantial time commitments by the governor. I had to take one agency at a time to painstakingly install both the systems and the requisite follow-up procedures. By mid-1975, after many months of hard work, there were five code departments firmly on both MBO and ZBB.

All this, to me, constituted a management Camelot. I was so proud of these achievements and wanted nothing more than to simply continue this work. Politics reared its annoying head, however, and made its incessant demand: You must fight for reelection.

*Fight. Dan Walker is a fighter. Dan will fight for you. Dan fights the Machine.*

I couldn't say, "Dan Walker will get in there and make bureaucracies more efficient." That wouldn't have excited anyone. It had to be fights piled on top of fights.

The legislature had adjourned for summer break, and Vic had retreated to his five-acre farm outside Springfield. One of the state troopers drove me out to talk to him.

It was hot when I arrived, and Vic showed me his very large vegetable garden, fruit trees, and livestock before we settled on the lawn in the shade of an old elm tree two or three stories tall.

"I don't know, Vic," I confided. "I'm really ambivalent about this next primary election. I don't spend nearly enough time with my family. I'm weary of the constant battles. A primary campaign will be one long, hard fight on top of all the legislature fights. There is a big part of me that just wants to say, 'Enough.'"

Vic nodded.

"I'm sick to death of Daley continually sabotaging my best work."

Vic said, "Dan, you know you can't quit now. You're really accomplishing things. Our people believe in you and the cause. They've worked so hard for you. You can't even consider stopping here. You just cannot let them down."

I basically agreed, yet I didn't know if I could muster the same zeal I had brought to the last campaign. I loved being governor and trying to make lives better through intelligent governing. Yet, I sometimes shuddered at the immediate fights ahead and then four more years of battle with that damn Daley machine.

## 23

## *Losing in the 1976 Primary*

Another sleepless night in my cell. I can't read or work on the manuscript for my Jesus book with the lights dimmed, so I'm stuck with my thoughts. I think too much. I haven't had a conversation of more than a sentence or two with anyone in days.

My bronchitis is back, so I think about my chances for parole to distract myself. I've worked hard drafting the petition, and my lawyer thinks my chances of early parole look good because of all my public service. But even if I do get out early, I still face a long stretch of nights such as this one. Days and days of depression and drudgery are still ahead of me under the best scenario, along with time away from my wife and any chance of rebuilding our future. I choke up and start coughing, prompting one of my three roommates to swear at me.

Okay, I must not think of my wife. My thoughts turn once again to 1976.

I believe that I am only now, over twenty years after the fact, facing up to the reality of the momentous—for me, at least—days of that 1976 campaign and election. Swept along by events that so drastically affected my life during and after that election, I was either unable or unwilling back then to face the facts and engage in a realistic assessment of what happened.

The Duluth weather is still below freezing at night, and the days have been dark and cloudy. I seek an escape from the bleakness of the moment and of my future. My past is less troublesome, and I crawl into it, finally able to distance myself from its grip. Night after night, I have been carefully reconstructing the events leading up to that election.

One question I still ask myself: Did arrogance play any part?

———

### TOP DOG

Even though I had not officially committed to running again, I spent an increasing amount of time in 1975 beginning to campaign for the March 1976 primary election. Actually, in a sense, I had been campaigning ever since I took office, always renewing my contact with the people, especially downstate. I worked the town squares as I had in 1972. Taking along my sons Dan and Charles and often my youngest son, Will, I used the red-white-blue jeep as a trademark vehicle.

In September, Vic and Dave told me that according to the polls, "It's close, Dan, but we're a little ahead." Actually, it is very hard—virtually impossible—to use polling as an accurate measure in a primary election since everything depends on who turns out to vote, so making decisions based on the polls was iffy.

I still performed my gubernatorial duties as best I could, but much of what I did was politicized to an even greater extent than it had been previously. I positively dreaded the fall "Veto Session" because I would have to make some very difficult decisions on which my opponents could criticize me, no matter which way I went. I knew because it had happened earlier in my administration over decisions on the death penalty and the lottery. Both raised the age-old issue facing conscientious elected officials: To what extent should an elected official heed popular opinion when it runs contrary to firmly held personal beliefs?

Condemnations often occur today of poll-bound politicians who make decisions on issues based on the latest poll results or even the outcome of focus group sessions. But surely, all thoughtful students of government would agree that in a democracy, people are entitled to expect that elected officials will carry out the wishes of the electorate. So, why shouldn't a conscientious elected official pay attention to what the voters want?

The legislature had passed the death penalty and lottery bills by veto-proof margins. The public overwhelmingly supported them. I abhorred the concept of the death penalty and had occasionally said so publicly while campaigning. On a statewide referendum, people were asked to choose between total abolition and total acceptance of the death penalty. They voted for total acceptance by a large margin. I had opted for total abolition but never made it a clear campaign issue.

The death penalty issue sat on my desk as a bill limiting its use to severe crimes such as murdering policemen, rape-murder of a woman, or killing an obviously pregnant woman. I was severely torn. I had great difficulty in reconciling my views favoring a tough approach to crime with my belief in the sacredness of human life and my continuing concerns about the too-frequent lack of fairness in our criminal justice system.

As to the lottery, I had learned as president of the Chicago Crime Commission about the severe problems that could result from legalized gambling. For example, it invited Mob infiltration. Add to that my intense dislike for the use of gambling as a revenue source. I felt strongly then (and still do, despite the current waves of casinos and slot machines inundating the nation) that we are much better off relying on taxation to support social programs rather than gambling. The former helps focus voters' attention on the costs of government; the latter enables voters to avoid responsibility and perhaps even to advocate gambling as a means to avoid increasing taxes.

I finally signed both bills. Was I pandering? Or making conscientious efforts to resolve difficult dilemmas posed by our democratic system? Tough calls. Obviously, in these two instances, I garnered popular approval. But I was also condemned as a turncoat by the liberals, who remembered my campaign stance against the death penalty, and by others who recalled my campaign opposition to spreading gambling in Illinois.

Another bill for me to sign or veto would improve compensation for on-the-job injuries—which were considerably below current injury and disability standards—but which would also require a worker to relinquish the right to sue for further damages. The whole system needed reform, but we had many other battles on our hands, and I thought this bill was a good temporary fix. I signed it, and the business establishment promptly and angrily protested that I had been "bought by labor," referring to labor union political contributions to my campaign.

Signing the bill wouldn't do me much good in any case, because all major unions in Chicago—and that was most of them—would vote the way Mayor Daley told them to, which would be for my opponent in the primary, though in late 1975 he hadn't yet made any move toward backing anyone.

Certainly I believed in various labor causes and believed in the merits of my action, and, being human, I did hope for some political reciprocity. How does one assess the degree to which personally advantageous considerations affect a final decision? I think it is too often assumed that an official's action is responsive to campaign contributions rather than personal convictions buttressed by facts. Certainly this happens, but it is basically unfair to assume that given a choice between good and bad motivation, the latter explains the elected official's decision. I can think of no consequential decisions I made as governor that were motivated by campaign contributions. No matter; the media constantly concluded that they were, even when, to me, it was patently ridiculous.

Of course, the media were anxious to spotlight campaign contributions deemed questionable; however, their spotlight was not necessarily the light of impartial truth. The *Chicago Daily News* ran a headline, "Mob Gave Walker Cash." The story revealed a few instances where individuals who made campaign contributions had at one time been allegedly connected with hoodlum figures. The newspaper killed the headline as soon as we complained, but because it had such serious implications, I held a series of press conferences, each time holding the headline before the camera and refuting its implications as "misleading and inaccurate." A subsequent report concluded, "Walker's TV impact is astounding." We did undo the damage that headline caused.

However, in a very short span of time, I had alienated both Chicago liberals and the Chicago business community and failed to win the support of important labor union leaders, all while having to battle the legislature and defend myself in the press. By late 1975, contributions were not pouring in, but we did have enough to launch a campaign. In Illinois, filing for statewide office happens in December to allow three months of campaigning before the March primary election. So, in October of 1975, the final commitment deadline loomed for the 1976 primary. Should we really make the stupendous commitment of time, money, strength, and energy, and ask the same of our volunteers?

Daily, I equivocated. Should I run? Shouldn't I? Go? Not go? I summoned my team with a memo: Decision time. As Dave Green, Bill Goldberg, Vic, and Norty filed in and sat in four of the office's leather armchairs, I lit my pipe.

Dave often set the tone with the results of his analysis and Jewish arithmetic. "The polls are still looking good. We're at 53 percent. It's possible Daley isn't going to fight us. He may just go ahead with your name on the top of the slate, because he doesn't really have anyone who's a sure thing to put against you. He's not going to waste time on a campaign he doesn't think he can win from the get-go."

"Huh!" Vic said. "Daley's got so many dirty ways to win. A little thing like an opponent's popularity wouldn't stop him."

We analyzed Daley's options and concluded that in a fair fight—which was unlikely—I could defeat any of them.

"This is good news," Norty said. "We can waltz out of the primary and focus on November."

"I also don't see any strong Republicans out there," Bill Goldberg said. "Not any who can beat Dan. And if Daley doesn't commit, we've got it, right?"

"Well, wouldn't that just be lovely," I said, knowing there was something very wrong with this assessment.

Vic shattered the daydream. "If Daley doesn't endorse anyone for governor, you can bet your butt he'll still join the Republicans in hammering us hard on the fights in the legislature."

Dave knew right where this was going. He pulled at his tie and leaned forward. "Daley knows we don't have the time and resources to run our campaign and mount another fight to support independents in the Assembly."

"The smoke in the hack ward offices is probably so thick already it won't clear until New Year," Vic said, gesturing as if to clear smoke away. "They're already lining up candidates who'll kill us on the floor."

"And that's exactly what I dread," I said. "The cost to me and my family is just too high. I just don't want another four years like that." I took a long, calming pull on my pipe.

Vic stood up and paced a bit and then stood behind his chair, bracing himself as he leaned forward. "The Democratic Party, the media, and some of the public still see Daley as top dog."

There were mutters of protest, but Dave said in his calm and logical voice, "Sad, but true. Yet, if we could defeat a Daley candidate in the primary, that would be a two-time win over Daley and his Machine—something that's never been done before. Dan would become a national political figure."

Heads nodded, Norty's especially.

"An undeniable power mandate," Bill agreed.

Vic sat down again. "With that kind of victory behind us, we might just get what we want through the General Assembly."

Norty fiddled with his glasses. "What if Daley doesn't run anybody?"

We were all thoughtful for a second. Bill cleared his throat. "If Daley doesn't run anyone, it will seem like a de facto endorsement of Dan. That would give Daley credit for the win."

"And *that*," Vic said, "would obligate Dan to him." He shook his head. "Jesus, it's almost like Daley had a brain. He does have amazing instincts, I'll give him that. But even if Daley couldn't plan all this, he'd smell the power coming back to him, and he'd grab it."

I made a few decisive puffs on my English-blend tobacco. "Call a press conference, Norty," I said. "I think I can provoke him so he has to run someone. Vic's absolutely right. Dead on. I've gotta be the top dog in this state or quit."

Norty summoned the press, stating that I was going to announce my official decision as to whether I would run for reelection. I made a carefully drafted statement in the affirmative and then concluded, "And as to any possible opponent, I have a direct message for Mayor Daley." I waited until I had undivided attention. "I challenge you to convene your clique of slate-makers and pick a puppet to run against me."

### DAMAGE CONTROL

Publicly, Daley ignored my challenge, but we began hearing rumors that machine wheels were turning toward the governor's office. They wouldn't announce until December, but everything would be in place by then. I couldn't believe I'd provoked the fight—the very thing I'd wanted to avoid—and yet, the possibility that this one push would grease the way for my whole administration had invigorated me. I could do this one more time. I had not even considered how foolish my dare might look if I didn't win.

Campaign success, as well as administrative success, demanded long days of leaving the office in the late afternoon and spending many evenings in various parts of the state, attending events, meeting people in small groups, and appearing on local media outlets where I could reach the public directly without the middleman effect imposed by Springfield reporters. This meant very few evenings with my family during the week. Then, on Saturdays and often on Sundays, I continued to work small towns during the day and spoke at events in the evening.

A schedule such as this left few days off for family recreation. All in all, Roberta, Margaret, and Will were too often neglected. Yet, the kids were wonderfully good sports about it. It helped that the staff in the Executive Mansion made them the center of attention and spoiled them, and even though Margaret and Will hated the constant state police escort, they loved the men of the security team, and the men loved them.

I did occasionally take time off for a hunting trip in the fall, but even that turned into bad press, at least initially. I was ticketed by a federal game warden for shooting doves over baited ground. When I protested that I knew nothing about the corn that was loosely covered with dirt, he became positively insolent.

"Knowledge is immaterial, Walker. I nailed Hubert Humphrey last year, and I'm getting you this year."

The incident was widely publicized downstate, and I anticipated adverse reaction until I learned that many thought I had been set up for the arrest. This proved to indeed be the case. The corn had been scattered the night before my arrival. Locals weren't too happy about a federal official being in charge of their hunting grounds. So, they sympathized, and whenever I walked into a small downstate café, I paused at the door until people looked at me, and then said in a loud voice, "Anyone here know a good place to go dove hunting?"

It was a sure winner, and the laughter and applause reassured me. I paid the hundred-dollar fine. Ignorance of the baiting was not a legal defense.

The frequent need for me to participate personally in damage control missions and also to constantly maintain my visibility around the state resulted in too frequent absences from home. Unfortunately, this led to gossip. Once, I flew down to southern Illinois to speak at a major fund-raising dinner where more than a thousand Democrats were expected. Pete Wilkes, my security chief, drove me to the hall. I planned a dramatic entrance, deliberately coming in solo and a little late through the back entrance and then working my way up to the head table, with applause mounting all the way.

On this occasion, I had been met not by the expected party official, but by a buxom brunette who said her boss had designated her to escort me. I was a little surprised, but went right ahead with my planned entrance. Ladies were often flirtatious with me, so I didn't think too much of this woman's behavior at first, but she annoyed me by repeatedly taking my elbow to steer me to particular tables for handshaking, and I finally brushed her off. Following my usual practice, I left the event immediately after speaking and jumped into the car for Pete to take me to the airport to catch my plane to Springfield.

On the way, I asked Pete, "Who was that woman who met me?"

Pete looked back over his shoulder and said lightly, "Governor, who you trying to kid?"

Tired and a little irritated by the question, I brusquely told Pete to knock it off and answer my question.

He said, "Governor, if you insist I'll say it out loud. Everyone knows that sexy lady is your mistress."

I learned later that the woman, anxious to have people see her holding my arm, had steered me to the tables where her family and friends were seated. All of them were aware of the gossip. I was *flabbergasted* (a word my grandmother taught me) and ordered Pete to tell me more. He informed me that the gossip about my "affair" with the woman was widespread all over southern Illinois. She was a secretary for one of the local political bosses, an employee I had previously met once or twice in his office. I never succeeded in stopping that gossip. How do you kill a false rumor that you have a mistress?

### KERNEL OF TRUTH

Perhaps the public had noticed that I seldom made appearances with my wife, the exception being formal occasions. They may have also noted the lack of any outward sign of affection between us. This was largely because my passion was for my work and the campaign. I typically put in fourteen-hour days and would come to bed exhausted. There would be Roberta, reading with the overhead light on, which she refused to turn off.

One night I said, "You know they make those little lights you can take to bed with you, just for this purpose. How about getting one?"

"No," she said. And that was that.

A little thing, but those little things really added up with me—perhaps because of so much pressure. My passion for my work, fatigue, niggling irritations, and my general malaise had all combined to erode our marriage. Yet, I wasn't unhappy and continued to charge ahead into the upcoming election.

On one campaign event, I encountered Roberta Nelson again. A fund-raising luncheon for her developmentally disabled children's center honored Paul Butler, a very wealthy man who lived in the village of Oak Brook, a western suburb of Chicago that he founded. I had met Paul at other fund-raisers, and he had contributed to my campaigns. Mrs. Nelson had made it her business to schmooze Paul to get his financial support for her cause.

I spoke briefly at the luncheon, and Mrs. Nelson approached me afterwards. "Governor, would you like to see the DuPage facility?"

I found I enjoyed again my moments with the woman. "That sounds interesting, Mrs. Nelson."

"Please, call me *Roberta*," she said, smiling. "It involves three separate sites. Can you fit that into your busy schedule?"

Whatever I had planned could wait. "I'll have my driver take us."

I'm sure I was impressed with the sites she took me to, and then I had my state trooper drive us to her home in nearby St. Charles. It was time to say good-bye.

"Would you like to come in and see my home?"

Again, I agreed to her suggestion. I had not been inside long, however, when the doorbell rang. It was my state trooper.

"Governor, Mr. De Grazia is upset. He says your schedule has been badly disrupted. He needs you to get back on schedule."

It had been a pleasant interlude, one that reminded me I was a man who enjoyed women. But I felt I would probably never see this married lady again.

During this time, I had to push all personal feelings aside. Vic constantly reminded me to provide all the energy and concentration I could muster. To that, I added my own compulsion for self-discipline. I had to be the best candidate I could possibly be.

### GET WALKER

That autumn, in addition to the governor's race, speculation began building about possible 1976 presidential contenders. And I was increasingly being mentioned in both Illinois and national media as a possible candidate. *Fortune* magazine, for example, ran a long article speculating that I would be "the best campaigner of the lot."

In November, Team Walker gathered to reevaluate our position: Vic De Grazia, Dave Green, Bill Goldberg, Norty Kay, and Mort Kaplan. Mort, a public relations professional, had participated in the original 1970 "go" decision and, while taking no position in state government, had often been consulted on strategy and tactics, sometimes in meetings and often by telephone.

"I have a proposal," Dave said. "I don't think Dan should run for reelection."

All heads turned toward him in surprise.

"I think," Dave continued, "he should boldly enter the New Hampshire primary early in 1976 as a formally announced presidential candidate."

I, along with the others, was stunned, but a serious discussion followed in which Dave revealed various poll numbers and projections and said he had already had some quiet conversations with top politicians in other states and in Washington.

Vic repeated his main concern. "This would mean giving up the battle against the rotten system and the Chicago machine. We just can't do that."

"This whole discussion is undeniably exhilarating but seems a little too far-fetched," I said. "I don't want to run for president. I wouldn't mind *being* president. Who wouldn't? But I've got all I can handle right here."

Finally, the prevailing argument was that I should continue the battle, win another dramatic Illinois primary battle against Daley's candidate—whoever that might be—and then, with a primary victory under my belt, take another look at the presidential possibility.

We felt confident of winning a second battle with the Daley machine. I felt particularly secure about downstate, what I often called "the other Illinois." With my solid record supported by statistics, I could claim credit for holding the line on taxes, stemming the tide of welfare spending, and substantially reducing the state payroll. All would be widely appreciated downstate even more than in Chicago. And we had taken great strides in giving downstate more power in both the legislature and the Democratic Party.

In the event, I did less downstate campaigning than I would have liked. I had marched in parades throughout my campaigns and while in office, all over the state. That fall, I marched in the Harvard Milk Parade. My public expected to see me walking, and I didn't disappoint them, eschewing the comfy convertibles of most politicians. I zigzagged back and forth, working both sides of the street, even dashing up to nearby doorsteps for a handshake and a good word. This was my element, but as it turned out, not what was most needed.

We knew that the Chicago area would prove more of a challenge, particularly in the machine-controlled areas of the city, but also with Chicago liberals who were dissatisfied with me, and among the many people who believed, wrongly, that my budget reductions had cut educational spending. In the Chicago area, I was again constantly at the factory gates and shopping centers along with the bowling alleys and restaurants.

In December, the Daley slate was announced. My opponent would be Mike Howlett, the incumbent secretary of state, a heavy-set, old-style politician who had failed to obtain even a high school diploma. Howlett flatly refused to debate and followed the usual campaign pattern favored by the regular organization, attending occasional public events downstate and emphasizing Chicago ward meetings.

I took the immediate offensive and attacked Mike on ownership of race-track stock, refusal to back away from the abuses of the patronage system as secretary of state, never stopping the practice, as I had, of forcing employees to obtain political contributions, and other similar matters related to the Illinois political system that I had fought to reform.

Predictably, all the regular Democratic organization, all the county chairmen, all the township committeemen, all the ward committeemen, all the precinct captains supported Howlett. So did all the major union leaders. I had hoped for divisions in the union ranks, and some courageous downstate labor leaders, notably Don Johnson, a trade union official I had installed in my cabinet as director of labor, helped me. Overwhelmingly, the top guys did as Daley wished and supported Howlett—no matter that I had a stronger pro-labor record than any governor of Illinois before me, including Adlai Stevenson.

I began looking for as many sources of support in Chicago as I could find. One nearly certain endorsement would come from my friend, Congressman Abner Mikva.

"Oh, yeah," Vic said. "Ab's a sure thing."

So, I called and asked for Ab's endorsement.

Abner hesitated. "Dan, I'll have to think about it and call you back."

I was surprised but readily agreed. Several days later, Abner called.

"I'm sorry, Dan, but I can't help you. I'm going to support Mike Howlett."

I was shocked into silence. Recovering, I said, "Ab, I just can't believe this. I've been a friend and supporter of yours for years, and when the chips were down, I saved your seat in Congress by vetoing the Daley bill that would have killed you. Why? Why are you doing this to me?"

Abner responded, "It's because you signed that death penalty bill."

I was again shocked into silence. Then I said, "Abner, I'm just flabbergasted. You mean that just because we differed on one issue, after all the work we've done together for good candidates and the cause of political independence in Illinois, and after I saved your congressional seat, you're going against me?"

"Yes," he said.

Badly shaken, I reported the conversation to Vic, and he too was amazed. He called Abner directly, but Ab was adamant.

"I just can't believe this," Vic said. He set the phone down and paced, stating the obvious: "It's not like Mike Howlett and the rest of the Machine are against the death penalty."

"Just the opposite."

"And nobody thinks Howlett can beat *any* strong Republican candidate," Vic said.

"Let's see how Abner's liberal supporters like the way the Republicans handle the death penalty."

Vic and I looked at each other, knowing the obvious explanation. Abner did not want to cross Daley.

I thought again of Adlai Stevenson, Paul Simon, and Otto Kerner. Independents in talk, all of them, until the power of the Daley machine reined them in. "Another independent caves in to the Machine."

"They do come to heel when Daley cracks his whip," Vic said.

A friend betrayed a friend. Such was the power of the machine.

Furious, I kept up my aggressive campaign and confessed to "baiting" Mike Howlett in speeches, charging that he only did what Daley told him to do, or that he was a machine hack, or that he was Daley's puppet. At one point, he lost his cool, calling me publicly before television cameras a "lying son of a bitch."

When Howlett was criticized by some in the media, Daley defended him by attacking the reporters. The *Chicago Tribune* called it a "dirty campaign" by both candidates. I disagreed, finding nothing below the belt in the hard-hitting campaign I waged based on charges I could prove against Howlett in my attempt to change the face of politics in Illinois. In fact, our television commercials weren't hard-hitting enough, featuring nothing more than my governmental record: Elect me because I'm a whiz-bang administrator.

"I'm disappointed in our TV spots," I said at a meeting with Vic and Dave. "They have no bite. I'm not getting the kind of feedback during my face-to-face campaigning as I used to get."

"We probably should have reshown shots from the walk commercials," Vic said.

Meanwhile, Daley went all out, making it abundantly clear to all the ward committeemen and precinct captains that this was a "get Walker" campaign that he was determined to win. On the Sunday before the election, cards were distributed after church services in some heavily Catholic precincts stating, "Vote for Howlett because he's opposed to abortion." No matter that my position on abortion was exactly the same as Howlett's. Both of us were quoted throughout the campaign as being personally opposed to abortions but recognizing the nation's need to abide by the decision of the U.S. Supreme Court in *Roe v. Wade.*

We had not built the volunteer organization we'd had before, but our people worked extremely hard, and despite the loss of key support—liberals, Chicago unions, Catholics, and other voter blocks—both field reports and polls appeared encouraging. The surveys right up to election-eve gave me confidence, showing a statewide lead with 53 percent to Howlett's 47 percent.

On Election Day, Daley very cannily sent large numbers of his captains in "safe" wards out into the Cook County suburbs to work the precincts against me. We didn't have the numbers of poll watchers we had enlisted in 1972 or the volunteers to get people to the polls.

Still confident, our usual crowd gathered at the Allerton Hotel in Chicago to watch the results. After hours of reports that the race was too close to call, Vic and Dave told me that we had lost. Downstate, I carried almost all the counties (94 of 102). Outside Cook County, I received 70 percent of the vote, carrying the rest of the state with a plurality of 113,434. It wasn't enough; Cook County beat me. A narrow margin elected Howlett as the Democratic candidate for governor. Clearly, I lost the election in the Chicago area—Daley's turf.

One of the toughest times in my public life came when I called the family into a conference room in the hotel. All were there: seven children and Roberta. All were apprehensive, but the media had only reported that the race was exceedingly close. Numb, almost in physical shock, I told the family that we knew better, that we had lost, that the fight was all over. There was dead silence, and then several of the girls broke into tears.

I had to leave, though, to face my supporters in the ballroom downstairs. Still shocked, I thanked them for fighting the good fight and said something about wishing I could have done better for them, but the scene was nightmarish. As the gloom deepened, so did the silence. Finally, they left.

The March weather was cold and blustery when we returned to Springfield. We pored over the returns, precinct by precinct, in critical parts of the state. What the figures clearly revealed was that too many of "our voters" stayed home. Our study pinpointed the areas where Howlett ran substantially ahead, such as the heavily Catholic neighborhoods. The results demonstrated once again that surveys cannot predict a primary election that depends on voter turnout.

The critical fact was that in the Chicago area, Daley turned out the Howlett vote, and we failed to get out the Walker vote.

Coffee grew cold in cups where Vic and I had holed up in my office.

"We should have realized by 1974, after experiencing all those bitter fights, that Daley would never stop being such an implacable enemy," Vic said. We looked at the statistics and gazed outside, watching the wind push the spruce trees back and forth.

"Our worst political mistake was that we should have built our own grassroots organization in the critical Chicago area precincts back in 1974." I could only shrug, sigh, and agree.

The media concluded, "Walker was rejected by the voters." That statement really should have said that Chicago Democrats rejected Walker. The evidence is conclusive that had it been a general election, rather than a primary election, I would have won by a decent margin—for whatever that's worth.

## THE EXCRUCIATING LAME-DUCK MONTHS

The months from March to January passed rapidly. I kept my vow to spend more time with my family, particularly in visits to our getaway place on the little lake in Taylorville, Christian County. We went east for Charles's graduation from Brown University, and on return, I went under the knife for removal of my gall bladder and appendix. Because of unexpected infections, I was kept in a recovery mode for two months. I did my utmost to throw myself back into the governing routine, though it was difficult to accomplish as much as I desired.

When Dan came to Springfield after law school graduation to be sworn in as a member of the Illinois Bar, I invited all the new lawyers to a reception and lunch at the Executive Mansion. I was delighted when Robbie was chosen to be a First Scholar at the First National Bank in Chicago and began her courses to achieve an MBA at the University of Chicago, where she had first met her husband, Taki Okamoto. Margaret, finishing high school, threw a big party at the mansion for her friends and classmates. She and I took delight in working in the vegetable garden we created on the mansion grounds—the first and last it has ever seen.

I splashed with Will and Margaret in the Montgomery Ward aboveground swimming pool outside the mansion. The *Springfield Journal-Register*, never a fan of mine, editorially deplored both this and the tire swing that, for Will's use, I had hung from a large tree visible to the public. Will often joined me for jug fishing at out little Taylorville lake, and Margaret came up with a great beer batter for frying the catfish fillets. We bought one of those three-wheeler, all-terrain vehicles, and I joined them in driving it around the grounds, until one day, going too fast, I could not make a turn and drove right off the bluff and into the lake. Will filmed what he called "The Great Jewel Robbery," working with a friend to write the screenplay, and then shot the action at the mansion with him and his friends as the actors. The staff particularly enjoyed watching this; they had kind of adopted Margaret and Will.

Meanwhile, back at the office, critical people were leaving my "lame-duck" administration, and it was hard to work up enthusiasm for the tasks at hand. I had announced early in 1976 my support for Jimmy Carter for the Democratic nomination for president, actually much earlier and more strongly than Mayor Daley, who remained coy until June, after Jimmy already had enough delegates to clinch the nomination.

Jimmy Carter and I had been at the U.S. Naval Academy together and had worked together pleasantly at several governors' conferences while he was still governor of Georgia. So, I spent numerous days campaigning for him. When she visited the state singly, I escorted Rosalyn to political affairs. I even made some dutiful campaign appearances for Mike Howlett in his race against Jim Thompson for governor—distasteful though it was, he was still better than a Republican. Yet, to nobody's surprise, Howlett lost by a large margin. And, perhaps more critically, the machine did not deliver in November its usual heavy margin for Carter. That was when Jim Thompson, the Republican candidate for governor, called Daley "a wounded old lion—bloodied, but dangerous."

I still accomplished a few things in the legislature. Having worked hard on a bill to provide bond money for a series of home-style centers around the state for the developmentally disabled, it passed before the legislative session ended for the summer. Surprisingly, even people like Daley's man Jerry Shea supported the bill—the one who thought nothing we did was "for real." Roberta Nelson had also lobbied actively for passing this bill and attended the formal signing. After the ceremony, we chatted.

A thought struck me. "Would you like to have lunch with me?"

"That sounds terrific," she said.

The Bismarck Hotel was across the street. We went to its dining room. I enjoyed being with her. However, there was nothing I would remember as "electricity" between us.

The White House was holding the Mental Health Conference at a large hotel-motel in Rock Island in the fall of 1976. I was invited to give a speech and found myself unprepared. I wanted to talk about Illinois facilities for the developmentally disabled, and so I asked someone to have Roberta Nelson come to my room to work on the speech with me. She did so, and I again found her attractive, but there was no physical contact of any kind, and I didn't give her personally any serious thought. Later, in the course of my speech, she was sitting in the front row. I publicly thanked her for her help and also pledged to the gathering that after I left office, I would devote considerable time to causes for the mentally handicapped. If I was angling to be around Roberta Nelson, it was an entirely unconscious process.

Also in the fall of 1976, I accepted an invitation from the Democratic candidate for governor in Indiana to spend a day campaigning for him. He said that I could help because voters liked me based on my appearances on the Chicago television stations that also served northern Indiana. While campaigning, I was surprised when told that Mayor Daley was trying to reach me by telephone.

"Guv," he said when I came on the phone, "this is Dick Daley. Need to talk a little politics with you."

"Good to hear from you, Your Honor," I replied, a little taken aback by this unusual conviviality.

Daley then described a recent meeting with some of his key guys. "We talked about what a great campaigner you are, Guv, and how we need you at the top of our ticket."

Amazed, I thanked him for the compliment.

"We discussed your running for the United States Senate, Guv. We could help you, and I thought I'd just pass this on for your thinking."

I was really taken aback; I had given little thought to running for that office in 1978, and it had never entered my mind that the Chicago machine would support me. I thanked the mayor for his flattering remarks and said I would give it some thought.

Then, when I thought the conversation was ended, he suddenly said, "One other thing I'd like to mention."

I wondered what was coming.

"Guv, do you think it would be possible for you to consider changing your position on the Crosstown Expressway? If you'd go for it, we might just get the appropriation through Congress."

Immediately, I realized the ploy. He was offering a deal. If I would give up my diehard opposition to his pet expressway, he would put the machine behind me for the next Senate seat. I couldn't help admiring Daley's chutzpah in offering a deal where, obviously, I would have to deliver first, with no guarantee that he would in turn deliver for me when the Senate election came up. But that was immaterial. There was no way I could make such a crass bargain, turning my back on the thousands of people who had helped me after I promised to protect their homes and businesses from the Crosstown.

Actually, I had no interest in running for the Senate. I had thought about it over the years, and the combination of constant travel to and from Washington, plus the nature of the life of a senator, just did not appeal to me. I never discussed the matter again with Mayor Daley or anyone else. He died of a heart attack later that year. I attended the funeral, a High Mass that went on and on, giving me time to think of his role in my life, his success at the expense of principles, how no one mentioned his flaws and found so many good qualities. I felt too much frustration to mourn his passing and knew also that machine politics in Chicago would not die with him.

One memorable event during those months was the annual governor's conference in Washington, D.C. At the conclusion of the conference, Queen Elizabeth invited all the nation's governors to a reception on the imperial yacht that had sailed from England to Philadelphia to be a part of America's 1976 bicentennial celebration. The queen and her consort prince received us in the yacht's grand salon, where a delightful brunch was served.

In Springfield, we did some pleasant entertaining in those closing months. I recall one dinner for the Illinois Supreme Court, a very formal white-tie-and-tails affair to which I also invited some members of my cabinet. Socializing with the Supreme Court was limited to this annual dinner, since mingling of the executive and judicial branches of government was never encouraged—although I did on occasion play tennis with Justice Walter Schaefer; but we had a personal relationship that long preceded my becoming governor.

Anyway, this dinner was stiffly formal with dignity and protocol, and when the dinner ended and coffee was served as a prelude to dessert, I leaned back in the fancy, antique Louis XIV chair to relax. Unexpectedly, the back of the chair went out when my back hit it, and over I went backwards, topsy-turvy, with a loud crash, landing on my back with my feet sticking straight up.

Standing near me was the mansion butler we called "B. I." who was a favorite of mine. Tall and straight, with a broad smile showing gold-embedded teeth, he was the epitome of a southern butler. B. I. was balancing a large tray holding crystal dessert dishes.

When I crashed to the floor, B. I. was aghast, crying in a loud voice, "My god! Look at the guvnor!"

Silence fell on the formal gathering. At the same moment, the tray slipped from B. I.'s grasp, and the crystal dessert dishes hit the floor with another loud crash. An even deeper silence fell over the room.

The wife of the chief justice saved the day. In a loud, high, falsetto voice, she cried, "Gawd, lucky it wasn't me. Imagine my feet sticking up, my skirt down, and all my bloomers showing!"

That brought down the house.

After things quieted down, in an effort to restore some sense of normalcy, I told my guests that such a faux pas was not unusual for me. I recounted the story of attending a similar white-tie dinner in the White House, where I was seated next to Mrs. Nixon. "As you know," I said, "everyone stands when the president and first lady enter the dining room, and when she reached our table, I moved to pull back Pat Nixon's chair. But I was shouldered aside by a strapping Marine Corps officer in full dress uniform. We sat down, eight of us at the table, all behaving properly. Glasses of wine and the salad first course were already on the table.

"Pat Nixon was saying something polite to the gentleman on her right, an honored guest. The lady on my left was also in conversation, so with nothing to do, I casually picked up a salad fork and absent-mindedly reached for the salad nearest my right hand. I was startled when Pat Nixon tapped me on the shoulder, and when I turned toward her, she spoke loudly and sternly in a cold voice clearly heard by everyone at the table, 'Governor, you're eating my salad.' Silence. What in the world does one say after being called to task by the first lady of the land? All I could think of was to mumble, 'I'm sorry, Ma'am,' as I placed my fork back on the table." I ended the story by saying it was rare for me to be at such a total loss for words.

### HOWLETT LOSES

In November, Jim Thompson handily defeated Mike Howlett. I did some hunting that fall, but again, as in previous years, I avoided private hunting clubs and lodges where former governors had shot geese, duck, dove, quail, and pheasant. Most often, I hunted on farms with the landowner, often with downstate legislators like Vince de Muzio and Kenny Boyle and small-town businessmen like Wally Heil, who owned a furniture store, and Jerry Gross, who operated a haberdashery.

I tried not to allow emotion to surface as January of 1977 approached and my term as governor came to an end. I would focus instead on my accomplishments. Not as many legislative programs as I would have wished, but, withal, there were some notable victories. The first campaign contribution disclosure law, the modern mental health code, the modernization of the penal code, a new mine safety law, a new strip-mining reclamation law, a strengthened Environmental Protection Agency, increases in awards for work-related injuries, the nation's first antiredlining law, a state bond issue to build regional home-style centers for the developmentally disabled, creation of the Regional Transportation Authority for the Chicago area, passage of the right-turn-on-red law, and lottery proceeds dedicated to education.

Not enough, surely, but still enough to generate some pride. But my greatest pride was in holding the line on taxes, substantially reducing the state payroll, and greatly improving the transparency, honesty, and effectiveness of government through the operating departments and agencies. This, perhaps even more than through new laws, is where peoples' lives can be more directly impacted. And it is here where most top governmental executives fail.

With my series of executive orders, we dramatically improved the ethics and honesty of the executive branch of government operating under the governor. With the accountability budget, a new series of governor's action offices, and four years of monthly accountability sessions, taxpayers could see and assess their state government at work. With hard political spadework, we measurably redressed the balance of power between Chicago and downstate in the halls of state government, giving downstate more political and governmental power than it had ever had.

I should mention other steps taken with executive power. I left office with a surplus of $168 million in the state's coffers. There were 4,000 fewer employees on the state payroll than when I took office. What other governor can make that claim? Significantly, the number of state employees has skyrocketed since then. Other executive accomplishments were collective bargaining for state employees, stopping the Chicago Crosstown Expressway, aggressive steps to improve flood control in the Chicago area, moving away from institutional care for the mentally ill, major enhancement of the community college system, substantial elimination of unnecessary regional offices in operating departments, and establishment of overseas offices to improve trade with Illinois.

I have no hesitation in saying that Illinois was, during my four years, far ahead of other states in efforts to improve governmental efficiency, ethics, and transparency. And I have even less hesitation in saying that no governor who has succeeded me has done as much to make such improvements in ethics in Illinois government.

If my term as governor were a scrapbook, among my favorite pages would be those executive orders and the people I brought into government as a result of personal contacts. For example, to take just one small thing, on the campaign walk I met a farmer named Davidson, and because of my conversation with him, I managed to remove the requirement that fishing licenses be obtained in both Illinois and Kentucky to fish in the Ohio River.

A small matter, yes, but there were many, many others that stemmed from my walk through the state, like strip mining reclamation. Then there were the minority members I brought to state government, like Roland Burris, a black bank official I named director of general services, the state's large and important "housekeeping" department. Roland was later elected the state's attorney general and came within an ace of becoming one of the nation's very few black governors.

Sid Marder, a plant manager I met on the walk, went to work with me when the gasoline crisis hit Illinois in 1973. He did such a good job that he became my energy consultant. The Marders moved to Springfield, and though I would not be staying there, Sid would stay on and build a national reputation in the energy field. I met Don Johnson as head of a small tradesman labor union downstate and made him director of the Department of Labor. He went on to become president of the Illinois A.F.L.-C.I.O. And there were campaign workers, like Mary Lee Leahy who so capably ran Children and Family Services, and Beverly Addante on my staff. I could name many more dedicated and amazingly competent men and women, white and black, who joined me in this grand fight for better government. I was depressed that my term of office had come to an end, but I firmly believed that the state was better because I had been governor.

But now what?

## 24

## *A Dramatically New and Different Life*

I return to the barracks from my workstation at noon, stopping to pick up mail before heading to the mess hall for lunch. I am dispirited and the weather doesn't help. Bitterly cold days like today make me wonder why anyone would live in this part of the country. Iron ore comes from the mining area around here, but when the wind off Lake Superior cleans the air, it's not too unpleasant. There is no wind today, however, and the air is grimy and humid, the overcast sky leaden in its gloom. There is nothing from my lawyer; on his last visit, he said he didn't think the time was ripe for early parole, but that he was going to go to Kansas City and meet informally with some of the parole board members.

My spirits are a bit low, but then the handwriting on one letter jumps at me. It is from Roberta—R2. I haven't heard from her in many weeks, and my first reaction is one of simple joy. I tear the envelope open hastily, hungrily scanning the first page. There is no "Dearest Dan," not even a "Dear Dan." Just "Dan." Then, "I'm very troubled." Then, "You've wounded me, wronged me."

This isn't what I had expected and not at all what I had hoped for. As I read further, I remind myself that she has never been very good at handling adversity of any type, and this letter only proves that she still isn't. That's okay, I tell myself, she's just going through the stage I've heard about from other inmates who got similar letters from their wives.

"Everything that happened is your fault."

God, I've got enough already to depress me, to make me wonder whether this time is worth living through. I'm at the bottom. And now this. Why? Why can't she be strong enough to control her emotions and try to help me instead of hurting me? I love that woman but cannot understand why she's doing this to me.

Why?

Why?

How in God's name can she say everything is my fault?

I read on, growing more depressed. Complaints, complaints, complaints. There are several pages of dismal description of our financial affairs. Two pending lawsuits to collect money. Each, she wrote, is my fault.

"Why did you lie to me about the amount of money you were making?"

This is a new one, and I don't know what she is talking about. Our income, lavish at times, had come from our businesses, before they dried up. The lawsuits she complains about are routine collection actions and could easily be handled, but she has made a mountain out of them. My feelings begin to move from sorrow to anger. What the hell is she talking about? Why is she exaggerating everything? Why are her words almost screaming, "Everything is your fault"? What about those times we said to each other during the seemingly endless investigations, "We're in this together, and we'll see it through together"?

Finally, I reach the last page of her diatribe of several pages. I can hardly believe my eyes as I focus on her final words: "I want a divorce. Right now. I have a lawyer, and the papers are already on file." She enclosed the lawyer's card. "Have whomever you want talk to him. There's no point in communicating with me. It's all over and that's final. We're through. Period."

I am distraught. Shocked. Stunned. It has never occurred to me that she would do this. I sink down to sit on the bunk, holding my hand to my forehead. *Jesus, I don't believe this.*

I read the last page again. And again. And then I reread the whole letter two more times. This can't be happening. She can't be doing this to me. The thought of her has been my main hold on sanity. Why won't she come up here so we can at least discuss this?

I get hold of myself. *She's probably gone. Face it.*

But then . . . *No. I'll at least give it one last try. Probably a waste of time, though.*

I don't want to eat anything, so I don't bother going to the mess hall. I don't want to see anybody, talk to anybody. I curl up on the bunk and sort out my thoughts. Then I get up and write a quick letter, asking her to reconsider, begging her to come up and talk with me. I mail it without much hope.

Somehow I go back to my job cleaning toilets and scrubbing floors, trying unsuccessfully to banish her from my mind. Next day, I destroy her letter.

A week passes and I don't receive any answer to my letter or any other communication from her. Finally, I call my son Dan to act as my lawyer. In total depression, I tell him about the divorce action and ask him to contact her attorney.

"Give her whatever she wants," I say. I have no fight left in me at all.

---

### HONCHO

The day arrived in January of 1977, my last day in office. Turnover day. I admit that it was a tough day for me. All our belongings had been moved out of the Executive Mansion, except for the bare necessities to complete the day's protocol. What had been familiar living quarters now seemed more like a hotel. Roberta, first lady for a few more hours, must have spoken to me, but I wasn't aware of any words of cheer or sympathy, and I offered none. The suit I had selected would be equally appropriate for a funeral. We dressed in silence, ate breakfast in silence. Each ordinary function carried me a step closer to the end of my tenure as governor, the best experiences of my life along with some intensely disappointing ones.

We descended in the elevator for the last time and then stood waiting in the foyer. Things had been tightly arranged, but I went through the necessary motions, unaware of all the careful coordination. We waited in silence several minutes, a montage of memories flickering in my mind like ghosts of a bygone era.

When my successor, Jim Thompson, and his wife arrived, I somehow managed enough cordiality to do the necessary handshaking. I was symbolically handing him the keys to the Executive Mansion. Jim's expression remained stern as we proceeded to a limo alone, followed by our wives in another limo. A light snow covered the ground and the sky was as gray as my spirits.

"You know, Jim," I said, once we were under way in the spacious limo, "I can't resist telling you that you're getting much more cooperation than Dick Ogilvie gave me back in 1973."

The man showed no visible sign of having heard a word I said.

I tried again. "I hope to meet with you soon so we can work out as smooth a transition as possible."

No response.

The rest of the ride and subsequent ceremony in the State Armory Building were agonizingly slow and awkward. In the ensuing weeks, Thompson and his staff told my people he wanted none of their input. Quite the contrary. I chose not to dwell on this hostile snubbing, however, as Roberta and I set about creating a new home. We had decided to rent a condo in Springfield while we worked out our transition plans.

Vic stopped by after a couple of weeks, and the state trooper assigned to me for another year took us to a Springfield café for lunch. We ordered simple burgers and, inevitably, talked politics.

"One of the new aides told me that Thompson and his team plan to 'show up Walker,'" Vic said.

"Why, for God's sake? It's not enough that they won?"

"They can't stand it that you got so many votes downstate in the primary. They're going to do their best to knock down your popular standing."

"That doesn't make a lot of sense, Vic," I said. "I wasn't his opponent. I said nothing negative about him in the few appearances I made for Mike Howlett. When I met Thompson in connection with the Crime Commission years ago, he was friendly enough."

"They're scared of you, Dan. It's pretty amazing just how scared."

"Of course; they consider downstate essential to their power base," I said.

"Exactly. I've heard from several sources about a memo outlining steps to, quote, 'kill any chance for Walker to ever come back.'"

I shook my head. "A comeback. Could anything be further from my mind right now? I've got to have an income, a career, a professional life."

"Well, they're thinking about this freak two-year term." Vic's expression was both solemn and intense. "To tell you the truth, I am too."

"Ah, Victor." The 1977 term for governor of Illinois was constitutionally limited to two years on a one-time-only basis so that gubernatorial campaigns would no longer be in competition with presidential campaigns. Vic already had notions that I should think about running again. "I'm so numb, I can't think of anything political."

"Right." Vic grinned and scoffed. "That should last a good two or three months."

Yet, it lasted far longer than that. I had suffered shock and disappointment, a severe blow. I told myself I deserved to get some enjoyment out of whatever I chose to do next. In the closing months of office, I had given considerable thought to my future. Several large Chicago law firms sent out feelers, offering full partnerships.

Still, I wanted something to look forward to, and working in a big firm inspired no such enthusiasm. Forming my own statewide law firm did inspire me. I dreamed of working out of a Chicago-area law office, attracting good clients with interesting problems, being the honcho over the law firm. I could call it "Dan Walker Law Offices" and bring Dan and Kathleen in to join me. My income would be far from assured, however.

Hunting was another of my loves. I hatched the idea of forming a club to offer hunting and fishing opportunities around the state. The "Outdoor Club" would lease sites for fishing in Lake Michigan and on downstate lakes and rivers, plus places for hunting geese, ducks, quail, pheasant, and doves. Sales of memberships would cover expenses, and the members would pay modest trip-fees for hunting and fishing. The Outdoor Club would give me opportunities to enjoy the hunting season and spend time downstate, mostly in the southern Illinois area that I liked so much. Surely there were lots of frustrated outdoorsmen around the state, particularly in the Chicago area, who would welcome the opportunity to easily get good places to go hunting and fishing.

I thought Roberta would like the idea of a family law firm, but she was busy working with the Executive Mansion Historical Society and had brought a wonderful lady named Edith, who had been a housekeeper at the Executive Mansion, with her to our condo. She kept harping on moving back to the Deerfield home we still owned. I flat out refused.

I finally turned down the big Chicago law firm opportunities and set about putting together the Outdoor Club and the Dan Walker Law Offices, with principal offices in Chicago and Springfield and outlying offices in other cities around the state—including the existing law offices of my son Dan in a suburb of Chicago and my daughter Kathleen with her husband David Vaught in Fairview Heights in southern Illinois. A sense of purpose again invigorated me as I set to work. However, Roberta wanted to sit in on the partners' meetings where we discussed the law business. To keep peace, I allowed her, though she understood little of what was going on.

Governor Jim Thompson had commenced publicly "bad rapping" my administration. For example, he repeatedly charged that the state was in a near bankruptcy condition when he took office. That was demonstrably untrue, since I had left him with a $168 million cushion in the state treasury. Often, when problems cropped up, he said to the media, "It's not my fault. This problem was created by Walker."

"This could hurt my ability to draw clients," I said to Vic over the phone.

Vic and Bill subsequently made discreet inquiries at the U.S. Department of Justice and were told that Thompson's staff had circulated a seventy-page memorandum suggesting areas where they should investigate me along with the people in my administration, trying to dig up dirt. This one took me completely by surprise. We never saw the alleged document, but there were enough reports of its existence to convince us it was more than rumor. A grand jury investigation poked around and came up with nothing.

I drove out to Vic's new home in Long Grove, a Chicago suburb, one summer day, frustrated and wanting to discuss the whole business. Vic, together with his wife Nancy, fixed a lunch of pasta and served it with glasses of wine. Nancy left us afterwards, and I began my rant.

"Thompson has done nothing but glad-hand legislators and media people—"

"And they eat it up," Vic said. "They think the guy can do no wrong."

"—yet he doesn't have time to spend making his government accountable. He pits business against labor, upstate against downstate, school boards against state-level education people. The man is incapable of coming up with solutions and plans, so all he can do to justify his miserable administration is throw stones at ours." I was burned up.

"It's what he does best," Vic said.

Jim Thompson had achieved his early fame as the U.S. attorney for the Northern District of Illinois, headquartered in Chicago. He had personally prosecuted, convicted, and sent to jail Democratic governor Otto Kerner for law violations based on his ownership of racetrack stock.

"Look, we're five months away from the December deadline to declare for the next election," Vic continued. "Thompson's watching us like a hawk. Talk is rampant. People are saying that Thompson can't afford to let you get into a position where you could run against him. It's common knowledge he considers you his most formidable opponent."

I pooh-poohed the idea, expecting Vic to give me a pep talk on running again, but he had something else in mind.

"I just don't think they're going to leave this alone. They're going to keep hounding you. If not now, then before the next election."

I relaxed. "They're wasting their time." And I didn't give it any further thought.

Roberta continued to argue for returning to our life at the Deerfield house, as if we could simply turn back and resume the old way of life we had before my first primary campaign. I disagreed strongly and urged a new home in Oak Brook, where I could work with our son Dan in one of the Dan Walker Law Offices. Roberta and I were at loggerheads continually, and I found little comfort whatsoever in our marriage, which had rapidly deteriorated during my last year as governor, when I spent very little time with the family. So, the breakdown was considerably my fault. The home-front situation became even worse after I left office, when I tried to adjust back to private life from the fast-moving, exciting job as governor. Some of my ex-governor compatriots had warned me that the "decompression" process would take several years. And it did.

And then a phone call came that changed my life and Roberta's as well.

### R 2

"Governor," a soft female voice said in greeting. "This is Roberta Nelson of the Illinois Epilepsy Society."

Though my world had changed so drastically, I still remembered Roberta Nelson as a beautiful, vivacious lady. She was some fifteen years my junior and had successfully operated several nonprofit organizations. She also knew the world of society from her work with benefit balls for various charities.

We exchanged a few pleasantries, and then she said, "The reason I'm calling is because of your public promise to work for the handicapped after leaving office. Do you still plan to honor that promise?"

I hadn't really thought about it, and I did eventually plan to become involved with the handicapped, one way or another. "Yes, I do, Roberta," I answered. "What did you have in mind?"

Vic—had he been with me at that time—would have said she had plenty in mind, but I sensed no ulterior motives. As I said, women were often a little flirty with me as governor. I enjoyed it, gave as good as I got, and let it go.

"We would love for you to serve on the board of directors," she said.

I agreed and attended several meetings. Later, she asked me to help establish local chapters for the society in major cities in Illinois. I readily agreed to that, too. On those trips, we booked separate rooms. At first.

Meanwhile, I worked hard bringing to fruition the statewide law firm and the Outdoor Club, traveling frequently around the state. Having set up first with my son Dan in Oak Brook, I began temporarily staying with him—a conscientious attempt at separation from my wife, which Dan seemed to accept, although he did not know about my growing attachment to Roberta Nelson. I also worked at bringing into our statewide law firm my daughter Kathleen and her husband in Fairview Heights, opening the Chicago and Springfield offices, and finalizing arrangements with lawyers who had existing practices, including Jim Gende in Rock Island, Jim Hatcher in Peoria, Mike Berz in Kankakee, and Paul Giamonca in Mt. Vernon. All of us were optimistic as we worked hard throughout 1977 and 1978 to make the new venture a success.

In early 1978, the state trooper assigned to me for the customary year after leaving office no longer drove me places. So, on trips with Roberta Nelson, I drove my own car, and we stayed at motels in various cities. As we became more involved, I started to fall in love with her. She was in the process of divorcing her husband, and in November of 1978, I resolved to ask my wife for a divorce.

As the lady she has always been, Roberta Marie very reluctantly consented when she became convinced that I was determined to go my own way. She moved back into our former Deerfield home, taking Edith, the housekeeper, with her. For myself, I leased a small apartment in the Oak Brook area. Our children had all been aware that for several years the marriage was on shaky grounds and that Roberta and I had argued far too much when I was governor. Despite our attempts at discretion, the staff at the mansion overheard our angry exchanges at dinner and gossiped about it. The children's initial reactions to the divorce almost paralleled their ages. The older ones saw it as "past due" and "almost inevitable" and "a long time coming." The middle children were stunned and dismayed at first, but then acknowledged that the gulf between their mother and me was just too wide. The two youngest were openly upset and angry with me. I called each of them and explained what I was doing and why, and eventually they came to see it as certainly unavoidable and possibly for the best. However, they properly remained very supportive of their mother.

My love affair with Roberta Nelson progressed rapidly. Actually, I became obsessed with her. She seemed to offer everything a wife should be. Beautiful, intelligent, easy to engage in both light and serious conversation, well informed about politics, government and foreign affairs, and on top of all that, always fun to be with. She was able to make me relax, something that was very hard for me to do. She could even make me laugh, something no woman had ever done. She reawakened a part of me that had been virtually comatose. And to all appearances, she had the same experience with me.

People began telling me I was a different man. Vic, who was acquainted with her, saw things differently. We met for lunch at an Italian restaurant in Chicago one day. He seemed rather quiet. Finally, he said what was on his mind.

"What you do with your private life is your own business, Dan, but as your friend, I gotta say I really don't think Roberta Nelson is your type."

"Why not?"

"Well, don't get me wrong. I've seen you as a stiff Annapolis guy, as a man of the people, as a polished governor and expert lawyer. It's not that you aren't in her league; it's more like she's only interested in rubbing elbows with high society and men in power. I've seen her lobbying with the legislators, working them expertly. Dan, I frankly think she'll end up . . . hurting you."

I muttered something about appreciating his concern, and then I simply ignored him. By this time, my family had learned of the relationship and was not happy about it. When I traveled with Roberta Nelson on our trips for the Epilepsy Society, the room reservations kept getting fouled up. We would arrive at our night's lodging only to be told that we had cancelled our reservation and that they had given the room to someone else. I eventually found out why. My youngest daughter, Margaret, then eighteen, proved to be a bit of a detective. She would somehow discover my plans and sabotage them. Bless her.

I was so thoroughly smitten, I didn't care about others' opinions. Publicly, Roberta Nelson had a way of subtly flaunting her figure when she wanted to. Never too much, though, and I thoroughly enjoyed showing her off, wanting her to wear sexy evening dresses. We were mad about each other, holding hands publicly to the point that someone told me we were kind of obnoxious about it. As soon as our divorces were final, I asked her to marry me. She accepted.

At the same time, I continued working hard at seeking clients for the new Dan Walker Law Offices. I hoped, based on my prior legal record, that I would be retained for major litigation, obtain some good corporate clients, and be offered posts on a few prestigious boards of directors. Disappointingly, none of this happened. Also, unhappily, the Outdoor Club failed during this time. I did manage to line up the needed hunting and fishing opportunities, but a statewide mailing did not yield enough members to support the operation. It was great fun for a while. I leased at very low cost an old duck-hunting club on the Illinois River where I had the pleasure of introducing my son Will to duck hunting. Reluctantly, after months of work, I folded the club.

### A NEW MAN

In November of 1979, Roberta Nelson and I were married in an Episcopal church in Elmhurst before a gathering of about forty guests, with my son Dan as best man. The press covered the event. The reception took place in our new, unfurnished home in Oak Brook. A band played while each of five different rooms offered a different motif and cuisine: Mexican, Oriental, Italian, Continental, and American.

Afterwards, the new Mrs. Walker and I—together with her teenage daughter and two sons—moved into our new home during a heavy snowstorm. Our happiness subsided when it became apparent that the Dan Walker Law Offices could not survive. I was unable to attract enough new clients, and the existing law practices of my downstate partners could not support the heavy expenses of a statewide firm. Unfortunately, the concept of a multicity law firm was too new an idea for clients to accept. Added to this was the fact that my antiestablishment reputation did not sit well with Chicago-area businessmen who still catered to city hall. And even after Mayor Richard Daley's death in late 1976, I was *persona non grata* in city hall. Also, corporate lawyers had forgotten my original business-law practice and must have assumed I would be trying to practice mostly "influence" law—and what good was a Democrat in handling compliance and other matters in which a Republican administration held sway? The final coffin nail was the Thompson administration's ongoing investigations into anything they could think of in my administration. While the rumored grand jury investigations came to nothing, leaks to the press continued.

In the end, my downstate partners went their own ways, the Chicago and Springfield offices closed, and Dan and I were left with an office in Oak Brook. This failure deeply disturbed me. I kicked myself for not going with the major law firm. This was the first time I had failed professionally, and my confidence was shaken.

I was still trying to recover, when one night at the dinner table, Roberta said, "Honey, I've got my eye on a mink jacket."

She still worked at a center for developmentally disabled children and received only a small salary. I had told her that as senior partner of my law firm, I would be entitled to a $100,000 draw.

"You know the firm isn't doing well," I said to her that evening. "You'd look beautiful in a fur jacket, but we just can't afford it right now."

"Sure we can," she said. "You're earning a hundred thousand a year."

"No, I'm not. I'm entitled to that as a draw, but it's not guaranteed."

"You never said anything about conditional income."

"Well, I didn't want to upset you."

"How can you not tell me something like that? "

"Just be patient, dear. We'll have enough money."

"This is a double-cross, Dan Walker," she said. "You misled me. And how much are you paying your first wife every month?"

I told her the agreed-upon alimony amount.

"What? We can't afford that! How can you pay her that much when we don't have the things we need?"

"The alimony is fixed. I cannot and will not change it. She has to have the money to live on. She was my wife for over thirty years and raised our seven children. I couldn't hold my head up if I abandoned her financially. My children would despise me."

Roberta didn't really yell or cry or pout, but she sort of smoldered. Her anger carried over into the bedroom, but after a couple of weeks, she accepted the situation.

"Sweetheart," I said to her, "I'm going to make some money somehow. I'm always an optimist. I would like you to be, too."

She brightened, and our romance returned. I gradually became involved with a new venture, the fast oil-change centers that were catching on elsewhere in the nation. I learned about the potential from a client and worked with him to get the business started in the Chicago area. However, my client moved to Indiana, so Roberta and I persuaded a wealthy friend, Paul Butler, to join us in launching our own Butler Walker Fast Oil Change centers.

As that business grew, I finally decided to stop practicing law and turned the Oak Brook law office over to my son Dan so I could concentrate on the oil change centers. Paul and his son Frank took a 50 percent interest in the new company, but even with Paul's help, start-up was difficult. Bank financing for land and construction was exceedingly hard to obtain for a new business during a time of rapidly increasing interest rates. But when the first two "BW 10-Minute Oil Change Centers" became outstanding successes, financing became easier to find.

Roberta took a salaried job as vice president of the national Easter Seal Society. She also had a good head for business, and we worked well together. After several years, the profits from the business grew, and we commenced a much more active social life, attending formal balls, polo games, opera, symphony concerts, and parties—first in Chicago and later in Palm Beach, Florida, where Paul Butler maintained a home. At Oak Brook and at Wellington, near Palm Beach, we enjoyed polo games with famous patrons of that sport, including Prince Charles. We both attended and hosted fancy dinner parties, and our names and pictures often appeared in the society pages.

I was somewhat incredulous at this new lifestyle, which I had never aspired to. Indeed, despite my years in the limelight, I still felt more comfortable with the downstaters and the kind of people I met on the walk than with the Chicago society types. However, I was a willing learner and readily followed Roberta, who loved the publicity, showing off a governor husband. She was a natural for this kind of life. My racy white convertible bore the vanity license plates "GOV DAN," and, yes, I did enjoy some people continuing to call me "Governor." Why not? Protocol says, once a governor, always a governor. I remembered encountering my former boss, Governor Adlai Stevenson, when he was serving as ambassador to the United Nations during the Carter administration. Attending a meeting in the Waldorf Astoria Hotel in New York City, I saw Adlai standing in an elevator when the door opened. Other men were with him, obviously from foreign nations.

Taken aback, I said, "Adlai, great to see you!" as he and his associates walked out of the elevator. We shook hands and chatted for a couple of minutes. "I'm embarrassed," I said to Adlai. "I should have addressed you as 'Ambassador' or 'Excellency.'"

"No, Dan," he responded. "Please call me 'Governor'; that's the title I prefer."

I would later learn that Jimmy Carter and Ronald Reagan shared his preference; both insisted on being addressed as "Governor," even after they no longer held that office and right up to the day they were inaugurated as president. Thus, there was nothing unusual about a former governor being addressed as such.

It has been suggested that all this change of lifestyle was an antidote to the nagging depression that followed my loss in the 1976 primary, that I was reinventing myself subconsciously to put great distance between the present and the past. This may be the case, but I never thought like that, so I couldn't say if it has the ring of truth or not. I still felt disconnected to the "society" crowd, never as comfortable with them as with the plain folks. Yet, I think I needed to go through this phase of my life, even though I never would have come up with it on my own. It was my new wife's vision of what constituted the good life, and I was so in love with her that I wanted to give her the moon if I could. At first, we didn't have the money to do much, but as the profitability of our businesses increased, we spent it lavishly. Roberta got the full-length mink coat she wanted.

My sons and daughters visited us from time to time, or we sometimes visited their homes. Roberta made an effort to fit in, and both our families seemed accepting. My grandchildren visited often, and Roberta played "dress up" and "make up" with the little girls. She also staged events such as grand Easter egg hunts and Christmas parties for all the numerous children and grandchildren. Everyone tried to get along. I was happy during this time, yet I still couldn't drive the possibility of returning to political office out of my mind.

### RED BANDANNA

Sometime in 1981, I read in the newspaper about another grand jury investigation of my campaign fund-raising as it related somehow to liquor. I called Vic right away.

"What's going on with this Anton Valukas?" I asked Vic.

"He's Jim Thompson's man. Thompson has made no secret of his desire to control presidential appointments to the Office of the United States Attorney in Chicago," Vic said. "He has clout with the Reagan administration and got Anton Valukas."

"Valukas. The guy who used to be his director of corrections?"

"Yeah. And personal friend." Vic sounded concerned. "Right on schedule. They want to smear you before you even think about the next election. They've got you in their sights."

I also called Bill Goldberg, who had already been following the publicity.

"A number of people in your administration are being investigated, Dan, and Valukas is openly saying he's going to 'get' them. He's talking about threatening them with indictments and then offering possible immunity to get them talking." This angered me deeply—personally, professionally, and politically.

And then, when Thompson drank beer openly with students at a Northern Illinois University football game, I made public some of that anger. A reporter called to ask my reaction.

"Governors just should not do that kind of thing. It's a line you don't cross if you're the chief executive of the state. It's plainly illegal, and the students, if caught by an authority from the university, would be promptly expelled."

Thompson was rarely snappish with reporters, but he was on this occasion when they confronted him with my charge. Normally he treated them as his cronies. I had clearly struck a nerve. I received some supportive letters from both students and parents. And then, as if in defiance of anyone who would dare criticize him, Thompson again drank publicly with minors at a university sports event. And again, I criticized him. And again he was petulant and defensive with the press.

"It's a damn football game!" he yelled at a reporter who questioned him. "This is just Walker incessantly politicizing everything. He's just trying to take the heat off any investigation of his administration, and this is the best he can come up with."

The U.S. attorney's office had continued to plow the same infertile grounds the investigations of 1977–78 had covered, despite the fact that they had yielded nothing prosecutable. I learned from Bill Goldberg that Washington had even sent an attorney out to assist Valukas, and I contacted him.

"This is harassment, pure and simple. The Republicans are trying to prevent me from being a candidate for governor." My complaint had no effect, however.

In November of 1981, Vic called me from his office in Chicago, where he and Dave Green had set up a consulting firm. "I think it's time to get out your red bandanna, Dan."

I laughed.

He didn't.

"You can't be serious," I said, although the thought had crossed my mind.

"Thompson's up for reelection next year," he said. "Adlai can't beat him. You can. And there's no Daley to stop you."

Jane Byrne was by then mayor of Chicago. She had served on Daley's cabinet but had broken away from the regulars somewhat and seemed like a more independent mayor.

"But the regulars are still in control, right?" I asked.

"Yeah, but they're sorta biding their time, hoping to put the old guy's son, Richie Daley, in office as mayor sometime in the future. So a window has opened a crack—if you want to run." Vic was quite serious. "Let's huddle, Dan." The old excitement surged inside me, although I forced myself to remain calm and objective.

Rumors of ongoing investigations still buzzed with vague accusations. The best way to really smoke my accusers out into the open, where the media would be forced to cover my side of things as well, was to go ahead and run a tough campaign. And of course, I itched to finish many of the tasks I had begun while in office.

I contacted many old friends downstate. They seemed supportive, so I drove over for the meeting with Vic and Dave Green.

"We have good support in the African American communities," Dave said.

"Downstate Democrats are eager to get rid of the Republican governor," I reported. "And they still like me a lot."

After long talks, Vic, Dave, and I decided that I should try for the Democratic nomination. Basil Talbott of the *Sun-Times* said I was the one candidate who really got under Jim Thompson's skin and would therefore give him the best run for the money. If I ran unopposed in the primary, we felt strongly that we could beat Thompson in the fall general election. And I was pleased when Roberta said she was delighted at the prospect.

I met with Mayor Jane Byrne, and she said she had an open mind. Then I hit the streets in downtown Chicago and on the South Side. "I'm Dan Walker, and I'm considering running for governor again. What do you think?" The reactions were uniformly positive. "We need a strong guy to beat Thompson" was the frequent response.

Mayor Byrne gave a party one evening that included many individuals active in Democratic politics. Hundreds of influential Democrats attended, and the event earned a lot of press. I chatted with Byrne's husband privately.

"Dan," he said, "Jane's going for you. You are our candidate."

Surprised, but pleased, I reported this to Vic, and we redoubled our efforts. Yet, several days later, rumors appeared in print that Jane Byrne was considering supporting Adlai Stevenson III. I was astounded. I called Jane and made an appointment to see her at her office.

"Dan," she said, "I'm afraid that Adlai will—as he has threatened to do—wage a primary fight on his own, if the regulars don't pick him."

"Adlai will never take such a risk, Jane, believe me. He's bluffing. He really doesn't want to upset the regulars. He knows he can't beat me. And he couldn't stand to lose in a primary, and especially not to me. Most important, Jane, he can *not* beat Thompson."

My attempt at convincing her was a wasted effort. She was dealing with the disasters created by Daley's years of what might charitably be called "deferred maintenance."

"Nobody has any idea how many problems came out of the woodwork," Jane said. "Calling Chicago 'the city that works' is nonsense." The Daley administration had plastered over problems with public schools, the police department, O'Hare Airport, and the whole infrastructure of Chicago. "I'm worried that a primary battle of this magnitude led by Stevenson would seriously disrupt the party and divert attention from what I'm trying to do with the city. I just can't risk that."

She was obviously intent on backing Stevenson, and I certainly had no interest in raising money for and fighting another primary battle, so I dropped all notions of running. Adlai received the nomination but ran a losing campaign, and like Mike Howlett, was defeated by "Big Jim" Thompson.

### THE GOVERNOR'S LADY

I plunged back into my life as a socialite. Once, we made arrangements with the Chicago Brookfield Zoo to use the lion house for a cocktail party and buffet while the lions roared. On another occasion, we hosted a "traveling dinner party for twelve" on Chicago's near North Side, with cocktails at the Ambassador East Hotel, dinner and dancing at an elegant nightclub, brandy and dessert at a popular disco place, and finally breakfast in our hotel suite with guests transported from site to site in decorated white horse-drawn carriages.

Roberta Nelson had a friend, Sam Wanamaker, a well-known Hollywood actor then living in London, where he had started a project to rebuild Shakespeare's original Globe Theatre, involving wealthy sponsors and entertainment-world stars. We were invited to London, where we enjoyed cocktails and dancing at Buckingham Palace and were served high tea at Blenheim Palace, the home of Lady Diana's parents.

I was talking with Prince Philip's aide, who had attended the British military academy called Sandhurst. The man was curious about my time at Annapolis, yet he stopped looking at me as we were talking and was looking wide-eyed at something. I turned to see what he was looking at. It was

Roberta, holding hands with the prince in blatant public violation of the "do not touch royalty" rule.

Bolder still, she took the prince's arm and said, "Your highness, I want you to meet a very lovely old lady." She practically pulled him across the room and introduced him to a woman friend of hers who had donated to the Old Globe Theater.

The aide was absolutely horrified, but the prince seemed to be enjoying himself. Roberta could schmooze anyone. She was a sparkling woman. My love for her was undiminished.

I shrugged and said to the man, "That's my wife."

Later, at a grand party in Hollywood at the Beverly Hills Hilton Hotel hosted by Sam Wanamaker, we were pictured with Prince Charles, Elizabeth Taylor, and her husband, Richard Burton.

We commenced our downfall by buying a small, downstate savings and loan association where I had served on the board of directors. We moved its headquarters to Oak Brook, and it did quite well, as did the oil change business. With the blessing of the state regulators, the S & L invested money in real estate mortgages to help our independent franchisees build oil change centers. No danger flags were flying.

We took profits from the oil change centers we owned personally and paid ourselves reasonable salaries. Experienced executives were hired to handle day-to-day operations. Roberta liked the financial end and became a financial officer for both businesses. I concentrated largely on the oil change business, doing all the legal work needed to qualify for franchising in various states and obtaining the necessary clearance from the Federal Trade Commission. We sold franchises in Illinois, Texas, and Florida. After renting a small home in Fort Lauderdale, we toyed with the idea of purchasing a powerboat in Florida, both for our pleasure and to entertain business guests interested in becoming BW franchisees. I had always wanted a boat, and we looked at several.

Back in Oak Brook, I awoke one night with severe chest pains, and Roberta rushed me to a nearby hospital in Elmhurst, where I stayed several days. I came home, but the chest pains persisted and became worse. The cardiologists concluded I was suffering small heart attacks. Fearing that the end was coming, and wanting to live out my remaining days with as much gusto as possible, I called the yacht broker from my hospital room and ordered a powerboat, feeling that I was entitled to humor myself.

After another episode of severe chest pains, my long-term doctor moved me by ambulance to a hospital where a nationally known cardiologist ran lengthy tests and took extensive X-rays. When finished, he entered my room and brusquely ordered the nurse to disconnect me from all the wires and tubes.

"Doctor, we can't do that," the nurse said.

"Yes, you can. Disconnect him."

The nurse hesitated. "I'm sorry, doctor, but we can't just disconnect him like this."

"I'm telling you to disconnect him now."

She did so, while the doctor watched.

Then he turned to me. "Put your clothes on, governor, and leave this hospital," he said, grinning slightly. "There's nothing wrong with you other than a pinpoint hole in your esophagus extremely hard to see on an X-ray. But it produces exactly the same symptoms as a heart attack."

I was going to live. All the more reason to have the boat! This was the first major expenditure that was strictly for something I had always wanted. We went ahead with the purchase. One boat led to trading up for another, as it often does, and soon we had an eighty-two-foot, diesel-powered yacht named *The Governor's Lady*, with captain, mate, engineer, and chef. It had cost $650,000, but our businesses were doing amazingly well. Roberta happily spent another $250,000 refurbishing it—including small diamond chips embedded in the dining table, which our elegant guests sometimes stole along with the silverware.

We used the yacht for entertaining on Lake Michigan in the summer and then cruised down to Florida for the winter, defraying some of the expense by chartering the boat. There were pictures of *The Governor's Lady* in *Town and Country* magazine featuring my wife and me drinking champagne and dancing on the upper deck. We used it to entertain socially in Miami Beach and Palm Beach, as well as Chicago.

I was invited to join in honoring Mike Royko at a grand convocation and ball when the Lincoln Academy of Illinois made him a Lincoln Laureate. I am a lifetime regent of the academy as a former governor, but I boycotted the formal ceremony because of Royko's open contempt for downstaters, whom he repeatedly called "boors" and "rubes" in his columns. Abraham Lincoln, a downstater himself, would never have applauded this man.

There are those who say the high life led by Roberta and me went to my head. Perhaps so. I felt happy in a relaxed, self-satisfying way, but I didn't have the down-to-earth relationships with people I had become accustomed to in downstate Illinois, who were much like the people with whom I was raised in the San Diego backcountry. My mental compass was disoriented, and I lost touch with reality. I also lost touch with my old friends—Vic, Dave, and Bill. There was nobody to bring me up short.

I know that I was curt from time to time with retail people, for instance, and the incidents found their way into the gossip columns. I often got impatient with poor service, and so I came across as overbearing and arrogant. Vic had warned me about this, and even the *Chicago Sun-Times* ran an editorial chiding me for my manner. Well, okay, I had it coming. But was it really newsworthy? What was especially annoying was that the editorial criticized my height, posture, and strong voice—none of which could have resulted from my new lifestyle.

Connected to that sense of having been governor was something that resonated with me more deeply than the fancy lifestyle: an obligation for public service that had become almost a compulsion for me. It must have begun with my always-compassionate mother, certainly not from my rough-hewn father. Her teaching and her constant care for those around her, including the Mexican farm workers, and her dedication to Alcoholics Anonymous on behalf of my father made a deep impression on me. Then, in law school, I was indoctrinated with the duty of a successful lawyer to give of himself to public service. I used to point out in speeches to businessmen and other lawyers that Chicago—with its rough heritage as "hog butcher for the world," its tolerance of the Mafia, its impoverished immigrants working the slaughterhouses—was historically weak in the tradition of public service, especially by successful attorneys. Lawyers and top business executives in eastern seaboard cities—Boston and New York, for example—recognized that obligation much more often than they did in Chicago.

So, all the time I was living the high life, I was engaged in community activities. For three years, I served as president of the DuPage Council, Boy Scouts of America—the largest council in the Chicago area. I became a lecturer at the Loyola University undergraduate campus and school of law, both in Chicago, conducting classes in state government. I was invited to join the national boards of both the National Epilepsy Society and the American Foundation for the Blind, the organization originally started by Helen Keller. In the former position, I led the attack on the insurance companies' practice of charging excessive rates to people suffering from epilepsy. Calling on my prior legal experience, I drafted a long legal complaint suitable for filing in federal court, telling the long story of discrimination against epileptics from ancient times to the present and detailing the stories of some world-famous epileptics. The complaint ended with facts detailing the discrimination against epileptics practiced by the major insurance companies, all of whom were named as defendants. Before filing the complaint, I sent it to the general counsel of major insurance companies, suggesting that we meet to discuss the situation. The meeting proved unnecessary, since all contacted me and stated that their companies would review and redress their practices and policies. And they did.

Meetings of the charity boards took me often to New York and Washington. Admittedly, I also thoroughly enjoyed both the work with my talented, beautiful wife and the social life I had never before experienced. I have always been a driven person: driven to achieve, driven to accomplish, driven to set goals and meet them, driven to pursue "upward mobility," driven to succeed in a public/legal career. Having reached a peak as governor after an uphill struggle, and having been "driven" for so long, I thought I had earned a right to indulge myself in some pleasurable pursuits. I quickly concede that, to use an old expression, I was "riding high," but I honestly felt back in 1986 that after all those years of hard work I was entitled to enjoy this new lifestyle. We had flourishing, highly profitable businesses, and I gave back to the community. What could go wrong?

## 25

## *The Sad Trail to Jail*

Two days ago, the prison mail brought details of the arrangements for my divorce from Roberta Nelson Walker. I will be left with no assets, considerable debts, and, obviously, little prospect for gainful employment after the time in prison. There is one thing that keeps me from falling apart, and that is the prospect of early parole. A letter from my lawyer now sits in front of me. At first, my hopes soared, but if it were good news, he would most likely have called, not written. I can barely bring myself to open the letter. My hands shake as I finally tear open the envelope.

The words jump around at first and then settle.

*Dan, I hate to tell you this, but there is no chance for parole. None. The Board has adopted a new policy. A petition will not even be considered this early on a multiyear sentence like yours, so we're wasting our time.*

He goes on to say that the board had become aware of the prison turmoil that had resulted from some inmates getting parole much earlier than men who had committed the same crime but were sentenced under the new law. The old "one-third of the sentence" rule of thumb is dead. He makes a reasoned guess that I will serve at least half of my sentence. That would mean three and a half or, more likely, four years.

I am devastated. Heartsick.

I have already endured a long free fall. From being governor of one of the mightiest states in the Union, which—if it were an independent nation—would constitute roughly the tenth largest economy in the world at the time, and from being a recognized contender for the presidency, all the way down to being a convict who is doomed, after years in prison, to spend the rest of my life as a branded felon. At age seventy upon release, I would be unemployed, penniless, divorced, humiliated, disgraced, and ruined.

My descent has finally ended, and I am at the rock bottom of a black pit.

### LOSS OF THE OIL CHANGE BUSINESS

The first disaster was with the oil change business. The business had continued to grow rapidly and produce very substantial profits. The trouble started with our partner, now Frank Butler after the death of his father, Paul. Frank, an open homosexual, persisted in finding pleasure with the young men still in their teens who worked in the oil change centers, and this became a severe business problem. I barred him from the centers and, in retaliation, he refused to attend any directors' meetings. This paralyzed our corporation, since no board decisions could be made on critical financial matters without participation by the 50 percent owner who controlled half the votes on the board of directors.

In desperation, I obtained a court order entitling us to sell the stymied business over Frank's objections. Unfortunately, the facts became known in the industry, and we had to accept a "fire sale price" for the business. Jiffy Lube, then and now the nation's largest chain of fast oil change centers, was the purchaser. At the time of the sale, BW had about forty centers either open or under construction. After the company sale, my wife and I still held the franchises on eight centers—now Jiffy Lubes—jointly with our children. For a while, the income produced by these centers was steady, though drastically reduced.

So, we still weren't too nervous, though we had refinanced our home to remodel it, and the yacht was more than qualifying as "a hole in the water into which money is poured." The savings and loan association still produced income. If we had sold it right then, we could have gotten at least a million dollars for it and for its charter, since there were only a limited number available, but we thought it would eventually yield a nice profit that would provide enough to repay our debts, allow us to live comfortably, and retire.

S & Ls were soon to encounter severe problems, however, stemming from the unusually high interest rates that ballooned in the 1980s.

Traditionally, S & Ls make profits (if any) on the difference between what they pay for money (usually, savings accounts, at that time paying around 3 percent) and what they receive from loans (usually, home mortgages, then about 7 percent). The difference is called the "margin." Ordinarily, at least a 3 percent margin is required to cover overhead costs. First American, being new, had almost no savings base, so it had to borrow in the open market to make loans and, hopefully, become profitable. With home mortgages bringing in 7 percent, we could not pay out more than 10 percent. When market interest rates climbed far above 10 percent, we were obviously in trouble, along with many other S & Ls. For many, including First American, unprofitability resulted not from bad management but from soaring interest rates.

At the same time these dark financial clouds were gathering, my political enemies continued to cause problems. For example, my wife and I left Chicago to spend a long weekend with an elderly lady friend at her home on Lake Geneva in Wisconsin. Unbeknownst to me, the FBI had been asked to serve a subpoena commanding my appearance as a witness before a grand jury. Not finding me at home, teams of FBI agents descended at night on the homes of several of my children, demanding to know where I was. My children did not know, since I was not in the habit of telling them where I spent weekends.

Somehow, the FBI tracked me down. The agents (as I later learned) chartered a helicopter and flew to Lake Geneva. There, local FBI agents met the Chicago team, so there were six armed agents in all. Late Saturday night, they descended on the lakeside home where we were staying. The loud pounding on the back door awakened everyone, and our elderly hostess went to the door. She described to us later how the agents, all of them, did the well-known "badge flop," dramatically flipping open wallets to display the FBI badge.

They demanded, "Is Walker in this house? We've got a subpoena for him."

She responded politely, "Yes, Governor Walker is a guest in my home. I'll tell him you're here."

Bathrobed, I came to the door. "What's going on?"

"We're here to serve a subpoena."

"Six armed men in the middle of the night? Why didn't someone just call and tell me you had a subpoena?"

I appeared before the grand jury several weeks later, as directed by the subpoena, yet never received an explanation for that almost Keystone Kops behavior of the FBI agents. The questioning before the grand jury related to campaign finances and was desultory, not accusative. Actually, I could perceive no point to it. Months later, three men who had worked in my administration were indicted. (Their names had never been mentioned when I was questioned.) The charge was that they had solicited campaign contributions from an individual (Allen Bahn, an Indian computer businessman) who later received a modest state contract to perform outsourced computer work. Vic De Grazia was also told that he was being investigated for having received one anonymous campaign contribution. All of these "cases" later died; nobody was ever convicted of anything. But we learned from reliable sources that the U.S. attorney's office, under Anton Valukas, was unhappy about not being able to pin anything on me.

## MORE BUSINESS PROBLEMS

Meanwhile, interest rates had climbed to 12 and then 14 percent. We had to try harder and harder to find investments or make loans at higher rates in order to cover our costs of operation. All over the nation, S & L institutions, commonly called *thrifts*, were struggling. Forced to pay high rates to attract depositors but dependent on low-interest home loans for revenue, the struggling thrifts saw their profits disappearing.

The federal S & L regulators began questioning the construction loans made by our savings and loan to independent businessmen who were BW 10-Minute Oil Change Center franchisees, a practice that had been approved by the Illinois governmental agency when our savings association was state-regulated at the time of purchase. These loans produced needed revenue for our association, which was having trouble surviving the extremely high interest rates that made it difficult to acquire the capital needed to make loans. And market interest rates continued to soar, reaching 18 percent—levels never before experienced. The narrowing gap between cost of capital and interest income from loans finally drove our S & L into insolvency.

With Butler Walker gone and the S & L insolvent, we found ourselves in deep financial trouble and used up our savings. We were receiving some small income from chartering the yacht and from our oil change center franchises, but this wasn't nearly enough to cover expenses, which were already huge and growing. We tried desperately to sell the yacht and couldn't find a buyer. As the expenses continued, we went further and further into debt, always hoping we could turn it around. I could not personally borrow more money from First American, having borrowed up to the legal limit, so I borrowed $45,000 from a general contractor whose business had loans of $279,000 outstanding at the association, the idea being that this money would last until we could sell the yacht, and then I would quickly repay him.

This contractor had routinely borrowed from other institutions as well—hundreds of thousands of dollars to finance his construction activities, which included schools and hospitals. He had also attended the Naval Academy, and our connection was businesslike but friendly. We did no paperwork on the loan, and I considered it a personal loan. I knew this was against regulations, but, like most businessmen, I saw a huge difference between a law and a regulation. Regulations change all the time and come from a government bureaucrat who isn't in touch with the real business world. Businessmen routinely live with government regulations, trying to adhere to them as much as possible, though sometimes finding it necessary to bend them. When they do, they do not feel the same weight of morality that is felt about violating a law. When desperate, you can readily convince yourself, rightly or wrongly, about the necessity and morality of this type of thinking. Roberta, though she later denied it, knew about this loan. However, neither she nor I believed that the loan was criminal to the point of being a felony. If anyone had suggested that it constituted bank fraud, I would have laughed.

### A NASTY TURN OF EVENTS

When the insolvency of our First American Savings and Loan continued for months, federal regulators abruptly took it over, removing my wife and me as officers. There were no bondholders to be affected by the federal action. No depositors lost any money, and new government-chosen executives kept the association operating. The only financial losers were the stockholders—my wife and me. Not one depositor lost one red cent under our watch. This was in stark contrast to other savings associations in Illinois and elsewhere around the nation that went under during those years of extremely high interest rates. Often, both depositors and bondholders lost significant amounts of money.

Despite the fact that there were no such losses at First American, the federal S & L regulators conducted a routine postfailure review of our books and records. And then a copy of the report was sent to the U.S. attorney in Chicago: Anton Valukas. I learned that his office had commenced an investigation of me and, becoming more and more concerned as the investigation continued, I finally retained counsel—Tom Foran, a highly regarded criminal lawyer who had achieved fame prosecuting the Chicago Seven. As previously noted, he had also been considered a potential opponent in my race for governor. He ascertained that my wife, who had been chief financial officer for the S & L, was also under investigation. Both of us were named by the U.S. attorney's office as targets, not just potential witnesses.

I went home with a knot in my stomach and told Roberta the news. Her eyes widened with disbelief and anger. "Me? They're targeting me?" Roberta asked. "Why me?"

"Because, Roberta," I said, "we've been in this venture together from the beginning. We were both officers of the S & L. I was chairman of the board, and you were a financial officer. Roberta, with us it has always been a 'we' situation. We were both officers together. Every major decision was a joint decision."

"Well, I sure didn't do anything unlawful."

"I could say the same thing. The point is that we did it together. The only way we can get through this is to work together."

"But I didn't do a goddamn thing wrong."

"I feel the same way. These people are determined to get me and are perfectly willing to stick you at the same time. So, darling, we've just got to stick together."

Roberta remained obviously deeply troubled, but she finally shook her head and sighed. "Yes, you're right, Dan." She put her arm around me. "Of course, we're in this together."

She retained independent counsel, but that was normal for this kind of situation. Tom Foran told us that Anton Valukas had taken the unusual step of overseeing our case personally. Did he discuss this investigation with his old boss, Jim Thompson, who was still governor? I don't know, but since Valukas was also Thompson's personal attorney, I have very little doubt that he did.

Negotiations began in earnest between Foran and Valukas. I met Tom at his office, and he told me how the conversation went.

"Dan, this guy is determined to nail you," Tom began. "When I told him his case against Roberta is damn weak, Valukas actually said, 'No matter. Look at all the publicity I'll get.'"

"The man is a snake. But he will get publicity, all right."

"He also pointed out to me that two of your children received loans."

I blew up. "Those were car loans, small personal loans—all fully collateralized and above suspicion!" I yelled.

"The media will have a field day if the case goes to court," said Tom.

"I can see the headline: 'Walker, Wife Charged; Son and Daughter Implicated.'"

We cooperated fully in the investigation. Eventually, the possible charges were narrowed to a few, and the decision we faced was whether to fight or plea bargain. The adverse consequences from a public trial would be enormous. Roberta would be indicted, and the negative publicity would be very hard on her and her children. My son and daughter, Dan and Kathleen, were both practicing attorneys in the Chicago area. Being publicly named in the trial of the case could cause substantial harm to their law practices. Then there was the cost. Our counsel estimated that a trial would cost well over $50,000 in legal fees, expert witness fees, and other costs. We simply did not have that kind of money.

I had made in the course of a long, sworn deposition a statement that could be characterized as false. I stated that I had not received financial benefit from loans made by the association to members of my family. My son Dan had used loan proceeds to pay off an old note ($5,000) that he and I had negotiated when we were still practicing law together. When we terminated our partnership, he took over that debt. However, my name was still on the note, so technically his paying it off was a "financial benefit," although when I testified at the deposition that I had received no benefit, this had never entered my mind. The charge was perjury, carrying a maximum penalty of five years in prison.

Another charge was that my wife and I had overstated income and understated contingent liabilities on financial statements submitted with loan applications. When we first signed the loan applications, we looked at our past earnings and projected earnings and stated the projected earnings on the optimistic side, as many people do. However, things had not followed the rosy trajectory that we envisioned, so the disparity was substantial. The contingent liabilities we failed to mention were the loan guarantees we signed for the BW businesses operated by franchisees. These loans were solid, and we knew we would never have to be financially responsible for them. And, in fact, they were duly paid off. But when we applied for our loans, they hadn't yet been paid off. The charge was false financial statements, carrying a maximum penalty of one year.

The final charge involved my personal loan from my contractor friend of $45,000. It was argued that in borrowing from a borrower of First American, I did indirectly that which I could not legally do directly. They interpreted this as bank fraud, carrying a maximum penalty of five years. I'm a lawyer, and I never once thought this was a criminal act, let alone a felony, nor did Tom Foran.

We had a decent legal defense. Each charge required proof of criminal intent, and we could argue that we had no such intent. Later, I learned about the Silverado case involving Neil Bush and the Colorado-based Silverado Savings and Loan Association that made front-page financial news across America about the same time as my S & L troubles. Neil Bush, son of one president and brother of another, was a member of the board of directors of Silverado. Neil's friend, an extremely wealthy Denver land developer, had borrowed over $100 million from Silverado, and Bush voted as a board member to approve the loans, without disclosing his relationship with the developer. Then, the developer friend loaned Neil Bush personally more than $2 million.

After Silverado went under, the senior general counsel of the Federal Deposit Insurance Corporation concluded that "Silverado was the victim of sophisticated schemes and abuses by insiders and of gross negligence by its directors." As one of those directors, Bush was paid $120,000 per year, plus undisclosed bonuses, together with a lavish expense account.

All this and more is described in detail in *Silverado: Neil Bush and the Savings and Loan Scandal,* by Steven K. Wilmsen (Washington, D.C.: National Press Books, 1991), a gripping account of how officers and directors of Silverado became involved in "fraud, deception, and greed that cost depositors and bondholders millions of dollars" and ultimately caused Silverado to "come crashing down into a pile of wreckage." Actually, when it went under, the government spent $1 billion to bail out Silverado. *Time* magazine called it "the $1 billion debacle."

The U.S. attorney in Denver forwarded criminal charges against Bush and others to the Department of Justice in Washington. The sorry chapter closed when the attorney general of the United States concluded that borrowing from someone who borrowed from the S & L was a violation of regulations, but *not* a criminal offense. This was precisely what I had done in the main charge against me.

I don't know whether knowing all the details of Neil Bush and Silverado would have altered my final decision to plead guilty. My father had taught me to take the consequences of my mistakes, and I had believed in this all my life. No rationalizing could change the fact that I had been irresponsibly careless about money matters. I didn't want my family's names in the papers because of me. I didn't have the money to defend the case. And, though I didn't see how the prosecution could prove criminal intent, I didn't trust the potential gullibility of juries. Former governor Otto Kerner probably held no criminal intent when he acquired his racetrack stock, and that was his defense. The jury didn't buy it. A lot would depend on how a jury saw me as a human being. I feared that on top of my often negative press image, they would look at my lifestyle, my knowledge of the law—all of which Valukas would hammer home—and conclude that I knew what I was doing.

My counsel, Tom Foran, advised me that if I pleaded guilty, I would most likely get probation, no prison sentence, since we were still under the old laws. He said he had discussed the matter with the U.S. attorney. I assumed he meant Valukas.

With the understanding that the charges against my wife had been dropped, I entered my plea in September at an arraignment before Judge Ann Williams: guilty as charged. She set the sentencing for November 19, 1987, in the Federal District Court, Northern District of Illinois, located in Chicago.

### THE FINAL BLOW

A grand, high-ceilinged, dark wood-paneled courtroom is the domain of each federal judge. The imposing, desklike dais, elevated over the rest of the courtroom, awaited Judge Williams. On the wall behind the dais hung a huge Great Seal of the United States, flanked by flags of the state and the nation.

The area in front of the elevated dais is called the *well*. In it, tables and chairs separated the opposing prosecution and defense attorneys. A single podium stood in the center for them to use when addressing the court. A low wooden partition divided the well from the rest of the courtroom. Only attorneys, bailiff, court recorder, defendant, and witnesses were allowed within it. It is here that I sat nervously at defense counsel's table beside Tom Foran, one of his associates, and my son Dan, who, as an attorney, was permitted to join us. My son Charles was among the spectators. Neither my wife nor any of my daughters were present; I did not want them there. At the other table, the government attorneys waited with a neat dossier before them. Since this wasn't a jury trial, reporters crowded the jury box containing fourteen seats. Spectators packed themselves into the rows of benches that occupied the remainder of the courtroom.

In her black robes, Judge Ann Williams, an African American recently appointed by President Reagan, entered through the rear door from her chambers. Her bailiff cried in a loud voice the "All rise" I had heard so many times before as a trial lawyer. Yet, his command and the reverberation of sound as the multitude in the courtroom stood all at once lifted the hairs on my neck and arms. The judge was seated, and then everyone else.

The bailiff pounded his gavel. "This Honorable Court is now in session."

The clerk then called out, "People v. Daniel Walker. For sentencing."

The judge asked, "Is the defendant Daniel Walker ready for sentencing?"

Tom Foran stood and responded, "Defendant is ready, Your Honor."

After a few perfunctory questions, the judge then announced, "The court will hear matters in mitigation or aggravation."

On this occasion, the U.S. attorney called witnesses. One was the president of the Florida S & L that had taken over our yacht when it was repossessed. He testified to the amount due and the expenses (a figure startling to me) they had incurred in making the yacht fully operational as an "entertainment facility" for clients—which it already was. My contractor friend testified to the amount of his loan to me. The federal official who ran the S & L after it was taken over by the FSLIC testified to its financial condition at that time. Except for the expenses for the yacht, there were no surprises.

Tom Foran stood and said he had filed with the judge over a hundred letters written in my behalf, all asking the judge for mercy in sentencing. Judge Williams said only that she had received them. Tom then made a statement recounting my life of public service, asking that this be taken into account in determining the sentence. And then, inexplicably, my attorney adopted a different stance and spoke with a sort of confidential tone in offering what he considered to be mitigating circumstances.

"The former governor was spoiled by success and the perquisites of office." He went on in that vein, and I could hardly believe my ears. Why the hell, I wondered, was he saying this? We never discussed this as a mitigating circumstance.

"Are there any witnesses for the defense?"

"No, Your Honor," Tom said.

Judge Williams then asked the government attorney, "Does the government have any recommendations regarding sentence?"

Customarily, when the prosecution and defense have made an agreement, the government attorney makes no recommendation and merely states, "No recommendation, Your Honor." This is an unofficial signal of sentencing agreement by counsel. So, based on what Tom had told me, "No recommendation" was the answer I expected to hear that morning. I further expected to hear that the resulting sentence would be probation on all three counts; no jail sentences.

The government attorney did not say that. He stood, walked to the podium, and said loudly and firmly to Judge Williams, "Your Honor, the United States recommends the maximum sentence on each of the three counts."

A few spectators gasped, and the reporters in the jury box made a small rustling as they shifted to full alert. Otherwise, there was dead silence.

I had never even considered this possibility. I reached out my hand and grasped Tom's wrist. He shook it off and raised himself a little as though he were about to stand up, but apparently changed his mind and sat back down. He said nothing.

The judge then picked up a sheaf of papers and read her sentencing statement. "I received all of the letters written on the defendant's behalf, but they are immaterial. I will read only one letter that I received by mail." The letter was highly critical of me as a candidate and governor and was obviously written by someone who intensely disliked me politically.

"You ask that I take the defendant's years of service into account?" the judge said to Tom. "What I will mostly take into account is that the defendant was a governor and a lawyer and should know better than to violate the law." She began reading her statement. "He will be held to a higher standard *because* he has served as governor. This overcomes whatever good public service he may have provided throughout his life. This man is a disgrace to public officials and public service. This man thinks he's still a governor who can get away with things. Witness his automobile license plates that read GOV DAN . . ."

Could this be me she was talking about? Could this African American judge possibly be talking about the Dan Walker who had marched with Martin Luther King Jr., fought residential segregation in his own neighborhood to the point of family members being ostracized, the Dan Walker who ended the practice of redlining African Americans out of the homes of their choice? This judge was reading an outrageously unfair statement about me.

And then I went into denial. Oh, wait, I thought. She's deliberately overstating the case just to show how tough she can sound, that she is acting like a judge should. I can live with this tongue-lashing. When she finishes, she'll sentence me to probation.

She went on. "This man placed himself above the law. His fall from grace, loss of stature, embarrassment, and humiliation are of his own making."

As she reached the end of her statement, the judge's voice rose. "Defendant Daniel Walker, stand."

I stood with Tom and Dan beside me. A pall of silence had fallen over the courtroom. The judge spoke loudly. "Defendant Daniel Walker is hereby sentenced to serve four years on count one (bank fraud), three years on count two (perjury), and five years' probation on count three (false financial statements.)" She wasn't smiling exactly, but her eyes narrowed with the intensity of pleasure, and the corners of her mouth lifted slightly as if with satisfaction. Her voice rang out. "All sentences to be served consecutively."

*Consecutively. Not concurrently.* This final blow seemed aimed at my gut. Beside me, Dan held my arm. This meant a total of seven years. Then, after release, probation for five more years.

"Defendant is also sentenced to five hundred hours of community service. And finally, Defendant will repay the $45,000 loan in full and will guarantee the contractor's loan of $279,000. Defendant will report to the U.S. marshal on January 2 to commence serving sentence. Confinement will be at the United States prison in Duluth, Minnesota." Judge Ann Williams banged her gavel and marched out of the courtroom.

I went into shock. I could hear the reaction of reporters in the jury box and people in the courtroom. Several exclaimed, "Oh my God," and "Jesus, that's tough."

I rocked back, and Tom and Dan reached out to steady me. I could not believe this wasn't a dream. Right up to the moment of sentencing, I had persuaded myself that she would only place me on probation. But I fought to get control of myself. *Head up, shoulders back, be a man. Take it, Dan, don't let the bastards see how you feel. Don't say a goddamn thing to anybody.*

Dan put his arm around my shoulder, hugging me. "It'll be okay, Dad, you'll get through it. Let's get the hell out of here."

My son Charles joined us as Dan, Tom, and I walked out of the courtroom and into the corridor. Reporters, television cameramen, and photographers swamped us, all yelling and trying to get me to say something. Charles jumped out in front of me and forced the clamoring reporters and photographers to move back so we could walk into the corridor. Surrounded, I had to stop when I faced a solid row of television cameras. Numerous microphones, from both radio and television, were thrust into my face.

I said firmly, looking right into the television cameras, "I have violated the law and I will serve my sentence." And that was all I said to the media, either that day or thereafter, until after I had served my sentence.

With Tom on one side and Dan and Charles on the other holding my arms, we pushed our way though the reporters, through the crowd of on-lookers, and out of the federal building, where more photographers waited on the sidewalk and more people gawked, until finally I was able to get into Dan's car. He drove me home.

Even columnist Mike Royko, never a fan of mine, wrote that the sentence was grossly disproportionate to the crime. But certainly U.S. Attorney Anton Valukas must have been pleased at receiving the same publicity his former boss and client Jim Thompson had been given when he sent Governor Otto Kerner to jail. And no doubt Thompson himself joined in the congratulations to his protégé and personal attorney.

Naturally, I thought about comparisons, and not just the Silverado case and Neil Bush. As noted earlier, literally hundreds of savings and loan associations had failed at that time, and the media were full of reports on cases where both owners and executives reaped huge personal benefits worth millions of dollars while bondholders and depositors suffered multimillion-dollar losses. And in all of these scandals, only one man in the nation other than me was ever indicted and punished. That man was Charles Keating, whose Lincoln Savings and Loan in California was driven under by a series of bad loans and money-losing, million-dollar manipulations that violated the law. Keating piled up huge profits while his bondholders and depositors lost millions. I have the distinction of being the only one punished for losing money while my depositors lost nothing.

Over the Thanksgiving holidays, many friends called or visited, offering sympathy and sharing their frustration.

"Selective prosecution is inexcusable," Bill Goldberg said, "and that's clearly what this was."

"Of all the S & L failures and mishandling, Dan represented maximum publicity value to Valukas," Dave Green said.

"It was mainly a political prosecution. If you'd been a Republican, we wouldn't be having this conversation," Vic said.

All my friends agreed. Even people on the street would come up to tell me what a shame it was that the sentence was so unfair and that I was the victim of selective political prosecution.

I decided to let the chips fall where they may, hoping the public would examine all the facts before reaching a conclusion about me. Distortions appeared in the media, however, the wildest one reporting that "Walker stole millions of dollars." Even if I'd had money to sue for libel, I could not.

Public figures are fair game. You can say anything about them without fear of a libel suit.

Publicly, I have kept my feelings to myself until this writing. While I was guilty of violating the law as a businessman, my actions hurt no one. It was truly a victimless crime. I took solace in the undeniable fact that I was never charged with any wrongdoing arising out of my actions as either a practicing attorney or governor.

I had to go in for fingerprinting at Metropolitan Corrections in downtown Chicago. Fortunately, my former security trooper, Pete Wilkes, was the U.S. marshal, and he let me come in on my own, allowed no handcuffs, and personally escorted me through the building, tolerating no harassment and shielding me from the press.

For the Christmas holidays, a final interval before prison, Roberta Nelson and I drove west, crossing the Rockies and staying at the mountain cabin of a friend of my son Charles in Taos, New Mexico. The days were peaceful and sad, Roberta warm and comforting, seeming to have every intention of standing by her man.

# 26

## *Suicidal Thoughts*

Every military base of any consequence in the nation had one during and after World War II: a large water tower, a cylindrical tank supported by four seemingly spindly and slightly spread legs. The tank was high enough so that the water could flow by gravity to supply all water needs for the base. The bright red and white of the tower at the old aviation base in Duluth, now my prison, was originally painted to make it plainly visible to planes taking off and landing. Its metal ladder rungs run up one of the legs and straight up the outside of the tank to a narrow, circular railed walkway along the rim, perhaps forty-five to fifty feet above ground.

I know all the details of that tank, its supports, and that ladder. Every single detail. Walking around the prison camp, I have studied them many times. In the light of day, under the spotlights at night—wet in the rain, white in the snow. Sometimes I even stand still and gaze intently at those details for minutes at a time. I often think of that tank while in my bunk at night. I wake up seeing it plainly in my mind's eye.

My fellow inmates and I are kept outside during one of the routine night-time prisoner counts when all bunks are checked. As I am doing now, I have often imagined myself climbing those rungs all the way up to that walkway and then jumping off to my certain death. I have a fear of heights, always have. I couldn't handle walking along that walkway at the top, so I would have to jump as soon as I got to the top of the ladder, before I lost my nerve.

Should I go feet first or dive? Will my body twist as I fall? Will I stay conscious throughout the fall, or will I black out before I hit the unyielding tarmac? Ah, but why in the hell am I even thinking about such things? If I jump, I jump, and it's over before I'll have a chance to think about it. Just don't look down, Dan.

Death, that wonderful, peace-bringing oblivion, will be easy, man, easy. Right there before me. I wouldn't even have to jump. All I would have to do is take one step into infinity. I would not even see the darkness that would envelop me in seconds. The pain is not worth thinking about. It would be but a flash and then gone. No more pain forever.

*Suicide.* I have never used that word in my nightmarish daydreaming. I think of it only as "finding death." Jumping to find, to meet, my death. To find, yes, nothing. To be enveloped by blackness. Total surcease from life and all of its disasters and all of my mistakes. I give no thought to a hereafter. Death is not to go somewhere. Death is an escape from an unacceptable earthly reality. Death is an escape from this pit I have somehow dug for myself, an escape from this cage made up of the tight bands that formed around my life. I am sick to death of this life, of this damned prison. With one little step, this reality, this pit, this cage, this prison will simply not be there anymore. Gone forever, thank God!

Suicide is supposed to be a cowardly way out, but finding peace in death is not cowardly to me. Indeed, it will take courage: I am so desperately afraid of heights. I know I will find it terribly difficult to climb those rungs to the top.

Can I do it?

Yes, I tell myself, as I have over and over, with the self-discipline that I have always prided myself on having.

What would my Old Man say? "You were dealt the hand, son. Now play it as best you can." What will my first Roberta say? "I hope he's found peace with God." What will R2 say? Probably, "Good riddance." What will my children say? This one stops me. I just do not know. What would the courageous Jesus say? Maybe, just maybe he would understand. After all, he confronted his own death and never dodged his fate.

Time and again, many days and on many such nights, I have pondered all these questions as I stared at that damn water tank and its long, spider-like legs and that ladder I would climb. I have never failed to look up as I go by, mesmerized in a death-seeking trance. Even when I try not to stop, I inevitably do. To stare and say to myself, "Yes, I could and I would climb. And jump."

Why am I hesitating? Still just staring?

The days are longer now, but the water tower is spotlighted against the cool purple evening sky. I slowly wander along the road to the tower, which is about a hundred yards from my barracks. I will dash across and climb up before anyone can stop me.

I close my eyes for a few moments in my deep despair. What I experience is not blackness, but a face, looking directly at me. It is the face of Jesus. A real man, not a picture. I immediately open my eyes. No one there. I close my eyes again. There he is, looking into my soul. There is no movement. His face is immobile, unsmiling, yet he is real. He is there. Every time I close my eyes, he's with me. A feeling of profound peace envelops me.

I record the phenomenon in the prayer book that I keep under my mattress.

In these difficult days, I am able to exist moment by moment in this way, knowing that I can summon this face, and time passes. I do my prison jobs, and take a break to lean against a wall, and close my eyes. He is there. I slip away to the chapel after my work shift ends. I close my eyes, and he is there. I lie on my bed at night and see him before I sleep and again when I wake. There is no message or even words, no judgment or forgiveness, only steady comfort. Peace.

I am well aware that this phenomenon is not unknown, that psychologists say it can be created by a deeply disturbed mind. That may be so, but no matter what those experts say, I shall always remember the face of Jesus being there when I needed Him.

I tell this story to the prison psychiatrist not as a formal patient, but because I have gotten to know him, since his office is in the chapel building.

Several months pass, and I record the day, September 9, when I can no longer close my eyes and summon up that picture of Jesus. I enter the single word *gone* in the prayer book. The face was there when I needed it and gone when I reclaimed my balance and achieved peace within myself, a peace that has never left me.

### WALKING AWAY

Winter came again, the cold hitting like a hammer. My bronchitis returned, worse than it was last year. The weeks went by, and members of my family visited regularly. I somehow got through my work and the loneliness. The spring returned slowly, and then summer came.

One day, I was given permission to make a telephone call to my attorney, Tom Foran, who had previously written asking me to call on this day after a scheduled appointment he had set up with the sentencing judge. From a wall-mounted telephone in a large, noisy, and crowded prisoners' public room, I placed the call, not knowing what I would hear.

When I reached Tom, he said, "Dan, the judge has just reduced your seven-year sentence to the time you've already served."

I was silent. Could I possibly have heard him correctly?

"That means you're free!"

"Would you repeat that?"

"You are a free man, free as a lark. Scot-free."

Voice quavering, I ask, "Is the order signed as being effective immediately?"

"Yes!"

I yell at the top of my voice, startling everyone in the room, "I'm free! I'm a free man!"

"Thank you, Tom, thank you," I said into the phone. "I just . . . can't say it enough. Oh, thank you."

I went immediately to the warden's office. "The federal court has set me free, Warden," I said. "Now I want my Naval Academy ring back along with my other clothes and immediate clearance to leave the prison."

"No way, Walker," he said. "You'll stay right here until I receive the papers. That'll take about three days."

I said, "Warden, I don't give a damn what you say. I'm leaving. I'm walking out of this prison right now, right through the main gate. The federal judge in Chicago this morning signed the order, effective immediately. Immediately means *immediately*. If you stop me, I'll make a call to my lawyer son and get a writ of habeas corpus issued real fast by the federal court in Chicago."

The warden glared but subsided. He knew I could do just as I threatened, that federal judges do not take lightly a prison official ignoring their orders. So, I made the rounds, collected my stuff and my ring, and asked my friend Evan Miller to call a taxicab to take me to a downtown hotel. I then called my son Dan and he, Charles, and Will arrived in Duluth some hours later—the same three who had walked the state with me, the same three who brought me to the prison the previous year. We stayed at the hotel that first night and bought a bottle of Johnnie Walker Black Label. I thoroughly enjoyed it. Then, next morning, what a joyous trip home!

I have no idea whether it is true, but I was later informed that I owed my release to a group of distinguished African American professionals and businessmen who had known me over the years. I was told they called on the federal judge who sentenced me and reminded her of my many years of involvement on civil rights issues. They also informed her that I was in poor health and concluded by asking her for mercy. The judge then decided to reduce my seven-year sentence to time served—eighteen months. I never learned the identity of those wonderful friends, but my gratitude is boundless.

### GOING HOME

Once out, I reunited gloriously with my family, including Roberta, my first wife. Roberta Marie, former first lady of Illinois, had sold our house, bought a small condo, and taken a job in a Marriott Hotel gift shop. Edith, the housekeeper, was still with her. Roberta somehow looked just the same as she always had. It was good to see her.

"I know I didn't seem happy about your visits to Duluth," I said to her. "You know I didn't want any of my family to see me. But I always appreciated your presence. Thank you, Roberta."

She smiled. "I was glad to come." All her years of faithfulness came through in that quiet statement. She had never even considered the possibility of remarriage. She was a one-man woman, and I was still her man, though "for worse" and "for poorer" had both come to pass. "Have you thought about where you'd like to live?" she asked.

I knew that she would make room for me in the Deerfield condo if I asked her to. "The only thing I'm sure of," I said, "is that I have to get out of Illinois."

Her smile dropped at that, as I knew it would. I might always be her man, but Deerfield was her home. She would never leave it. So there was no possibility of attempting reconciliation.

I decided to live with my brother Waco in Virginia Beach. His wife, Angela, had died of cancer the previous year, and his grown children lived elsewhere. Waco and I fantasized about building a place on the Chesapeake Bay where we could hunt, fish, and live to ourselves. But that, too, was not to be, because a few months later, Waco found a new wife, lovely Ellie, whom he had gotten to know on antique business tours.

I still had five years of probation with five hundred hours of community service to work off. I was used to being on the administrative and fund-raising end of public service, so I confess, I wasn't looking forward to working at the base level. But in Virginia Beach, I came into contact with people trying to establish a center for the homeless and went to work with them. We raised the necessary money and built the Virginia Beach Outreach Center for the Homeless. It felt wonderful to be free to do what I wanted to do and be in charge of my life again, to decide where I wanted to go and what I wanted to do. I cherished my personal independence as never before. I was living on Social Security and hadn't yet begun to repay the $45,000, so I needed to find work. With most of my community service hours worked off and my brother enjoying his life with his new wife, there was nothing to keep me in Virginia Beach. I needed to find a new home.

## 27

### *More Travail and Finally Peace*

The Chicago area was not a place for me. I found that I still could not handle the recognition that showed in people's eyes when I encountered them in stores or on sidewalks. Wondering what they thought of me now as a convicted felon was a question that still tormented me. My bones still retained the memory of eastern winters, particularly those in Duluth, so I decided to head for southern California and start life anew. Surely, I thought, I could get a job as a paralegal with a corporate law department or law firm.

In Los Angeles, I stayed with a longtime friend, Vivian Monroe, who had founded a national organization called Constitutional Rights Foundation that worked with young people and schools on programs stressing constitutional rights. Years earlier, she had persuaded me to become a member of its board.

The job search, unfortunately, was in vain. After numerous law firm and corporate legal department interviews, I reached a dead end. I just could not overcome the combination of age, now almost sixty-eight, and felony status. Even men whose careers I had helped launch as governor said, "Sorry, Dan, I can't help you."

#### RETURN TO SAN DIEGO

This was a blow, but an insignificant one in comparison to what I had already endured. I turned my search to San Diego, my old hometown, hoping that it would make room for me. Drawing on my service with the Boy Scouts in DuPage County, I contacted the local Boy Scout executive and asked if he could help me with any members of his board, all prominent citizens of San Diego. The scout executive suggested Father Joe Carroll, a Catholic priest who ran a large, successful center for the homeless in San Diego. Thanks to the talents and charm of Father Joe, his Joan Kroc Center had attracted widespread community support and achieved national recognition as one of the most successful operations for the homeless, combining food and shelter with outstanding rehabilitation programs. I called on Father Joe and made a simple proposition: I would go to work on his fund-raising programs if he would pay me just the amount I could receive without reducing my Social Security benefit. That would give me a total monthly income of about $1,600 before taxes.

Father Joe said, "You're hired, Dan."

He needed someone to start a planned-giving program, raising funds from people who could achieve tax savings from making substantial and regular or designated contributions. I had the legal background to run such a program. I coupled that work with helping on the food lines—serving the homeless men, women, and children who came to the center every day for a free meal. I rented a small apartment and fortunately had a used car that my brother had provided. It was subsistence only, but nonetheless a pleasant life in San Diego.

This continued for about eighteen months, and I was able to add more than a million dollars to Father Joe's endowment fund. One day, I was enjoying a hamburger in a sports bar in downtown San Diego and noticed that it featured Chicago sports paraphernalia. The owner was from Chicago, and I kidded him about posting pictures of Mayor Daley but none of me. He remembered me, apologized for not having a picture to display, and said effusively, "Dan, you were my governor, you are my governor, you always will be my governor." I don't know if he remembered my conviction; it never came up.

Soon thereafter, I received a telephone call from his attorney, who had learned about my legal background from his client and wanted to talk about my doing paralegal work for his firm. I met with Joel Pressman and found that we had a perfect fit. His trial practice was expanding, and he needed help on some major cases. This was exactly what I had done in Chicago for years. I explained some of the unusual trial preparation techniques we had developed for major-case litigation, and Joel offered me a job at a good paralegal salary. When I told Father Joe, he urged me to accept the offer, satisfied that his planned-giving program was now off the ground.

Joel and I worked together very well. Our first major contingent-fee case involved a dispute among business partners, and the jury came in with a very substantial verdict in favor of our client. There were other successes, and we also lost a few as the months rolled by. I resumed playing tennis, had a comfortable small apartment in a seaside town named Del Mar, bought a convertible, and enjoyed life. I even managed to pay off that $45,000 loan.

I also decided to try to patch things up with my former wife Roberta Nelson. She flew to San Diego, and we talked endlessly. I finally forgave her for divorcing me while I was in prison. We even wondered whether there might be any basis for a renewed relationship but decided that would be impossible. Then, wanting some female companionship, I tried in a variety of ways to meet women my age in an effort to find a suitable match. The search included a variety of get-togethers, including lunches and dinners with quite a few women over a period of many weeks, and I found the process enjoyable. One quality lady, Lillian Stewart, stood out, and she and I had a number of fun dates together in different places around San Diego.

During this time, though, I also was enjoying phone conversations with my first wife, Roberta, remembering old times fondly, sharing experiences about our sons, daughters, and grandchildren, and perhaps imbuing the past with more happiness than it warranted.

When we were raising our children, Roberta and I had attended classes in the Confraternity of Christian Doctrine, or CCD, and it was through these classes that I began my intense interest in, and subsequent study of, Christianity. So when I finished my religious book, *The First Hundred Years, AD 1–100: Failures and Successes of Christianity's Beginning*, I dedicated it to Roberta Marie. The book describes modern scholars' analytical views on the story of Jesus's life and message and the authors of books of the New Testament, the denigration of women in the early churches, and the beginnings of Christian anti-Semitism. I submitted the manuscript to traditional publishers and received repeated rejections with the explanation, "It's a well-written book, but you're not qualified to write it." Spelling it out, they said that marketing a religious book requires an author with a background in theology or divinity, neither of which I had. So, I resorted to electronic, print-on-demand net publishing, and it achieved a modicum of success. I used it as the text in adult Sunday school classes I taught at the local Presbyterian church.

I was enjoying the law office work and finally decided that I should ask for restoration of my law license in Illinois. Former attorney general Bill Scott, who had been convicted of income tax evasion and had consequently lost his law license, was able to get it back after a few years. As required, I applied to the Illinois Attorneys Registration and Disciplinary Committee (ARDC). While the ARDC was chaired by the brother of my lieutenant governor, Neil Hartigan—a Daley guy with whom I had experienced considerable difficulties—I thought I would still get a fair hearing. And in any event, the petition would end up in the Illinois Supreme Court, and it was there that I thought I had the best chance of prevailing on the merits. The crucial argument was that my offenses were unrelated to the practice of law and that I had led a blemish-free life in San Diego, making considerable contributions to the community by working for the homeless and being active in church-related programs.

Bill Hart, a distinguished Chicago attorney with a brilliant record on civil rights matters who had admired my public career, agreed to handle my case on a pro bono basis, since I clearly could not afford his fees. We completed all the necessary paperwork and were ready for the ARDC hearing, which we thought would consist of my describing my clean record and public service activities since leaving prison, with supporting letters, witnesses, and so on. Then, Bill called me to say that there was an unexpected development. ARDC staff had notified him that an expert witness would testify that my former savings and loan association was a part of the national scandal of failing institutions and that I personally contributed to that scandal by mismanagement.

Astonished, I said, "That's just not so, and besides, this has nothing to do with my right to be reinstated."

Bill responded, "Dan, you're right, and I don't know why the top guys are insisting on this, but they are, and we'll have to call a counter expert." He explained that we would have to have an expert testify that the crimes of which I was convicted had nothing to do with the failure of my S & L and explain, with facts and figures, how it went under for business reasons related to the prevailing, extraordinarily high interest rates. I said to Bill that bringing in this expert was ridiculous; that the only issue at the ARDC hearing should be whether my renewed life established that I was entitled to rejoin the legal community, the test applied to Bill Scott and others before me. Bill Hart told me he had argued this position unsuccessfully.

Bill then reminded me of the ARDC rule that I would have to pay all costs of the hearing, whether I won or lost. This would be bearable if the hearing went as we expected, short and simple—just my telling my story. But expert witnesses were a different matter. I asked Bill for his estimate of the costs. At least $20,000 for each expert, he responded. That did it. There was no way I could come up with that kind of money. So, I said simply to Bill Hart, "It's obvious that we'll have to quit. Withdraw the petition."

I continued the paralegal work, but during this time, first wife Roberta Marie and I decided a reunion might be possible. We could have full family gatherings again. I hated not to see Lily, but she definitely did not want to be around if I was interested in starting over with my first wife. I flew to Chicago, and this time Roberta agreed to come to San Diego for a while to see if such an idea might be possible. Roberta and I were making good progress.

And then disaster struck once again. Somehow, someone in Chicago who did not like me learned about my work with the law firm in San Diego. I believe that I know the identity of the Chicagoan but cannot prove it. He called a justice of the California Supreme Court who had responsibility on ethical issues and told him about me, saying that in Illinois a disbarred attorney could not work in a law office even as a paralegal because clients might assume that he was an attorney. He suggested that even though California had no such rule, it should still be applied to prohibit me from working in a law office, arguing that since I had been disbarred in Illinois, California should honor the Illinois rule.

Joel Pressman's senior partner was contacted and told about this complaint, concluding that the matter would be left up to the law firm. But the implicit suggestion was enough. I lost my job. To put it bluntly, I was fired—for the first time in my life. Who did it to me? The Chicagoan whom I suspect made the call to the California court was a "machine guy." I could not help but remember Mike Royko's book *Boss*, where he wrote that the machine "will wait years to get revenge."

Unemployment compensation kept me going for months while I searched for other paralegal work. Having become reasonably computer competent, I pointed out that I could work out of my apartment, using the county law library for research and coming to the law office only for occasional necessary meetings. My job search came to naught. Despite weeks of contacts, advertisements and applications, there were absolutely no job offers. I couldn't support Roberta, and so she returned to Chicago.

### A NEW LIFE

Sadly, I had to give up my apartment and live on Social Security. I wanted the companionship of a woman and thought warmly of Lillian. Would she still be single? Would she still be interested? She was a widow, having enjoyed a happy marriage for seven years, during which her husband worked as a psychiatrist and she as a registered nurse, having obtained an MBA degree in nursing administration. Lily had worked on rehabilitation cases for insurance companies in her own business and was also rehabilitation coordinator for the City of San Diego, finally retiring with many nursing and rehabilitation certifications.

Money was a severe problem for me at that time, but I decided to call her anyway. We talked and then met a few times. It was obvious the chemistry still bubbled between us. Finally, after many discussions back and forth, we decided to combine homes. But we were not comfortable with this arrangement, even though our feelings for each other continued to grow. I felt that the loving and honorable thing to do was to ask her to marry me, and I did so. She accepted, but before we were married, I had the first early warning of a heart problem. I offered Lily the chance to break the engagement, but she refused, saying, "One takes the bitter with the better in any solid relationship." We had a lovely wedding in Lily's beautiful backyard on June 14, 1996. My brother Waco was best man, and some of Lily's children and a granddaughter of mine were in the wedding party.

This true story may surprise some of our friends and family members. At the time we were married, we used a different account in answering the constant "where did you meet" questions. Perhaps understandably not wanting to relate the "personal ad" facts, we said that we had met at the copy machine in a law library where I was doing research on a law case and she was using the machine to copy estate papers.

The years with Lily have been extremely good ones.

In 1999, President Clinton was considering pardon petitions in the closing days of his administration. Lily encouraged me to try to completely clear my name in this way. Abner Mikva, a former friend whom I had helped when I was governor, had served as judge on the U.S. Court of Appeals for the District of Columbia and then as legal counsel to President Clinton in the White House. When I decided to apply to President Clinton for a pardon, I turned to Abner, who was in a position to help me. He had turned me down when I asked for his support in the primary in my bid for reelection.

Surely, I thought, he must feel guilty about caving in to machine pressure and would now make it up to me.

I contacted Vic, who thought it was a good idea. As one of his oldest supporters, Vic called Ab to ask him to help only to the extent of seeing that my pardon petition came to the personal attention of the president, a request Ab could easily fulfill.

Vic related the conversation to me. "Ab said to me, 'As a former appellate court judge, it would be improper for me to support a petition for a pardon when a lower court judge had convicted Dan of the offense.'"

"That's a strange thing to say. He hasn't been on that court for years!" I said.

"That's what I said. And I also said that a pardon is not a reversal of conviction, so it does not reflect at all on the trial judge. Also, I told him again, 'We're not asking you to endorse or support Dan's petition, just see that it comes to the President's attention.' Mikva answered, 'No matter, I won't do it.' I'm stunned that he turned you down, Dan."

And that was that. The conviction would stay on my record forever. At least it had been good to talk to Vic.

As I look back over the now eighty-four years of this roller-coaster life, I naturally try to draw some conclusions. I remain very fond of the men who have played such a major role in my public life. When I meditate on the trio of Vic De Grazia, Dave Green, and Bill Goldberg, the words of Henry Adams come to mind: "Friendship needs a certain parallelism of life, a community of thought. One friend in a lifetime is much, two are many, three are hardly possible." I have treasured three: Vic, Dave, and Bill have certainly held a community of thought with me. Together with many others, who worked hard in high positions and low, they are the ones who deserve credit for whatever successes I achieved in politics and government. Sadly, Vic has passed on. Dave has retired and lives with his wonderful wife, Mary, in a beautiful home in Winnetka, a suburb of Chicago on Lake Michigan. Bill still practices law as the head of the litigation department in a successful Chicago firm and lives with his talented wife, Judy, on the near North Side of Chicago.

I was content with my life, but because I love staying active and using my mind, I decided that I would attempt writing as a last career. I recalled that *Rights in Conflict: The Walker Report*, describing the tumultuous demonstrations at the 1968 Democratic National Convention, had been a million-copy best seller and that the Society of Midland Authors had even given me an award for that book. And, of course, there was also *The First Hundred Years*, the book I described earlier.

Lily and I coauthored and self-published *Delicious Walks: Picnicking with Exercise in San Diego*. Then I wrote *San Diego: Home Base for Freedom*, telling how San Diego became the nation's premier military port, describing all of San Diego's military bases, installations, and industries that have sent fighting men, women, ships, planes, and equipment to the far corners of the world for combat, most recently in Afghanistan and Iraq.

Next came *Thirst for Independence: The San Diego Water Story*, which relates San Diego's search for a reliable water supply, beginning with the primitive dam built by Father Junipero Serra and ending with an epochal agreement in 2003 that imported water from Imperial Valley and the development of a major program for desalination of ocean water. That book has attracted a good deal of attention, winning in 2005 an award from the San Diego Book Awards Association as best book about San Diego.

Completed and awaiting publication is my sixth book, *Barefoot to Spacecraft: Travel and Transport in San Diego*. Remarkably, San Diego County has experienced firsthand more modes of transportation than any other county in the United States. All of them, 189 by my count, make up a fine human-interest story, ranging from the Kumeyaay Indians to my Naval Academy friend Wally Schirra's globe-encircling space mission. I'm now working hard on a novel titled *VETO!* based on the interaction between politics, legalized gambling, and the Mob in Illinois.

Appreciation for family has taken on greater significance in the years after the pursuit of career. The greatest satisfaction comes to me from the kind of men and women my children have become, and the families they have raised. I always hope to see in them that they are becoming better human beings than I have been. I sadly admit causing the greatest hurt to my first wife. Life is hardly ever what one bargains for, but in selecting me, Roberta Marie Walker, the former first lady of Illinois, got far more and far less than she bargained for. She passed away in 2006, and I repeated my apologies to her before the end.

My two eldest, Kathleen and Dan, are both successful practicing lawyers. Kathleen specializes in bankruptcy law, working out of her office in Aurora, Illinois. Dan's office is in Hinsdale, where he has a well-rounded law practice with his partner, Joe Cesario, while Dan specializes in court work. Charles, who also went to law school, left that profession and is a highly successful venture capitalist, living in Hillsborough, California. The other kids have all made their homes in Illinois. Julie Ann has her master's in education and teaches the seventh grade. That's where my youngest son, Will, also has his home, working as part owner and general manager of a chain of auto repair shops. Robbie Okamoto lives near me in Rosarito, Mexico. She is an accomplished writer and bilingual teacher in Japanese, often working with her husband, Taki. Margaret, who graduated from Southern Illinois University with her brother Will, is a talented landscape architect, living in Lake Bluff. I'm particularly proud of her husband, Bob, who has worked hard to become a chief petty officer in the Naval Reserve.

Lily and I maintain homes in Escondido, a suburb of San Diego, and in Rosarito, Baja California, where our condominium overlooks the Pacific Ocean. With thirteen children between us and twenty-seven grandchildren (twenty-two of them mine) plus three great grandchildren, our normally quiet life sparkles in celebration with frequent family visits.

I can honestly say that I have never climbed over the backs of others to achieve success. I am proud, too, that everything I have gained has been the result of my own hard work and that of the many who worked with me. Good luck has rarely been a factor. In fact, I have had pretty bad luck at times, and perhaps the worst was making grievous mistakes when a political enemy was acting as U.S. attorney.

Outside government, overall, I think my track record is good. As a trial lawyer on business lawsuits, I proved that I could hold my own with the best in Chicago. At Montgomery Ward, I became a successful executive in the big league of the business world. And in starting and developing the fast oil change business in the Chicago area, I proved that I could find, grow, and manage a public-oriented business. In the not-for-profit world, I am very proud of the results of my many years of work with the Chicago Crime Commission, the Metropolitan Housing Development Corporation, the Constitutional Rights Foundation, the Boy Scouts of America, the National Society for Epilepsy, and the National Foundation for the Blind. One of the emoluments hanging in a prominent place on my wall is the Roger Baldwin award given by the American Civil Liberties Union.

I can also say proudly that to me, from the beginning, the allure of government and politics was not just holding high public office. I had also a strong desire to improve the system and make it work better for the public. It cannot be gainsaid that I fought harder for stronger ethics in government than any governor before or after me. And it cannot be gainsaid that I invested more or lost more in my fight to open up the Illinois political system to balance Chicago power with downstate power than any governor before or after me.

And now I hope I have earned the reader's attention for some final perspectives.

# Conclusion

Some commentators have labeled me a "confrontationist" governor who "created too much turmoil." However, it is puzzling to me how a corrupt, entrenched, bipartisan political system could be challenged without confrontation and turmoil.

Surveying the political landscape in Illinois since I left office, I have seen many good things being done in Springfield by governors after me. Former friends and associates have served capably, like Jim Houlihan as legislator and Cook County assessor, Roland Burris as state comptroller and attorney general, and Pat Quinn as treasurer and lieutenant governor. Some good men and women from both parties have served capably and honestly in state office.

Today, the greatest governmental abuses more often involve what is often called "pay to play" schemes. Money is more important than jobs. There is also "pinstripe patronage": not just handing out jobs but awarding government business to the favored few. Job patronage remains, but its impact on government pales in comparison. Most subject to abuse are engineering, consulting, and legal contracts where a particular expertise is required, so that a bidding system is deemed unworkable. Also subject to abuse are the "set-aside contracts" in which government business is restricted to minorities and women to make up for past discrimination. The rip-off comes when a minority member or a woman is installed in name only, while the business is really owned and operated by favored nonminority individuals who reap the financial benefits of the government contract.

Patronage abuses continue, and campaign contributions still provide power, but with new twists. A major one works this way: An elected official has favored lawyers whose identity is well known. Private interests seeking help on legislation retain those attorneys, paying high fees. The lawyers, in turn, regularly make substantial contributions to the campaign chest of the elected official. The official then parcels out the money to the campaigns of other officials who know that, to continue receiving this largess, they must abide by the official's wishes.

The Chicago "pay to play" system is extremely diffuse. Both Mayor Daley and the famed Eleventh Ward Democratic organization presided over by the mayor's brother, John Daley, a Cook County commissioner, have taken very substantial campaign contributions from city employees convicted as part of the infamous hired truck program. The mayor has a political fund that receives huge sums from the business establishment, including particularly the lawyers who are essential to any project, large or small, in which businessmen are involved. The money flows through political contributions or to foundations established to help finance public projects.

In the introduction, I quoted the judgment of the *Chicago Tribune* that Chicago may be the most corrupt city in the nation and the description of the state as a "petri dish for corruption." Then there is the Mob, still active, as shown by the federal indictments of numerous Mob gangsters. Columnist John Kass has revealed that as a result of the $40 million hired truck scandal, city hall was crawling with Mob-connected truckers from the Eleventh Ward. He writes that certain individuals who like to boast of their Mob connections drink with Mayor Richard Daley at the Como Inn, a well-known Mob hangout. Then, for a nightcap, he writes, they "get $100 million affirmative-action contracts." Also in the introduction, I cited the recent federal investigations of the administration of the current governor, Ron Blagojevich, a Democrat.

One of the twenty-eight counts on which the former Republican governor George Ryan was convicted in federal court charged him with using state employees to fuel his political organization through fund-raising events. His finance director testified that campaign funds raised by coerced state employees were the biggest source of money for Ryan's political campaigns. This practice, a variant of the "pay to play" intertwining of government and politics, has for many years been endemic in state government. As earlier discussed, I put a stop to that practice by executive order as soon as I took office in 1973 and enforced the order for four years. None of my successors had the guts to follow my lead.

At his trial, former governor George Ryan used in his defense the same cry heard often from the friends of the Daleys, father and son, in response to charges of corruption: "He never took a dirty dollar." No matter that, as the evidence showed, his cronies, like the Daley cronies, grabbed those dollars while Ryan and the Daleys looked the other way. It has always been a bipartisan game in Illinois.

Nobody commented on the supreme irony in 2006 when Ryan was convicted. Former governor "Big Jim" Thompson's law firm gave Ryan an estimated $10 million gift in providing *gratis* Ryan's legal defense team. By the way, reporters are still asking whether that $10 million is a taxable gift by the law firm or taxable income to Ryan. But going back to the irony, it was the same Thompson as U.S. Attorney who convicted and jailed for corruption Ryan's predecessor governor, Otto Kerner.

Perhaps Thompson had in mind the embarrassing fact that for fourteen years as governor, he had in his numerous campaigns regularly condoned pressure on his state employees to raise millions of dollars in campaign funds. This practice avidly followed by Thompson was precisely the same as that utilized by Ryan in his many years as a state official working with Thompson as governor. No wonder, then, that Thompson was willing to protect Ryan and visibly stood by him personally as Ryan was sentenced to jail for, among other things, violating federal law by engaging in those practices.

The Democratic Party in Illinois is still dominated and controlled by Chicago. Downstate is still held in thrall by Chicago. I fought constantly to give downstate a stronger voice in both politics and government. But today, any downstate legislator who seeks success in passing legislation for his district still must beg for help from the Chicago-controlled leadership. And any downstater who seeks high office still must make obeisance to fifth-floor city hall in Chicago.

True, both the mayor of Chicago and state officials of both parties have produced some excellent programs. *Time* magazine recently reported that the second Mayor Daley is widely viewed as "the nation's top urban executive." He certainly has beautified Chicago to an extent far exceeding anything done by his father, and visitors exclaim over the vast improvements in the downtown area. His twenty-year plan for downtown is on track, and already the area feels alive and vibrant, day and night. He promises "more museums, more theater, more jazz and futuristic transportation programs." He has shown courage and delivered results by tackling long-standing problems in such critical areas as public housing and education (e.g., Renaissance 2010 promises by the end of the decade to produce seventy new public schools out of one hundred failing ones). Mayor Daley has also demonstrated a surprising degree of governmental sophistication in supervising the many young achievers he has brought to city government and in giving headroom to a few highly capable and totally honest administrators, like Cook County Assessor James Houlihan, who has courageously modernized an antiquated property tax assessment system to make it no longer a fertile field for granting favors to the privileged few. Indeed, overall, some of the rough edges of Chicago politics have been sanded off and smoothed down so skillfully that even critics have difficulty in finding fault.

But make no mistake. That system I fought is still there, still very much alive, as the current U.S. Attorney has vividly demonstrated with over 126 indictments. In the nitty-gritty workings of city hall, in the fiefdoms of the aldermen and ward committeemen, the wheels of the new machine grind on, as the numerous federal investigations have amply demonstrated. Out of the Eleventh Ward, original home of the Mayors Daley, tentacles of old-fashioned machine-type politics still reach out.

The Seventeenth Ward Democratic organization, it was recently revealed, has in the last three years received donations totaling a quarter of a million dollars from more than sixty firms holding contracts with the Chicago Housing Authority. Yet there *is no* public housing in the Seventeenth Ward. What is in the Seventeenth is a powerful resident, Terry Peterson, chief of all Chicago public housing, who has also served as the ward's Democratic alderman.

In some critical ways, the same Boss Daley lives inside the skin of the present Mayor Daley. Money counts. Big money. And it must flow in the right direction. Richie, like his father, Richard, before him who defeated me in 1976, will not leave office a rich man, but many around him will take the money that, so to speak, is still left on the table. "Pay to play" remains the name of the game.

John Kass, *Chicago Tribune* columnist, has written repeatedly that the real rift in Illinois is not between Republicans and Democrats but "between the political insiders and the rest of us." This is the same gap I have repeatedly stressed over the years as being created by a club system between members and outsiders. Kass calls it a "combine" and describes the bipartisan political insiders just as I have over the years: "the power brokers in both parties who—through their clout, connections, consulting contracts, and political contributions—manipulate our political system for their personal gain." They are the "ruling elites" who make the club system of politics work—for them, not for the taxpayers. Just as I call them the bipartisan leaders of the "club system of politics," Kass calls it the "combine of City Hall Democrats and the Republican power interests." Thus, the system that fosters "pay to play" government remains largely the same in both parties, and the combine continues. But the Daleys have been "smart" enough to let their associates take personally the financial benefits while they contented themselves with the political benefits of the system.

Classic examples of the bipartisan "club system," or "combine," are William Cellini, "Big Bob" Kjellander, Antoin "Tony" Rezko, and Stuart Levine. Cellini is chairman of the Sangamon County Republicans (that's where Springfield is located) and a powerhouse in the state Republican Party. Kjellander is treasurer of the Republican National Committee and has made millions on deals during the administration of Democratic governor Ron Blagojevich. Rezco, a top fund-raiser, adviser, and friend of Blagojevich, has pleaded guilty to felony charges of seeking millions of dollars in kickbacks and campaign contributions from individuals working with state pension funds. Levine has pleaded guilty to kickback schemes involving his position on the state teacher retirement pension board.

In Levine's plea agreement, Cellini's name as the unindicted "Individual A" appears more than thirty times. Says former Republican senator Peter Fitzgerald (no relation to U.S. Attorney Patrick Fitzgerald), "No one in the history of the state to my knowledge has made more money off the taxpayers than Bill Cellini." Cellini has made his millions on deals sanctioned by both Republican and Democratic governors going back to Richard Ogilvie, under whom he served as secretary of transportation and "bag man" for campaign contributions from highway contractors. I am the only governor in more than thirty years who never succumbed to Cellini's blandishments. He once tried back in the 1970s, but my deputy spurned his advances.

Many of the practices spotlighted in the more than 120 felony indictments brought by U.S. Attorney Patrick Fitzgerald to date, as well as numerous plea agreements and the felony conviction of former governor George Ryan, were prohibited by the series of tough executive orders I signed in 1973.

A rising star on the political horizon is Illinois U.S. senator Barack Obama, who has raised hopes that he can restore luster to the land of Lincoln. He opened his campaign for the presidency with generous praise for Mayor Daley, carefully sublimating the existing Chicago scandals in his statement. This was in striking contrast to his hard-hitting attack on the corruption in Kenya when he was recently in Africa. Is the Kenya corruption worse than that involving more than 120 criminal indictments, which helped label Chicago "the most corrupt city in the nation"? Regrettably, Obama seems to be following in the footsteps of Illinois "independents": Democrats before him who ended up kowtowing to a Boss Daley. If Obama quails before a political boss in Chicago, how will he as president deal with powerful major malefactors abroad?

Yes, I was a "confrontationist." But I have no regrets for having boldly confronted a rotten system that has prevailed in Illinois for far, far too long. I have no public buildings or streets or anything else paid for by the taxpayers of Illinois named after me. But, like my Texas father whose genes and teaching are largely responsible for what I am, I hold high an independent head that has never "cottoned to bowing." I can proudly say this and perhaps only this. I have left a marker.

# Index

**Dan Walker**, the governor of Illinois from 1973 to 1977, graduated from the U.S. Naval Academy at Annapolis and served in the navy during World War II and the Korean War. He was a law clerk to Chief Justice Vinson at the U.S. Supreme Court, a successful trial lawyer in Chicago, the vice president and general counsel of a major national corporation, and the president of the nationally known Chicago Crime Commission, all the while fathering seven children. He is the author of six books and the famed Walker Report on violence at the 1968 Democratic National Convention. Walker lives with his wife, Lillian, in Escondido, California, and in Baja California.